CITIES OF KNOWLEDGE

POLITICS AND SOCIETY IN TWENTIETH-CENTURY AMERICA

Series Editors
WILLIAM CHAFE, GARY GERSTLE, LINDA GORDON, AND JULIAN ZELIZER

A list of titles in this series appears at the back of the book

CITIES OF KNOWLEDGE

COLD WAR SCIENCE AND THE SEARCH
FOR THE NEXT SILICON VALLEY

Margaret Pugh O'Mara

PRINCETON UNIVERSITY PRESS   PRINCETON AND OXFORD

Library of Congress Cataloging-in-Publication Data

O'Mara, Margaret Pugh, 1970–
Cities of Knowledge : Cold War science and the search for the next Silicon Valley / Margaret Pugh O'Mara
p. cm.
Includes bibliographical references and index
ISBN 0-691-11716-0 (cloth : alk. paper)
1. Research institutes—Location—United States. 2. Research parks—Location—United States. 3. Research, Industrial—Location—United States. I. Title.

Q180.U5M63 2004
607'.2'73—dc22   2003066082

British Library Cataloging-in-Publication Data is available.

This book has been composed in New Baskerville

Printed on acid-free paper. ∞

www.pupress.princeton.edu

Printed in the United States of America

10 9 8 7 6 5 4 3 2 1

For Jeff

Contents

Illustrations and Tables

Illustrations

Tables

Acknowledgments _____

WASHINGTON, D.C., was my first graduate school. I won admission by having the luck to work on a winning presidential campaign, which landed me in the White House less than a year later. It was a heady experience, and one that provided a sometimes painful crash course in politics and government. My time there showed me how much government matters, but also how public policy has limitations and shortcomings as a mechanism for social and economic change. I learned how much of this public-sector influence flows through policies flying well below the political radar screen, their profound effects largely unnoticed even in the age of twenty-four-hour news channels. Working in politics showed me how the implementation of federal policy at the local level can have effects quite different from those originally envisioned by national policy makers. I saw how policy making is often a process of imitation—one that takes promising practices and models and creates public frameworks to support their replication—and how differing local and institutional conditions make this imitative process quite difficult to pull off. As I continued my education in American public policy by becoming a historian of it, I began to find corroborating evidence for these observations and hunches. The "new federalism" of the 1990s was the continuation of familiar patterns. Ground-level implementation has long been the crucial second phase of national policy making, and tactics of private-sector persuasion—not government mandates—are often the way the U.S. state gets things done. The "public-private partnership" is not some facile invention of late twentieth-century policy makers, but has been a hallmark of American state-building throughout the nation's history.

All these lessons form the underpinning of this book, and I learned them because of the mentorship and encouragement of many extraordinary people. I first thank the advisor of the dissertation from which this book is developed, Michael Katz. Michael was the dream graduate advisor, unfailingly supportive and extraordinarily responsive, and he remains a valued mentor and colleague. Tom Sugrue also has served as a terrific advisor and friend; my many conversations with Tom about intersecting currents of politics, policy, and social history helped shape my approach to this topic, and his subsequent comments and ideas have enriched the results. This book also benefited greatly from the insights of David Kennedy and Richard White, who, despite towering piles in their in-boxes, provided critical readings of the entire draft. I profusely thank Richard, David, and the rest of the Stanford History Department for providing me with a welcoming home in which to work, and for providing me with the time and the resources to complete the project. This book had a wonderful editor in Julian Zelizer, who provided invaluable guidance throughout the writing process, and thoughtful readings of manuscript drafts.

Additional people provided comments on earlier versions of this work that helped sharpen its arguments and its prose. Two anonymous readers from Princeton University Press provided important early comments on the manuscript. Many thanks to Bruce Schulman for his insightful critiques and for his enthusiastic support. The comments I received from another author I admire, Ingrid Roper, made this book better, as did notes on individual chapters from Ron Bayor, Rich Combes, and Bruce Kuklick. I am grateful to those panelists and audience members who provided comments on presentations of the portions of the book, including those at the Newberry Library Seminar in Technology, Politics, and Culture, the Stanford University Social Science History Workshop, the Policy History Conference, the Miller Center Fellowship Conference, the Berkeley Center on Globalization and Information Technology, and the University of Pennsylvania History and Urban Studies Works-in-Progress Series. Conversations with other scholars are also one of the best ways to make a project better, and I'd particularly like to thank Brian Balogh, David Hollinger, Michael Kahan, Michel Laguerre, Lynn Lees, Tim Lenoir, Alice O'Connor, Peter Siskind, Anne Spirn, Clarence Stone, Larry Summers, Michael Teitz, Lorrin Thomas, Fred Turner, and Margaret Weir. You may not have always known you were giving me good ideas, but you were.

While researching and writing this book, I was supported not only by a Postdoctoral Fellowship in the Study of the North American West at Stanford University, but also a fellowship from the Miller Center of Public Affairs at the University of Virginia and a graduate fellowship sponsored by the University of Pennsylvania's Program in Non-Profits, Universities, Communities, and Schools, funded by the Kellogg Foundation. Many thanks go to all the people and institutions that made these fellowship opportunities possible. My research took me to many places, but I was particularly lucky to work in the rich university archives of Stanford, Penn, and Georgia Tech. I am grateful to the archivists at all these institutions, and give special thanks to Maggie Kimball for her assistance on this project and my related research in Stanford's Special Collections and University Archives.

I learned much of what I know about public policy from my former colleagues in the Clinton Administration, including Sheryll Cashin, Peter Edelman, Dave Garrison, Kumiki Gibson, Olivia Golden, John Monahan, Donna Shalala, and Gene Sperling. Of this group, John Monahan deserves particular thanks for his friendship, his masterful grasp of the nuances of policy and politics, and for talking me out of going to law school. I am also grateful to Bruce Katz, who knows how to get academics and policy makers to talk to one another, for the intellectual and professional opportunities he has offered me at the Brookings Institution Center for Urban and Metropolitan Policy.

Many thanks to the editors and staff of Princeton University Press for making this such an enjoyable process, particularly Brigitta van Rheinberg, who has helped me sharpen the central arguments of the book and create something that effectively brings together the history of high technology, political development, and urban change.

No one could write a book without the support of friends and family, and I consider myself extraordinarily fortunate in this regard. My parents, Joel and Caroline Pugh, have given constant encouragement during all my professional and intellectual endeavors, and their great talents as writers, public speakers, and teachers continue to serve as an inspiration. Friends from all phases of my life, and from all the places I've called home, helped make this book a reality and provided some of the best "eureka moments" I had during this process; the list is too long to enumerate here, but you know who you are. The last and biggest thank-you goes to the person to whom this work is dedicated, Jeff O'Mara. No author could be luckier than to have an in-house editor who is a careful reader, an incisive critic, and an untiring cheerleader. He always saved my sanity when I was drowning in tangential arguments and tangled prose, and he inspired some of the smartest ideas in this book. He is the most wonderful and important thing in my life, and I could not have completed this project without him.

CITIES OF KNOWLEDGE

Introduction

Discovering the City of Knowledge

In the second half of the twentieth century, a new and quintessentially American type of community emerged in the United States: the city of knowledge. These places were engines of scientific production, filled with high-tech industries, homes for scientific workers and their families, with research universities at their heart. They were the birthplaces of great technological innovations that have transformed the way we work and live, homes for entrepreneurship and, at times, astounding wealth. Cities of knowledge made the metropolitan areas in which they were located more economically successful during the twentieth century, and they promise to continue to do so in the twenty-first. Magnets for high-skilled workers and highly productive industries, cities of knowledge are, in fact, the ultimate post-industrial city.

Plenty of people know about the city of knowledge, but they do not call it by that name. It's a "high-tech capital" or a "science region"; it's Silicon Valley; it's Boston's Route 128.[1] Business leaders across the nation and globe want to become cities of knowledge and replicate their economic success. The allure of high-tech development does not diminish in economic downturns; even as the high-tech economy languished in a long and painful economic recession after the burst of the Internet bubble, CEOs and state and local politicians from Washington, D.C., to Albany to Shanghai continued to try and turn their metropolitan areas into the next high-tech boom town.[2] In doing so, these local leaders followed more than half a century of tradition. Ever since the growth of the Cold War defense complex and the consequent expansion of American scientific research and high technology sectors, cities, states, and regions have sought to imitate the magic formula that Silicon Valley and Route 128 seemed to have stumbled upon. Few have succeeded.[3]

Understanding why high technology thrived in certain places, and why these regions have proved so hard to replicate, requires looking at their evolution *historically* and *spatially*. In doing so, it becomes clear that these places are not simply high-tech regions that resulted from fortuitous combinations of capital and entrepreneurship. They are cities of knowledge: consciously planned communities that were physical manifestations of a particular political and cultural moment in history, and shaped by the relationship between the state and civil society in late twentieth-century America. The city of knowledge was a creation of the Cold War, whose policies and spending priorities transformed universities, created vibrant new scientific industries, and turned the research scientist into a space-age celebrity. And it was a product of the suburban age, when economic realignments, demographic changes, and public subsidies transformed patterns of living, working, and economic opportunity. Suburbanization created ideal environments for science to grow and prosper, creating spaces where university, industry, and scientist could create new networks of innovation and production, away from the distractions and disorder of the changing industrial city. The Cold War made scientists into elites, and mass suburbanization reorganized urban space in a way that created elite places. The result of this intersection is that cities of knowledge did not just spring up anywhere, but rose up amid the larger landscape of the affluent postwar suburb.

The American research university was at the heart of this process, as economic development engine, urban planner, and political actor. Universities and their administrators were central to the design and implementation of cities of knowledge, and successful scientific communities often depended upon the presence of an educational institution that not only had extensive research capacity, but was also an active participant in state and local political power structures. The government-university relationship that emerged as a result of Cold War politics did not simply affect the "inside game"—the internal workings and research priorities of universities—but transformed the "outside game" of land management and economic development in the communities in which these institutions were located. This relationship was a two-way street in which federal programs influenced university choices, and academic institutions and traditions had an important effect upon the design and implementation of public policy.[4]

These intersections of policy and place, and the role of universities within this process, are evident in the highly particular industrial geography of high technology at the beginning of the twenty-first century— geographic patterns that endure in times of high-tech bust as well as high-tech boom. For most of the twentieth century, the places that provided desirable residential environments for high-tech workers were suburban in look, feel, and location.[5] High technology grew up as a world of office parks, freeway commutes, and proximity to residential subdivisions; high-tech workplaces looked more like college campuses than factories or downtown high-rises. This was more than a case of suburban "sprawl," however, for high-technology activities grouped together in distinct clusters—a pattern particularly evident in Silicon Valley, which one observer labeled a "remarkable petri dish of industrial innovation."[6]

High-technology location choices also take into account where educated workers prefer to live, and as a result, these sectors cluster in some

TABLE I.1

Decentralization, Density, and Income Levels of Some Leading Concentrations of High Technology Industry

Region	Distance from Region's 1950 Central Business District*	Population Density, 2000 Census (High-Tech Counties vs. 1950 CBD)	Median Household Money Income 1999 (High-Tech Counties vs. State Average)	Leading Research Universities in Area	Leading Universities Federal R&D Income, 1968 (National Rank)
Silicon Valley: San Mateo and Santa Clara Counties, San Francisco–San Jose, Calif.	32 miles	1,439.2 people per square mile [City and County of San Francisco: 16,526.2]	$72,577 [California: $47,493]	Stanford University	$41.1 million (2)
Route 128 Corridor: Middlesex and Norfolk Counties, Boston, Mass.	10 miles	1,703.6 people per square mile [City of Boston: 12,172.3]	$62,127 [Massachusetts: $50,502]	Massachusetts Institute of Technology (MIT) Harvard University	MIT $79.8 million (1) Harvard 39.2 million (3)
Eastside Seattle: King County, Seattle-Tacoma, Wash.	16 miles	817.0 people per square mile [City of Seattle: 6,714.8]**	$53,157 [Washington: $45,776]	University of Washington	$27.9 million (10)
Silicon Hills: Williamson County, Austin, Tex.	18 miles	222.6 people per square mile [City of Austin: 2,610.6]	$60,642 [Texas: $39,927]	University of Texas at Austin	$10.3 million (40)

Sources: Distance from 1950 CBD to High-Tech Concentration is the driving distances from downtown districts to the following towns: San Francisco to Palo Alto; Boston to Waltham; Seattle to Redmond; Austin to Roundrock. Density figures from U.S. Department of Commerce, Bureau of the Census, *County and City Data Book 2000* (Washington, D.C.: Government Printing Office, 2002). Median household money income from U.S. Department of Commerce, Bureau of the Census, *City and County Quick Facts*, quickfacts.census.gov, (accessed 8 September 2003). Federal funding figures from national Science Foundation, *Federal Support of Research and Development at Universities and Colleges and Selected Nonprofit Institutions, Fiscal Year 1963*, NSF 69–33 (Washington, D.C.: Government Printing Office, 1968), 15–17.

*Central Business District, defined as the city with the largest population in the region according to the 1950 U.S. Census.

**Seattle is also part of King County and is included within the countywide figure.

of the most affluent, and economically homogeneous, places in the country. The connection between patterns of wealth and of high technology explain the infrequent exceptions to the suburban trend at the end of the twentieth century, which occurred after cities began to regain some of the wealth and middle-class residents they had lost to the suburbs decades earlier. Multimedia districts like Lower Manhattan's "Silicon Alley" and San Francisco's South of Market district—that grew during the 1990s Internet boom and shrunk significantly in the subsequent recession—emerged only after these city neighborhoods had become attractive to educated professionals. But changing urban economic dynamics have not been enough to trump the powerful connection between high technology and the suburb. Would-be Silicon Valleys, domestically and internationally, follow the model established by existing high-tech capitals and create homes for industry in largely affluent areas at the fringe (or beyond the fringe) of cities.[7]

American high-technology activities cluster in defined communities, simultaneously decentralized and proximate, diverse in function but not in socioeconomic composition. Communities of scientific production are places to live as well as work, home to a range of related and complementary production activities, cultural amenities, and services. In metropolitan areas with high concentrations of science-based industry, the rise of this kind of community has served to shift the focus of economic activity away from the central cities that dominated the regional economy up until the middle of the twentieth century and turned sleepy agricultural areas and bedroom suburbs into internationally influential concentrations of industrial production and commercial capital. By placing the history of high technology within the larger history of postwar urban and industrial change, we can trace the institutional and political origins of these fundamental—and inherently contradictory—geographic and socioeconomic characteristics and understand why they have been so economically important. This investigation shows how the process of high-tech growth was actually a process of city building. The suburbanization of science in the late twentieth century helped to *urbanize* American suburbs by making these places closer to classic definitions of cities in terms of their economic diversity and self-sufficiency.[8] No longer adjuncts to the central cities around which they grew up, the high-tech suburbs of the early twenty-first century are a new and influential kind of urbanism. They are not just amorphous "regions," but cities of knowledge.

Discovering the city of knowledge requires moving between the national scale and the local, identifying the complex interaction between public and private, and taking the story of high technology and giving it clearer geographic dimensions. The development of the city of knowledge has been so hard to see because it stemmed from choices made not only in Washington, D.C., but at the local level as well. And the role of policy in this process is difficult to trace because it involved programs that did not dictate, but *encouraged*, certain institutional and industrial choices. This study traces these programs from inception to implementation, beginning with the Cold War politics of the late 1940s, moving through the local economic development efforts of the 1960s, and taking an intense look at the experience of three very different metropolitan areas and their research universities.[9] It finds that:

Cities of knowledge are products of Cold War spending patterns. The Cold War defense complex created new hierarchies of political influence and a giant new source of capital, both of which came with geographic strings attached and created fierce competition among regions and institutions for these funds. Cold War geopolitics prompted new political attention to science—not just the kind of research that could build better bombs, but also basic scientific exploration of the kind going on in universities. Scientists and university administrators became key political players in Washington, and unprecedented amounts of money began to flow to research laboratories and universities. In turning university science and industrial research into "big science," Cold War politics took an inherently elite and historically independent scientific sector and made it an increasingly public and governmental one, supported and shaped by national political priorities. It also reinforced long-standing hierarchies of scientific excellence, giving the vast majority of research money to a small pool of elite institutions that already had significant scientific capacity. Pork-barrel politics compounded this favoritism by steering the bulk of defense research and development dollars to certain regions of the country. For reasons both strategic and economic, deliberate and accidental, Cold War politics privileged a select number of places and institutions, leaving them much better situated to build economies of high-tech production.[10]

While institutional and regional favoritism might be a familiar story to students of Cold War history, its effect upon the intra-metropolitan geography of science has been little explored. However, there are some important connections. The patterns of national defense spending that funneled the majority of investments to certain regions of the country had the ancillary effect of shifting scientific activity to the suburbs because the Sunbelt states receiving the bulk of the funds were places experiencing rapid and largely untrammeled suburban growth. Federal defense spending—the "seed money" for later high-tech development— went to parts of the country where state and local leaders were particularly hospitable to the idea of this industry being located in the suburbs. Civil defense policies provided another connection between Cold War defense spending and high-tech suburbanization. Concern about the vulnerability of central business districts during nuclear attack prompted officials to build in a number of powerful incentives into federal defense contracting policy that encouraged contractors to choose suburban locations over urban ones. The structure of these "industrial dispersion" policies, built around tax incentives and other private-sector encouragements, was quite similar to other federal mechanisms that indirectly encouraged postwar decentralization.[11] In this case, such subsidies explicitly targeted the expanding research-based industries that did business with the federal government. Although the civil defense concerns that prompted these incentives diminished in political and strategic importance over time, the preferences served as a federal endorsement of the idea that those sorts of industries should be decentralized and suburbanized and helped set in place enduring geographic patterns. The Cold War gave scientific institutions the money and clout to generate vibrant high-tech economies, and the geographic and institutional preferences embedded in Cold War defense contracting and research grant competitions contributed to the fact that these economies were more likely to emerge in suburban settings than urban ones.

Cities of knowledge are the product of university-centered economic development policies. As Cold War investments in research and development grew, state and local economic development policies began to increasingly orient themselves toward attracting clean, productive, and progressive businesses of science and technology. Because of its new wealth and research capacity, and its ability to act as a magnet for high-tech industries and workers, the research university became the economic development engine at the center of these efforts. Seeking in part to rectify the skewed economic geography of Cold War scientific research programs, by the early 1960s federal policy makers had created new public subsidies encouraging universities to expand their campuses and form collaborative partnerships with government and industry. States and localities complemented these programs with further incentives of their own. Many of these strategies centered on leveraging the power and resources of the university to create a very particular kind of industrial district, the research park. Through high architectural standards, extensive landscaping, and careful tenant selection, the research park mimicked the aesthetics and demographics of both the American college campus and the white-collar suburb.[12]

Although university-based economic-development strategies often aimed to shore up the declining economic fortunes of inner cities and poorer rural areas, and even though many prominent universities were in fact urban in location, the engagement of the university in economic development was crucial in mapping high-tech's exclusive and decentralized-but-clustered industrial geography. These efforts promulgated an industrial model that was immensely well suited to a suburban setting, and that complemented the larger trend of industrial decentralization—a phenomenon that was itself heavily subsidized by public funds. Federal, state, and local governments provided tax breaks, infrastructure subsidies, and other persuasive mechanisms that pulled all kinds of firms out of central cities; public efforts to foster the growth of high-tech regions thus occurred amid a giant suburban building boom spurred in part by these federal incentives.[13]

The presence of these other policies indicates that science would have likely suburbanized to some degree, regardless of the geographic biases of Cold War defense spending and science-based economic development policy. The *degree* of this suburbanization, and the clustering of these institutions and firms in affluent places, however, are patterns that reveal the influence of science-based industrial development campaigns and the engagement of the university in these processes. By placing the university at the center of their high-tech development strategies, policy makers made an economic development model out of institutions that—despite often being located in cities—had long-standing preferences for low-rise, intensively landscaped campuses. And by making inherently exclusive and inward-looking institutions into agents of social and economic change, public policy reinforced the idea that communities of science should be places reserved for a highly trained and highly educated class of people.

Cities of knowledge are the product of local action. Federal policy built the framework for the city of knowledge, but the translation of this framework into real economic success depended on local implementation. And the preexisting social context at the local level, and the geographic and institutional preferences built into federal policy, had a massive effect on the ability of a region to win the high-tech economic development game. Areas with large defense industries and with the ability and willingness to develop modern research parks and desirable residential areas—like the suburban areas of the South and West—had huge competitive advantages. Regions receiving less defense money or with an aging and economically declining infrastructure—such as the large industrial cities of the Northeast and Midwest—faced huge hurdles in attracting high-tech industry. Geography wasn't everything, however. The centrality of the university in these kinds of economic development efforts meant that localities and regions fared much better if they had a wealthy, entrepreneurial, and politically savvy research university at their heart. These distinctions were lost on the designers and implementers of science-based economic development strategies. Policy makers instead approached this process as one of *imitation* that presumed universities had similar economic development capacities, and cities and suburbs could be equally attractive to high-tech industries and their workers. The importance of the local political and economic context, and the drawbacks of this imitative strategy, become clear in the second half of this study, which takes an intensive, ground-level look at the experiences of three metropolitan areas and their leading research institutions.

Stanford University set a powerful early example of university-driven high-tech development and was widely imitated even though its success was due to rather extraordinary circumstances. Blessed with a massive endowment of undeveloped and economically desirable land, entrepreneurial administrators, and location near key defense facilities and amid one of the nation's more rapidly growing affluent suburban areas, Stanford built a research park adjacent to its campus that became, in the eyes of many government officials and university administrators, the gold standard for this kind of development. Stanford's development not only created even more rigorous criteria for architecture and landscape design that would blend into affluent suburban residential areas, but it also imbued the idea of the research park with a particularly Californian and Western architectural and landscape aesthetic—a look and feel that its imitators transposed in areas far removed from the Western habitat. At the University of Pennsylvania, in Philadelphia, local officials and university administrators used urban renewal funds as well as other sources of public money to attempt to transform a racially mixed and economically deteriorating urban neighborhood into a home for scientific industry and workers. Class and race often became conflated in the various attempts to develop scientific communities in these kinds of urban neighborhoods, where so many of the poor happens to be African American. The Penn example demonstrates that the racial and class politics of urban neighborhoods—not simply their physical infrastructure and location—created often insurmountable challenges to science-based development and were important reasons that Rustbelt cities like Philadelphia had such difficulty competing with Sunbelt suburbs for high-tech firms and personnel. The experience of the Georgia Institute of Technology, in Atlanta, demonstrates what happen when a region is advantaged by defense spending, and interested in creating suburban homes for high-tech industry and professional workers, but lacks a politically empowered and economically engaged research institution.

The experiences of Stanford, Penn, and Georgia Tech are more than merely case studies; these kinds of local-level processes formed a crucial second phase in the development of cities of knowledge and in the geography of American high technology. The experiences of these three places—a booming Western defense hub, a struggling Northeastern industrial city, and a rapidly growing and racially divided Southern metropolis—vividly illustrate the unevenness of the high-technology playing field, and the way in which Cold War politics spurred tremendous opportunities for some places and closed off economic possibilities for others.[14]

Singling out three examples for in-depth exploration means, of course, leaving out others, and one city of knowledge that does not appear in this group is Boston, home to Harvard, MIT, and the East Coast high-tech region stretching along—and beyond—suburban Route 128. In many respects, 1950s and 1960s Boston demonstrated the processes of the city of knowledge at work: universities enriched by massive amounts of Cold War defense spending, research parks springing up at the outskirts of the metropolitan area, scientific professionals and firms flocking to the region to take advantage of its universities and research facilities. Yet Boston is in many regards an exceptional case and, because of this, a less apt fit for this kind of study. Taking one place that succeeded in its efforts to both become a top national research center *and* generate a high-tech economy—Stanford—and comparing it with two places that, despite valiant efforts, were not as successful—Penn and Georgia Tech—provides a more interesting comparison that reveals the importance of place and space. In addition, Harvard and MIT did not influence high-tech architecture, design, and university-centered land development practice to the same degree as Stanford. For reasons we will further explore, the universities of Boston were so uniquely privileged in the Cold War competition for scientific industry that the rules of economic development and economic competition that applied to other cities of knowledge (and would-be cities of knowledge) did not apply to them.[15]

The story of the city of knowledge is a revealing window onto the relationship between state and society in twentieth-century America. The choice of postwar policy makers to implement science policy through a loose and decentralized network of academic and industrial partners and interest groups, rather than through consolidated state power, was consistent with other aspects of U.S. welfare-state formation and economic policy—and a marked contrast to other industrialized nations. While an in-depth comparative analysis is not feasible here, it is worth noting that both Japan and Germany, two nations who rivaled (and at times surpassed) the United States in industrial and technical innovation during the late twentieth century, have had more visible and centralized science policy structures. However, these nations and others did not become home to geographic clusters of scientific activity on a par with Silicon Valley. The communities of this sort that now exist in other countries are the products of conscious imitation of American models rather than being organic outcomes of national policy structures. The implication of this is that strong states may lead to strong national industrial policy, but they do not lead to cities of knowledge.[16]

The city of knowledge is a quintessentially American form, and is one that developed because of—not in spite of—the federalized and privatized American political system. The city of knowledge is, in fact, the product of the contradictions within this system, and within Cold War statebuilding policies in particular. The Cold War required a strong state, but American political traditions demanded a weak one. The solution was to empower universities and scientific industries to become agents and partners with the federal government, a choice that gave these local actors new influence over local economies and politics. It also created fiercely competitive dynamics among these partners, which in turn made institutions and industries more entrepreneurial and creative in devising strategies that could place them in favored positions economically and politically. While high-tech entrepreneurship is something often considered to have emerged in spite of government involvement, not because of it, the entrepreneurial drive of high-tech sectors and postwar universities may have stemmed in significant part from the competitive dynamics set up by the state.[17]

Examining these political and economic currents provides additional perspective on the question of how the United States implemented far-reaching, defense-driven policy agendas during the Cold War without becoming a "garrison state."[18] Through persuasion and partnership, the development of the Cold War science complex became a process in which federal decision makers, university administrators and scientists, and corporate research leaders all managed to have a voice. These power structures and policy networks enabled leaders to quietly and significantly increase the power and influence of the federal government while simultaneously condemning the idea of "big government" as dangerously communistic.[19]

Such political structures, involving institutions and industries with planning traditions that emphasized isolation and exclusivity, created a firm association between scientific activity and low-density, suburban working environments, and helped embed this association into the design and implementation of federal public policy. In doing so, Cold War research and economic development policies joined the ranks of a host of other public programs that "pulled" people and jobs out to the suburbs by creating economic incentives for the recipients of government money—whether they were states, cities, businesses, or homeowners—to behave in a particular way. While consumer preferences and market trends already favored urban decentralization and would have likely effected some decentralization even without this public intervention, government incentives accelerated and widened this process by making the automobile-dependent suburb a much more economically sensible location choice for families and employers. This same pattern of incentive-based policies and market influence marked the Cold War science complex and its component institutions, particularly the research universities that would become cores of significant concentrations of high-tech production. The outgrowth of these public-private collaborations was that these new suburban landscapes became home to an overwhelming proportion of the institutions and industries that made up the Cold War science complex.

Federal policies created a new political order in which scientific institutions were ascendant, and they built an institutional framework in which certain areas became the most economically attractive locations for scientific activity. They empowered and enriched certain institutions and certain places, reorienting the focus of American science and engaging universities in affairs of state and commerce like never before. In less than twenty years, the top American research universities went from being institutions with few financial or political ties to the federal government, to being entities crucial both to the federal defense complex and to state and local economic development campaigns. The way federal, state, and local governments contributed to this new spatial and economic order was not through large and centralized public programs, but through persuasive mechanisms that flew largely unnoticed below the political radar screen.

The political discourse around the American welfare state has long focused on what the federal government didn't provide its citizens (such as universal health insurance, wage subsidies, or family services like child care). By broadening the definition of "welfare" to include both means-tested and non-means-tested programs, and both public and private funding sources, new scholarship has demonstrated that the American welfare state is much more far-reaching and complex.[20] The case of the city of knowledge attests to how much the federal government *did* provide, and how these subsidies were disguised to such a degree that they often went unrecognized by their beneficiaries. These "strong-state-as-weak-state" policy frameworks—from basic research policy to economic development incentives to tax and infrastructure subsidies—allowed local actors to shape policy and tailor public funds to meet their own ends. Sometimes this worked, spurring explosions of science-based economic growth in certain regions; sometimes it did not. National policy intent and local policy implementation were equally important to the evolution of these communities and to the growth of the institutions and industries housed within them. This policy structure allowed a stronger state to masquerade as a weak one, and at the same time allowed local flexibility, institutional entrepreneurship, and opportunities for innovation. The end result is a high-tech sector that has become a world leader in science and technology, but that seems to have collective amnesia when it comes to acknowledging the role of the federal government in its growth.

Uncovering the city of knowledge in the suburb reveals that the history of high technology has far more to do with government choices than is commonly realized, and it also shows how much local-level implementation of this policy matters. It explains why high technology is so often in the suburbs, and why this geography is so important to the history of technology and the history of American cities. For the influence of the city of knowledge goes well beyond high technology. At the outset of the Cold War, the notion that, in so many major metropolitan areas, more Americans would go to work in the suburbs than in the central city by the year 2000 would have seemed somewhat unbelievable. Today, the decentralized landscape of production, where millions of Americans go to work in office parks and lush "campuses" at the fringe of metropolitan areas, is so normal that most people rarely question how it came about. The historical and geographical dynamics underlying the development of the cities of knowledge help explain this. This story shows the complex interactions of policy, economics, and culture that spurred industrial suburbanization, and it also shows that this process was far more complicated and deliberately planned than is commonly supposed. The city of knowledge stands as a further example of a type of postwar urban development that, while often suburban in location and low-density in design, was not unplanned "sprawl." Instead, cities of knowledge were the products of careful and deliberate planning that involved both residential and industrial development. It also provides additional evidence of the profound influence of the Sunbelt and Pacific West in twentieth-century urban development patterns, and lends support to the argument that influence and imitation in postwar American city planning and development radiated from west to east rather than vice versa.[21]

"If the dominant figures of the past hundred years have been the entrepreneur, the businessman, and the industrial executive," wrote Daniel Bell in his 1973 treatise *The Coming of Post-Industrial Society,* "the 'new men' are the scientists, the mathematicians, the economists, and the engineers of the new intellectual technology."[22] This book is about how the rise of these "new men" became reflected in the American urban landscape, and traces the way in which federal public policy was instrumental in both the growth of high technology and the decentralization of high-tech industry and its workers. This is not a paean to the entrepreneurial brilliance of the Silicon Valley businessman—although it readily acknowledges the fundamental role individual innovation played in the growth of high-tech industry in the United States. Instead it places government and politics at the center of its narrative of how and why high-tech communities evolved the way they did. It was neither coincidence, nor a natural outgrowth of the market, that suburban landscapes became home to an overwhelming proportion of the institutions and industries that made up the Cold War science complex. The complex interactions between public and private created frameworks and incentives for high-technology production that moved the most rapidly growing sectors of the economy to the low-density, affluent fringe of the metropolis and redefined the American city for a post-industrial Information Age.

Part One ————————————————————

INTENT

1

Cold War Politics

B UILDING a city involves money, power, and the right location. In the case of the city of knowledge, these required elements flowed from an American Cold War scientific research and development (R&D) effort that created giant new streams of federal financing for academic and industrial science. While the United States had long valued science and technology for its important role in industrial production and contributions to intellectual life, the Cold War made science more important than ever before. It enlarged and refocused the definition of "science" to encompass activities that were now in the interest of national security as well as economic well-being: academic disciplines ranging from physics to chemistry to mathematics and engineering; a wide spectrum of industries that developed advanced consumer products like transistors, military hardware like warplanes, and specialized equipment like semiconductors and computers. The military buildup, the new emphasis on educational excellence, and the desire for significant economic growth all worked to privilege—to an unprecedented degree—American scientists and the institutions and industries in which they worked.

The city of knowledge came to be because of the new opportunities that the Cold War presented to research universities and the professional scientists who worked in and around them. And the city of knowledge came to be *located* where it was because of the way Cold War strategic concerns intersected with economic ones, the way in which power and money was distributed institutionally and geographically, and because of the larger social and economic context in which the Cold War defense complex grew. Cold War politics did not occur in a vacuum. As scientific professionals and institutions became highly valued and celebrated members of American culture, the shape of the nation's urban landscape underwent radical change. Suburban areas benefited at the expense of central cities, and the South and West grew as the Northeast and Midwest stagnated or declined. Within the context of these changes, policy choices made in the earliest years of the Cold War vested scientific institutions and industries with the power to transform regional economies, while creating dynamics of institutional and regional competition that made this transformation more likely to occur in some places than in others.

Frameworks, 1945–1950

The Politics of Science

During the Cold War, "R&D" was a blanket term that encompassed a huge array of governmental activities and whose definition shifted over time. It included scientific research activities taking place in university laboratories, government facilities, and corporate research branches. The vast majority of this work, particularly in the early Cold War years, was "applied" research conducted for the purposes of developing technology with specific, relatively short-term military or commercial uses. The remainder was "basic" research: scientific inquiry conducted for the sake of greater scientific understanding. The basic research projects supported by the federal R&D effort included medical and social-scientific research as well as projects in the physical sciences; while applied research often occurred in government and industrial laboratories, basic research usually took place in universities. Beyond these activities, and occupying a far greater share of the national budget in the Cold War years, was the actual procurement and manufacture of military equipment, a process that created a powerful constituency of defense contractors and transformed regional economies through the influx of billions of dollars of federal spending. Taken together, all these activities made up a state-funded economic juggernaut that President Dwight D. Eisenhower famously and ominously labeled the "military-industrial complex" as he left office in 1961.[1]

Although basic research was, in fiscal terms, the smaller part of the Cold War R&D apparatus, the process by which this kind of research became a Cold War priority marked an important step in the engagement of universities and their administrators in postwar politics and public life. During the 1920s and 1930s, the strength and scope of the postwar alliances between academia, industry, and the state was hard to imagine. Universities (particularly private institutions) and the scientists who worked in them tended to be highly suspicious of federal government involvement in their affairs. In contrast to the federally sponsored entities that would dominate American research in the latter half of the twentieth century, prewar science's most influential representative body, the National Research Council, was a private, nongovernmental entity made up of "the elite of university science, industrial research, and the foundation world."[2] Too much "outside" involvement could taint the research process, some academics and administrators argued. The less a scholarly project was influenced by nonacademic interests, the higher the quality of the scholarship.[3]

This profession of fierce intellectual and fiscal independence belied the fact that universities and their scientists were, in fact, already beholden to outside private- and public-sector interests. The U.S. government had subsidized university research activities for as long as there *had* been research universities in America. Beginning with the Morrill Act of 1862, which established the land-grant college system of technical and agricultural educational institutions, the federal government had devoted considerable funds to foster the advancement of science, the development of new technology, and the education of scientific professionals.[4] Many large state universities, whose laboratories were funded largely by public dollars, had impressive research reputations. Yet private universities tended to be less significantly dependent on public money, and instead relied upon the contributions of American corporations and corporate-founded philanthropies.[5]

The corporate patronage of prewar universities reflected the fact that, during these decades, private industry, not the government, was at the center of the action when it came to the research and development of new technology. While federal grants and subsidies formed a crucial, if often hidden, underpinning of the American university system, direct support of scientific research was anemic at best. In contrast, American industry had engaged in industrial research efforts since the nineteenth century, and by the early twentieth century housed some of the world's most innovative research laboratories and industrial scientists.[6] Not seeing a role for government support of their own institutions, administrators of some of the nation's top private universities saw little irony in their protestations of academic independence and their fear of government control of academic research agendas, while welcoming corporate support.[7]

The Second World War changed everything. The outbreak of war created an urgent need for the rapid production of new military technology. Roosevelt Administration officials and the military leadership marshaled the forces of American research universities and their top scientists through a flurry of research grants and contracts. The administration coordinated wartime research efforts through a new agency, the Office of Scientific Research and Development (OSRD). Over the course of the war, the OSRD funded hundreds of military research projects, many of them secret. It became one of the most visible signs of the quiet revolution in the relationship between the members of the scientific community and the federal government.[8] Now, with huge wartime research projects under way, America's top scientists went to work for the government and, in some cases, found themselves thrust into a highly politicized public spotlight.

The men of science who gained the most celebrity (or notoriety) as a result of the war were the atomic-bomb builders of the Manhattan Project. Scientists like J. Robert Oppenheimer—the quintessentially detached academic who was so absorbed in his work that he had not bothered to vote until 1936—suddenly found themselves in the national limelight after the war-ending 1945 bombings of Hiroshima and Nagasaki.[9] The breathless prose that popular accounts often used to describe these men and their work built public awareness and support for the idea of federal financing of research, military and otherwise. Scientists "acquired something of the position in our society of the Mathematician-Astronomer-Priests of the ancient Mayas," wrote journalists Joseph and Stewart Alsop, "who were at once feared and revered as the knowers of the mystery of the seasons, and the helpers of the sun and the stars in their life-giving courses."[10] Some of these scientists were reluctant celebrities. Most seemed to harbor deep uneasiness about the morality of using their scientific talents to create such murderous technology. But the lure of the military's abundant resources for scientific research work was often more powerful than their moral qualms about performing it.[11] Military work not only gave scientists a lot of money, but it could allow plenty of creative latitude. As General Eisenhower wrote in a postwar memorandum on "Scientific and Technological Resources As Military Assets": "Scientists and industrialists must be given the greatest possible freedom to carry out their research. . . . [They] are more likely to make new and unsuspected contributions to the development of the Army if detailed directions are held to a minimum."[12]

The highly successful mobilization of university scientists during the war convinced President Truman and many in Congress that the federal government should stay in the business of scientific research in peacetime. Even when it was no longer necessary to manufacture thousands of airplanes and armaments, or quickly develop more advanced military technology to respond to the new weapons developed by the enemy, the United States had a vital interest in maintaining national technological strength. Germany and Japan had been vanquished, but now Soviet Russia posed a new and potentially greater threat. As U.S.-Soviet tensions heated up over the course of the late 1940s, government officials recognized that research was fundamental to preparedness. Even before the war had ended in the Pacific, the Truman White House and Democratic leaders in Congress were working on legislative efforts to establish a permanent government agency that could support peacetime scientific activity similar to the way OSRD had supported science in wartime. "No nation can maintain a position of leadership in the world of today unless it develops to the full its scientific and technological resources," argued President Truman as he addressed Congress exactly one month after the atomic bombs fell on Hiroshima and Nagasaki. "No government adequately meets its responsibilities unless it generously and intelligently supports and encourages the work of science in university industry, and its own laboratories."[13]

Scientists themselves stood at the center of this effort, drafting policy, testifying before Congress, and using publications to build public support for government science.[14] The universities from which many of them came also lent their institutional support to the effort. University administrators now recognized that expanded government spending was not only in the government's interest, but also in the economic and academic interest of universities. Institutions' experiences in housing research projects during the war helped build this kind of political support, but universities had more pragmatic reasons as well. More than a decade of Depression and war had meant declining enrollments, reduced levels of support from a struggling private sector, and cost-intensive wartime mobilization activities; after this, even the most well-endowed universities needed more money. The situation became more dire after passage of the 1944 GI Bill that gave returning servicemen money for college and created a huge new student population that required new housing, new classrooms, and new services. Universities were getting much bigger, and they needed money that only the federal government seemed to be able, and willing, to provide.[15]

One of the most important figures in this process was Vannevar Bush, a physicist, former vice president of MIT, and head of the Carnegie Institute who already had a long and impressive record of government service. Bush had chaired the National Advisory Committee on Aeronautics (NACA), the only significant research-oriented federal entity of the interwar period, and during the war he headed the OSRD. Through this work, he became a full-fledged scientific celebrity, appearing on the cover of *Time* magazine in 1944 as the "General of Physics."[16] In early 1945, Truman asked Bush to draft a report outlining a political rationale for a permanent science agency and proposing its structure and function. Published in July of that year, *Science, The Endless Frontier* articulated a sweeping vision for government-funded academic science. The report forcefully argued that scientific innovation would be essential to political and economic success in the postwar world, and recommended that the federal government establish a National Science Foundation (NSF) to fund scientific education and basic research in universities. Bush's choice of the term "foundation"—rather than the more familiar "agency"—revealed his strong feeling that the new entity not be just another government bureaucracy, but an independent body run by professional scientists rather than federal bureaucrats, whose mission centered on the promotion of basic research.

Picking up on a metaphor used two decades earlier by former president Herbert Hoover, whose corporatist views he shared, Bush employed the powerful and evocative idiom of the "frontier" of science.[17] "The pioneer spirit is still vigorous within this nation," Bush wrote. "Science offers a largely unexplored hinterland for the pioneer who has the tools for his task. The rewards of such exploration both for the Nation and the individual are great. Scientific progress is one essential key to our security as a nation, to our better health, to more jobs, to a higher standard of living, and to our cultural progress."[18] The report argued that the foundation should not only support research that could have military applications, but that it also fund medical research and university education in the sciences. Another hallmark of Bush's thought—and a strong undercurrent in the report—was an attitude best characterized as meritocratic elitism. Bush was hardly alone in his ideas about the existence of a ruling class based on talent, not birth, but he particularly emphasized the scientist as the epitome of this elite type. As a Bush biographer has noted, "he ranked the engineer as first among equals, a sort of super-citizen who could master virtually every activity essential to the smooth functioning of a modern nation."[19] Their professional expertise gave scientists a *responsibility* to guide policymaking; as Bush put it in a 1946 speech to MIT alumni, "government by the people is really government by that portion of the people which takes the trouble to participate actively in the forming of public opinion . . . . professional men realize that theirs is a special obligation" and "the physical scientist . . . must accept the responsibility that mark[s] the professional man as distinguished from the simple scholar."[20]

Bush's artful rhetoric about the merits of an entity run by scientists, for scientists, aimed to sway ongoing legislative debates around science policy. West Virginia Democratic senator Harley Kilgore, chair of the War Mobilization Subcommittee of the Senate Committee on Military Affairs, had proposed a series of bills throughout the war that sought to centralize government research functions in one permanent agency. A New Dealer "elected on Franklin Roosevelt's coattails" in 1940, Kilgore envisioned a national science agency as a necessary solution to the lack of coordination in federal research efforts as well as the favoritism that concentrated these resources within a select group of elite universities and contractors. Starting with the introduction of the Technology Mobilization Act in 1942, Kilgore argued for a single, central agency that sponsored applied research projects and created technology on which the government itself held the patents.

Military officials and OSRD-affiliated scientists quietly expressed deep reservations about this liberal vision of state-sponsored research and planning. Science should remain in the hands of scientists, not bureaucrats, they argued. Private-sector voices weighed in with a similar verdict about the danger of government control of academic science. Bell Laboratories' Frank Jewett condemned the bill, saying that it "would set the stage for the complete domination of the life of the nation by a small group of federal officers and bureaucrats."[21] On the other side of the debate, government officials expressed reluctance to hand over control of this new agency to industrial scientists, "a group of citizens who are at the same time employed by private institutions or organizations."[22]

Disagreements about whether government science should be the province of public servants, independent academics, or industry representatives were one thing that bogged down the Kilgore proposal and subsequent science legislation. Another was the political fracture of the Democratic Party. The battle between conservative Southerners and more racially moderate liberals over civil rights overshadowed Congressional debates, pitted the White House against the powerful Southerners who held leadership positions on key committees, and led to legislative stalemates.[23] Rising anti-Communist sentiment—a feeling that crossed regional and partisan boundaries, and that most infamously manifested itself in the Congressional hearings orchestrated by Senator Joseph McCarthy—further compounded the legislative difficulties. The Kilgore-style plans, with their proposal of a large new government bureaucracy, were out of step with the new political mood, where projects of this sort seemed suspiciously socialistic. On the other side of the issue, scientists faced heightened scrutiny of their past and present political attitudes by those looking for signs of "subversion"; the most famous victim of these investigations was Robert Oppenheimer, who retired from public life after questions about his alleged Communist sympathies left him stripped of his security clearance.[24] The transfer of both the House and Senate to Republican control between 1947 and 1949 did not help matters, increasing the partisan divide between the legislative and the executive (Truman called it the "Do-Nothing" Congress) and diminishing the possibilities of finding a framework for science policy that was acceptable to all.[25]

While the efforts to create the NSF remained stalled in Congress, the executive branch attempted to move forward in elevating scientists and science policy on the national agenda. In 1946, in a move signaling a willingness to give scientists an unprecedented high-level role in day-to-day White House policy making, Truman established the President's Scientific Research Board (PSRB), headed by one of his White House assistants, John Steelman. The new organization produced a massive report on federal science policy that echoed the ongoing debates in Congress in recommending continued government funding of basic research, and reiterated sentiments about the public responsibilities of scientists. "The democratic ideals of our society have fostered science and helped to give it its present place in the world at large," the Steelman report observed. "It is the obligation of the scientists, in turn, to give willing aid to the tasks involved in making our system work well."[26]

While the diverse interests involved in this early stage of the science debate may have differed in their visions for the execution of science policy, they rarely questioned the fundamental premise that the federal government should become the major patron of scientific inquiry. In a time of unprecedented global tensions and rapid technological change, a strong science policy was in the national interest. Congressional hearings brought together a broad assortment of witnesses—representing business coalitions, labor unions, professional associations, and a wide array of research universities—who gave testimony in enthusiastic support of the NSF idea. "Organized to maintain a sustained program of research for national welfare and progress, [the nation] will be ready to conquer the endless frontier of science, not in competition, but with the cooperation of all groups and finally all nations," testified the American Federation of Labor's (AFL) Lewis Hines.[27] Harvard University president James B. Conant predicted: "If the proposals before you become law and Congress appropriates the money, we will see a flowering of scientific work in this country the like of which the world has never seen before."[28] Yet supporters also warned that maintaining scientific independence was essential; Polaroid camera developer Edwin Land reminded lawmakers that "the great discoveries in pure science arise spontaneously and unpredictably in the minds of scientists who are not usually on organized programs" and that the government should "help to educate and to create a large number of good scientists who are then helped economically but are left free to work in their own way."[29]

Even before the passage of a single piece of science legislation, this assortment of government officials, scientists, academic administrators, and industrial allies built a case for science whose presumptions about the relationships between public and private, and scientific and economic, had lasting effects on the design and implementation of science policy—and, by extension, the places where scientific activity occurred. Although these supporters of government science emphasized the responsibility of scientists to serve the greater good, and advocated massive public investment in an area heretofore supported primarily through private funds, the scientific-expert vision of the role of the state in this process was distinctly different from the activist, redistributive model of the New Deal. Scientists and scientific institutions would be agents of the government rather than dependents. As the Bush and Steelman documents pointed out, important research was already under way at American universities; the purpose of government funding was to recognize and support this activity in ways that increased its strategic and economic value to the nation. A quiet recognition of the enduring wariness that the scientific community felt about government control ran throughout these early Cold War arguments about science policy, which consistently emphasized the accomplishments of the independent *individual* or of *an elite team of individuals* as the means by which to achieve collectively beneficial ends.

The decentralized, expert-run vision of publicly sponsored science fit well with the postwar direction of national economic policy. In the late 1940s, Americans were only a few years removed from the Great Depression and remained deeply uneasy about their economic future. An October 1945 Gallup poll reported that 42 percent of respondents identified jobs as the most important problem facing the country during the next year. Only 2 percent cited the atomic bomb. An August 1946 Gallup poll found that 60 percent of respondents believed there would be another serious economic depression within the next ten years.[30] Government officials shared this unease. A mild recession in 1949 made President Truman and his economic advisors even more concerned about maintaining high levels of production and increasing the standard of living. Although the recession soon ended, the 1950 Economic Report of the President recommended using government expenditures—the biggest of which were defense related—to prevent further sluggishness in the economy.[31]

Economic health depended not simply on increased production, however—but also on increased productivity. "There is left but one possible source of new wealth to replace the wealth lost in war," one independent analyst noted in 1942. "The source of wealth is the discovery of new products to manufacture and sell. It is on this source of wealth that we must now and in the future depend for the means to maintain and raise our standard of living."[32] The well-developed R&D infrastructure within the private sector by midcentury meant that American industry would have developed the ability to produce and distribute many of these innovative, time-saving, and affordable consumer goods even if the federal government had not gone into the scientific research business during and after World War II. However, by the late 1940s, compelling examples existed of the way in which government investments in university research resulted in technology with important nonmilitary and consumer applications.

One example that showed both the catalytic effect of military research upon civilian technology and the pivotal role of the research university as a site for technological development was the world's first supercomputer, the Electronic Numerical Integrator and Calculator (ENIAC), an invention unveiled at the University of Pennsylvania in 1946. In the 1940s, the term "computer" meant, to most people, not a sophisticated machine but a worker (during the war years, most often a woman) who painstakingly calculated hundreds of mathematical equations using brainpower and perhaps an adding machine. The war effort generated a huge demand for these human computers, as calculating the probable trajectory of a missile could mean the difference between winning or losing in battle. As the demand for operations research grew, military officials increasingly sought mechanized solutions to the problem. Only a few years earlier, the advent of vacuum-tube technology had opened up the possibility of creating a mechanized calculator that would have the capability of computing thousands of equations in a fraction of the time it took human workers. ENIAC's postwar unveiling was met with great press attention and professional acclaim, making headlines at the same time as the NSF continued to be debated in Congress. For both technical and administrative reasons, the supercomputer had very little commercial success and was soon eclipsed by faster, more agile machines. It was, however, a landmark in the history of computing—not only for its role in the development of computer technology, but also for being an early, prominent example of a federally funded, university-developed product with both military and commercial uses.[33]

Another persuasive model of military-academic-industrial cooperation was the RAND Corporation, founded in 1945 as a research arm of a major wartime contractor, the Douglas Aircraft Corporation, and spun off into an independent nonprofit research organization in 1948. Commanding General of the Army Air Force "Hap" Arnold and General Curtis LeMay were key movers behind the founding of RAND, as was MIT's Edward Bowles, then a consultant to the Secretary of War. Charged with the task of linking high-level research and development to military strategy, RAND's early projects included a report on earth-circling satellites, analyses of likely domestic nuclear targets, and research into intercontinental missile technologies. By the late 1940s it had over two hundred staff members—scientists and social scientists from a range of disciplines—doing quite ambitious and forward-thinking projects in the name of improved military technology. While RAND later took on some nonmilitary contracts with private foundation support, its primary customer was the U.S. military; the firm served as "the ideologist of the national security state" throughout the Cold War.[34]

The cooperative examples of ENIAC and RAND validated the usefulness of the "hands-off" model where the government provided funds but let scientists and industry provide the homes for this research and retain a good deal of control over its execution. These two examples also reflected another crucial characteristic of early Cold War science: institutional exclusivity. The people and institutions involved in the political conversations swirling around Washington during the late 1940s made up a very small portion of American scientists drawn from a tiny pool of the top research universities. Most prominent among these were Harvard and the Massachusetts Institute of Technology (MIT). Wartime research activities centered upon these institutions—top scientists and engineers had traveled from their home universities to Cambridge for the duration of the war—and in the immediate postwar years, the two institutions solidified their positions as the preeminent research universities in the nation, as indicated by the ubiquity of past and present leaders of these institutions in policy debates over the NSF. Recognizing this favoritism, Kilgore's legislative proposals had contained strong provisions for a more equitable distribution of resources among institutions.[35]

While legislation to improve institutional competitiveness remained stalled in Congress, the high-ranked institutions that were *not* Harvard and MIT had to become more aggressive and entrepreneurial in getting the attention of policy makers. Geographically distant universities quickly recognized that long-distance lobbying was difficult to impossible, and an office in the nation's capital was now a necessity. One of the earliest universities to establish a permanent Washington office (in 1945) was Stanford, an institution whose leaders had long expressed disdain for "big government"-style programming and who paid little attention to cultivating relationships with federal policy makers.[36] Despite the fact that the campus was then home to a former U.S. president, university alumnus and lifelong Stanford booster Herbert Hoover, university officials tended to characterize themselves as Washington outsiders. "It wasn't 'respectable' to know somebody who was in politics," reflected one administrator several decades later.[37] Yet it became obvious to university administrators that the key to joining the highest ranks of national research universities in the postwar era was to have a full-time advocate in Washington.

The legislative debates over the NSF embodied the ideological divide between "the people" and "the interests" at the core of American politics and gave it a Cold War twist. Senator Kilgore, his fellow Congressional liberals, and sometimes parts of the executive branch put forth a populist vision of science in which the central state controlled the development of new technologies, and the bounty of federal research money was not restricted. Military officials, industrial researchers, and scientists from elite universities argued that the country was best served by leaving scientific research policy in the hands of the "best men" and best laboratories, rather than centralizing it in the hands of government officials, or dissipating scientific projects and talent over too wide a range of more middling institutions.

Even before passage of any comprehensive science legislation, it was clear that the elites were going to win. The military and scientific establishments were ascendant interests in late 1940s Washington; liberals and

New Dealers were losing ground, compromised by the regional divisions in the Democratic Party and muffled by rising anti-Communism. The United States had already won a war and developed breakthrough commercial technologies without the existence of a large, centralized federal agency. And in a Cold War world, where American-style democracy faced off against Soviet-style socialism, the U.S. government needed to find means of expansion that did not create the appearance of too much state control. These political conditions allowed Cold War science to remain an exclusive place where the power to determine policy and allocate research money lay in the hands of relatively few institutions and individuals. When the NSF finally overcame various political hurdles and became law in 1950, its administrative structure reflected the vision of the scientists, not the populists, and as a result, the science complex stayed under the control of a relatively limited number of people and institutions.

A hierarchy *within* this hierarchy also emerged during this period. In a small and elite pool of research institutions, Harvard and MIT sat firmly at the top, needing to do little active or overt lobbying to get the attention of policy makers or win federal funding. The other universities in this pool were discovering that, in order to tap into the expected bounty of federal research funding, they needed to work a little harder: establishing Washington offices, adjusting their academic missions, becoming more entrepreneurial and political in their approach. These patterns of power and privilege—and the competition they engendered among universities for prestige and resources—had critical bearing on the eventual geography of scientific production. Because science became the domain of elites, scientific places came to be elite as well.[38]

The Incentives to Disperse

At the same time that Congress and Truman Administration officials were debating the merits of the NSF and determining who should have control of scientific spending, they also were engaged in a separate political conversation about the strategic necessities determining where these activities should take place. The U.S. experience in World War II had convinced policy makers of the importance of research, and it had also convinced them of the need for powerful mechanisms to keep these and other defense-critical activities safe from enemy attack. The advent of the atomic age made this threat even greater. In an era when the majority of businesses and factories were inside city limits, a well-placed atomic bomb could strike a huge blow to American productive capacity. In the doomsday scenarios outlined by military planners, large cities would be ground zero of a hypothetical nuclear attack; the Air Force estimated that ninety-two cities with populations above 100,000 would become "prime targets."[39] Although the United States was still the only atomic superpower in the first years following the end of the war, scientists, business leaders, city and regional planners, military tacticians, and national politicians alike seized upon the idea of urban decentralization as an important and crucial way to combat the threat of outside nuclear attack. Many of the same people concerned about the nation's scientific capacity were also concerned about the need for dispersal; in a 1945 memorandum to Truman, Vannevar Bush wrote that: "some degree of passive defense—or of passive retention of the power of retaliation—is offered by dispersion of population and of essential industries."[40]

In the late 1940s, the Truman Administration took a series of administrative steps to establish a policy of "industrial dispersion" and encourage manufacturers to move out of potential vulnerable central cities. A quiet effort that operated largely below the political radar screen, the dispersion campaign focused its attention on the dispersion of defense contractors and other customers of the military—firms that made up the most "defense-critical" sectors of the economy and that had the most financial dependence on the federal government. Dispersion policy became one piece of a complex bundle of public and private drivers of postwar industrial location patterns for these firms that depended upon the federal government as an important customer. Dispersion's significance to the eventual geography of high technology results not only from the subsidies it created but, perhaps, even more significantly, its providing a governmental stamp of approval on the idea that suburban places were logical homes for science.

Industrial dispersion received its first official federal endorsement with the passage of the National Security Act of 1947, the law that comprehensively reorganized the federal government's military and foreign policy apparatus and created an institutional infrastructure for waging the Cold War.[41] One of the new agencies established by this act was the National Security Resources Board (NSRB), which, among its other civil-defense duties, was charged with "the strategic relocation of industries, services, government, and economic activities, the continuous operation of which is essential to the Nation's security."[42] The NSRB was in existence only during the Truman administration; President Eisenhower abolished it in 1953 and had the Office of Defense Management take over its civil-defense functions. While short-lived, the NSRB was a politically important organization in the Truman years run by leaders personally close to the president—for a time, his science advisor John Steelman held the post, as did fellow Missourian and former Secretary of the Air Force Stuart Symington. These personnel choices demonstrated the overlap between the policy communities engaged in scientific research matters and those developing the national civil defense strategy.

Although the NSRB was at the center of industrial dispersion efforts, publicizing the issue through widely distributed pamphlets and press releases, the agency itself did not have the legal authority to force firms and industries to disperse to safer areas. Rather, the Truman Administration and its allies in Congress began to enact a series of provisions that embedded incentives for dispersion in the federal tax code and in military procurement laws and regulations. During the late 1940s and into the early 1950s, these provisions did not necessarily *mandate* that firms be dispersed, but they *indirectly* fostered dispersion by providing a host of financial incentives for new construction. Because new facilities were more likely to be built in lightly settled areas than in congested central cities, these incentives became a useful encouragement for decentralization.

The Armed Services Procurement Act of 1947 gave "the armed services power to use negotiated procurement as a dynamic instrument of preparedness and to take into consideration such factors as geographical location, avoidance of over-concentration in a few companies, and maintenance of a basic core of plants, facilities, skills, and personnel, *around which there can be expansion when it is urgently needed*" (emphasis added).[43] Subsequent guidelines released by the Defense Department's Munitions Board made a clear connection between such preferences for expansion-ready facilities and industrial dispersion. The Board released a directive entitled "Policy Guidance in the Location and Dispersal of New Construction" in January 1949 recommending that contractors and potential contractors take advantage of the need for new facilities to relocate themselves to safer, more remote locations.[44]

The preference for new over old, and the dispersed rather than the centralized, had the potential to significantly affect the behavior of private defense contractors, as the Defense Department allocated billions of dollars not only for R&D projects, but for direct construction costs as well. "According to an early estimate, expansion under the program is expected to reach a $5.9 billion total," noted the Congressional Joint Economic Committee in 1951, and "a considerable proportion will be used for new structures."[45] The Truman Administration further encouraged contractors to locate in dispersed areas through an executive order that made "the location of the facility with due regard to military security" a criterion for the awarding of Defense Department direct loans and loan guarantees to industrial contractors.[46]

Changes to the tax code also proved to be a useful policy vehicle for industrial dispersion. One change with potentially far-reaching effects on industrial location was an October 1950 amendment to the Internal Revenue Code that sped up the tax amortization process and allowed certain firms to write off up to 100 percent of "the costs of new capital equipment." Firms awarded "certificates of necessity" attesting to their defense-critical functions could take advantage of this accelerated tax amortization. Geographic dispersion was one criterion for the award of such certificates, making firms more likely to win this tax write-off if they were decentralized. Yet beyond this direct incentive, by providing a rich reward to firms who built brand-new facilities rather than rehabilitate existing ones, the write-off created additional economic incentives for firms to move from older plants to new, modern facilities in less-congested—that is, suburban—areas. Within six months of the establishment of this new program, over $4 billion worth of tax amortization had been awarded to U.S. firms.[47]

Procurement and tax-amortization incentives made up one prong of the dispersion strategy up to 1950; an extensive public relations effort made up the other. The NSRB released several widely distributed and slickly produced pamphlets on dispersion during this period, the first being September 1948's "National Security Factors in Industrial Location." Dispersion would not only reduce the potential for destruction in atomic attack, the report argued, it might prevent such attacks altogether: "If the industrial facilities of the United States were effectively dispersed, that fact alone would make an incalculable contribution toward the maintenance of peace because of the prohibitive expense of any enemy attempt to destroy this country's ability to defend itself. Dispersion could contribute significantly toward outlawing war."[48]

The federal government was not alone in making such grand statements about the potential of dispersion. These policies, in fact, gained publicity and political momentum partly because dispersion was an idea very much in keeping with prevailing "expert" opinion about what was best for American cities and for the American economy. In the late 1940s, many urban planners did not consider suburbanization to be particularly harmful to central cities. On the contrary, many of the most prominent urbanists of the day considered the decentralization of people and industry an essential measure to ensure the continued health of the central city. The gospel of decentralization was well entrenched in the city-planning profession by 1945, having some of its roots in the "garden city" ideas of the Victorian planner Ebenezer Howard, who had proposed the breakup of large urban agglomerations into smaller satellite communities separated by parks and countryside. While it was not feasible to abandon modernity and return to the rhythms of pre-industrial life, Howard had argued, society could be vastly improved if urban areas were decentralized into multi-nodal garden cities that were both residential and industrial. Howard's vision was not a rejection of urbanization altogether, but was one that proposed that the most modern and efficient urban model was one that integrated the best of the city and the best of the country.[49]

These ideas had inspired several prewar community planning experiments, one of which was the 1920's development of Radburn, New Jersey, by leaders of the Regional Plan Association of America (RPAA), a group cofounded by the prolific author and critic Lewis Mumford. During the New Deal, the federal government actually tried to get into the business of garden-cities through a Resettlement Administration effort called Greenbelt Towns. Unlike the quintessentially suburban experiment at Radburn, the Greenbelt Towns program attempted to revitalize poor and depopulated rural areas through planning along garden-city principles. While both Radburn and the Greenbelt Towns had limited success, the ideas of the self-described "decentrists" of the RPAA—thinkers who believed "in thinning out the dense cities and dispersing businesses and people to smaller places"[50]—continued to dominate the discourse around urban and regional planning in the early postwar period. Even before the U.S. entry into World War II, the leaders of the RPAA were quick to pick up on how urban decentralization and garden city ideas could be relevant to military planners. As one RPAA leader argued in a 1940 memorandum to federal officials: "limited size communities are a necessity of wartime security as well as peacetime economy of government and living."[51]

The common interest in decentralization held by city planners and defense strategists created interesting crossovers and collaborations between the two communities. By 1948 *The Bulletin of the Atomic Scientists* was featuring articles by the former president of the American Institute of Planners Tracey Augur, who neatly united arguments for dispersal and urban decentralization. Industrial dispersion policies would not only reduce vulnerability, Augur argued in these essays, but they would "increase capacity for production . . . by giving [industry] a modern urban plant." Such policies would also have social benefits in that they could "minimize the danger of fifth column activity based on internal unrest [resulting from] the slum and near-slum environments in which many millions of Americans are now forced to live."[52] In 1949, the American Institute of Architects (AIA) made "American Life and Architecture in the Atomic Age" one of the central themes of its annual meeting and invited members of the U.S. Atomic Energy Commission to be among the speakers on this subject. They and the other speakers at that year's AIA meeting reiterated the themes expounded by Augur and other leading lights of the city planning profession: urban decentralization was a two-for-one policy solution, strengthening national security as well as "creating well-rounded, modern centers for living and working."[53]

The mainstream press, in the course of reporting about developments in civil-defense policy in Washington and in special reports on the subject, began to draw similar links between the atomic threat to cities and the social and economic effects of urban congestion. In 1949 the magazine *U.S. News and World Report* predicted that the atomic threat would fundamentally change the spatial composition of cities. The "net result of Russia's getting the atomic bomb is likely to be a gradual change in the pattern of city and country within the United States. . . . [A]s time goes on, there will be a noticeable shift toward a smaller, fringe type of city, with low buildings and plenty of space for traffic, parking, recreation, and gardening." In a vivid parallel to contemporary accounts urging urban redevelopment and renewal, the article featured photographs of the skyscraper-dominated downtowns of New York, Chicago, Pittsburgh, and Detroit all sharing the ominous caption "a new element of danger."[54]

The identification of dispersion policy as a solution for urban problems helped the policy gain a wide-ranging, and sometimes unlikely, assortment of allies. Dispersion made sense to people and groups who were worried about social problems in the inner cities. The 1949 program of the CIO's (Congress of Industrial Organizations) National Committee on Regional Development and Conservation argued that urban decentralization was in the best interests of working people and their families, who "know better than anyone else the misery which comes from overcrowding in big cities," and endorsed industrial dispersion for national defense as an expeditious means of bringing this about.[55] And dispersion made sense to those who were concerned about regional industrial development. The idea of industrial decentralization was consistent with the pro-growth—and pro-decentralization—approaches of many local business coalitions during this period; in a 1950 speech to one of these groups, the San Francisco Bay Area Council, San Francisco's director of city planning observed: "It is more than a great piece of good fortune for city planers that policies which best serve the nation's security are also best for urban development. . . . We claim that this is good for our people and economical for our industry and business."[56]

Academics outside the city-planning community helped publicize the issue of dispersion through books and speeches, strongly advocating for the idea even while warning that it would be slow and costly. Physicist R. E. Lapp published a treatise on the issue entitled *Must We Hide?* in which he proposed that a long-term, voluntary program of urban decentralization occur over the subsequent ten to twenty years.[57] University of Chicago sociologist William F. Ogburn noted that one study performed by his colleagues had estimated that " 'rapid dispersion would cost something like 500 billion dollars!' " and suggested that the solution be "a gradual dispersion over a period of 25 to 150 years" whose initial phases would revolve around "locating new industry outside of cities and . . . moving old industries as their present plants become obsolete."[58]

Just as the political debates around the NSF articulated a political rationale and power structure for government science, the early conversations around dispersion revealed two important political realities underlying the relationship of science, government, and the shape of urban space. First, the Cold War effort turned the federal government into an immensely powerful customer of industry and gave it a vested interest in where its contractors located within a given metropolitan area. Because of strategic concerns, the federal government worked actively—albeit through low-profile persuasive tactics rather than large-scale planning— to encourage firms to move out of central cities. Second, economic, social, and spatial changes in mid-twentieth-century American cities created a political context in which these efforts were welcomed and encouraged, and gave the effort crucial outside support and political momentum.

Not only was urban dispersion a principle consistent with expert opinion and with pro-growth industrial development philosophies of local business coalitions, but it was one in an array of postwar policies that, both intentionally and indirectly, were making suburban locations more affordable and practical for thousands of employers and millions of workers, even those with very modest incomes. Placing dispersion in the metropolitan context of the late 1940s shows the neat overlap between "strategic" and "economic" functions. Although the American "urban crisis" is often characterized as a phenomenon beginning in the late 1960s, the urban economic and demographic transformations that spurred this were well under way twenty years earlier. This was, in good part, the result of new technology, some of it seemingly mundane. Cars and trucks, marketed aggressively to postwar consumers and made more affordable through new financing mechanisms, were becoming the dominant form of personal and commercial transportation. Public transit systems, whose fixed routes had often determined a regular and radial spread of urban settlement, fell into disrepair as improved road and highway networks began to spread out of central cities, opening up remote areas for residential and industrial development. Innovations like air conditioning made it possible to manufacture goods in a controlled climate regardless of outdoor heat and were beginning to encourage migration to warmer parts of the country like Texas and Florida.[59]

By this period, demographic changes were also leaving their mark on large American cities. The oppressive segregation of the South prompted hundreds of thousands of African Americans to migrate to northern cities beginning in the 1940s. Once they arrived there, racial discrimination in housing and in employment often prevented upward mobility and forced African Americans to live in crowded and deteriorating ghettos. As black migrants came into central-city neighborhoods, the whites who lived there fought to keep their communities white through racial covenants prohibiting selling homes to blacks, and, when that was ineffective, they resorted to violence. White households moved to more racially homogeneous outlying neighborhoods, or moved out of cities altogether. Demographic change also prompted industries to move out of central cities, following white professional workers and escaping the rising costs of doing business in increasingly poorer communities.[60]

Urban decentralization occurred not simply because of these "push" factors, but because of immensely powerful "pulls" as well. White households and employers left the cities because they had opportunities and the incentives to leave. Some of these were already in place by the late 1940s. The GI Bill of 1944 provided returning veterans with a generous mortgage guarantee for buying a first home. This and other federal home-mortgage subsidy programs made home ownership affordable for a majority of white Americans for the very first time, but favored new, single-family construction and economically homogeneous communities, preferences that effectively shut out urban neighborhoods and minority home buyers from the process. While the passage of the Interstate Highway Act was a decade in the future, public subsidies were already building the roads and highways that made car and truck transport so practical, and made living and working in suburbs and exurbs infinitely more feasible. By the early 1950s, tax amortization for new commercial construction—mechanisms similar to those used to encourage industrial dispersion but more far-reaching in their execution—prompted the construction of suburban shopping centers and other kinds of industrial developments, creating retail magnets that drew even more people and jobs to outlying areas. State and local public subsidies also facilitated the rise of the suburbs by paying for an essential infrastructure of roads, sewers, water mains, and public services in new, privately developed residential subdivisions.[61]

Because of these changes, dispersion arrived on the domestic policy agenda at a moment when political and business leaders were not only embracing decentralization as a sensible economic and social strategy, but were also turning their attention to the physical renewal and redevelopment of older urban centers. The efforts to redevelop distressed urban areas had local roots, and dated to well before the Second World War. Although depression and wartime mobilization stalled the implementation of schemes to renew urban areas, after 1945 public and private coalitions in a number of large cities began to develop and implement comprehensive redevelopment plans. New York and Philadelphia, already well-established centers of housing activism, were among the first to embark on such efforts.[62] Philadelphia's Redevelopment Authority, in its first annual report in 1946, articulated the high hopes local officials had about the potential of urban renewal: "redevelopment affects the life of the entire city and is affected by the life of the city, just as dropping a pebble in a pond sends wavelets out over the pool."[63] Passage of federal urban renewal legislation boosted local efforts politically and financially. Title I of the Housing Act of 1949 authorized $500 million to cities for urban land clearance for redevelopment and for low-income housing. Intended to alleviate a long-standing and severe housing shortage in cities, Title I also made low-income housing construction and slum clearance profitable by allocating money to private developers and quasi-private redevelopment authorities.

This local and national push to redevelop urban centers helps explain why the political dynamics around dispersion during the late 1940s sometimes seemed like those accompanying an urban economic development initiative. Dispersion gained active support from a range of interests outside the government who, for various social and economic reasons, were interested in making cities more low-density, decentralized places. Urban planners put an intellectual seal of approval on the government's plan to disperse industry to the suburbs. While the motivation for the program was civil defense, the program was consistent with and complementary to larger political and economic trends. Federal officials acknowledged internally that the redevelopment of urban slums complemented civil defense and urban dispersion efforts. One program officer urged his superior "to call to the attention of the Civil Defense Administrator the fact that conditions in urban centers—that is, slums and blight— toward which the slum clearance program is directed are those which may be the most vulnerable in event of attack." He continued, "local programs directed to the removal of these conditions can therefore contribute to the security of the communities."[64] The official's words reflected a common undercurrent between defense-related dispersion ideas and urban renewal programs—that *renewed* and *safe* cities also happened to be *less dense*. As the campaign for industrial dispersion continued, the major economic and spatial changes occurring in American cities became increasingly important to dispersion policy's design, implementation, and ultimate effects.

Policy and Geography, 1950–1965

Dispersion Meets Suburbanization

While Washington policy makers managed to put in place some key elements of urban economic development strategy by 1950, ongoing political infighting and budget concerns continued to bog down the various policy proposals of the nascent national security state. Despite forceful and high-profile arguments for increased government support of basic research, the various proposals relating to the NSF continued to languish in Congress; despite a wide range of outside support for dispersion, the policy appeared to have little visible effect on private-sector location patterns. Although the Truman Administration had already articulated many of the ideological underpinnings of Cold War security policy, most notably the goal of the "containment" of the spread of Communism to other nations, these ideas had not translated into broad-based changes in domestic appropriations. The partisan split between the Republican Congress and the Democratic president between 1946 and 1948 had a good deal to do with this state of affairs, but even after Congress returned to Democratic control relatively little legislative progress occurred. In the late 1940s the United States remained the only nation possessing atomic weapons; without the Bomb, Soviet Russia was an abstract menace around which it was hard to mobilize public attention and political action.[65]

This changed dramatically in 1949, when the Soviets performed a successful test of an atomic bomb. Following close on the heels of this event, in 1950 the United States entered into a war to suppress a Soviet-backed Communist takeover of Korea. Now the threat of Communism and of nuclear war moved from a hypothetical scenario to an urgent crisis. In 1950 President Truman's seminal policy directive, NSC-68, called for a rebuilding of the American military apparatus to defend the nation and contain the spread of Communism abroad. The emergence of the Soviets as a second atomic superpower and the conflict in Korea ushered in an era in which the Cold War was an integral, looming part of everyday life in the United States. While only 2 percent of citizens polled in 1945 cited the atomic bomb as their chief worry, by 1952 another poll found that 53 percent of Americans thought that "general war"—atomic conflict—was likely.[66]

These events turned industrial dispersion—and the larger civil defense effort of which it was a part—from a somewhat moribund political side issue into a matter requiring immediate action by policy makers at all levels of government. Using the World War II mobilization of cities as a model, military agencies, state governments, and local authorities began to implement far-reaching, well-publicized campaigns of citizen preparedness—from recruiting volunteer air raid wardens to stockpiling supplies to improving evacuation plans. Many of the protective measures would have been of little defensive use in an actual nuclear war, however. The large institutional buildings designated "fallout shelters" in cities would likely have provided little or no protection from the powerful bombs and no protection at all from radioactive fallout. While the air-raid warden system could be effective in conventional bombing raids, volunteer wardens on city rooftops had little usefulness in scenarios under which a single high-flying aircraft had the power to drop an atomic bomb that could annihilate an entire city.[67]

The underlying impracticability of the civil defense effort may have been the reason the U.S. Congress never funded the program to the degree its military advocates would have liked. But the widespread publicity garnered by preparedness campaigns made civil defense in cities a compelling issue, particularly for people living in large cities. By 1951 the Gallup organization had found that 56 percent of residents of the largest cities (100,000 population or more) did not feel safe living in their communities in event of atomic war.[68] Local governments and civic organizations, who bore much of the responsibility for organizing and supporting civil-defense efforts, often became the most vocal proponents of continuing such measures. Local newspapers were full of photographs of mayors and city councilmen proudly opening a new fallout shelter, or looking on approvingly as tons of canned goods were unloaded into city stockpiles.

As urban leaders intensified their preparations for the possibility of "total war," Washington policy makers redoubled their efforts to redirect federal money *away* from the "ground zeroes" of central cities and into the suburban periphery. Stung by Congressional criticism about the low rates of industrial dispersion up to 1950, during the last two years of his presidency, Truman used executive-branch powers to create even more incentives for firms to disperse. In crafting these incentives, the Administration sought to increase industrial participation in the dispersion program by adapting a looser, more generous definition of what was considered an adequate degree of dispersion, and by more carefully targeting these incentives to firms that were most likely to use them.

President Truman signaled this shift in strategy with an August 1951 executive memorandum ordering all government agencies "to enact concrete measures encouraging industries to move out of dense urban cores."[69] The memorandum departed from earlier federal recommendations on dispersion in two respects, both of which stemmed from an acknowledgment of the economic factors restricting wholesale urban decentralization. Prior dispersion policy had drawn little distinction between industries, arguing that any sort of urban concentration was a bad thing and indicating that dispersion measures should target all industry. Yet large, established industries were hardly "footloose": they had huge capital investments in existing plants, or needed to be near particular natural resources like mines or water sources. Picking up and moving was easier, the memorandum reasoned, for new growth industries that had fewer ties to a particular place. "Our policy, therefore, must be directed mainly toward the dispersal of new and expanding industries,"

Truman wrote. In 1951, the "new and expanding"—and mobile—government contractors were often small firms in the business of developing and manufacturing sophisticated electronic equipment like semiconductors that lacked any significant consumer market. In short, these were the firms that would later develop into some of the giants of the late twentieth-century global high-technology industry.

The other policy shift evidenced by the memorandum was a redefinition of what was considered a safe area in which to disperse. Rather than move to distant rural areas, industries could disperse into "local marketing areas adjacent to industrial or metropolitan districts in all sections of the country." These areas should be ten to twenty miles from nuclear ground zero, the city center. Dispersing industry to suburban areas was not economically harmful to a region, the memorandum reasoned, because production facilities and jobs would stay in the same "marketing area" and have easy access to the central city.

The NSRB amplified the message of the presidential memorandum with simultaneous publication of a widely distributed pamphlet that picked up on the themes of security and urban health made over the past five years by planners, academics, and interest groups. Entitled *Is Your Plant a Target?* the publication emphasized that dispersion policy was in keeping with existing market trends. "The long-range objective of industrial deployment is to carry out a natural industrial expansion away from congested centers," the report wrote. "This movement has been under way for a number of years. A speed-up of this natural expansion is an urgent security measure."[70]

In the matter of industrial location, the report went further than the Truman memorandum in outlining criteria for proper dispersion of industry. Not only should facilities be ten to twenty miles from the city center, but they "should be located a sufficient distance from one another so as to avoid clusters creating new targets" and "should be limited in size to avoid any concentrations which would create new targets." Industrial dispersion would be ineffective if it simply created new urban concentrations; settlement must be more diffused than it had been in the past in order to be properly dispersed. Thus, the ideal location for defense-crucial American industry, as defined by the president and by his chief civil-defense strategists, was in a small community that was at a certain distance from the central city but was still connected to a regional metropolitan economy. The ideal location, really, was a suburb.

Although Congress was now back under Democratic control, some Congressional resistance to the idea remained. The measure made little economic sense to these legislators whose districts contained few if any areas low-density enough to qualify as properly dispersed. Connecticut Republican James T. Patterson introduced a bill to stop the dispersion

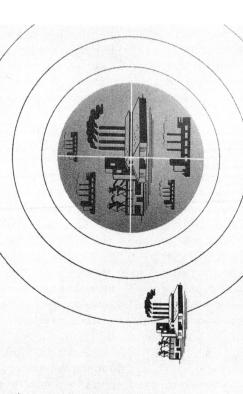

YOUR PLANT
CAN HAVE GREATER PROTECTION . . .

In the event of all-out atomic attack upon the United States, dispersion of new or expanded industrial facilities within your local marketing area is one of the keys to:

● Continued essential production—the backbone of national security.

● Maintenance of our production superiority.

● Ultimate victory for our free world.

Figure 1.1. The frontispiece of *Is Your Plant a Target?* The NSRB brochure was an important tool in convincing American business of the economic and strategic usefulness of industrial dispersion. National Security Resources Board, *Is Your Plant a Target?* (Washington, D.C.: U.S. Government Printing Office, 1951), 2.

1.

THE PROGRAM IS DESIGNED TO DISPERSE NEW AND EXPANDING INDUSTRY—

NOT TO MOVE ESTABLISHED INDUSTRY

A dispersal trend in production centers has been apparent for a number of years. This has not been an upheaval of whole populations, factories, and economies, but a gradual growth from and around around metropolitan centers. Industrial dispersion for national security is a speed-up of this natural process by deploying new and expanding industries.

This dispersion program does not call for moving of established industry from one section of the country to another. Nor does this program discourage voluntary relocation to any section if desired by individual companies.

Industry has concentrated its production in areas where raw materials, labor, housing, transportation, and access to markets were adequate for economical and efficient operation. These location factors cannot be ignored.

The Nation's industrial strength for defense, however, is being expanded. With the increasing destructiveness of atomic weapons, industrial dispersion can provide improved security for new industrial capacity.

Newly created industries or expansion of established industries offer the best opportunity to carry out orderly industrial dispersion within a local marketing area.

2.

NO REGION OF THE COUNTRY IS TO BE BUILT UP AT THE EXPENSE OF ANOTHER

All areas of the Nation, working together in the common objective to build superior industrial production, make the Nation strong.

Each region and section of the country is making its particular, essential contribution to the total strength of the Nation.

An industrial dispersion policy that would weaken any single region or section would weaken our over-all strength.

It is the policy of the National Government to disperse defense production as widely as possible. No section of the Nation should be weakened. All should be strengthened and expanded.

Figure 1.2. *Is Your Plant a Target?* emphasized that "new and expanding industry" was most able to follow dispersion procedures. The publication also sought to reassure its readers that dispersion would not favor one region of the country over another. However, such favoritism was already being exhibited in the defense contracting process generally. National Security Resources Board, *Is Your Plant a Target?* (Washington, D.C.: U.S. Government Printing Office, 1951), 7.

order in late August, but the measure gained little attention or legislative traction. Newspapers like the *Washington Post* came out in favor of Truman's proposed strategy of targeted dispersion and used the opportunity to further chastise legislators for dragging their feet: "Congress' hostility to such a plan can only be construed as part of general lethargy that seems to be affecting every aspect of civilian defense."[71] What was more remarkable, given the scope of the memorandum and the bold proposals of the accompanying NSRB publication, was the relatively little amount of attention these acts garnered in either Congress or the press. Truman Administration officials must have been aware of the political advantages to releasing a possibly unpopular directive in August, when Congress was in recess, Washington's summer heat was in full force, and most decision makers and pundits were on vacation.

From then on, industrial dispersion efforts remained firmly in the hands of the executive branch. The Truman, and subsequently the Eisenhower, Administrations used the tools at the disposal of the executive branch and altered military procurement policies over the course of the 1950s so that dispersed industries had an advantage in the contracting process. Incentives no longer revolved merely around the financing of new construction, but they were crafted in ways that made "proper location of a new defense plant a condition to receiving defense-production assistance."[72] Defense Department directives in 1954 and 1958 further reminded procuring agencies to consider geographic dispersal in their decision-making process, the 1958 directive instructing the military to "plan production among dispersed production and maintenance sources, utilize alternate sources and effect such other feasible measures that will reduce vulnerability and maximize the possibility of survival for any period subsequent to the initial stages of a general war."[73]

At the same time, changing defense concerns and economic realities served gradually to change the standards and definitions of "proper" dispersion. A revision to dispersion policy in 1955 changed the geographic standards defined in the Truman memorandum to make them better tailored to the needs of individual metropolitan areas. "Dispersion or spacing," noted one bulletin, "must be balanced with the basic needs for a properly functioning urban economy."[74] The new guidelines empowered states and localities to take a greater role in determining how dispersal should progress, "No hard and fast rule can be provided by the Federal Government that would be equally suitable in all situations and in all parts of the country," testified one defense official in Congressional hearings on this issue.[75] Perhaps the most important sign that dispersion had become a policy shaped as much by economic considerations as it was by strategic ones was the designation of the chief federal economic-development agency—the Office of Area Development—as the entity in charge of the dispersion effort. Even though the guidance policies established by the Defense Department remained in force, the day-to-day administration of the dispersion effort—including the awarding of the all-important certificates of necessity—now was the responsibility of the federal government's economic development office.

The accumulation of such policies appeared to further sweeten the pot for firms choosing to move to suburban areas. And it spilled over into industries that did not necessarily depend on defense dollars for their survival. Beginning in 1956, the IRS further refined tax amortization policy to allow manufacturers (whether they were contractors with "certificates of necessity" or not) to claim tax write-offs for all costs associated with moving to a dispersed location. "The write-off is based on the outlay over and above the investment normally required if he chose an economically sound but inadequately dispersed site," noted the Department of Commerce.[76] While high-profile political discussions about dispersion largely died down after the mid-1950s, the executive branch continued to reinforce dispersion guidelines well into the 1960s through memoranda and internal actions.[77]

Did dispersion accomplish what its designers intended? Did it make defense contractors behave differently than other kinds of firms? These questions are difficult to answer conclusively because of the under-the-radar-screen structure of dispersion incentives, and the fact that they appeared on the scene at the same time as other public incentives and economic and technological shifts that encouraged industrial decentralization. But as early as the mid-1950s, signs began to emerge that dispersion policy was having its intended effect on some sectors of American industry. A 1956 Commerce Department report noted that the traditional geographic concentration of the electronic industry in a few large cities began to break down after 1950 and disperse over wider geographic areas. "Governmental policy on industrial dispersion has undoubtedly encouraged this move," the report noted. "All other things being essentially equal, a firm with well-dispersed facilities has a definite advantage in securing military electronic business over competitors whose facilities are in critical target areas."[78] The small, new companies in the business of making high-tech electronic equipment like semiconductors and early computers had no significant consumer market for their products in the late 1940s and 1950s. Contracts from the military were essential to their survival and future growth. By 1957 federal funds made up 61 percent of electronics industry R&D, 54 percent of communication industry R&D, and 30 percent of R&D dollars in the professional and scientific instrument industry. Manufacturers of specialized electronics equipment and other sophisticated technologies were in many cases kept afloat entirely because of military research and development grants.[79]

But the persuasive mechanisms of dispersal policy affected larger defense contractors as well; when such firms needed to build new research or manufacturing facilities to accommodate increased military demands, they could greatly reduce their construction costs if they built in dispersed areas. One defense contractor, writing in an armed-forces journal, noted that even though his firm was based in Philadelphia, it had opened facilities in the city's outer suburbs as well as in the Sunbelt states of North Carolina and Florida. "Dispersal is more than defense against disaster," he argued, "it is good business, and good business insurance."[80]

Standing alone, dispersion incentives might not have convinced many contractors to move their facilities out of central cities. In conjunction with other economic and social trends and other federal policies, however, they presented a much more favorable economic proposition. Enabled by new technology and subsidized by new public infrastructure, millions of white Americans moved to suburban neighborhoods, and thousands of American retailers followed to serve them. Home builders capitalized on the availability of cheap mortgages by rapidly building huge subdivisions of suburban tract homes, each with a driveway in front for the family car. These developments—from Levittown on Long Island to the towns of the San Fernando Valley in Los Angeles—became cultural shorthand for the economic and social promise of postwar suburbia. Suburban, auto-dependent living created new geographies of consumption as well, and shopping malls blossomed near highway interchanges and obviated the need for suburban shoppers to travel downtown.[81]

These changes were particularly fortuitous for dispersion policy. The 1955 revisions to the Truman memorandum abandoned the ten-mile dispersion standard, stating that such a standard was infeasible given the power of more sophisticated thermonuclear weapons.[82] However, this expansion did not contradict dispersion's economic considerations, for less than five years after Truman's memorandum, some American metropolitan areas had decentralized to an extent that the metropolitan "marketing area" reached beyond the ten-mile dispersion boundary. Firms could decentralize further, placing themselves out of reach of new and more powerful bombs, yet still remain within the boundaries of the urban economy.

Federal policies encouraging dispersion may have paled in comparison to the other incentives encouraging industry to move to the suburbs in the 1950s, but they formed a crucial element in the suburbanization of science. In this case, intent matters as much to our story as actual outcome. Dispersion was, in effect, a political endorsement of the idea that defense-critical work—of which scientific research was a central element—was best conducted away from the urbanized commercial center. These policies targeted generous economic incentives to encourage the suburbanization of a highly persuadable group—"new and expanding" industries with little commercial market for their high-tech products. In doing so, the policies helped *normalize* the idea that scientific activity should occur in the suburbs. Dispersion was also a rather ingenious example of persuading private-sector businesses to act in the states' interests, while simultaneously allowing firms to maintain the illusion of independence from government control. The Philadelphia defense contractor quoted above also proclaimed that his company had dispersed "without government meddling. It may honestly be said that [the firm's] management planned it this way, and has proved that it is profitable."[83] Because of the number of tax breaks and competitive advantages in the procurement process given to decentralized facilities, it is not surprising that this business leader and his counterparts in other contracting firms found dispersion so beneficial to their bottom lines. Business leaders might have concluded that their decisions simply followed market trends, while failing to fully acknowledge that the state had a great deal of control over these market forces.

The Cold War University

The developments at home and abroad in the first years of the 1950s jump-started dispersion policy and civil defense, and they also turned Cold War science policy into a programmatic reality. When the NSF at last became law in 1950, its mandate was not only to develop a national program of basic research and scientific education but also, when requested by the Defense Department, to "support specific defense research activities."[84] Its passage marked the beginning of an era of rapid (and, it seemed to some, exponential) increase in government investments in R&D. Within a very short time, federal expenditures in this area began a rapid upward trajectory that would last for well over a decade. Between 1950 and 1955, R&D expenditures more than tripled, reaching over $3.3 billion, or 3.3 percent of the entire U.S. budget.[85]

However, while the aggregate growth of R&D skyrocketed, the rates of expansion were not consistent among the different parts of the Cold War science complex. In the early 1950s the vast majority of funds and the highest rates of growth lay on the "D" side of the equation, a category whose grantees were large private contractors and military facilities, not universities. The expenditures on development made the "R" side—and especially the basic research with this "R"—appear rather puny by comparison, even though federal research expenditures had risen to unprecedented levels. Although the political rhetoric of the science debate had emphasized the fundamental role of basic, university-based research in

Table 1.1
Federal Research and Development Expenditures as a Percentage of the U.S. Budget, 1950–70 (millions of dollars)

Fiscal Year	Total Budget Outlays	R&D Expenditures	R&D as Percent of Total Budget
1950	43,147	1,083	2.5
1951	45,797	1,301	2.8
1952	67,962	1,816	2.7
1953	76,769	3,101	4.0
1954	70,890	3,148	4.4
1955	68,509	3,308	4.8
1956	70,460	3,446	4.9
1957	76,741	4,462	5.8
1958	82,575	4,991	6.0
1959	92,104	5,806	6.3
1960	92,223	7,744	8.4
1961	97,795	9,287	9.5
1962	106,813	10,387	9.7
1963	111,311	12,012	10.8
1964	118,584	14,707	12.4
1965	118,430	14,889	12.6
1966	134,652	16,018	11.9
1967	158,254	16,859	10.7
1968	178,833	17,049	9.5
1969	184,548	16,348	8.9
1970	196,588	15,736	8.0

Source: National Science Foundation, *Federal Funds for Research, Development, and Other Scientific Activities* (Washington: U.S. Government Printing Office, 1972), 3.

the postwar world, most of the new spending went to applied research taking place in government and industrial laboratories. By 1955 only $169 million of the more than $3 billion the government spent on research and development went to university projects.[86] The level of federal expenditures on basic research elicited public criticism from Nobel laureates like atomic chemist Glenn Seaborg, who argued that "pure research should be encouraged as the best training for the nation's short supply of young scientists and engineers."[87] Similar calls came from other "expert" quarters. The Commission on Organization of the Executive Branch of the Government, known as the Second Hoover Commission, argued in a May 1955 report that "the foundation of the greatest sector of human advancement in modern times is basic research into nature's laws and materials" and that the public sector needed to do much more to support such research.[88]

It took another international crisis to bring the Cold War science complex closer to realizing the ideals of government-sponsored basic research articulated in the legislative debates over the NSF. On 4 October 1957 the Soviet Union launched the Sputnik I satellite, an event that shocked the nation's political leadership and set off a barrage of criticism in the mass media and self-recrimination in Washington government circles.[89] Political leaders interpreted the Sputnik debacle as evidence that the American system of scientific education lagged far behind that of the Soviets, despite the great investments that had been made in scientific research since 1945. Consequently, not only did President Eisenhower and the Congress greatly increase the overall funds for research after the fall of 1957, but they also refocused federal spending to provide more support for the educational and research activities of universities.

Some Eisenhower Administration officials had previously "scoffed at" the basic research conducted by university laboratories, finding basic research "a kind of academic 'boondoggle.' "[90] In the post-Sputnik world, however, basic research won new respect and political support, and new federal grant programs for graduate education and the construction of university facilities further enriched institutional coffers. More than ever before, national leaders saw scientific excellence as key to winning the Cold War, and recognized research universities as the chief producers of scientific innovation and talent. A 1960 report by Eisenhower's chief science advisors provided an eloquent summary of the new attitude of the federal government toward the university. "With all their irritating faults," the advisors wrote, "universities are essential agencies of our national hopes, and they must be treated accordingly."[91]

One of the first responses by the Eisenhower Administration was to propose increased funding for the NSF, whose budget nearly tripled, reaching $136 million in fiscal year 1959.[92] Other federal funding streams began to creep steadily upward. In 1955 the federal government spent $286 million on basic research. By 1960 this sum had more than doubled to $693 million; by 1965 that figure had more than doubled again to reach nearly $1.6 *billion*. Between 1955 and 1965, basic research had grown from 8 percent to 12 percent of the total R&D budget.[93] Government publications of the time made the connection between basic research and university education explicit. "The process of graduate education and the process of basic research belong together at every possible level," wrote the President's Scientific Advisory Committee (PSAC) in 1960. "We believe that the two kinds of activity reinforce each other in a great variety of ways, and that each is weakened when carried on without the other."[94]

Because the vast majority of basic research monies went to universities and affiliated institutions, the proportional increases in basic research at universities and colleges were much greater than what is indicated by the overall totals. These institutions went from receiving $169 million in federal R&D funds in 1955 to receiving over $1 billion in 1965; $879 million of the 1965 total (an incredible 82 percent) were for research activities classified as basic research.[95] With this rise in grant money also came a deliberate effort to share the wealth among a larger pool of institutions. The PSAC's 1960 report continued: "we urge the importance for the country of an increase in the number of universities in which first-rate research and graduate teaching go forward together. . . . we must hope that where there were only a handful of generally first-rate academic centers of science a generation ago and may be as many as fifteen or twenty today, there will be thirty or forty in another fifteen years."[96]

The new emphasis on basic research benefited American research universities well beyond the research laboratory. Politicians and the media interpreted Sputnik as a failure of U.S. scientific research and a sign that the nation's educational system—from elementary to graduate level— was deeply flawed.[97] In the months after Sputnik, academics, politicians, and the media expressed deep concern that Soviet schools and universities were "grinding out double the number of technically trained people that ours are producing."[98] Sputnik turned the political leaders of the national defense effort—including the most powerful legislators in the land—into active supporters of scientific education. In the fall of 1957, Senate Armed Services Committee chair Lyndon B. Johnson proposed a series of educational funding initiatives to address the American deficiencies in science education. For the first time, the federal government would allocate money directly toward college and university teaching and scholarships. President Eisenhower signed the bill into law in September 1958 as the National Defense Education Act (NDEA). The NDEA marked the first time that the federal government gave this kind of funding solely to educational institutions (the NSF's programs affected government and industrial laboratories as well as academic ones), and it set the precedent for later federal investments in university education. The NDEA was unlike its successors, however, in that its provisions characterized these educational measures in terms that were directly related to the competition with the Soviets for trained scientific manpower.[99] Reflecting upon the NDEA ten years after its passage, President Johnson remembered telling his Senate colleagues, "history may well record . . . that we saved liberty and saved freedom when we undertook a crash program in the field of education. . . . I hope this bill is only the forerunner of better things to come."[100] Although the NDEA was a seminal federal education policy, it was generally understood that, as one official later put it, the NDEA "could not have passed at that time without the 'defense' label."[101]

Although the scientific manpower problem was often interpreted by the press and by politicians as a matter of inadequate numbers, what American science really faced by the beginning of the 1960s was a problem of quality rather than quantity. While the number of M.A. and Ph.D. programs in science and engineering had expanded significantly since the 1940s, there was a growing perception that Americans were far behind their Soviet counterparts in the caliber and level of scientific training. As Stanford provost Frederick Terman pointed out in 1962, the issue was that "companies are in general able to find warm bodies for their basic billets. However, far too often employers fill positions at bachelor's degree level when men with master's and doctor's training are desired but not available."[102]

Changes on the development and production sides of the military-industrial complex also increased pressure for more highly trained scientists and engineers. During the early 1950s, the large-scale production of conventional armaments to fight the war in Korea and build up military capacity at home had given the Cold War effort a distinctly blue-collar cast. Defense workers were more likely to work on an assembly line than in a laboratory. Over the course of the decade, increased technological sophistication in weaponry—such as the development of new missile technologies—and the new emphasis on space exploration called for a higher-skilled workforce. "Traditional metal fabricating processes give way to more intricate and sophisticated techniques," NASA official Earl Hilburn testified to Congress in 1964, reflecting on the changes of the past decade. "Consequently, blue-collar workers are fewer; while scientists, engineers, and technicians have gained in numbers in establishments serving defense and space procurement needs."[103]

The new federal money available to universities translated not simply into funds for new experiments or new graduate scholarships, but also into new *buildings* in which to house these activities. The third prong of the post-Sputnik strategy to improve higher education and address the scientific manpower shortage was the Higher Education Facilities Act of 1963, which provided generous federal grants and loans for facility construction at all kinds of colleges and universities. Administered by the states, the program paid one-third of the construction costs of science and engineering facilities and offered loans for up to three-fourths of the cost of any kind of campus facility, for scientific purposes or not.[104] In the same year, Congress passed the Health Professions Education Act, another initiative with significant implications for campus expansion. This initiative sought to expand the pool of medical professionals in a manner similar to the campaign to increase the supply and quality of scientists and engineers; to meet projected rates of the expansion of medical research, one estimate found, the nation would need double the number of medical personnel by 1970.[105] Among other things, the Act allocated funds for the construction of medical and dental schools—

an additional boon to major research universities, most of which had affiliated medical facilities and teaching hospitals.[106]

This was not the first time the federal government had supported education and medical-facility construction. The Hill-Burton program, enacted in 1946, provided funds to states for hospital construction, particularly in economically depressed or underserved areas, and was an important moment in federal support of public health and hospitals. Between 1948 and 1961, federal Hill-Burton funds had accounted for twelve percent, or about $1.2 billion, of the total spent nationally on hospital construction.[107] Since 1949, the department of Health, Education, and Welfare also had administered a surplus property program that transferred unused government facilities to nonprofit educational or public health institutions at huge discounts, and sometimes completely for free.[108] The post-Sputnik facilities programs were a departure from past practice, however, as they gave universities and their affiliated medical institutions unprecedented flexibility and control over construction funds. Unlike Hill-Burton, whose funds were allocated by state agencies, universities had control over how the new facilities money would be spent. Unlike surplus property transfer, which required that universities adopt their facilities needs to older buildings that might be at some distance from their campuses, the facilities programs of the 1960s supported new construction on or near university complexes.

Despite the new incentives and opportunities created by the NSF, NDEA, and facilities construction programs, some observers continued to worry that persistent stereotypes of "antihumanistic" scientists discouraged students from choosing scientific education.[109] Forty percent of respondents to a 1959 University of Michigan survey agreed with the statement "scientists are apt to be odd and peculiar people."[110] The gender segregation and racial homogeneity of scientific professions also posed a problem, as one Congressional report identified: "Women apparently find such careers unattractive. In particular, only 1 percent of American engineers are women (compared with 29 percent in the Soviet Union). Other social groups, such as Negroes, make a disproportionately small contribution to the national supply of scientific and technical manpower."[111] Dr. Edward Teller told the Preparedness Subcommittee of the Senate Committee on Armed Services that "the spirit in our schools is such that a kid who is interested in science is ridiculed by his fellow students, and he will very rapidly lose that interest." In contrast, Soviet students considered a career as a scientist "the best thing to be."[112]

The private sector joined in the effort to bring scientists into the cultural mainstream. By the mid-1950s, images of "normal" scientists proliferated in the media. A recruitment film produced by the chemical company Monsanto "displayed a group of scientists in white coats and assured the audience: 'No geniuses here; just a bunch of average Americans working together.' "[113] Social critic William H. Whyte later asked a Monsanto executive "why [the] company felt impelled to claim to the world that its brainwork was carried on by just average Americans. The executive explained that Monsanto had thought about the point and wanted to deter young men from the idea that industrial chemistry was for genius types."[114] The message was clear: scientists were ordinary folk, with extraordinary talent.

The laudatory media treatment of scientists may not have resolved the scientific manpower shortage, but it did foster a growing popular interest in science and in the leading university scientists of the day.[115] In 1960 *Time* magazine named fifteen American scientists—including some of the nation's most prominent atomic researchers—as its "Men of the Year."[116] This kind of media attention on scientists and their activities bolstered their visibility and their credibility; as one observer noted, "media treatments were almost uniformly on the side of the 'expert' who was depicted as 'objective, disinterested, uncorruptible [*sic*],' and an 'impartial searcher for the truth.' " By the early 1960s "most polls designed to rate professional prestige put the scientist close to the top."[117] A 1965 NSF report to Congress noted, "the adult population of the United States has increased by approximately 5 percent in the past 4 years. In the same period of time, subscriptions to the magazine *Science* have increased by 45 percent, to *Scientific American* by 60 percent, to *National Geographic* by 44 percent."[118]

The crescendo of popular excitement about scientific discovery and scientific men is hardly surprising given the great number of resources that had been flowing toward the American science complex. All of these investments were beginning to pay off—not only in increasingly sophisticated weaponry and the dazzling hardware of the space program, but also in new advances in medicine and other discoveries with the potential to improve the quality of everyday life. By the beginning of the 1960s, Americans may have had some trepidation about the size and scope of the Cold War military effort, but they could also see the results of the nation's unprecedented investments in scientific research and education—and the potential for even greater accomplishments in the future. And this shift meant that research universities played a distinctly different role in American life in 1960 than they had in 1940. Rather than being centers of privately sponsored activity, universities were now publicly subsidized institutions charged with key public responsibilities and provided with new and unprecedented opportunities for expansion.

Power, Money, and Location

By the early 1960s, Cold War policy had put in place several key elements
of the institutional framework that governed the development of high-
tech regions over the course of the next several decades. Accelerated and
vastly enlarged spending on defense-related research and development
increased the political and economic clout of research-based industry
and research universities. Economic and strategic concerns about the
rate of scientific innovation prompted new federal funding for basic scientific research and university education, and gave certain prominent
scientists a role in national politics and government that they had never
enjoyed. However, the national political and economic environment in
which the science complex grew meant that it did not bestow this new
power and money equitably.

First, not every university got to be a "Cold War university." Following
patterns of power and privilege established in the earliest years of the
Cold War, most of the government R&D largesse flowed to a small pool
of contractors and a small and elite group of research universities. Despite the escalation in this kind of defense-related spending during the
1950s and 1960s, the size and membership of this exclusive club remained remarkably unchanged. Corporations and research institutions
that won hefty research contracts in the early 1950s were, for the most
part, top defense contractors ten and twenty years later. In the case of
universities, government spending followed established patterns of scientific capacity. In 1939 and 1965, exactly the same group of twenty-five
universities (fifteen private and ten public) was responsible for producing two-thirds of the nation's Ph.D.'s in science. Not surprisingly, the top
twenty-five institutions received 60 percent of all funds spent by the federal government on university science, and "an even greater percentage
of the research grants and contracts of mission-oriented agencies." The
schools that were almost always at the top of both these lists, producing
the most scientists and receiving the most federal money, were the places
that had been at the top of the heap at the beginning of the Cold War:
Harvard and MIT.[119]

The institutional elitism that Harley Kilgore had tried to dissipate with
his NSF proposals had become deeply entrenched, resulting from a scientific grant-making process that was ostensibly meritocratic, but where
the "best" research institutions also happened to be the best connected.
At the outset of the Cold War, only a few research universities had the
capacity to conduct the sort of high-level experiments required by new
military research contracts. Not coincidentally, these institutions were
often ones whose scientists and administrators had been engaged in war-

time research efforts and the postwar organization of the federal scientific infrastructure. When the primary rationale for grant making was the qualifications and capacity of the grantee, it is no surprise that the best candidates were the places that had gained experience and resources as a result of earlier federal grants. Interestingly, scientists' insistence that federal research funds remain above the political fray and in the control of dispassionate professionals, rather than politicians or bureaucrats, contributed to this state of affairs. The biggest federal grant makers—the Department of Defense and the Atomic Energy Commission chief among them—used a process of "peer review" that allowed a select group of scientists and military officials control over who received research money. Many of these decision makers had close ties, if not institutional affiliations, with top-tier universities, creating the potential for a "go with what you know" tendency in grant awards.

The Department of Defense was not disturbed by the limited spread of its resources and stuck by its policy of contracting by expertise well into the Johnson Administration, when Secretary of Defense Robert McNamara went so far as to take the formal position that R&D expenditure decisions should not be attached to regional population or income.[120] Yet by continuing to award grants and contracts to the same set of institutions, the military's policy of locating their research projects in places of greatest expertise and resources became a self-fulfilling prophecy. The favored institutions reached higher and higher levels of excellence in science and engineering because federal grants allowed them to upgrade facilities, lure eminent faculty, and develop graduate programs. Such resources gave them a huge advantage in future federal grant competitions.

Second, R&D funds—and the scientific activity they spawned—did not go equally to every region of the country. From the beginning of the Cold War, there were dramatic geographic inequities in the distribution of military installations, defense-production facilities, and R&D resources. Mirroring the patterns of political power in the Congress during this period, the places that won the vast majority of contracts were in the South and West. The Southern Democrats who controlled key defense policy and appropriations processes steered a lion's share of military production to their home districts, thus amplifying a practice of geographically targeted federal spending that dated to the New Deal. Franklin D. Roosevelt used public works projects, then wartime military spending, as an opportunity to bolster the overwhelmingly agricultural economy of the South. During the early Cold War, the military and security agencies continued to build a disproportionate number of military facilities in the under-industrialized Southern states, responding to political pressure by the South's Congressional delegations to use the engine of federal spending to improve the infrastructure and long-term economic prospects of the region.[121]

More affluent regions also benefited disproportionately from federal funds, particularly the Pacific West. The flow of money to these regions originated in both Congressional politics and military necessity, but also followed a path-dependent pattern similar to that driving institutional favoritism in university research. California is a good example of this. Proximity to the Pacific theater made its major cities centers of military mobilization and production during the war, and left it with a built-in economic base of well-equipped companies and trained personnel. The presence of these kinds of firms—not to mention California's mild climate and modern metropolitan infrastructure like new housing and highways—led to a further influx of defense dollars during the Cold War. As in other Sunbelt states, success bred more success: by helping to spur massive migration of population and a giant expansion of total economic output, the defense economy in California contributed to a commensurate increase of the state's power in national policy making, making the state even better positioned to win and retain defense contracts.[122] In this way, the pork-barrel politics of Cold War spending became a major driver of a massive shift of population and employment from the Northeast and Midwest—the Rustbelt—to the Sunbelt states of the South and West.

The combination of institutional favoritism in the R&D process and geographic favoritism in both military production and R&D allocations meant that scientific activity and scientific professionals became concentrated in certain parts of the country. By 1963 one official estimated that only one hundred of the nation's two thousand institutions of higher education participated in federal research programs. Fifty percent of the nation's scientists worked in only six states: California, Illinois, New Jersey, New York, Ohio, and Pennsylvania. The Western states had twice the density of engineers per million than the South, and 50 percent more than the Midwest.[123] Of the $1.5 billion given in fiscal year 1963 to colleges and universities for scientific research, California institutions alone received 28.6 percent of the total. In contrast, the entire Midwest received only 13.9 percent.[124]

Members of Congress from Northeastern and Midwestern states began to question the military's selectiveness in awarding grants and contracts, and by the early 1960s found the situation dire enough to hold hearings examining the "geographical distribution of the Federal research dollar."[125] As *Science* magazine noted in 1965, "Congress in effect concluded that science was too important, or at least too rich, to be left to the scientists."[126] At one hearing, in response to an official's testimony that the Department of Defense sent research money where the competence was greatest, frustrated New York Republican congressman R. Walter Riehlman mused, "as far as I am concerned, it looks to me as though it is a sealed situation. The people that do not have some competence in certain areas of the country are not going to have a chance to participate in these programs unless this situation is broadened."[127] Senator Gaylord Nelson of Wisconsin, chairman of the Senate Labor Committee and one of the most outspoken legislators on this issue, remarked at another hearing: "I am not suggesting that where the money is going there is no competence; but what I am suggesting is that I wonder whether all the competence that is available has an opportunity to get some of the money."[128]

Nelson's remark revealed the degree to which federal spending on science had become an economic development proposition and showed the frustration Rustbelt legislators felt about being largely left out of the Cold War science complex's economic bounty. Yet the origins of these inequities made solving them somewhat complicated. Institutional favoritism could not be explained away purely as the result of Congressional pork-barrel politics, but stemmed from mechanisms more deeply embedded in the grant-making process, where a small and select group of "experts" had control over the allocation of money and tended to award research grants to the same places, year after year. The "competence" in universities was becoming more and more concentrated, making it harder for other institutions to break into the top tier of government contractors. And while geographic favoritism clearly reflected the Congressional power structures of the 1950s and early 1960s, where partisan rifts and regional cleavages added to the power of Sunbelt legislators to steer defense money to their districts, these patterns complemented more general economic and demographic shifts toward the Sunbelt. Just as industrial dispersion incentives dovetailed neatly with under trends toward residential-industrial decentralization, patterns of defense spending fit well into regional industrial realignments predating the Cold War. The institutional and geographic disparities in R&D allocations were difficult to reverse once established. Despite some Congressional efforts to spread the scientific wealth, the flows of power and money had very much to do with the right location.

Conclusion

In ways both deliberate and indirect, for reasons both strategic and economic, Cold War politics laid a foundation for the city of knowledge. The Cold War made science a political and economic priority, and made the research university into a key political and economic actor. Strategic concerns motivated policy makers to encourage scientific activity to decentralize into new industrial districts outside the central city and spurred new programs to support university education and research. More political motivations led policy makers to steer federal defense dollars, including money for basic research, to a select number of contractors and to certain regions of the country.

These Cold War policy decisions emerged amid the context of larger economic realignments, technological changes, and new patterns of residence and work. Public spending on science made sense in a national economy that was increasingly dependent on technological innovation. Industrial dispersion fit neatly with prevailing patterns of urban decentralization. Defense spending in the South and West complemented technological and demographic changes that encouraged the migration of people and industry to these regions. Coupled with these larger trends, Cold War science policy had a much more significant effect on the shape of urban space than it might have had otherwise.

The Congressional debates about the uneven distribution of federal R&D dollars honed in upon its obvious regional inequities, but they did not investigate the metropolitan dynamics of these spending patterns. However, had they chosen to look into this issue further, they would have noted that parts of the country receiving the most R&D money also happened to be places whose cities were suburbanizing rapidly, and where there were few economic or political constraints on the decentralization of industrial activity. They would have also found that the location patterns of industrial sectors most dependent on federal R&D—electronics, telecommunications, and the research arms of major defense contractors—were strikingly consonant with the aims of industrial dispersion policy, which had provided rich incentives for these kinds of firms to move out of cities and into new facilities in the suburbs. The spatial dimensions of American science were not simply regional and institutional, but intra-metropolitan as well. Yet these dynamics were hard to identify amid the clear-cut geographic favoritism in federal R&D spending, and Congressional remedies to the uneven distribution of defense money remained concerned with regional inequities rather than metropolitan ones.

The political relationships at the heart of the Cold War science complex were part of what made these patterns difficult to see, and the role of public policy so difficult to trace. Although transformative in effect, policies were subtle in execution, using persuasion of the private sector—rather than government mandates or public-sector expansion—as a means to effect broad-based and ambitious ends. The central state grew dramatically during this period, not simply in terms of increases in direct spending, but also through alliances with nongovernmental entities like universities and scientific industries. Cold War policy made scientific industries and institutions partners with the federal government in ac-

COLD WAR POLITICS   57

complishing mutually beneficial goals. In doing so, it gave these partners
the power to affect the way science grew, and where it grew.

The institutional and geographic favoritism of scientific spending created competitive and sometimes adversarial relationships among research institutions. For universities, winning federal R&D funds became
a matter of political access as well as intellectual merit, and it became a
matter of location as well. While some institutions would continue to win
defense dollars irrespective of their regional location—Harvard and MIT
being the most prominent examples—the combination of institutional
and regional dynamics placed certain universities in particularly fortuitous positions. If a university had prestige and research capacity *and* was
located in a defense-rich regional economy, it found itself particularly
well positioned to take advantage of the rich financial opportunities created by the Cold War science complex, and to turn these opportunities
into catalysts of local and regional economic growth. How universities
chose to respond to this situation, and how states and localities contributed to these efforts, forms the next part of this story.

2

"Multiversities," Cities, and Suburbs

I N a series of lectures published in 1963 as *The Uses of the University*, University of California chancellor Clark Kerr outlined a new conception of the American research university—one increasingly integrated into the economics and culture of the rest of society and having a responsibility to apply its knowledge to the problems of the world outside its walls. It was, he argued, no longer simply a university but a "multiversity." The tremendous increases in federal expenditures on research and development since 1945, particularly the rapid upswing in spending on basic research since Sputnik, had turned universities into powerful agents of social and economic change and created a new correspondence between the goals of the university and the goals of Cold War–era public policy. "It is interesting," Kerr noted, ". . . that universities which are part of a highly decentralized and varied system of higher education should, nevertheless, have responded with such fidelity and alacrity to national needs."[1]

One of the consequences of the new influence of the "multiversity," Kerr observed, was that universities—and the knowledge they produced—had become an important economic asset for the places in which they were located. In a society that placed a high economic and political value on scientific knowledge, universities had become not only places of teaching and learning, but also centers of growing economies of scientific production. Large research universities were now institutions that, if they chose, could have a dramatic impact on the shape and composition of regional development. They now had more money, more employees, and more potential to generate capital for the communities in which they were situated. Thus, wrote Kerr, "universities have become 'bait' to be dangled in front of industry, with drawing power greater than low taxes or cheap labor."[2]

However, several tensions underlay the engagement of universities in economic development. The first was one of *location*. As America suburbanized, many of the nation's most prominent research institutions—including those at the top of the list of federal R&D contractors—remained in cities. In an age of science-based economic development, these urban universities became economic saviors who might be able stem the exodus of middle-class residents and white-collar jobs. Universities could not only bring the city back, some argued, but they also could make it better by serving as models for urban development. The university was no longer like a "one-industry town," Kerr noted, but had spilled outside its traditional boundaries to become the center of a larger "City of Intellect."[3] "If our universities are to enjoy the advantages of their urban position," historian Henry Steele Commager wrote in the *Saturday Review* in 1960, "if they are to be to American society what the great urban universities of Europe have been to their societies, they must assume responsibility for the development of urban and regional civilization. . . . What they need is an awareness of their opportunities and potentialities; what they need is a philosophy."[4]

In redefining the university both as a city in itself and as an integral part of the urban landscape at large, however, Kerr and Commager captured a second, *spatial* tension inherent in the new role of the American research university as an engine of economic development. The university had turned its focus outward, engaged in politics, and become charged with greater social and economic responsibilities, yet it remained an exclusive place whose fundamental intellectual mission was predicated, in part, on separation and isolation from the world outside. This separation was communicated through long-standing campus planning and architectural traditions that infused both the choices universities and scientific industries made about the design and architecture of expanding university campuses and the shape of industrial districts and surrounding communities.

A third tension running through the process was one of *definition*. The "research university" was a monolithic term that actually encompassed a broad and varied range of institutional types. The definition included top-ranked institutions that were winning the bulk of federal R&D grants, and low- to middling-ranked schools that were attempting to break into this elite group. It included universities in the middle of cities, and universities in suburbs and small towns, schools in the declining Rustbelt, and schools in the booming Sunbelt. And, importantly, the definition included private, independent universities as well as public, state-sponsored ones. A university's ability to act as a positive force for regional economic-development depended greatly on where it fell within this broad definition—a distinction that often was lost on the federal, state, and local leaders attempting to build industrial development strategies around these institutions.

The university engagement in economic development was a two-way street: politicians and business leaders seized upon these institutions as essential tools in larger economic strategies, and university administrators used these new economic policies to shore up their economic fortunes and become, in effect, a new breed of city builder. Yet the tensions that underlay these economic-development efforts had a profound effect upon where these new kinds of cities would grow, who would live in them, and what they would look like.

The Scientist in the Garden

From Campus to Industrial Park

Campus planning traditions begin to explain why the postwar engagement of the university in economic development, and urban economic development in particular, had such important spatial implications. For the institutions that became the economic saviors of the American city had, from colonial times forward, established themselves as alternatives to the corruption and chaos of the mercantile and industrial city.[5] The prevailing design and architectural choices of American colleges and universities reflected the deep-seated cultural presumption that the urban environment was no place for intellectual discovery. Students needed peaceful, natural settings that would uplift them intellectually and morally. Henry David Thoreau once commented that "it would be not a small advantage if every college were . . . located at the base of a mountain."[6]

Rather than building institutions of higher education in the centers of cities, as continental Europeans did, Americans instead imitated the English models of Oxford and Cambridge and tended to locate colleges and universities in the country, in small towns, or on the sparsely populated outskirts of cities.[7] At the time of their founding, the most prominent twentieth-century "urban" universities deliberately sited themselves in places that were accessible to the commercial center of the city, but at a certain remove from it. Harvard was in suburban Cambridge rather than the heart of Boston; Penn's original campus was a scant half-mile from the heart of mercantile Philadelphia, but in this "walking city" such a distance placed the campus on the urban fringe. More than a century later, Columbia University was founded in a lightly settled, suburban part of upper Manhattan, and Penn had left its now too-urban location for a new campus in the upper-middle-class suburban neighborhoods in the western part of the city.

The rejection of the city by the university went even further in the case of state university systems. State governments began to establish these schools amid the unprecedented urban growth and industrialization of the nineteenth century. Immigrant-supported political machines—rightly or wrongly presumed to be filled with corruption and cronyism—ruled the largest cities.[8] In many states, state capitals were not in these large urban areas but in more remote locations—Albany rather than New York City, Harrisburg rather than Philadelphia, Springfield rather than Chicago—creating a further political polarization between the big city and the rural hinterland. Policy makers often chose to locate the flagship campuses of state universities in these small-town capitals or in even more bucolic settings. There are plenty of examples of private schools that also chose to locate in more rural areas, as well as there being many examples of urban state university campuses. However, the universities that became the most prominent during the Cold War were often independent schools with a suburban-turned-urban campus (such as Harvard, MIT, Johns Hopkins, Penn, and Chicago), or large state universities in state capitals or college towns that were rural at the time of the university's founding (like the Universities of California, Michigan, Wisconsin, and Illinois).

For institutions public and private, urban and rural, the location choices were ones of both philosophy and utility, choices that physically announced the separation of the university from the corrupt and chaotic city and provided an adequate amount of open space on which to build. Institutions invariably incorporated large amounts of green space into their campus plans. The pastoral ideas undergirding the development of the American campus endured even as these institutions expanded their academic functions and increased their engagement in affairs of state and commerce. In the later nineteenth century and the early twentieth, many major American institutions were transformed from "colleges" emphasizing a traditional liberal education into "universities" with increased research capacity, academic specialization, and a new focus on professional and industrial training. During the late 1940s and early 1950s, as more students attended college and as the federal scientific complex grew, universities responded not only by considerably expanding their campuses but also by establishing entirely new institutions, particularly new campuses of large state university systems. Administrators used this institutional growth as an opportunity to plan comprehensively and add dramatic modernist structures to their campuses, which often became experimental templates for cutting-edge planning ideas like superblocks, common green spaces, and innovative architecture. In their multiple functions, and as places of both work and residence, universities operated like miniature cities. Yet in their low-density architecture and extensive green space, universities had more in common with newly emerging suburbs. Perhaps, some observers said, this hybrid was a new kind of city; the great modernist architect Le Corbusier, after visiting American college campuses in the 1930s, noted that each "is an urban unit in itself, a small or large city. But a green city."[9]

As these "green cities" grew, they maintained their physical separation from the world outside the university. Even as universities became more and more a part of white middle-class American life—increasing their enrollments beyond the traditional intellectual elite, performing huge research projects for the federal government—they continued to organize their campuses in a way that announced their distinctiveness from non-academic institutions, people, and places. As one prominent postwar architect observed: "Most campuses are planned using the concept of the old Roman military camps with a wall surrounding them, figuratively or literally, to protect the academic environment from the community, or the other way around, and to provide within the campus boundary an area of tranquility which, hopefully, leads to contemplation and the enhancement of the learning process."[10]

Well before the emergence of the Cold War "multiversity," the influence of American campus planning traditions extended well beyond academia, particularly in the case of industrial laboratories employing white-collar scientists. Although during the prewar period most research facilities did not look very different from ordinary factories or office buildings, there existed a number of well-publicized examples of "industrial campuses" that deliberately mirrored the look and feel of the college campus. General Electric was one of the first major American corporations to develop a facility of this kind when it built its Nela Park campus outside of Cleveland in 1913. Half a century later, planners continued to praise Nela Park for "its spacious and beautifully landscaped lawns [that] give it the appearance of a university campus rather than an industrial district."[11] Bell Laboratories' facilities in suburban New Jersey provided another prominent prewar example, having clusters of architecturally innovative buildings grouped within extensive landscaped grounds.

Some prewar research operations sought to replicate the American campus; others sought to group together in campuslike zones of scientific industry.[12] The emergence of the modern research university in late nineteenth-century Western Europe had prompted several community planning experiments that sought to create agglomerations of scientific industry close to university campuses. Outside the great industrial city of Manchester, England, local leaders established Trafford Park Industrial Estate in 1894. Trafford Park was "one of the earliest efforts to organize an entire geographic region toward the goal of scientific-technical integration," and deliberately grouped advanced scientific industries like electrical engineering facilities, automobile plants, and similar firms in a landscaped industrial complex.[13] Although planned industrial towns appeared in Britain and Western Europe earlier than they did in the United States, observers of the time seem to have considered such developments quintessentially American in form and industrial efficiency: "A puff piece from the early 1920's described Trafford Park as 'an "Americanised" corner of old jog-trot England.' "[14]

The pastoralism and separation that characterized campus development provided architectural models that fit comfortably with larger industrial trends emerging over the course of the twentieth century. As early as the 1920s, urban factories in significant industrial cities like Philadelphia and Chicago began to close their doors in the wake of reduced consumer demand and more streamlined productive technologies; widespread unionization and crippling strikes also created an incentive for industrialists to locate plants to non-unionized areas like the South.[15] In some sectors, new assembly line methods called for factories with a huge footprint, in which the square footage of older, multi-story manufacturing facilities became spread out over only one or two floors. The need for bigger facilities requiring more land drove many manufacturers to outlying industrial districts, suburbs, or outside the metropolitan boundaries altogether. By the early 1940s, many factories had moved to the green fields at the edge of cities, or rural areas of the South and West. In an age when technology and professionalization increasingly drove commerce, these facilities communicated their tenants' prestige, wealth, and commitment to modern production techniques.

After 1945, technological changes, economic realignments, and federal infrastructure and tax programs made the suburbs more desirable— and economically efficient—locations for households and firms. The process of industrial relocation and contraction sped up rapidly. Between 1947 and 1953, areas with fewer than ten thousand employees experienced about a 30 percent growth in manufacturing employment, well above the national average of 10 percent. The migration to the Sunbelt contributed to this suburbanization. The fastest-growing job centers were metropolitan areas that also happened to be suburbanizing the most rapidly; Los Angeles was highest in growth among the nation's nine largest metropolitan areas, with an over 77 percent increase in manufacturing employment. The old industrial capitals had more sluggish growth—Philadelphia had roughly 3 percent, for example—or lost jobs, like Detroit, Boston, and Pittsburgh.[16]

The facilities real-estate developers usually chose to build in these suburbs were modern, low-rise complexes surrounded by lush lawns, landscaping, and parking lots—space-eating elements that had nothing to do with the manufacturing activities inside. As the footprint of industrial buildings grew, so did the amount of green space surrounding them. "In years past, a ratio of one acre of plant space under roof to five acres of total site (4:1 ratio) was considered reasonable," noted one late-1960s industrial development report, "but today, the ratio continues to climb and 10:1 or 15:1 ratios are common."[17]

The new kind of American factory often did not rise up in isolation, but as part of a larger industrial zone. The emergence of low-rise, spatially deconcentrated facilities as the dominant form of U.S. industrial architecture during the postwar period was simultaneous with a rapid proliferation of "industrial parks" of all shapes and sizes. The 33 industrial parks in existence in the United States in 1940 swelled to 302 by 1957.[18] As parks increased in number, they also became less likely to locate within the political boundaries of very large cities. About 75 percent of the parks built during the first decade after World War II were "located in cities of between 25,000 and 500,000 population," reported a 1960 survey.[19] Most of these early parks were privately sponsored, often developed by consortia of large landowners (railroads, for example) and real estate developers.[20]

Although private interests owned and developed most of the new industrial districts, and they had chiefly private-sector tenants, public policy played a pivotal role in the proliferation of the suburban industrial park. Tax policies were crucially important. Using mechanisms similar to those employed in the Cold War industrial dispersion effort, the 1954 Tax Recodification established "accelerated depreciation" that allowed firms to write off large portions of their capital investments in new buildings, machinery, and equipment during the first five years of a facility's life. This translated into a huge tax break for firms who built new facilities in undeveloped areas at the edge of cities. By 1959 one-sixth of all businesses had switched to accelerated depreciation in calculating their tax returns.[21] At the local level, the growing disparity between high urban tax rates and lower suburban ones—differences that intensified as more and more employers moved outside city limits—created an additional lure. And suburbs themselves welcomed the new industries because of the tax revenue they could bring. For suburban governments, an industrial park brought in more taxes than a residential subdivision, and these taxes could pay for enhanced local amenities, particularly public schools. Tax structures prompted an economy-boosting surge in suburban construction and turned industrial parks into win-win propositions for both suburb and business. As one later report by the Congressional Budget Office observed, tax policy did not deliberately set out to create such lucrative tax shelters, "in large measure they just grew."[22] As jobs, workers, and tax revenue flowed to the suburbs, the only loser in this arrangement was the large city.[23]

When industry moved to the suburbs, it changed its appearance, both as a response to the generous provisions of new tax policy and as an attempt to blend in with more bucolic surroundings. Few of the postwar facilities labeled as industrial parks adhered to the architectural and landscaping standards of landmark prewar developments like G.E.'s Nela Park facility and the Bell Labs campus in New Jersey, but all were characterized by some degree of developer restrictions on the size and shape of buildings, and their density within the development. However, there remained variation in these standards, and even real estate developers themselves struggled to find a precise definition of what an industrial park *was*. Developers recognized that some parks—because of their location and because of their tenants—needed to adhere to higher design standards than others. Affluent suburbs in particular required a more refined sort of development; their homeowners might welcome the tax revenue brought in by industry, but they had little interest in living next door to a smoke-belching factory. In June 1958 the State of New Hampshire and real estate development consultants Arthur D. Little, Inc. co-sponsored a conference on industrial parks at Dartmouth College, whose participants eventually came up with this unwieldy, yet revealing, definition (emphasis added):

> An industrial park is a planned or organized industrial district with a comprehensive plan which is *designed to insure compatibility between the industrial operations therein and the existing activities and character of the community* in which the park is located. The plan must provide for streets designed to facilitate truck and other traffic, proper setbacks, lot size minimums, land/use ratio minimums, architectural provisions, landscaping requirements, and specific use requirements, all for the purposes of *promoting the degrees of openness and park-like character which are appropriate to harmonious integration into the neighborhood.* The industrial park must be of sufficient size and must be suitably zoned to protect the areas surrounding it from being devoted to lower uses.[24]

Implicit throughout this definition was the fact that industrial parks could serve as vehicles for introducing industry into affluent residential suburbs: places populated by new homeowners concerned about property values, and community aesthetics, and keenly interested in keeping the perceived ills of the crowded industrial city at bay. The industrial park was designed to be the anti-factory, a place whose design standards aimed to blend industrial and commercial functions seamlessly into the suburban landscape.

In aspiring to high standards of planning and architecture, maintaining a bucolic atmosphere, and removing itself from the more unsavory elements of modern life, the predominant form of postwar industrial development—the suburban industrial park—had much in common with the American university campus. The principles of separation, isolation, and pastoralism that guided the physical shape and location of both the campus and the industrial park had important spatial ramifications for science-based economic development. By the time policy makers turned their attention to the possibilities of university-centered development strategies, the institutions and industries around which this effort centered were already choosing low-density, cloistered environments in which to locate, a precondition that made it difficult to successfully execute such strategies in denser and more diverse places. The connections between campus planning and industrial architecture manifested themselves most clearly in an important and influential subspecies of postwar industrial development: the research park.

Industrial Park to Research Park

By the end of the 1950s, the new industrial parks springing up in the outlying neighborhoods and suburbs of American cities had helped draw many firms away from the city center. By relocating in suburban industrial parks, employers could enjoy new tax benefits and be closer to a ready workforce and farther away from the congestion, elderly infrastructure, and recalcitrant union members of the older industrial cities. To many a business executive, it seemed like a winning proposition. It is important to remember, however, that not all firms suburbanized. In fact, as the U.S. Department of Commerce noted in late 1957, the growth in office buildings in the center city still outpaced the growth in the suburbs, and many firms found compelling reasons to stay downtown. Businesses chose to stay in the city if they needed proximity to services like banks and public transportation, and if their customers and colleagues also remained in the central business district. They chose the suburbs, the Commerce study reported, if they desired "avoiding city congestion, space limitations, and reduced occupational efficiency," needed "undisturbed top-level concentration on policy matters," or were driven by "civil defense considerations."[25]

Scientific industries engaged in federal R&D work neatly fit this 1957 profile of the firm more likely to choose the suburbs over the central business district. While the Commerce Department couched its discussion in terms of private-sector choices, its survey revealed the influence of public policy—defense policy in particular—on the location decisions of certain firms. Not only were these firms and professionals affected by the incentives driving the defense contracting process, but their needs and desires regarding industrial location and amenities were catered to by public policy as well. Understanding how this happened first requires delineating the ways in which the "push" and "pull" factors reshaping the U.S. industrial map specifically affected the firms that made up the advanced scientific sector of the early Cold War.

One important influence on scientific location was the technology itself. The technological change that was partially responsible for the shift in the location and architecture of American industry had a particularly strong effect upon scientific firms. The experiences American industries had in wartime production ushered in changes in the geographic organization of production within industrial buildings as well as their outside appearance, and industrial research laboratories were among the facilities in which changes were most noticeable.[26] Immovable office walls gave way to open spaces and flexible partitions that were precursors of the "cubicle culture" of late twentieth-century offices.[27] The technological requirements of scientific research also necessitated sophisticated fittings like customized air conditioning and special furniture. All of these requirements not only meant that research needed new buildings, but that even the most modern of facilities quickly became obsolete.[28] For all these reasons, as one observer concluded in 1950, "research laboratories are fundamentally one of the more expensive types of modern commercial construction."[29]

However, the strong preference that research-intensive industry began to demonstrate for one-story facilities with extensive grounds was not purely due to technological necessity. Industries that did not necessarily need extensive floor space or technological sophistication also chose to move from high-rise facilities to low-rise ones. Scientific industry adhered to the landscaping and high land-to-building ratios seen in industrial parks generally, and occasionally veered toward having significantly more extensive green space. A 1966 Commerce Department report found that "a research manufacturing operation and an electronics plant have respective land-to-building ratios of 157:1 and 149:1."[30] Even contemporary observers noted that research-intensive firms used land to a degree that far exceeded economic necessity: "Site requirements both per plant and per employee are in the medium range. These requirements are inflated beyond the minimum because of the affinity of such electronics plants for landscaped, spacious sites," reflected one observer. "This is related to the type of personnel that the industries depend upon, the newness of the industries and the industrial park location of many of the plants."[31]

This observation pinpointed a key reason behind the desire of these firms to incorporate such a large amount of green space into their developments during the 1950s and 1960s: the scientific workforce. High-technology firms' "one critical requirement . . . is brain power, which they must attract to keep ahead of competition," noted another critic in

1961.[32] Operating on the well-entrenched assumptions about the connection between pastoral environments and intellectual creativity, firms used architecture and planning as a means of attracting an elite workforce, retaining it, and ensuring its productivity. The federal investments in R&D intensified the situation. The hot competition for scientific workers that resulted from the proliferation of federal research contracts created an economic calculus for scientific industry that was often diametrically opposite to the "cheap land, cheap labor" rationale driving other kinds of industries. Small high-tech manufacturers and small research-intensive branches of larger corporations tended to make location choices based on where the *expensive* labor force of scientific professionals was located (or wished to locate). Similarly, advanced scientific industries of all kinds needed land that was plentiful but not necessarily cheap. Even if rents were higher, these industries tended to prefer locations within or near high-income, white-collar communities because of their attractiveness to scientific professionals and their families. Exclusivity attached a value to land for which advanced scientific industry was willing to pay.[33]

Not just any high-income community would suffice, however. Advanced scientific industries were drawn by a "pull" factor absent in non-technical sectors—the presence of other scientific activity. For the emerging high-technology sector, whose companies were new and dependent on constant infusions of new technological knowledge, it was essential to locate in places where there were other scientists and other laboratories. A critical mass of scientific production also functioned as a potent community amenity in luring talented employees.

Luring high-quality workers was one goal of the new industrial architecture; keeping them productive and happy was another. In the discussions on worker productivity and its relation to design it became clear that the new designs for industrial facilities sprang from the same impulses that also underlay the American campus planning tradition: intellectual creativity required peaceful and pastoral landscapes in order to flourish. Industrial leaders seem to have wholeheartedly agreed with the intellectual premise that a pastoral atmosphere had a significant impact upon scientific innovation and productivity. Being surrounded by green space, they reasoned, made scientists happier, more creative, and more productive workers. A speaker at a 1961 conference on industrial research outlined the deliberative and workforce-centric thinking that lay behind the design of these facilities: "this is a very special productivity, that of the minds of men and women. While they must be given the proper tools and facilities (which is relatively easy), they must also be put in an atmosphere that will be conducive to concentration and creativity.

That is why every factor of the physical environment should first be intensively analyzed in terms of the individual."[34]

These technology needs and workforce concerns all served to heighten the planning and architectural principles behind the industrial park—low-rise modernism, landscaping, exclusivity, harmony with surrounding community—and create a new subspecies of industrial park, one that aimed to be populated exclusively by scientific or research-intensive firms. In an era of the glorification of American scientific achievement and scientists, the research park, as it was known, became one of the most desirable types of industrial developments, highly successful in disguising its industrial functions to fit into the new suburban landscape. As universities were industry's chief competitors in the competition for scientific labor, it followed that making work surroundings as much like college campuses as possible increased the private sector's competitiveness with universities in attracting highly coveted, and highly mobile workers.[35] As the American suburb also drew upon these planning ideas, it is not surprising that, in its look and homogeneity, the research park was barely distinguishable from the upper-middle-class suburb. The design elements of the research park, while seemingly having little to do with economic necessity, created "psychic income," boosting a company's place in economically beneficial networks of commerce by creating an amenity-filled and exclusive environment amid similar firms.[36]

Research parks were distinctive from other parklike industrial developments of the era in their relationship with institutions of higher education. The workforce and technology priorities of postwar private-sector science turned universities—the preeminent concentrations of scientific research and teaching, newly empowered and enriched by Cold War programs—into magnets for industry. A typical research park was located in close proximity to, or within easy driving distance of, a research university or universities. University administrators recognized the benefits of these new kinds of developments and often played an important role in designing and marketing these parks. Even in cases where the parks were privately managed, universities sometimes retained an equity stake in the developments.[37] Making industrial facilities look as much like extensions of university buildings as possible served as a tangible expression of the close relationship advanced scientific industries enjoyed with university science and engineering departments—and further distinguished them from the smoke-belching behemoths of the industrial age.

Research parks were also a mutually beneficial way for industry to operate in university communities. This was particularly true of primarily residential university towns or university-dominated suburbs that may have had aesthetic misgivings about allowing industry in their municipalities, but often urgently needed the tax revenues of industrial development.

One advocate of research-park development reminded a 1961 audience of "the problems encountered by suburban communities which have successfully resisted the introduction of any kind of commercial facility [and] which have found their residents in the most serious predicament of having to choose between inadequate school and other public facilities and prohibitive local taxes."[38] Research parks, deliberately designed to look like college campuses—and, by extension, like the residential areas of suburbs themselves—created what was essentially an aesthetically pleasing disguise for revenue-producing commercial and manufacturing activities.

The presence of universities was an especially powerful lure for scientific industry when surrounding areas offered corresponding community amenities. A 1961 poll of scientific researchers found that "social, cultural, and general living conditions of the area" were respondents' top priority in making location decisions, but coming in second was "accessibility to major universities and libraries."[39] Scientific professionals, many of whom had young children, also were concerned with living in a place with excellent public schools and high-quality housing. A 1960 survey by the State of New York found that "the physical location of housing and schools and their physical appearance and quality are of critical importance, as well as the social climate in the residential areas or the quality of education in the schools."[40] Top executives echoed their employees' preferences. Surveys of advanced scientific industry found that the presence of a vibrant university community was a top consideration for companies in the site selection process. A 1965 survey of five hundred industrial research directors and company presidents found that 75.8 percent of respondents listed "proximity to a university" as the most important factor; the second most frequently cited factor was "professional manpower available," cited by 67.7 percent of the respondents.[41] As Rice University chancellor Cary Croneis put it in 1965, "industry now goes where the scientific talent is—or where it can be trained."[42]

Yet because of the combination of other forces acting in favor of residential and industrial decentralization during this period, the universities that offered nearby *suburban* facilities in which scientists could live and work were the institutions most advantaged in the competition for scientific industry. American science grew enormously at the same time that tax shelters were helping to spur a giant suburban building boom. Suburban amenities—good housing, good schools, low taxes—also mattered. The severe shortage of professional scientists in the early Cold War period intensified the amenity-consciousness of industry, and enhanced the competitive advantage of industries and universities located in aesthetically and culturally desirable areas. Federal officials were well aware of this fact. In an analysis of the 1950s electronics industry, U.S.

Commerce Department officials noted: "Engineers and scientists have shown a preference for locations near educational institutions offering graduate study for professional advancement, and for the cultural advantages which are found in the larger cities. Under these present conditions of a large unfilled demand for engineers, attractive living conditions are an important factor."[43] If a firm could take advantage of new tax breaks and amenities of the suburbs *and* have proximity to a research university, they could have the best of all worlds.

All of these factors presented wonderful opportunities for the American scientist. Like millions of other white professionals (and, in this era, the overwhelming majority of scientists were white and male), the postwar FHA and VA housing programs enabled them to become homeowners and build personal wealth. The growth of suburban subdivisions provided their households with spacious and modern housing in pleasant neighborhoods with good schools. Less overtly stated, but always lurking in the background of any conversations about this almost entirely white workforce, was that scientists were like their white-collar peers in preferring to live in places away from poor and racially changing urban neighborhoods. On top of that, the overheated job market spurred by Cold War spending gave these professionals a good chance of getting a job with the perks they wanted, located where they wanted. More often than not, the communities having these desired qualities were outside the central city.

An Example and an Exception: Route 128

The rise of the research park, and the engagement of the research university in industrial development, was intricately intertwined with the geographic and industrial favoritism of defense spending. The institutions most favored by federal R&D spending often happened to be places that had already fostered small clusters of scientific industry prior to the war. Well before the Cold War made university and industrial research into a huge business, former students from the engineering departments of some of these places had founded new companies in the shadow of their alma maters, relying upon the expertise of their professors and university laboratories to help them in their entrepreneurial endeavors. This created small university-centered technology clusters to which new companies gravitated. In the postwar decades, the massive new influx of defense-related money turned these places into high-tech boomtowns.

In the 1950s and 1960s, one of the most prominent of these places was metropolitan Boston. In many respects, this region seemed to provide the ultimate example of new patterns of science-based industrial development. Harvard and MIT, institutions among those at the very top of the federal R&D heap, were research powerhouses and magnets for industries that located nearby to have access to their scientific resources, faculty, and students. The Boston area's scientific industries located in some of the earliest and most influential research park developments, places that won national attention and acclaim for their modernist architecture and generous landscaping.[44]

The spatial patterns that scientific activity assumed in Boston also made it something of a representative case. MIT and Harvard, like many other top-ranked universities, had urban campuses (Cambridge, while technically a suburb of Boston, was dense, centrally located, and socioeconomically diverse). Like other urban universities, they used their wealth and institutional clout to amass large amounts of land surrounding their campuses—by 1980, Harvard owned 10 million square feet, and MIT owned 8 million—and to lure other research facilities to the vicinity.[45] However, these land-acquisition efforts began in earnest in the mid-1960s, after more than a decade of science-based economic growth in Boston during which neither Harvard nor MIT made significant efforts to keep science-based industry in the city. The area's research parks had sprung up miles away, along a perimeter highway at the periphery of the metropolitan area, Route 128. While scientific industry moved to Boston to be near Harvard and MIT, the proximity to these universities seems to have provided corporate customers with *perceived* value as much as practical value. A 1963 economic development analysis discussed this paradox:

> In the course of our interviews in the Boston region, we were surprised to find that the frequency of direct contact between industrial research operations and MIT, Harvard, or the other universities is actually very low. . . . Yet these same people insist that they would not consider living and working anywhere but in the major scientific centers in the nation. In explanation, they cite the vital intellectual environment which makes them feel a part of an elite scientific community—a community whose influence extends to the schools, the arts, and a whole variety of social institutions which they deem essential to their way of life.[46]

In Boston as in other high-tech centers, industry wanted to be near universities, but the definitions of this "nearness" where quite broad. It was not necessary to be cheek-by-jowl with the research university; being in the same metropolitan area was enough. By locating on Route 128, high-tech firms might have been miles away from Cambridge, but they were "freeway-close," a quick drive away on the region's new urban thoroughfares.

While having some spatial and institutional characteristics in common with other cities of knowledge, the Boston case was less an example than an exception to prevailing patterns of university-centered development.

No other Rustbelt city was able to do so much to buck the larger regional patterns of defense spending and build such a significant base of scientific industry. The City of Boston itself was losing population and jobs; its suburbs, while prosperous, were not growing at the exponential rate of those in places like the Bay Area and Los Angeles. The region's exceptional ability to withstand prevailing economic trends stems in large part from the institutional power of Harvard and MIT. The two schools were quite different institutionally. MIT was a technical school with a long history of collaboration with industry, while Harvard "maintained a calculated distance from the industrial world."[47] But as Cold War universities, these two were in a league by themselves. Largely undisputed and unchallenged as the very top research universities in the nation well before the war, these were places whose prestige allowed them to grow and prosper with relatively little effort. While urban universities, their assets and prestige allowed them to become remarkably successful in luring federal and industrial research facilities to the urban area surrounding their campuses, while simultaneously maintaining strong institutional relationships with firms located in the research parks at the suburban periphery. In doing so, they built a metropolitan-wide network of high-tech development that was more extensive than was seen anywhere else in the country. This is an important distinction. In other places during this early Cold War period, urban development and suburban development was an either-or proposition. High-tech activity centered in Silicon Valley had little influence on the San Francisco economy until the Internet boom of the 1990s. Urban universities from Penn to Chicago to Columbia sought to effect urban economic development in their urban neighborhoods, but not actively to build ties with industrial clusters beyond city limits.[48]

The Boston area was also somewhat exceptional in the degree to which private real estate developers took an early lead in designing and building suburban research parks. Supreme among this group was Cabot, Cabot, & Forbes, the developer largely responsible for making Route 128 the region's high-tech corridor. The firm made itself a dominant force in the research park business by buying up open land along the highway well in advance of other development, and then building modern industrial facilities that won the attention of industrial development professionals for their high standards of architecture and landscaping. Although only some of the tenants along Route 128 were scientific firms, Cabot, Cabot, & Forbes emphasized the amenities and advantages their developments offered these sectors, and the area quickly became the preferred location for research laboratories and high-tech manufacturers.[49]

The embrace of the research park design by private real estate developers attested to the form's correspondence to the needs and wants of scientific industry, and to its profitability.[50] The research park met with relatively less community opposition because of its compatible design, and it provided the kind of setting desired by corporate clients. As one Cabot, Cabot, & Forbes official put it, "they are clean, highly attractive, superbly landscaped, easily sold to the local planning board. They are current with the times. They are one step ahead of the 'industrial' park."[51] The constant emphasis on isolation and solitude, while wholly consistent with prevailing ideas about scientific workplaces, served to further underscore the association of these places with suburban environments. Densely populated urban areas like downtown Boston and Cambridge simply could not provide this setting.

The exceptional conditions shaping the development of Boston and Route 128 set it apart from other regions. The dominance of the area's research institutions and industries in American science prior to the 1945 gave it something of a head start in the game of science-based economic development—a head start that allowed it to overcome the geographic disadvantages of being in the Northeast, a region that saw relatively less defense spending than the Sunbelt states, and of being centered upon two institutions with urban campuses. Harvard and MIT did not need to move early to become aggressive players in economic development strategies, either within the city or outside of it, in good part because they did not have to do so. The economic changes of the postwar period further enhanced their preeminence as research institutions, and the active role of real estate developers created desirable homes for scientific industry without university or government intervention.

In other cities and regions, the situation was different. Other universities needed to adapt a number of entrepreneurial strategies internally and externally in order to compete. As Clark Kerr noted, "the new connection of the university with the rise and fall of industrial areas has brought about an inter-university and interregional competition unmatched in history except by the universities and their Lander in nineteenth-century Germany. Texas and Pittsburgh seek to imitate what California and Boston have known; so also do Iowa, Seattle, and nearly all the rest. A vast campaign is on to see that the university center of each industrial complex shall not be 'second best.' "[52] Scientific industry and scientific workers may have already been inclined to cluster near universities, and real estate development trends were well suited to creating the kind of industrial and residential environments that these workers and firms wanted. But public subsidy was an essential element in this competition among the places that weren't Harvard, and didn't have the unique institutional assets that Boston had going into the Cold War.

The "second best" universities and regions that sought to imitate places like Boston got a healthy assist from federal, state, and local economic-development policies and programs in order to do so. As the industrial map of the United States shifted to Sunbelt and suburb, and as scientific industry proliferated as a result of Cold War defense spending, scientific activity became both a *means* through which governments sought to revitalize struggling cities and regions, and an *end* in itself. Governments and institutions focused considerable resources on the development of scientific industry and, along with it, campuslike environments for scientific activity and scientists. In their words and deeds, policy makers implicitly endorsed the assumption that scientific research and production was best conducted in quasi-pastoral settings that were separated, by physical boundaries or by actual distance, from the city.

Economic Development Solutions

The Multiversity and the City

The growth of scientific industry and the rise of the research park, occurring within larger trends of industrial decentralization, solidified the connection between science and suburban-like spaces: low-density, green, exclusive. However, the fact remained that many American research universities were located in central cities. During the 1950s and 1960s, parts of these central cities were becoming some of the most economically distressed places in the nation. How did science-based economic development strategies play out in urban settings? What was the role of urban universities? The answers to these questions demonstrate the many levels of governmental support that enabled universities to grow into institutions with important influence over metropolitan economic development, and show the convoluted relationship between the idea of the "multiversity" and the twentieth-century effort to renew and redevelop the industrial city.

The federal urban renewal program played a key role in this process. Industrial realignments, regional migration, and the tax and infrastructure policies pulling households and jobs out to the suburbs had left the large city governments (especially those in the Northeast and Midwest) reeling from lost revenues and burdened with new social problems. Big-city mayors and business leaders started to tackle urban redevelopment in earnest after passage of urban renewal legislation in 1949, shoring up downtown business districts in order to keep employers and retailers in city limits. Although tax structures and demographic changes were a large part of what was driving businesses away, urban redevelopers usually defined the problem as one of aesthetics, not of structural inequality. The core problem diagnosed by civic leaders and planners was "blight": unsightly, crowded, functionally "obsolete" buildings and infrastructure.

What was keeping cities from competing with new suburbs, officials reasoned, was their traffic congestion and lack of parking, their outdated commercial buildings, and their shabby inner-ring neighborhoods. Not surprisingly, the neighborhoods deemed the most "blighted" by planners and local officials were those populated by poor people, often the new African American migrants arriving from the South.[53]

City officials were right in diagnosing that the urban infrastructure needed help. The Great Depression and the war had created a more than fifteen-year period of minimal commercial construction and relatively few infrastructural improvements in many cities. Many city halls continued to be run by political machines, whose leaders were by this time often corrupt, wary of change, and fiscally inefficient. After the war, firms and residents with the financial means to improve and maintain their properties were following real estate trends and tax incentives and moving to the suburbs; the new migrants arriving in the cities had fewer means, and no access to the rich public subsidies provided by federal tax and housing policy. As they lost middle-class voters and employers, cities lost political leverage in statehouses and in Washington.[54]

Ironically, in finding solutions to this crisis, local officials turned to the same set of planning principles that encouraged decentralization in the first place: deconcentration of settlement, rejection of the traditional urban street grid in favor of "superblocks" that incorporated extensively landscaped green space, sweeping arterial roadways, and the location of residential, commercial, institutional, and recreational structures in close proximity with one another. One typical example was Pittsburgh, where the city announced plans to clear ninety-five downtown acres of housing and commercial buildings to build a massive complex incorporating a Civic Center, luxury apartments, parking garages, and other large structures.[55] As the Pittsburgh project made clear, urban renewal was not an anti-poverty program; it was an effort to inject economic vitality into central cities, boost the fortunes of downtown businesses, and reconfigure the demographic composition of certain urban neighborhoods to make them more middle-class and more white.

The need to present a particular image of the United States internationally was a constant, silent subtext in the slum clearance and redevelopment programs during the Truman and Eisenhower years. Urban slums did not present a good view of the much-heralded American way of life, nor did slowly dying retail districts in downtowns. The urban renewal program served not only a crucial economic growth function but also contributed to a positive image of America in a Cold War world. The high-rise residential towers, manicured parks, gleaming office complexes, and shopping plazas of "renewed" downtowns showed the Soviet Union—and the other nations that might be in danger of falling under the influence of communism—a modern, progressive, and affluent America.

Despite grand local plans and high political hopes, however, urban renewal proved to be more complex and controversial than its champions had expected. Redevelopment became synonymous with the wholesale eradication of neighborhoods, conditions exacerbated by the agonizingly slow pace at which funds flowed down to cities from the federal government, which often meant "renewed" areas remained vacant lots for years after homes and businesses had been bulldozed. Complaining of burdensome regulations and limitations on the use of funds, cities had only drawn down $100 million of the $500 million of Title I funds by 1954. By the end of the 1950s, despite modifications to the program that attempted to increase the rate of draw-downs, urban renewal was distrusted and resented by the urban poor and urban intellectuals alike. In a 1958 letter, Lewis Mumford expressed great disgust at what he saw as the perversion of the urban renewal program: "it has simply become a policy of lending government aid to assemble land for the private investor, who gets a further government subsidy in acquiring the land at a lower price than the market would demand. The whole business is scandalous: socialization for the sake of the rich accompanied by the expropriation and the expulsion of the poor! This use of the term has made renewal a filthy word—like 'love' or 'creativity' in the mouth of an advertising copy writer."[56]

The urban changes of the 1950s, and the general ineffectiveness of urban renewal in stopping them, were of great concern to the universities whose main campuses and other facilities were located in or near neighborhoods facing racial and economic transition. Most of these institutions were the private, independent schools whose formerly suburban campuses had become more densely settled and socioeconomically diverse. One business leader active in urban renewal remarked at the time, "higher education is being urbanized like the rest of American life, and unfortunately this urbanization coincides with the decay of American cities."[57] Universities were unlike many other large private employers and institutions in that it was very difficult for them to move; too much had been invested in the physical plants of many older universities to make it feasible for them to leave the city for the suburbs. However, conditions in some places had deteriorated to a point that there were periodic threats from university administrators that their institution might desert the city for safer, greener quarters.[58]

As centers of scientific production, these university complexes were becoming far too valuable to both the economy and the larger national political agenda for their growth to be retarded by surrounding urban deterioration. To shore up and placate urban universities, and to in turn

strengthen the urban renewal program by targeting funds to large, powerful, economically thriving institutions, Congress amended the Housing Act in 1959 to give universities and colleges special privileges and
lucrative incentives to become involved in urban renewal. For some time,
cities with large urban renewal investments—like Philadelphia, whose
former mayor Joseph Clark now served on the Senate committee with
jurisdiction over housing and urban renewal programs—had long com-
plained of the financial burdens stemming from their share of project
costs (cities paid one-third, the federal government paid the rest).[59] Yet
the Eisenhower Administration was highly reluctant to increase the government's match, and in fact had proposed that the federal share be
gradually reduced.[60]

The "Section 112" program, so named because of the section of the
Act that authorized these expenditures, provided a solution to these
funding problems and also fit in neatly with other post-Sputnik subsidies
for higher education by using campus expansion as an urban renewal
tool. The new provision allowed the costs incurred by a university in
acquiring property, clearing land, and relocating residents to be credited
toward the local share of the cost of a nearby federally assisted urban
renewal project. The definition of eligibility was rather loose; a contemporary handbook explaining the program noted: "an institution is considered 'near' a renewal area if more than 50 percent of the renewal
project area can be enclosed by a line which is not more than one-quarter
of a mile distant from the boundaries of an eligible institution." In addition, if acquiring land for educational purposes, institutions could purchase it at significantly below market price. This greatly increased the
incentive for urban universities, which were often already strapped for
space because of growing enrollments and research programs, to expand
their campuses into surrounding neighborhoods. Section 112 not only
served immediate urban economic needs, but geopolitical ones as well;
as the Committee's final report noted, "recent international developments have demonstrated the necessity for improved facilities at our colleges and universities."[61] Combined with the benefits of federal educational facility programs, this new subsidy meant that a savvy university
could undertake most massive construction programs with little or no
expenditures of its own.

After the authorization of Section 112, local urban renewal administrations—New York, Chicago, Boston, Philadelphia, Atlanta, among many
others—began to include university neighborhoods in their lists of "priority areas" for renewal. Within five years, more than seventy-five universities and other institutions of higher education had taken advantage of
the provisions of Section 112. It was a win-win situation. As one university
president noted several years later, the "benefits to the city resulting from

such an arrangement became increasingly evident" as university-centered urban renewal projects were begun. "As sections of the city were cleared near urban institutions, new residential and commercial development often opened up. Such redeveloped areas provided a substantial increase in property tax income, even though large portions of the renewal area were designated for university or college purposes."[62]

While the projects encouraged by Section 112 also attracted their share of controversy (as chapter 4's account of the University of Pennsylvania's urban renewal efforts will make clear), the involvement of large institutions in the urban renewal process often meant that redevelopment occurred more swiftly and more comprehensively than it did in projects spearheaded solely by private developers and city agencies. Universities had ready money for expansion—often money they had won directly from the federal government for scientific R&D activities—and they often already had comprehensive plans in place for new construction. The upsurge in federal funding and student enrollments made universities bigger and more diverse at precisely the same moment that urban renewal funds became readily available to these institutions. Within a program that had been marked by delays, bureaucratic mistakes, physical upheavals, and a sense of failure, the university-driven urban renewal initiatives fostered by the Section 112 program were promising successes.

Section 112 projects added to the growing conviction that research universities were key to urban survival in this new post-industrial age. "A new city form—heavily dependent upon our cultural and educational institutions—is clearly in evolution," wrote federal urban renewal commissioner William Slayton in 1962.[63] The next year, he went on to note in a speech in Philadelphia: "as universities have recognized their increasing dependence on the community, so the civic authorities have recognized the role of the universities in the cities' economy. Not only are these institutions important to the city's economy, but they are growing faster than most other sectors of that economy."[64]

Although by the early 1960s the federal government was almost entirely subsidizing the campus expansion of many public and private universities, officials found it a worthwhile investment. Federal administrators not only considered the physical growth of the research university a solution to urban problems, but a way to redress the larger problems of society as well. As Slayton urged his Philadelphia audience in 1963: "This, then is the task and the opportunity of the university: to live for and with its community, instead of merely in it; to contribute its share of manpower and brainpower to the solution of community problems, so that its own problems may be solved in the process; and to provide the leadership in local urban affairs that it so often does in the national arena."[65]

Officials involved in the scientific research complex echoed this call. NASA deputy director Hugh Dryden argued in a 1965 speech that it was necessary to "bring the university's great resources to bear on the complex social and economic problems of the neighboring community, the region, the nation, the global community of nations."[66]

To the leaders of university-centered urban renewal efforts, one outgrowth of the idea that universities should elevate "urban and regional civilization," as Henry Commager put it in 1960, was the notion that faculty and staff needed to live close to the university campus. As the leader of the University of Chicago's urban renewal efforts, Julian Levi, argued, the university "must be a community of scholars, not a collection of scholarly commuters. The cross-fertilization of many disciplines and fields, so essential to productive research and teaching, is possible only when a university community exists as a place of residence."[67] And, the reasoning went, if university communities became attractive residential areas to faculty, then they would in turn attract other desirable professional residents.[68] The desire among university administrators and local officials alike to provide facilities that would make universities into "communities of scholars"—places to live as well as work—created additional impetus to use urban renewal dollars for comprehensive neighborhood development around university campuses. Because of Section 112, many private universities became key players in the public-private urban renewal process, and cities' hopes for economic revitalization increasingly centered on the growth of these institutions—fueled by rapidly increasing government research and teaching grants, government-sponsored facilities construction, and urban renewal funds. Yet, by making universities central to urban renewal, cities also exported campus planning traditions—ideas with roots in the eighteenth- and nineteenth-century rejections of the city—to the urban environment beyond the university. The federal officials running these kinds of domestic programs did not see any contradiction in this mission and found the pastoral campus an admirable model and antidote for urban blight. In the urban university, the urban renewal program had finally found the strong institutional force that could rein in blight, transform the aesthetics and demographics of city neighborhoods, and make the city more competitive with the suburb. As a 1962 report from the U.S. Department of Health, Education, and Welfare noted:

> The campus, built to last and urbanely manicured, is by nature anomalous to the average city neighborhood whose private dwellings, tenements, commercial establishments, and industries are usually conceived for the current generation only. Deterioration sets in early and accelerates as the futility of the effort of any one owner in putting money into maintenance or renewal becomes

evident. The most improvident owner becomes the pace-setter in the race toward slumdom. Only massive corporate action will arrest the process of decay.[69]

Two hundred years of tradition and experience had made universities
deeply conscious of themselves as places that were different and physically apart from the city and its ills. Universities were not anti-urban, per
se; academics and administrators of this period demonstrated a deep
feeling of responsibility toward the city's welfare. But they were places
firmly wedded to the idea that a certain degree of separation from the
world outside was necessary for scholarly thought and intellectual innovation. Thus, the expansion of university influence over the urban neighborhood did not mean the tearing down of the "Roman wall" that defined this zone of separation. It simply extended it to include urban
spaces where professors and other professionals could live and where
scientific industries could locate; the "community of scholars" was a place
within the city, not *of* the city. With federal dollars, urban campuses became green oases with very distinct boundaries—places that offered educated people a shelter from the increasing decrepitude of urban life. By
doing so, they sent a clear message to their poorer neighbors to "keep
out." Despite Clark Kerr's great pronouncements about the integration
of the "multiversity" into the rest of society, college and university campuses often became more and more walled off from their surrounding
environments.

Competing for Industry, Competing for Science

Cities were not the only places in crisis during the 1950s and 1960s. Universities entered into the economic development game at a moment
when certain places and regions were becoming particularly desperate
for new jobs, new construction, and new vitality. The central role that
urban universities took in urban renewal was one response to this situation, but this was only a small part of the story, involving a relatively small
number of high-profile private institutions that had the resources and
the political power to manage large building campaigns. The American
system of higher education contained hundreds of other colleges and
universities, large and small, public and private, both privileged by the
federal R&D complex and left out of it. The engagement of this universe
in economic development evolved along a different track, emerging
from a national political debate over larger patterns of poverty and unemployment, and new questions about the institutional and geographical favoritism of federal science spending.

Clark Kerr's 1963 lectures, focusing on the economic and social benefits of university science rather than its military applications, indicated

the degree to which political and economic priorities had shifted since the late 1940s and early 1950s. While anxiety about Russian nuclear capacity remained high, reaching new levels of intensity during the Cuban missile crisis of 1962, other domestic concerns like civil rights, poverty, and unemployment dominated newspaper headlines and Washington policy debates. Policy makers recognized that these social inequities had a strong correlation with shifting patterns of industrial growth. The shift of economic activity to the suburbs and the Sunbelt bypassed central cities and swaths of rural America, particularly the areas of deepest and most persistent poverty like Appalachia. The unprecedented national prosperity of the 1950s and 1960s made the contrasts between economically developed and underdeveloped regions all the more stark, and the regionally skewed Cold War spending choices accelerated and exacerbated this highly uneven geography of wealth.[70]

The first responses to the changing industrial map of the United States came not from federal agencies, but from states and localities. As regional markets became national ones, industries became more footloose, and white-collar professionals became increasingly geographically mobile, state and local governments established economic development agencies and public-private interest groups to create aggressive economic development campaigns showcasing the entrepreneurial, environmental, and aesthetic advantages of their regions. Firms and workers were now up for grabs, and state and local officials quickly recognized that the right combination of tax breaks, other financial incentives, and savvy marketing could lure industries to places they had never considered locating. These state and local efforts were on the leading edge of public-sector responses to the geographically fluid postwar industrial landscape, and such sales pitches escalated in number and sophistication as years went by.[71] In the case of Southern and Western states and suburban localities, these campaigns aimed to take advantage of the growing tendency for industrial relocation in suburban and Sunbelt areas and acted as an accelerant of these processes by increasing the attractiveness of these states and localities to industry. For governments in the Northeast and Midwest and in large cities, organized economic development attempted to stem the exodus of jobs and people and focused on luring new types of industries as well as providing home-grown companies with compelling reasons to stay where they were.

The modern marketing and advertising methods of postwar consumer culture made up one significant prong of these state and local economic development campaigns. Just as the builders of new subdivisions, automobiles, and manufacturers of consumer appliances used advertisements in national magazines to create demand for these ranch homes, Buicks, and washing machines, government industrial development authorities placed sophisticated and glossy print ads in publications with executive audiences, like *Fortune* and *Business Week.*[72] As early as the 1940s, trade publications and mass-circulation periodicals were filled with advertisements whose flavor and emphasis varied by region. As one survey noted, the northeastern states aimed to retain companies as well as recruit new, and emphasized their skilled labor pool and mature industrial base with slogans like "Make it in Massachusetts where you get a good day's work for a fair day's pay!" and Pennsylvania's "A State Is Known by the Companies It Keeps." Southern states used advertising to convince skeptical industrialists that their region was a good place to relocate: "Louisiana has Surplus Natural Gas and Electric Power for New Industries—Investigate Our Ten Year Tax Exemption Plan"; "North Carolina—Conditioned by Nature for Industrial Profit!"; "There's a Different Attitude in Mississippi, the New Frontier!" Western states emphasized their amenities with slogans such as "Labor likes to work here and management does too." Sales pitches also conveyed some not-so-subtle messages about the fact that Southern and Western labor was more ethnically homogeneous and less likely to be unionized. Augusta, Georgia highlighted its "thousands of fourth generation Americans as dependable workers."[73]

The other crucial component of many of these state and local campaigns was the active support and subsidy of new industrial parks. Seeing the degree to which industries were embracing modern architecture and industrial park settings, governments entered into partnerships with local industrial developers to create new homes for industry. Often, local agencies became involved in industrial park development first, and were then given additional financial support by state agencies. This occurred in Pennsylvania in 1955, when the state established an Industrial Development Authority "to help [local] industrial foundations finance the erection of factories on single sites or group sites." New England states took similar actions in the 1950s, indicating a greater desire on the part of former industrial powerhouses to create new homes for industry that were at least as attractive as those being built by private developers in the Sunbelt.[74]

By the early 1960s, these state and local efforts had vastly increased in number and visibility. One publication termed the surge in industrial development campaigns "a veritable 'stampede.' "[75] By 1964 there were an estimated twenty thousand local economic development agencies across the U.S. These agencies could be nonprofit, independent organizations or branches of local, regional, or state government. Their board members and staff were usually drawn from the ranks of local business leaders and elected officials. "Never before," remarked *Duns Review and Modern Industry*, "has the competition among cities and communities across the nation to get in on today's onrush of plant expansion and movement been so great."[76] In an era of declining manufacturing employment and a nationalized and increasingly high-skilled economy, aggressive industrial development campaigns were a matter of economic life or death. As one observer put it, the attitude of economic development officials could be summed up as: "Either we get new industry—and soon—or we become a ghost town and get scratched off the map."[77] "Nearly every local and state government in the Union appears to be convinced today that prosperity (in some cases, survival) depends on the rise of manufacturing within its borders," noted *Fortune* in 1964.[78]

As state and local economic development campaigns increased in number and intensity, the federal government was coming to the gradual realization that the postwar economic prosperity was not touching all parts of the country equally. Eisenhower Administration economic policy adhered faithfully to neoclassical economic principles of market stimulus and to the economic benchmarks of high industrial productivity and full employment. The proper role of government, argued Eisenhower's economic advisors, was to create "promising conditions favorable to the exercise of individual initiative and private effort."[79] Under this rationale, the massive spending on defense and on infrastructure like interstate highways was not through public-works programs, but through mechanisms that ensured private-sector growth. This approach, while highly beneficial to well-positioned business sectors, did not address persistent, place-based poverty. Changing industrial patterns forced officials of all political stripes to recognize that, despite the unprecedented prosperity of the postwar era, some places continued to lag behind.[80]

As in the case of a national science agency, where West Virginia's Harley Kilgore proposed early legislation, the first policy maker to raise the alarm about the increasingly inequitable distribution of jobs and wealth was a crusading liberal senator. Democrat Paul Douglas of Illinois, long a champion of the poor and a leading advocate of civil rights legislation, began in the mid-1950s to argue repeatedly and vociferously for new federal programs that targeted economic aid to areas of high unemployment. Douglas's travels through Illinois during his 1954 reelection campaign had impressed upon him the intractability of poverty and chronic unemployment in rural areas, and the relative immobility of the people who lived in these places. Government intervention was necessary to jump-start these regional economies, Douglas argued, and in cases where people could not move to find work, jobs needed to come to the areas in which these people lived. In 1955 Douglas introduced a bill to aid "labor surplus" areas of high chronic unemployment and soon gathered the support of other Rustbelt Democrats (like Pennsylvania senator and former Philadelphia mayor Joseph Clark) whose states were facing not only chronic rural poverty but increased urban distress as well.[81]

Douglas's ambitious legislative proposals for depressed areas met with resistance from Congressional Republicans and the Eisenhower Administration, and repeatedly failed to win passage. The Southern Democrats, who continued to control the legislative agenda, had little interest in passing legislation sponsored by an ardent champion of civil rights. Moreover, Southern states were where many of these manufacturers were going; a federal program to encourage these firms to go back to the Rustbelt areas whence they came was certainly not in the interest of the newly industrialized South.[82] However, the debates in Congress, combined with the increasingly evident changes in industrial geography, began to have an effect on Eisenhower's thinking, even though he persisted in framing these economic dislocations as temporary phenomena. "We must help deal with the pockets of chronic poverty," he announced in his 1956 State of the Union address. "Such conditions mean severe hardships for thousands of people as the slow process of adaptation to new circumstances goes on."[83] Although Eisenhower continued to support the idea of some kind of area redevelopment legislation in subsequent speeches and in his annual *Economic Reports* to Congress, his fellow Republicans in the House and Senate continued to disagree with the Democrats on the size and expense of such a program. Partisan disagreements continued to bog down economic development legislation; by 1960, Congress finally managed to pass two area redevelopment bills, only to find them vetoed by the president in his final months in office. Despite this, all of the activity on this issue during the Eisenhower years placed regional economic development firmly on Washington's political radar screen.[84]

Liberal Democrats made area redevelopment a topic of Washington debate; John F. Kennedy turned the idea into a compelling public issue that rallied political support for his 1960 bid for the presidency. Kennedy's visits to Appalachia publicized the plight of under-industrialized, economically depressed communities and reminded the voting public that postwar prosperity had failed to touch certain regions of the country. The presidential candidate's case was helped by a short economic recession during the final months of the Eisenhower Administration, a downturn that reminded politicians and voters that national prosperity was not guaranteed.[85] With Kennedy's election, the executive branch became sympathetic to a more sweeping vision of area redevelopment, and within a few months of the new president's inauguration, his administration established a new Area Redevelopment Administration (ARA) in the Commerce Department.[86] The initial appropriations to the ARA created a $3 million revolving loan fund for both public facilities and private industry, all targeted to areas of unusually high unemployment. While the ARA focused its efforts primarily on rural development, under-industrialized urban areas also received help from its programs. In addition, many of the "rural" areas serviced by the ARA were close to large metropolitan areas and, particularly in the South, contained rural communities that later would become suburbs as neighboring metropolises spread outward.[87]

It was at about this time that Rustbelt representatives began to shift their attention toward the regional effects of defense spending. The debate revealed the degree to which federal science spending had not only fed uneven regional economic development patterns, but also created a distinct hierarchy within higher education in which a few top institutions reaped nearly all the economic benefits, and the rest had to scramble for the remainder. Resentment among less prestigious institutions was growing, as was the belief that top research universities were highly complicit in this imbalance; one state university faculty member called favored institutions "the academic Mafia."[88] Although the elitism of science had been clear from the beginning, changing political conditions gave the issue new momentum. The Southern stranglehold on Congress was loosening as support grew in Washington and among the American public for civil rights. While powerful Southerners could still steer defense monies to their home districts, the passage of the ARA showed that opportunities were widening for Rustbelt representatives to push some of this bounty toward their regions instead, in the name of economic development for distressed areas.

Initially, Rustbelt Democrats and their allies in the White House placed much of the responsibility for correcting the geographical imbalance of R&D-focused development on the ARA's shoulders, a delegation of authority that ARA officials found frustrating. "I strongly protest the implication . . . that the primary responsibility for developing a R&D capability in the redevelopment areas belongs with ARA," wrote one official. "This is a gross misunderstanding of the situation. The R&D capability which now exists in Massachusetts and California did not always exist there, and it did not come about because of local efforts. The R&D capability in these areas was put there by Department of Defense contracts."[89]

Seeking to help bring technology to wider markets, and observing the clamor among members of Congress for increased support of science-based development in their home districts, the Kennedy Administration proposed a large and ambitious remedy in 1963. The Administration's program was explicitly designed to support the expansion of scientific activity and industry in underserved cities and regions, and to widen the application of military-developed technologies in consumer markets. The program aimed to provide "new support of science and technology that directly affect industries serving civilian markets," Kennedy wrote.[90] With this proposal, the federal government signaled that its support of university-centered scientific production served not merely as a means to enhance scientific knowledge, but as a way to develop regional economies, channeling money and expertise to create new university research centers as well as new high-technology regional economies.[91] The underlying assumption of this approach to economic development was that communities of scientific production were, to a certain degree, *replicable.* Some experts doubted this conclusion. Noted economist Charles Tiebout, when asked to comment on the proposed program, replied, "I'm afraid my over all reaction is somewhat negative. I don't see quite how we are going to be able to wrap up a package of 32 units of technology and ship them to some area to help business."[92]

The proposal did not succeed in becoming law until after Kennedy's death, and then only in much more modest form, as the State Technical Services Act of 1964. The STSA distributed funds to states through a poverty-based formula, and designated public technical schools and colleges as information and economic planning centers for science-based entrepreneurship.[93] Any doubts about the ability of the public sector to effect technological development seem to have been swept away by the time of its passage. The program's emphasis on scientific education and scientific research widened its political appeal to legislators who had long been engaged in defense issues but had been less passionate about distressed-area measures. One of these people was now president: Lyndon B. Johnson. "This bill will do for American businessmen what the great Agricultural Extension Service has done for the American farmer," Johnson said at the bill's signing. "It will put into their hands the latest ideas and methods, the fruits of research and development."[94] Despite Johnson's grand rhetoric, the STSA remained very small—Congress appropriated only $3.5 million for the program's first year, compared to $2.5 billion spent on university research alone during the same year.[95] But limited as it was, the STSA codified assumptions about the value and desirability of R&D-based economic development into national public policy. What economically distressed regions needed was not simply industrial development, but *science-based* development, which not only brought good jobs, but also brought talented people and rich cultural life.

The provisions of the STSA, like other public sector involvement in R&D-based economic development strategies, were predicated on the assumption that science-based industry had higher levels of productivity than other kinds of activity. This idea was based more on wishful thinking than hard science. Certainly, the expansion of university facilities and the arrival of science-based firms improved the tax and employment base of the locality in which they were located, but not significantly more than other types of industrial or commercial activity. The federal government, even while advocating science-focused economic development, could not come up with statistics that showed significant productivity differentials. The assumption on the part of economic development officials that R&D-based activity gave more "bang for the buck" was inspired more by their observation of successful high-technology regions than by hard statistical evidence. Rigorous analyses of the productivity levels and relative economic benefits of R&D-based industrial activity and research parks proliferated from the mid-1970s forward, but at the time of the passage of the STSA, little hard evidence existed.[96] In addition, R&D-based economic development was extremely expensive. Job creation involved expensive training, recruitment, and equipment; the high costs limited the number of new jobs created by government programs. The ARA 1963 annual report, for example, documented that the agency spent an average of $5,200 per job in its efforts to create new jobs in R&D and over $5,700 per job to create positions in medicine and health services. In contrast, the ARA spent $990 to create a job in the apparel industry.[97]

What made university-centered R&D activity so valuable as an economic development tool, in the eyes of the politicians and bureaucrats who worked assiduously to bring this sort of development to different parts of the country, went beyond simple cost-benefit analysis. It was the *quality* of employers and employees brought to a region. Public officials were frank in acknowledging this fact. As one Department of Commerce official remarked in early 1964:

> The principal reason for encouraging R&D activity in a region is that such activity typically involves employees who would be very desirable citizens. Their incomes are above average and consequently they are likely to provide fewer social welfare problems than would lower paid industrial workers and they are more likely to support such services as education. They are also more likely to participate helpfully in solving community problems.[98]

The core of the STSA's agenda was the encouragement of entrepreneurship of a certain type: "we do not mean entrepreneurship, say, as applies in the context of opening a chain of miniature golf courses," said STSA official Paul Grogan, "but entrepreneurship in the celebrated examples of Route 128, near Boston, and the Bay Area, near Palo Alto and Berkeley, California, where many electronic and spaceage industries have been spawned."[99] Because the program targeted its resources to areas of high economic need, the implication of this emphasis on entrepreneurship is that new residents needed to be lured in to start these new companies. High-technology entrepreneurs were not, by and large, going to be home-grown. The corollary of attracting "desirable citizens" to a community was keeping the less desirable citizens out, or at least making them less dominant in community life. Places filled with brilliant scientific minds still needed service workers, of course, but these workers could be "uplifted" by their presence in a community of educated workers. As anthropologist Margaret Mead coldly observed in a 1961 speech about "the new technical communities": "All need for activities which involve bringing in groups of lower status labor, lower status employees, mainte- nance men, etc., should be avoided in favor of designing high-level ser- vices and, if necessary, training programs for immigrants, which will in- volve the residence in the community of intelligent, but unskilled and possibly illiterate service people, whose children can benefit by the schools."[100]

Educated professionals brought tangible economic benefits, as well as cultural improvement, to the communities in which they located. Noted one observer: "The higher income levels of personnel customarily em- ployed in a research facility will of themselves produce certain predict- able economic benefits, such as homes in the higher price class, built on larger parcels of land, more carefully and expensively landscaped, than would be true in a lower income settlement." Other benefits of having highly educated scientific workers in a community were "the more active interest and participation in community affairs by professional personnel usually employed in research facilities, or the encouragement and sup- port given to a variety of cultural and intellectual endeavors which make an identifiable contribution to the total attractiveness or value of a given community."[101] The benefits of R&D-based development went beyond regional economic prosperity—regional economies of scientific produc- tion added to the United States's global economic competitiveness as well. In an increasingly globalized economy, in which the United States was beginning to feel the pressure of economic competition with West- ern Europe and Japan, "improved technology offer[ed] an access route to increased export sales."[102]

The political arguments put forth in support of science-based eco- nomic development capitalized on the positive public image of scientists and engineers created by the Cold War science complex, creating stark contrasts between these workers and the residents of high-poverty areas. Federally sponsored publications repeatedly characterized the cities, states, and regions targeted by federal economic development as places whose inhabitants seemed to be the antithesis of the mobile, prosperous American workforce of the space age. As one study noted rather patron- izingly: "While there are many restless men—men ready to move any- where anytime—there are others that feel more attachment for the place of their birth, or long-time residence. And it may not matter how ugly, how dirty, how sleazy the surroundings—it's home and they feel comfortable there. They'll do anything—including becoming wards of the State—to stay there."[103] The contrast between old residents and new, current poverty and future, high-tech prosperity resonated throughout the discussions of science-based economic development—creating a strong delineation of "us" and "them" based on class, education, and (more implicitly, but just as importantly) race.

The Johnson Administration and the Congress gave states and localities a great deal of responsibility and flexibility in designing and administrating the program. Science-based economic development needed to be locally driven for two reasons, federal officials reasoned. "First, in order to make it possible for groups of companies to apply new technology, one must know the special problems and needs of that locale; what makes sense in New England is not necessarily sensible for the Pacific Northwest. Second, the best contributions will be made by those closest to the problems the program is designed to meet; the most effective transfer of technology will be made, at the local level, by people capable of working continually on the problem." Thus, "the program should be mainly a local one, based on local institutions and local initiative."[104] The federal government's choice to devolve the STSA program to localities was not only consistent with the federalized structure of other kinds of social policy, but also was an acknowledgment that local and state economic development councils were already busily involved in recruiting science-based industries and workers. Strategies that were not tailored to, and integrated with, ongoing efforts of this sort were unlikely to be very effective.

State and local governments had already started to shift their economic development campaigns toward science-based industry by the time the STSA came into being. Like federal officials, state and local leaders felt that this emphasis made economic sense: industrial research facilities, advanced scientific manufacturers, and research universities were considered highly productive, employed a desirable class of white-collar professionals, and tended to be very good neighbors as a result. At the local level, the growing association between scientific industry and the research park added to this sector's cachet. Industrial development of this kind—disguised within good-quality modern architecture and well-designed landscape planning—was an easy "sell" for communities who might be concerned about introducing other types of factories into their midst. Recruitment of not just any industry, but science-based industry, was a feather in any local politician's cap. "The increasing involvement," wrote one observer, "is evident in state legislation and promotion, the creation of science advisory groups and research centers, growing interstate cooperation on a regional basis, and even the political battles for state office."[105] States and localities retooled their publicity campaigns so that "advertising for engineers in *Scientific American* and in trade journals looks more and more like the vacation advertising in *Holiday*."[106] By the end of the 1960s, in a full-page advertisement in *Business Week*, Minnesota boasted about its high number of Ph.D.s and its educated workforce: "We have had the nation's lowest rate of Selective Service Mental Test rejection for 3 of the past 5 years. Think about that."[107]

Could the high-tech, university-centered economies of places like Boston sprout up in Minnesota, Montana, or Mississippi? Could these industrial development programs create what one official termed "a total regional and community environment which will be attractive to technical personnel"?[108] The public officials leading the effort seemed to believe it was possible. "The patterns of earlier successes are being replicated in some instances almost as if one were following a recipe in a kitchen with expectations of producing a culinary masterpiece," said STSA official Paul Grogan in 1967. "But there is always the risk that the potentials of the yeast or the baking soda may become lost during the elaborate preparations and that the masterpiece will not come off as anticipated." While Grogan acknowledged that communities might not accomplish their economic development goals, the implication of his remarks was that failure occurred only when there were mistakes in planning and management—slip-ups in the "cooking" process, so to speak.[109] Other observers were more skeptical. A *Harvard Business Review* analysis from 1965 warned, "it is dangerous to be unrealistic. [There are] a number of conditions and requirements necessary for the successful attraction and growth of a scientific complex. . . . [u]nless a community can satisfy enough of these to have a reasonable chance of success, it is better advised to abandon the idea of establishing a scientific complex."[110] "The Research Park that springs up so confidently in so many communities with seductively attractive planning and persuasively attractive promotion has rarely attracted research facilities at all—that is, real research facilities," Cabot, Cabot, & Forbes executive John Griefen reminded fellow developers in 1965.[111]

State and local officials involved in economic development made similar comments. "There is concern . . . that the present faddish appeal of research parks will result in bitter disillusionment for many who believe that marking out laboratory sites on an empty piece of land will result automatically in a research center surrounded by science-oriented industries," acknowledged one state official at a 1963 conference. "But the continued expansion of research in the United States will create both the need and opportunity for well-conceived research complexes based on sound environmental assets and such development will foster, or contribute to, vigorous industrial activity in the contiguous area."[112] Strong universities or research parks alone could not accomplish economic development goals; what could, officials indicated, was comprehensive community development aimed at recruiting and retaining scientific workers and companies.

The fact of the matter was that few people involved in these efforts understood what *was* possible, and which ingredients were absolutely necessary for successful R&D-based development. Existing studies did not show promising results. A Stanford University study commissioned by the Department of Defense "stated that forced feeding of research-poor areas would have little effect on the present pattern of R&D concentration," arguing that expansion of R&D capacity was "frustrated" by "the interaction of three factors: the nonstandardized nature of the industry's products; the high, and increasing, dependence of the industry's products on labor skills of a high technical order; [and] the contract-project nature of the industry's market."[113] The conclusions of the Stanford study provided perhaps too neat a defense of the military's position that the exigencies of the contracting process resulted in the concentration of resources in only a few places. Other types of contracting or scientific production might be more geographically replicable, but there was no hard statistical evidence in support of this. Federal, state, and local officials involved in science-based economic development founded their assumptions chiefly on anecdotal observations, hunches, and hopes.

Conclusion

The public policy efforts to bring R&D-based industry to struggling cities and underserved regions were fueled by a tremendous optimism in the power of government spending and expert thinking. Federal spending on science since 1945 had fundamentally changed the stature of scientists, the role of universities, and the technological capacity of the American manufacturing sector. The U.S. science complex could send men into space; surely, it could solve the problems of crumbling cities and dying regions. In this context, the inherent faith in the idea of the "community of scholars" is understandable. It also explains the public-sector support for initiatives that, while ostensibly about fighting regional unemployment and urban poverty, created "privileged" environments—green, pleasant, modern, homogeneous—for privileged scientists.

However, unrecognized institutional and geographic distinctions had a tremendous influence upon these kinds of economic development efforts—determining where they would grow, and the degree to which they could succeed. First, the growth of scientific industry coincided with a giant suburban building boom, making it easier and much more economically attractive for scientific firms and workers to locate in suburbs rather than cities. Programs like the STSA may have inadvertently become additional instigators of scientific suburbanization, by supporting the development of research park development in areas that were in the process of changing from rural to suburban. Given the rich incentives provided by public financing decisions at all levels of government, it makes sense that this new and vibrant sector would be drawn toward new suburban facilities and research parks.

Second, this type of economic development policy revolved around the American university, an institution that had grown—and thrived— around the idea that separation and isolation were crucial to intellectual innovation. It was, historically, an elite, inward-looking, pastoral place— and persisted as such even as it became charged with much greater public tasks, and engaged in economic and political processes with national and global implications. The planning traditions that were the spatial expression of the university's identity as a place apart from affairs of state and commerce endured, and intensified, as campuses grew and research activities expanded. Even though many of the universities most active in the economic development process had urban campuses, the prevalence of these pastoral models meant that university-centered urban renewal became something of a process of "suburbanization" of the city—expanding green, exclusive, and clearly defined oases within the urban fabric. The combination of these planning traditions and the extensive— and largely hidden—subsidies provided for suburbanization indicate that science would have found it difficult to become more "urban" even if the federal government had made more of a concerted effort to keep science in the city.

Third, all universities were not created equal. Some entered into the economic development game with vastly more resources and political power than others. Interestingly, although the public rhetoric about the economic power of the university seemed to lump all these institutions together, the differences among them becomes clear when comparing the intent and implementation of the two main strands of university-centered economic development policy. University-centered urban renewal involved institutions that were usually private, often well endowed, and frequently at the top of the federal R&D food chain. The STSA, on the other hand, was part of a deliberate effort to expand the pool of federal R&D beneficence to smaller and rural institutions, most of which were public.

The national story only hints at the effect that this unequal playing field had on the ability of universities to generate high-tech economic development, and the ability of certain places to become cities of knowledge. The full implications of the policy frameworks created by Cold War politics and university-centered economic development strategies become apparent by looking intensely at the varying experiences of individual universities and regions. The second part of this book takes the examination to the ground level, exploring how three very different universities sought to become cities of knowledge. These stories reveal the realities that national policy makers often ignored, and show that a successful city of knowledge resulted not only from the federal government providing the right tools, but also from local interests using these tools in the right way.

Part Two ────────────────────────────

IMPLEMENTATION

3

From the Farm to the Valley: Stanford University and the San Francisco Peninsula

THE growth of the Cold War science complex, the emergence of the "multiversity," and the new public programs using scientific research activity as an economic development tool all had a dramatic effect on the social organization and physical landscapes of the communities surrounding major U.S research universities. Universities themselves functioned as important political actors in the creation of the Cold War research complex and in its use as a force for local economic development. Public policy responded to the examples set by universities and their local allies in government and industry. Federal policy choices profoundly affected the size, shape, and composition of university-centered communities of scientific production, but these federal policies were themselves shaped by a few compelling prototypes. The most compelling of these—a community having a huge influence on the way policy makers thought about scientific communities, and greatly affected by the resultant public policy choices—was the area surrounding Stanford University, located amid the suburban communities of California's San Francisco Peninsula. Understanding this region's influence on the development of federal policy related to science-based economic development strategy, and on the development of other high-tech regions themselves, is a further step in understanding the evolution of the city of knowledge within the postwar suburb.

Over the second half of the twentieth century, this region evolved from a primarily agricultural landscape far away from the centers of industry and capital in to "Silicon Valley," a sprawling new industrial landscape that was the undisputed global capital of high technology. Stanford stood at the center of this economic growth, not only because it was extraordinarily successful in attracting major federal scientific R&D monies, but also because it was an important and influential land developer. Enriched and empowered by Cold War grant money, located near some of the largest concentrations of military spending in the nation, and enjoying the unique asset of owning vast amounts of desirable and undeveloped land, Stanford entered into a highly successful land development

and planning business. The centerpiece of Stanford's real estate development work was a research park whose architecture and design standards
became models for countless other industrial developments. Stanford's
was not the first research park, but it was the first to be so closely associated with, and physically proximate to, a major research university. This
connection between university and industrial development set an important precedent, as did the way that Stanford incorporated a particularly Californian architectural vernacular into the design principles of
the industrial park. Other universities and local institutions embraced
Stanford as a model city of knowledge, often overlooking the many
unique regional and institutional assets that allowed Stanford's economic development efforts to be so successful. Stanford was often the
example that policy planners had in mind when they talked about the
possibility of replicating areas of scientific production through programs
like the STSA. However, because of the unique assets of the university
and the region, replication of what one observer called "the miracle of
Palo Alto" was nearly impossible, particularly in urban environments that
had little in common with Stanford's bucolic suburban landscape and
advantaged location amid a booming regional economy.

The story of Stanford and the San Francisco Peninsula provides a vivid
example of how the concurrent forces of mass suburbanization and the
growth of the Cold War science complex interacted with each other to
map out a low-density, decentralized geography of high-tech production.
Here we can see how the federal policies of Cold War science and economic development played out on the ground, and how, in turn, local
institutions had a significant effect on the development and implementation of federal policy. The example also further illustrates the complex
interaction between public and private that mapped out the geography
of high-tech production in the late twentieth-century United States. In
this case, a private university, fueled by public money, created institutional structures and physical spaces that served as literal "incubators"
for private scientific industry—industry that, in turn, was immeasurably
enriched by the programs of the Cold War defense complex.

It is significant that the university whose actions were so influential
upon the development of other cities of knowledge was also an institution with unusually close ties to private industry. And it is ironic that this
region—which benefited so tremendously from federal largesse—and
the University that was its intellectual anchor were led by people with a
general distaste for activist government and a firm faith in private enterprise and the market system. Their pro-entrepreneurial sentiments led,
over time, to idealization (even idolization) of the private entrepreneur
in Silicon Valley. True, the high technology phenomenon would not have
happened without the innovation and management of talented individu-

als. However, the enduring myth of the Silicon Valley entrepreneur ignores the pivotal role that federal contracts played in the economic development of the region and ignores that way the interaction between public and private also shaped the physical appearance and demographic composition of Silicon Valley and other cities of knowledge.

A Western Retreat

The geographic, intellectual, cultural, and spatial context in which Stanford University was founded have had an immense effect upon its development as an institution, its emergence as one of the preeminent Cold War research universities, and its role in the development of Silicon Valley. Stanford was founded by a businessman who believed in training young people for the modern world of corporate capitalism. It was an institution that, from the start, was designed for teaching *and* research, and it was assumed that the fruits of these endeavors would benefit commercial enterprise and further the technological development of California and the West. At the same time, Stanford was removed from the urban environment, an environment where business was conducted but also where social turbulence and disorder would disturb the process of learning and prevent the creation of a controlled, secured community.

The University's founders, millionaire railroad baron and California governor and senator Leland Stanford and his wife, Jane, established the school as a memorial for their beloved only son, Leland Jr., who died of typhoid fever while traveling in Europe at the age of fifteen. As legend has it, the devastated Leland Stanford woke the morning after his son's death and pronounced: "the children of California shall be my children."[1] The Leland Stanford Junior University opened its doors to its first class in 1891.[2]

While candid about their desire to create a school that would rank among the best in the country, Leland and Jane Stanford saw the University not as a place for intellectual dreamers but as a place where future business leaders could learn practical skills. Science—creator of wondrous modern technology, source of the innovation that was making men like Leland Stanford millionaires—was an essential ingredient in providing this practical higher education. And research, not simply teaching, was an important component of a proper science curriculum. While it was a university, not a technical school, and would offer courses in a wide variety of subjects and disciplines, its "object [was] to qualify its students for personal success, and direct usefulness in life."[3]

Although the early emphasis on scientific research and its practical applications gave Stanford University an intellectual orientation that would prove highly valuable in the Cold War era, another institutional asset was more significant to Stanford's later influence on the shape and social structure of communities of scientific production. This asset was land—nearly nine thousand acres of prime agricultural countryside in an area that would one day become some of the most valuable real estate in the world. Like many wealthy Gilded Age San Franciscans, Leland and Jane Stanford owned a large farm in the Peninsula's rolling foothills, and it was on this Palo Alto Farm that they chose to establish their new university, bestowing the entire holdings to the university in the process.[4] This land, of which the campus took up only a fraction, could be leased to others, but it could never be sold. For better or for worse, the university owned the Farm permanently.

The Stanfords' gift of this particular piece of land, and the provisions they attached to its use, was both a personal and political statement. It was, on the one hand, an emotion-laden choice made by grieving Victorian parents. Leland Stanford Jr. had loved to come down to the Palo Alto Farm, ride horses on its trails, and hike through its hills; after his death, the Farm became forever associated in the Stanfords' minds with their son. For Leland and Jane Stanford, the land upon which they established the memorial University was hallowed ground that should never be corrupted by substandard uses. On the other hand, the land grant and its location were calculations demonstrating the Stanfords' status as members of the nineteenth-century urban elite, and reflecting a sensibility about relationships to nature that were particularly Western.

The Stanford's choice to locate the institution on the Palo Alto Farm, although chalked up by some observers as further evidence that the new university was merely a giant vanity project,[5] reflected the times: one of the most politically and socially turbulent—and anti-urban—moments in American history. The late nineteenth-century United States was reeling from the effects of massive, simultaneous social and economic transformations that had been under way since the Civil War. American cities doubled and tripled in size, and became filled with huge factories belching smoke and hundreds of thousands of new immigrants from southern and eastern Europe. The deep inequity generated by emergent corporate capitalism, where the rich got immeasurably richer and working people and their children toiled away under substandard working and living conditions, manifested itself in civil unrest on city streets, mass strikes, and violent behavior. Vast neighborhoods of slums sprung up in cities crammed with thousands of families. All these changes created deep cultural disquiet on the part of the white native-born citizens, and cities came to be the focus of this cultural anxiety.

The middle-class response to the social conditions of late nineteenth-century cities was a huge wave of social reforms generally referred to as

Progressivism.[6] One of the common themes running through progressive reform was improvement through the rejection of the urban and the embrace of the pastoral. An important manifestation of this was the widespread effort to create ordered and inspirational space within cities through the creation of parks. Undergirding the urban parks movement was the belief that placing persons in a green, "natural," and decidedly non-urban atmosphere would prompt good behavior and serve as an antidote to the tremendous stress and alienation of city life.[7]

San Francisco, while much smaller than New York or Chicago, was the largest urban settlement west of the Mississippi, and it shared many of their urban woes. The vast wealth generated by extractive industries of the Western states—gold, then silver, then lumber—made San Francisco the "Queen City of the West" but also a crowded, turbulent place. In the minds of Victorian-era capitalists like the Stanfords, San Francisco was hardly an appropriate place to start a university focused on educating and uplifting young people. Just as city residents needed to breathe fresh air and enjoy pleasing vistas in city parks, college students needed a peaceful, natural setting in which to learn. The Palo Alto Farm was part of the burgeoning agricultural area of the Santa Clara Valley, called the "Valley of Heart's Delight" for its rich soil and pleasant climate. While its agricultural activity made the valley far from "natural," the lightly settled area was a dramatic contrast to the crowded city to the north. The Valley's already established role as an upper-class retreat further distinguished it from San Francisco; while plenty of working-class residents toiled in its mines and on its farms, the area was notable for the number of significant estates owned by Western capitalists.[8]

The Stanfords' choice also reflected a particularly Western type of American anti-urbanism. Stanford University came into being at the same time as John Muir was writing some of his seminal work on the magnificence of the California landscape. These essays expounding on the glories—and the fragility—of places like the Yosemite Valley recharacterized the natural resources of the West as precious and finite treasures, not wildly abundant commodities, and the advocacy of Muir and other Western reformers became instrumental in the creation of state and national park systems. The Western environment, Muir and his fellow conservationists argued, needed to be preserved because of the important antidote it provided to the stress and toxicity of the industrial city. It was a place of solace, of uplift, of scientific education.[9]

The intensified Western variant of American ideas about the relationship of nature and educational uplift informed the location and design of the Stanford campus. Like other American campuses, the Stanfords sought to create an environment that retained yet carefully rearranged the "natural" qualities of the landscape to create an appropriately pastoral environment for study. As if to underscore their seriousness about good planning, Leland and Jane Stanford hired the premier landscape designer of the age, Frederick Law Olmsted, to design the campus.[10] Although both Stanford and Olmsted shared a vision of the University as an enclosed community of uniform and uplifting design, they disagreed on aesthetics—Stanford wanted a more monumental campus, Olmsted a more pastoral one. The end result was a campus plan that incorporated the straight lines and grand vistas popularized by the architects and planners of the contemporaneous City Beautiful movement, rather than the curving paths and hillocks of Olmsted designs like New York's Central Park.[11] While borrowing design inspiration from city planning ideas that were themselves European in inspiration, Stanford felt that the campus architecture should be reflective of the landscape in which it was situated and draw upon the history of the West, and pronounced that the buildings should be "distinctively Californian in character."[12] No Gothic or neoclassical structures here, but instead long, low buildings of California sandstone and red tile, incorporating Romanesque arches. The design evoked the mission architecture of colonial days, about as far from the look of Eastern campuses as one could get.[13] From the natural backdrop of rolling foothills to the spacious main sandstone-and-tile quadrangle to the grand avenues culminating in monumental gates, the campus of Stanford University projected a design aesthetic that was reflective of prevailing ideas about urban space and planning. It was simultaneously "natural" and highly planned.[14]

For the first sixty years of Stanford's existence, the Palo Alto Farm served academic purposes or was leased to cattle ranchers or farmers. The institution realized a small profit, as taxes were still low in the area, and there was little demand for using the land in any other way. Students, faculty, and alumni developed a fixed idea of Stanford as a rural oasis; years after graduation, alumni would still wax lyrical about long hikes in Stanford's foothills or leisurely paddles on its lakes. "Poppy fields, rolling green hills, and winding country roads! The 'Old Grad' loves to dream of them!" rhapsodized one Stanford writer in 1927.[15] The lands themselves became integral to the educational function of the University, as its biologists examined the flora and fauna of the undeveloped hills and ridges and geologists probed its schist and soil. Ray Lyman Wilbur, who served as University president from 1916 to 1942, wrote that "located as it is in the center of a large estate with a mile or so of free space on every side, [the University] has developed a spirit of the open air and a sense of freedom and independence which have become the background of the Stanford spirit."[16]

Until the Second World War, Stanford remained this rustic retreat in the middle of larger, relatively undeveloped countryside. Stanford administrators focused on developing its core academic campus and in recruiting talented young professors from the East and Midwest who were ready for a Western adventure. As a result of the emphasis on research and advanced training that the University had from the beginning, by the 1920s Stanford's scientific research facilities were becoming moderately distinguished. And the area surrounding the University began to witness the very faint beginnings of the high-technology era, as a small cadre of experimenters and smalltime scientists in and around Stanford became involved with the development of new radio technologies. Stanford president Ray Lyman Wilbur was one champion of these young entrepreneurial efforts emanating from Stanford laboratories, indicating an institutional willingness to support commercial technology that would be put to great and profitable use in the Cold War years.[17]

Hot and Cold Wars

The Second World War had a profound and lasting impact on the San Francisco region. Always a military hub, the Bay Area became a center of wartime production. War workers poured into San Francisco, Oakland, and the surrounding counties. Richmond, an industrial suburb of the East Bay, became known as the hometown of "Rosie the Riveter," the iconic figure representing the millions of women who came to work in the factories. Between 1940 and 1947, the nine-county region surrounding the San Francisco Bay became home to 676,000 more people, 330,000 more jobs, and $2.5 billion more in annual income.[18] The per capita wealth of the region reached the highest level in the nation. Between 1940 and 1945, individual incomes increased by 66 percent.[19]

As in other parts of California, rapid residential suburbanization accompanied the population boom. Military spending priorities played an important role, as many military bases, production facilities, and wartime housing projects located outside the city limits. Yet another important factor spurring decentralization in the Bay Area was the fact that industrial activity had long established what one observer has termed a "centrifugal" pattern of development. Since the nineteenth century, factories had located not only in the industrial part of San Francisco's downtown, but had moved farther south on the San Francisco Peninsula or across the Bay to industrial suburbs like Alameda and Richmond.[20] Compounding the scattering of industrial districts was the multinodal quality of the metropolitan area from the late nineteenth century forward, as Oakland grew to challenge San Francisco in size and economic supremacy.

Wartime growth reinforced industrial, residential, and infrastructural patterns, and created added incentives for the mass suburbanization of people and jobs in the postwar decades. By 1960 the Bay Area would have three people living in the suburbs for every person living within the city of San Francisco.[21] California was accustomed to huge population increases—the state's population has approximately doubled every twenty years, with the biggest increase coming not in the wartime years but in the 1920s, when the population grew by 66 percent.[22] But the changes of the 1940s were felt more deeply in the Bay Area, as the infusion of people and jobs strained the region's infrastructure well beyond its capacity. All of these new migrants needed new housing, new roadways, new public services. As in other "military metropolises," one offshoot of the wartime defense boom was new attention to regional industrial planning.[23] In 1943 federal officials established a Metropolitan Defense Council (MDC), led by local businessmen and politicians, to address the chaotic situation created by clogged urban roads and too few apartments. Internal squabbling kept the MDC from getting much done, but it did spawn a successor organization, the Bay Area Council, in 1944.

The structure and programmatic emphasis of the Bay Area Council provides a revealing look into the planning and economic development ethos of the region, a policy approach that created a highly favorable environment for the growth of industry in the Peninsula suburbs and gave Stanford yet another advantage in its land development efforts. The Council, started by public funds but soon incorporated as a nonprofit, was sustained by $10,000 annual donations from some of the most prominent members of San Francisco's corporate community. The leaders of these concerns sat on the Council's Board of Trustees and reflected the makeup of prewar San Francisco business: banks, oil companies, chemical companies.

Business interests had been incorporated into government policy making in California since the Progressive era, serving on boards and commissions and on other advisory bodies.[24] The public-private dynamics of state and regional politics during this period is perhaps best encapsulated through the philosophy of "business associationalism" championed by U.S. president (and lifelong friend of Stanford University) Herbert Hoover. Government worked best when it focused its efforts not on centralized planning or redistributive policy, Hoover and his political allies argued, but on supporting the healthy workings of the free-market economy.[25] The business and political establishment of the Bay Area tended to agree with this kind of approach: when business prospered, the whole economy prospered. Yet after the boom of the war years, these champions of the free market did not hesitate to take advantage of federal largesse when it could positively affect the business climate and regional economic growth. As one Bay Area Council publication acknowledged: "Close contacts between Federal and private business groups built up during the war should be continued and strengthened. . . . Government business—Federal, State, and local—is a big business in the Bay Area and is a vital factor in its economy."[26] In short, the political philosophy of the men who ran the San Francisco Bay region in the mid–twentieth century—men who often had professional and personal connections to Stanford—was one that respected the right of capitalist enterprise to operate freely with a minimum of government regulation but at the same time understood the value of public-sector investment for regional economic development in the Cold War world.

These leaders also were pragmatic about the limited new possibilities for development in the city of San Francisco itself. As the minutes of a 1947 meeting of the Council noted: "San Francisco has reached its peak in residence and industrial sites—this city must now have an area-wide viewpoint."[27] The Council announced that it was "dedicated to the proposition that the San Francisco Bay Area is an integrated economic unit. The economic opportunities of all counties and localities in the Bay Area are not only interrelated but are interdependent. The basic purpose of the Council, then, is the furtherance of this economic and social unity."[28] While the Council's activities over the next two decades demonstrated that it clearly was more interested in economic than social unity,[29] the recognition of the regional nature of economic development was an important reflection of how the suburban areas of the region had become an economic force by the end of the war.

The Council's interest in regional economic planning and boosterism also revealed the new spatial needs of industry. Not only were the region's large cities completely built up and prevented geographically and politically from further expansion, but also industrial and commercial activities required much more space during the automotive age. In accepting this reality, the Council became quite pro-suburban in its orientation and saw itself as the promoter of more extensive industrial development in the outer areas of the metropolitan region and took a particular interest in the enlargement of industrial districts farther south on the Peninsula. In their plans and actions, the leaders of the Bay Area Council reflected the pro-decentralization and pro-dispersal tenor of the times. One early report commissioned by the Council—published at about the same time as planners like Tracey Augur were advocating dispersion, and policy makers in Washington were beginning to write dispersion clauses in procurement policy—noted that "careful planning to utilize and develop potential industrial areas in the region will not only stimulate the more rapid development of 'foot-loose' industries, but in the long-run make for more economical operation both for individual industries and for the communities in which they are located."[30]

The decentrist mindset of postwar planning in the Bay Area had an important effect on the willingness of the towns surrounding Stanford to welcome industrial activity into their midst. And the local business community's activism in postwar regional planning gave an important boost to the political fortunes of Stanford, an institution founded by a past captain of industry, whose administrators remained closely connected to the regional business elite. The leaders of the Bay Area Council also saw that California was going to find its economic niche not through replication of the industrial pattern of the Northeastern and Midwestern United States but in fostering the growth of "new" industries whose employees would be attracted to a good climate, beautiful landscape, and cultural amenities. The Bay Area Council became one of the first local economic-development entities in the United States to "sell" its region. The Council's marketing pitches almost exclusively emphasized the cultural and environmental amenities of the region—in effect, marketing to employees rather than just employers.[31] One of these amenities—perhaps *the* amenity for professionals in science and engineering—was the emerging research complex of Stanford University. Stanford administrators welcomed this attention from the business community. In a 1945 speech, the University's president Donald Tresidder expressed the "hope that in the postwar period Stanford will draw very much closer to business and industry than it has in the past—by means of cooperative undertakings we hope to develop more and more projects in which both the University and business will have a legitimate stake."[32]

Yet in 1945, despite the small scientific community around it, the university as a whole was a regional school of a standing far below its aspirations. Its administrators worried about the school's reputation as a country club that afforded more social and athletic opportunities than academic ones.[33] Unlike its peers in the northeastern United States, Stanford had seen little in terms of wartime government research contracts. Its leading scientists had gone to other campuses like MIT and Harvard, or government laboratories like Los Alamos or even nearby Livermore (in the East Bay), for the duration of the war in order to participate in wartime research. Despite the fact that the Bay Area was a center of military activity, the key university-based R&D projects of the war occurred elsewhere. "Stanford emerged from World War II as an underprivileged institution," commented Frederick E. Terman, the dynamic engineer who served first as dean of engineering and then as University provost during the crucial Cold War years.[34]

Within the next decade, however, Terman and other high-ranking Stanford administrators and professors would not only transform Stanford into a nationally recognized research powerhouse but would also help make the quiet suburbs around the University a magnet for innovative technological and scientific companies and their highly educated workforce. Terman later was called "The Father of Silicon Valley" because of his pivotal role in growing a high-tech agglomeration economy in the area. However, the national ascendance of Stanford as a research university, and the emergence of a high-tech economy on the Peninsula, occurred because of factors external to Stanford as well. Terman and other Stanford administrators were able to capitalize on these conditions in a way that, for the time, showed an unprecedented awareness of the capacity of research universities to spur certain kinds of economic development.[35]

The first advantage was the University's location amid one of the nation's most booming Cold War economies. Stanford and its immediate area were the parts of the Bay Area that were among the most blessed by the magic combination of military spending, middle-class suburbanization, and new private-sector wealth that emerged during the postwar period. Building on the Peninsula's heritage as a suburban retreat for the very rich, Palo Alto and neighboring Menlo Park became home to upper-middle-class families who tended to be highly educated and employed in white-collar occupations. Menlo Park's population grew from just over 3,000 people to nearly 27,000 between 1940 and 1960; Palo Alto's grew from under 17,000 to over 52,000 in the same period.[36] Yet the commercial activity that existed in these and other Peninsula suburbs in the late 1940s and early 1950s was almost exclusively generated by retail and service firms that addressed the needs of the communities' residents. The suburbs of the Peninsula were still commuter towns, whose workers traveled to San Francisco or elsewhere for their jobs.

The few exceptions to this pattern on the Peninsula were the small but influential spin-off technology companies that had emerged from Stanford's prewar engineering programs. Perhaps the most famous example of these was Hewlett-Packard, a company started in a Palo Alto garage in 1939 by two former graduate students. Another example was Varian Associates, founded by two brothers, Palo Alto natives who began their scientific careers tinkering with radio equipment in their family attic. Unlike the "dirty" industries like shipbuilding and heavy manufacturing that were emerging around the perimeter of the San Francisco Bay, advanced scientific firms like Hewlett-Packard and Varian were unobtrusive neighbors in the residential landscape of Palo Alto and its neighboring towns. The people who worked in these firms (or at least those who were the most visible members of the workforce) were white-collar professionals, unlike the masses of blue-collar workers who filled the factories by the Bay.

The presence of these select advanced scientific companies, combined with the ecological, infrastructural, and demographic conditions on the

Peninsula, made the moment ripe for creating a whole new sort of economic base for the metropolitan region that would revolve around the scientific research programs at Stanford. Fred Terman recognized this potential. He made some frank comparisons with other institutions in a 1943 letter to a colleague: "The years after the war are going to be very important and also very critical ones for Stanford. I believe that we will either consolidate our potential strength, and create a foundation for a position in the west somewhat analogous to that of Harvard in the East, or we will drop to the level somewhat similar to that of Dartmouth, a well thought of institution having about 2 per cent as much influence on national life as Harvard."[37] Terman's comment is revealing not simply in its cognizance of how the war might change the fortunes of colleges and universities, but in its underlying message that the West would soon become a significantly more dominant region in the postwar period.

Stanford also found itself in an advantageous political position in the Cold War period, not only benefiting from the political ascendance of scientists in federal government affairs, but also enjoying close ties with the local civic leaders whose own power was increasing as a result of Cold War spending patterns. Terman had been a student of Vannevar Bush at M.I.T., and in 1942 Bush was a leading candidate (supported by Hoover and others) for the presidency of the University. While Bush turned Stanford down in favor of his job at OSRD, Stanford administrators continued to build their ties to national political figures. Thomas Spragens, the lobbyist that President Tresidder had hired in 1945 to give the university a full-time presence in Washington, helped the university capitalize on these personal connections, build new contacts, and win important government contracts that gradually elevated its stature and national reputation.[38] On the local level, the men who ran Stanford also traveled among San Francisco's civic elite. Every Stanford president received an automatic invitation to join the famous Bohemian Club, the men's organization made up of the top notch of San Francisco society; many of the city's leaders were Stanford alumni who would vigorously defend the University's interests in regional economic affairs. Stanford administrators, in turn, were perhaps more attuned to the university's role in guiding regional economic development and supporting business interests than they might have been otherwise. While the University's entrepreneurial, pro-market mindset had its roots in the philosophy of millionaire capitalist Leland Stanford, the midcentury local political culture served to solidify this approach. The business associationalism of the regional elite colored University leaders' attitudes about government intervention, but like their allies in organizations like the Bay Area Council, the university was quick to recognize the central role of government spending in the local economy. Although President Tresidder had warned in 1942 that "permanent government subsidy carries with it many disappointments and disposes to new ailments. 'Cursed is the gift that taketh away liberty,' " by the end of the 1940s Stanford administrators were working actively to win lucrative federal contracts.[39]

Their efforts paid off. Over the course of the 1950s Stanford's income from federal grants and contracts rose steadily, from less than $2 million in 1951 to $8.3 million in 1960. The bulk of these grants came from the Department of Defense and the Atomic Energy Commission and went to the School of Engineering, which rose to become one of the most preeminent departments in the nation, a quintessential "steeple of excellence" in Cold War university research and teaching.[40] By the late1950s, Stanford University was an undisputed research powerhouse and one of the federal government's most valuable resources in its Cold War–related research efforts. Yet Stanford administrators understood from the beginning that government contracting was not an end in itself, but rather a means by which to achieve commercial ends. Terman and others recognized quite early that federal grants and contracts not only contributed to the national defense effort but that these funds also served as seed money for industrial innovation. Their entrepreneurial sympathies gave them a keen understanding of the degree to which the university as an institution was becoming a more potent force in American cultural and economic life. Thus, their postwar approach to building Stanford's reputation focused not only on strengthening certain of its academic departments to attract defense dollars, but also on making them more conducive to the promotion of innovation and entrepreneurship, working in concert with the private sector and with government. At Stanford, the commercial potential of academic innovation was celebrated and encouraged—to a degree that was sometimes found excessive by certain members of the faculty.[41]

Stanford further beefed up its postwar reputation by aggressively recruiting faculty from the Ivy League colleges of the East. Good pay, plentiful research dollars, strong ties with high-tech industry, a good climate and natural amenities, and a pleasant, family-oriented community were all powerful selling points in luring talented junior professors to Stanford. The exodus that resulted from the University's recruitment effort was noticeable enough by 1961 to merit an article in *Newsweek*, in which one new professor was quoted as saying that he left Harvard to come west "because interesting things are happening . . . there's excitement in the air."[42]

It is a great irony that an institution with such a long legacy of antigovernment sentiment would use federal defense contracts to bring it fame and fortune and, in turn, foster hundreds of fledgling entrepreneurs in their work. Although Stanford had always relied on the federal defense industry to a certain degree in its research pursuits, the Cold War–era explosion of research was unprecedented. And when this money began to flow in the direction of Palo Alto, local officials and Stanford administrators alike celebrated the "new" local economy's reliance on government dollars. The "impact of the electronics-nuclear space-age upon America's research and technology is accelerating the transformation of the Palo Alto area into one of the country's most important national defense facilities," crowed *The Tall Tree*, a journal sponsored in part by the Palo Alto Chamber of Commerce, in 1958. "The Palo Alto–Stanford research community has grown to become an integral part of the science community of the nation. . . . These United States resources of science are tapped by the armed services in continent-spanning teamwork for defense. . . . This brings Stanford research and the laboratories of industry here into sharp focus in their considerable dependence on the armed services and federal funds."[43] During the 1950s and early 1960s, the dependence on defense was a good thing, a display of patriotism, and a sign that advanced scientific industry was "big-time"—doing important things for the country and the world.

Land Development

The Cold War gave Stanford administrators an unprecedented opportunity to build on the institution's strengths in the sciences and engineering. The concomitant urban decentralization of the period presented Stanford's leaders with another new opportunity—to turn its vast landholdings into extraordinarily lucrative real estate developments. Stanford's choice to develop its land, spurred both by economic necessity and its administrators' real desire to make the San Francisco Peninsula a preeminent region of high-tech activity, had lasting repercussions on the geography of advanced scientific production through the Cold War and beyond.[44] For the university sought not simply to create isolated and unconnected real estate developments, but to form a "community of scholars" that would be a center for scientific production and innovation. In order to do this, Stanford consciously and comprehensively planned its developments, using architecture and design to accomplish social and cultural ends. Like other developers, Stanford may have gotten into the real estate business because it saw the opportunity for a quick profit, but its administrators also saw that the University could provide an alternative to the sprawling and unplanned suburban tracts growing up across the Peninsula. As a developer, Stanford saw itself as an important counterbalancing influence; because the University owned so much land, its choosing to develop carefully and sparingly would preserve land values over the long term. Interestingly, a university whose leadership embraced entrepreneurial, free-market economics not only eagerly accepted large amounts of federal grant monies but also saw that comprehensive planning (of the kind often practiced by the state) could be a way to control social and economic outcomes.

Prior to the war, the University had leased the land that was not part of the campus to farmers and ranchers, the only possible tenants for property located so far in the country. This provided the University with a modest income, but one that was hardly significant to the institutional budget. Like many other universities in the prewar period, Stanford struggled for financial solvency; diminished class sizes and shrinking alumni donations during the Great Depression exacerbated this problem. The population and economic boom during and after the war changed all this and gave new value to the thousands of acres of land owned by Stanford. Alf Brandin, chief of business affairs at the University, later remembered it this way:

> I worked on fundraising before we went off to war and I didn't understand— if we needed some money, why didn't we do something with our land? We could lease it out. What I didn't understand was that there wasn't the growth that we had later. . . . on all sides of us we had open land. . . . So, the opportunity wasn't there. Now, the war changed all that. . . . After the war we then had an opportunity to do something.[45]

The University not only had an opportunity—it had a *need* to "do something." Rising land values also meant rising property taxes; while a nonprofit organization, the University was subject to tax on "unrelated business income," which applied to the Stanford lands whether they were home to grazing sheep or suburban subdivisions. Leaving the land undeveloped would mean cash-poor Stanford would have to pay high taxes without getting significant rents in return.[46] Another danger was that local governments—as an outgrowth of urban renewal legislation—had power to condemn unused land and take it over for public uses such as schools or parks. In order to avoid both high and uncompensated tax costs, as well as possible land condemnation, Stanford needed to develop its acreage.

Wallace Sterling's ascension to the presidency of the University in 1949 was the turning point in making this land development campaign a reality. As Terman later put it, "Sterling [got] the world behind Stanford interested in Stanford."[47] Another Stanford administrator remembered: "Wally was the one who made Stanford's emergence possible. He really looks to me like the giant, the giant of those times. There was nobody in the country that compared to Wally—and in my opinion there still isn't."[48] While engineer Fred Terman was undoubtedly a crucial figure in the national emergence of Stanford and the development of Silicon Valley, it was under the leadership of historian Wallace Sterling that Stanford became a great engine of science-based economic development.

The choices that Sterling and his fellow administrators made in developing the Stanford lands were not simply a response to mass suburbanization and attendant increases in land value. In their design and planning, Stanford's land developments show the influence of prevailing modes of thought about urban decentralization and the design of places of scientific production. The first evidence of this connection is the postwar development and expansion of the campus itself. Carefully planned and designed from the start, the University continued this tradition after the end of the war. Stanford was the first university to establish a campus planning office, which enforced the University's stringent architectural and landscape standards.[49] Just as Leland Stanford had brought in the preeminent planner of his day—Frederick Law Olmsted—to design the original campus, in 1947 the University hired the famous urbanist and advocate of decentralization Lewis Mumford to assess potential development options for the campus and its surrounding land.

"Stanford owns the last large open area in what has become practically a single great suburban development," Mumford wrote after his visit. "For the sake of Stanford's future development as a University it is important that this area should be conserved exclusively for University uses." But Mumford was liberal in his definition of what these uses might be, finding that "housing developments to serve the staff and faculty of the university" would be acceptable uses and suggesting that the University further try to enhance its land values by obtaining strategically located parcels of land that could later be developed for business or residential use in a way that would not "reduce the value of nearby university land." Unlike the earlier planning recommendations laid down by Olmsted, which sought ways to best suit Stanford's unique landscape and convey its higher academic purposes, Mumford's memorandum reflected pragmatic concerns about how best to maximize the value of Stanford's land. Mumford argued that the land was most valuable when it was kept open or used for academic purposes and was strongly against subdividing acres on the border of the Farm for housing subdivisions.[50]

In the short term, Stanford administrators seem to have ignored Mumford's advice completely.[51] Within a few years, the University's leadership had commissioned a variety of other reports to assess the feasibility of residential, commercial, and industrial development of its acreage. Yet Stanford's longer-term choices for the land, while not exclusively academic in purpose, reflected Mumford's concerns about preserving the value of Stanford's property with the "right" sort of development. It is clear that Stanford's administrators also saw that the financial benefits of development would be maximized through comprehensive and conscientious planning.

University planners drew their inspiration not only from urbanists like Mumford but from concurrent city-planning movements such as the New Towns Movement in Great Britain, a public sector initiative that aimed to improve working-class housing conditions and urban congestion by building satellite cities from the ground up that incorporated industrial, commercial, residential, and recreational land uses.[52] A 1951 Stanford report authored by planning official Elmore Hutchinson noted "it is fortunate that the entire area is held in one ownership, as almost all planning now for new cities, especially the new city developments in England, make it necessary for a sort of redevelopment to take place and the ownerships gathered from many holdings into one, either publicly or privately." Sole ownership, Hutchinson continued, "is a deterrent to uncontrolled development that has in mind only the greatest amount of money return and it makes possible the ultimate stabilization of land values."[53]

Hutchinson's observations echo the American campus planning traditions that valued single ownership and comprehensive, multi-use planning; they also reflect prevailing thought about city planning in general. Other university communities had to employ public sector tools like urban renewal to obtain ownership and control of land beyond their campuses; Stanford had a huge advantage in that it already owned vacant and desirable property. Stanford administrators were also cognizant early on of the way in which the right sorts of jobs and the right sorts of people added to the value of land. Hutchinson's 1951 report expressed the hope that "we can develop a final plan where more work areas are made available, such as light industry of a non-nuisance type and which will create a demand for technical employees of a high salary class that will be in a financial position to live in this area. If this be possible, it will add greatly to our plan and make possible a more economically sound community."[54]

In 1953 the Stanford Board of Trustees voted to make available for development all of the lands except for the areas required for Stanford's future campus buildings. To determine how best and most profitably to use this land, the University hired the San Francisco architectural firm Skidmore, Owings, and Merrill to survey the region's economic potential and suggest land uses. The 1953 Master Plan that resulted showed Stanford administrators how fortuitous conditions were for high-end residential, commercial, and industrial development on Stanford lands. The Plan noted that between 1940 and 1950 the Peninsula had grown 105 percent—twice the rate of growth of the metropolitan area as a whole. Those who moved to the Peninsula tended to be higher income; San Mateo County had the highest per capita income in the metropolitan area. Once again, the plan noted the appropriateness of high-tech industry to this kind of area, as "these high-income residential communities do not want heavy industries, but they have become increasingly desirous of obtaining small, attractive, light industry plants to relieve their residential tax load, particularly if such industries can be developed in controlled industrial districts with rigid regulations governing land coverage, architectural design and adequate open areas for parking and landscaping." Careful planning should also guide the construction of residential development on Stanford lands: "The development criteria for the residential areas . . . reflect the application of contemporary planning concepts to attain a high order of living environment and at the same time render the University the highest economic return compatible with this aim. However, the ultimate character of the residential communities will be determined by the imagination and skill with which the development criteria are applied to the detail[ed] planning of the neighborhoods."[55]

While this evaluation was extremely useful and reflected the University's concern with high planning standards, the precise recommendations of the report were somewhat unsatisfactory to Stanford administrators. Skidmore, Owings, and Merrill persisted in thinking of the Peninsula as simply a growing and wealthy commuter suburb of San Francisco rather than an economic center in its own right. As a consequence, the 1953 Plan was heavily skewed toward high-end residential development and less concerned with the development of "small, attractive, light industry plants." The Plan recommended that up to 6,000 acres of the Stanford lands be developed as residential subdivisions, while only 350 acres be devoted to commercial or industrial uses. In its eagerness to develop such a massive portion of Stanford's acreage, the 1953 Plan was typical of its times. If the Stanford administrators had accepted this recommendation, not only might the economic history of Silicon Valley have taken a different course, but the landscape of Palo Alto also would have been strikingly different. Residential development on such a scale would have nearly obliterated the open spaces on the Stanford reserve, and perhaps would have set a precedent for further subdivision and development of open spaces elsewhere. In subsequent decades, the "growth-is-good" philosophy evident in the Skidmore, Owings, and Merrill document gave way to rising concern about environmental preservation and new growth control and land-banking practices that prevented large-scale development on the Peninsula's coastal mountains as well as in other parts of California and the West.[56]

Stanford administrators, seeing how federal defense contracts were greatly accelerating the creation and rate of growth of high technology spin-off companies around Stanford, disagreed with the Skidmore, Owings, and Merrill assessment and argued for a strategy that focused more of its attention on industrial development and on housing and retail components that responded to the future industrial functions of the region.[57] "If Stanford retains ample uncommitted land, in an area where land shortage is clearly looming, it will be in a position to attract to the University community a wide variety of national and regional activities which have a direct and immediate value to the University," an administrative committee wrote in a report to President Sterling. "They are likely to provide income from rentals, and provide as well both income and professional opportunities for students and staff."[58] The administrators' implication was that such activities would revolve around advanced scientific industry.

The Stanford leadership's emphasis on high-tech industrial development was not entirely due to economic foresight, as leasing land for industrial purposes gave the University more long-term flexibility than giving the acreage over exclusively to residential development. Industrial firms, with little grumbling, could be persuaded to sign 51-year or even shorter leases. Residential developers, however, could hardly be persuaded to sign anything less than a 99-year lease, locking up Stanford's land and limiting more lucrative possibilities in the long term.[59] But the Stanford administrators' response to the 1953 Master Plan also reveals their allegiance to the comprehensive planning ideas first proposed by Ebenezer Howard and later promulgated by their planning consultant Lewis Mumford. Sounding very much like garden city planners, the administrators argued that the University needed to take advantage of "the unique opportunity which the Stanford lands present to develop a community in which work, home, recreation, and cultural life are brought together with some degree of balance and integration."[60] In the context of the San Francisco Peninsula of 1954, which was in the process of turning from a sleepy rural area into a mostly residential commuter suburb, this was a bold vision.

In response to these criticisms of the Skidmore, Owings, and Merrill report, President Sterling, Provost Terman, and other University leaders embarked on a building program by the mid-1950s that had three chief components: high-end housing that would be attractive to professional families, a large regional shopping center that would take advantage of local purchasing capacity, and—most importantly—an industrial park made up of businesses and manufacturers who desired the cachet and the technical support gained by a location very close to Stanford. Reflecting the University's concern about long leases as well as Fred Terman's desire to increase the presence of high-tech industry in the area, nearly half of the total developed acreage was earmarked for this "Stanford Industrial Park."[61] The University stated "that the aim of the development shall be to produce in the ultimate a community of which the University Trustees and all those who have its welfare at heart can be proud

Figure 3.1. As the San Francisco area suburbanized, Stanford University's vast and largely undeveloped landholdings became more valuable. In this 1960 aerial photograph, the Stanford campus appears at the center, framed by the University's two major land developments: the Stanford Industrial Park (top) and the Stanford Shopping Center (bottom). Courtesy Stanford University Archives.

and that will, by reason of the fact that it is a University project, serve in an important way as an educational example in the field of community development."[62]

In the 1950s, the political dynamics between Stanford and local government worked in the University's favor in making this "educational example" a reality. Town-and-gown tension was never entirely absent in Stanford and Palo Alto, even though the University was the center of the town's economy and community culture. Outwardly, the town usually assumed an attitude of cheerful cooperation: "Stanford and Palo Alto have always been a single community in spirit, utilizing each other's resources and cooperating for mutual benefit," wrote a *Palo Alto Times* editor in 1953.[63] Palo Alto readily agreed to incorporate the land developments into the city, thereby providing Stanford with public utilities and road upkeep (and providing the city with tax revenue). The mayor of Palo Alto pronounced this "one of the finest annexations Palo Alto has had in its history." "I can't conceive of any opposition to the plan," said the mayor. "I feel the entire community is in favor of the annexation, and in the future it will become a greater and greater benefit, both to the city and university."[64]

The reality was a bit more complicated. Palo Alto officials were somewhat distressed by the idea of a large shopping mall siphoning off revenue from its downtown merchants and, at one point, attempted to wield power over the Stanford developers by threatening not to provide sewer service to the site.[65] The town seems to have quickly given up on this attempt to influence Stanford's plans, however, and made no further efforts to control the path of development. The hard political reality was that—as in many other small university-centered towns—Stanford administrators had much more political clout than Palo Alto elected officials. The University's political power was further enhanced by the tireless boosterism of the Palo Alto Chamber of Commerce, whose motto was "Palo Alto: The Home of Stanford University." Also working in Stanford's favor was California's heritage of a highly localized legal and regulatory environment that fragmented political power and tended to champion the rights of large private-property owners.[66]

The residential and retail components of Stanford's development plan, while seeking to adhere to higher architectural and planning standards than the usual kinds of postwar construction on the Peninsula, were not particularly innovative or remarkable aside from the fact that their leaseholder was a major research university. For these developments, Stanford administrators turned the tasks of construction and marketing over to private real estate development firms, but the University still remained an important influence on the projects. The commercial element of the development scheme, the Stanford Shopping Center, was the first regional shopping mall on the Peninsula and one of the first of the inward-facing shopping centers in the nation. While the University administrators were only nominally involved with its day-to-day operations, they maintained a strong interest in maintaining a prestigious and profitable group of tenants in the mall and in keeping the development from having significant commercial competition.[67]

The first phase of residential development was a small tract of single-family housing in Menlo Park, on the northern side of the campus near the new shopping center. The homes were designed to appeal to the educated white families already residing in the area, and many of those who moved in were Stanford alumni.[68] Stanford got deeper into the residential real estate business in 1957 with the development of "Stanford Hills," a subdivision whose houses cost between $33,000 and $75,000 and where lot sizes varied from the standard one-quarter-acre up to five acres. This development was significantly more upscale than those proposed in the Skidmore, Owings, and Merrill plan and built in Menlo Park.[69] The developer trumpeted the exclusivity of the tract in a 1959 advertisement: "Enjoy Peninsula Living at Its Best . . . in the lovely, rolling 'Stanford Hills,' our largest and most beautiful development. All homes INDIVIDUALLY PLANNED for the most discriminating buyers. No stock plans . . . no repeats. . . . You, too, can now join our 'Who's Who.' "[70]

In 1959 the University embarked upon a development called Willow Creek Apartments, a facility that marketed itself to the mobile, urbane professional who desired proximity to amenities like the University and the Shopping Center—a person who might otherwise choose to live in San Francisco. At the groundbreaking, developer Howard J. White remarked that "these luxury apartments were the result of innumerable requests on the Peninsula for true apartment living in a country setting" and said that he "expect[ed] his tenants to come from New York, from Florida, from the Northwest as well as Palm Springs and Arizona."[71] In all cases, the University's residential developments were for individuals and families of a certain income level; they were far beyond the means of blue-collar workers and often out of reach for ordinary middle-class families as well.

Despite the success of these commercial and residential projects, the greatest achievement of the Stanford real estate development effort—and the part with which Stanford administrators were most closely involved—was the Stanford Industrial Park. Like the Shopping Center, the planning and development of the Park was already underway prior to the 1953 Master Plan; the University first designated the area as a "light-industrial" district in 1951, and the first tenants moved in the year after.[72] The story of the Park is a vivid, real-life example of how the American campus planning traditions of pastoral isolation, separation, and comprehensive design were applied to industrial real estate development in the Cold War period. The Stanford Industrial Park was the exemplary research park, managing to become an industrial facility with the look and feel of a college campus. By 1960 Stanford's effort at this disguise had been so successful and so influential upon its neighbors that the local newspaper editor commented: "The research centers of the Mid-peninsula, with their architectural buildings and landscaped lawns, look more like college structures than factories. In fact, I've seen many college buildings, and attended classes in a few, that resembled those factories of old more than do the industrial plants of today."[73]

The purpose of the Stanford Industrial Park was to strengthen Stanford's position as a top national research university through the economic development of its surrounding region. Creating a home for high-tech industry next door to Stanford's campus enhanced the reputation of the University and created profitable connections to the business community. Yet Fred Terman and his fellow administrators recognized that

this goal would be accomplished only if the University's Palo Alto neighbors were persuaded that industrial development was a good thing, and
if the development was sufficiently attractive to advanced scientific firms
and their professional employees. The administrators thus set out to
make the park a model for suburban industrial planning. If the future
of the San Francisco Peninsula lay in high-tech industry, as Fred Terman
believed, there needed to be an example to show how this kind of industrial development could peacefully coexist with an affluent suburban
community. If the Park looked markedly different from other industrial
parks, it would underscore the fact that advanced scientific industry was
different from other kinds of industrial production—and thus better
suited to a town like Palo Alto. The new high-tech industries used modern, "clean" facilities rather than smoke-belching factories; their employees were white-collar professionals rather than blue-collar workers. Because of physical plant and personnel, most manufacturing activities
were highly inappropriate for exclusive suburbs like Palo Alto, reasoned
the Stanford administrators. On the other hand, if contained in the
proper setting, advanced scientific industry could blend in well with the
landscape of the suburban college town. Palo Alto officials supported
Stanford in its recruitment of this kind of industry and agreed that this
growth could "fit in with the residential character of the city and with
Stanford University."[74]

In order to attract advanced scientific industry and placate nervous
suburban neighbors, administrators designed an Industrial Park that
mirrored the lush greenery and low-rise, architecturally compatible
buildings of the Stanford campus. In doing so, the administrators also
demonstrated their allegiance to the idea that scientific creativity required a pastoral atmosphere in order to flourish. Having ownership to
a huge, undeveloped expanse of land, and enjoying a generally supportive and cooperative relationship with local authorities, Stanford administrators had the luxury of translating the pastoral ideals of the college
campus into an entirely new and comprehensively planned industrial
development.

To these ends, Stanford took the architectural and planning standards
of private industrial parks and intensified and tailored them to an unprecedented degree. The University instituted stringent architectural
and planning restrictions and maintained close control over the design
of every facility. Prospective tenants had to "submit an overall plan spell-
ing out in some detail the type, size, location and setbacks of buildings,
roads, off-street parking and green areas."[75] There had to be ninety-foot-
wide buffer strips of green space between the road and buildings at the
front of every lot. Buildings had to be low-rise structures, and all structures had to incorporate ample green space. The open land around the

buildings had to be 60 percent larger than the buildings constructed on it, making the park extremely low-density. Some of these lands, naturally, had to be taken up with parking lots, but in order to maintain the illusion of uninterrupted greenery, companies had to place their lots behind their buildings rather than toward the street. Tenants had to gain University approval for any alterations to their facilities and had to maintain the neatness and cleanliness of their buildings and grounds.[76]

The buildings that resulted were not particularly architecturally innovative, but they were cleanly modernist and generally unobtrusive. Some companies chose to articulate their connection and proximity to the University through architecture that evoked the colonnaded sandstone of the University's buildings. Varian Associates, a Stanford spin-off company and an early tenant, was one of these; a contemporary description of its facility used language that emphasized the psychic benefits of the building's design and environment: "The architectural qualities of serenity and repose—somewhat forgotten in today's stress on dynamics and drama—which the rhythmic pattern of the structural columns gives to the building, have a special appropriateness in the more or less rural area in which the building is located."[77]

In echoing Stanford's campus buildings—sometimes down to the red tile on the roof—the structures in the Industrial Park were not only creating a campuslike atmosphere but one that drew on the romanticized history and architectural traditions of the American West. The influence of the regional vernacular extended beyond imitations of the Mission Romanesque of the Stanford main quadrangle, to industrial buildings in the park that looked remarkably similar to the modernist suburban homes springing up throughout California subdivisions during this period. Some buildings in the Park incorporated the strikingly modern and distinctly Californian architecture seen in the homes of Joseph Eichler, a Bay Area architect whose mass-produced and cleanly modern ranch houses became architectural symbols of postwar California. Others used gently sloping landscaping and the incorporation of natural features, such as trees and shrubs (not always native, but characteristic of the region), to convey a particularly California feel. When we examine photographs of the earliest Industrial Park structures, it is hard to imagine these buildings being located in the suburbs of New York or Boston. The University also controlled the park's environment through careful selection of tenants, attracting a rarified group of innovative scientific manufacturers and research laboratories. Reversing the usual economic development model, where localities and developers wooed industry through extensive marketing campaigns and other enticements, Stanford required tenants to apply for admittance to the Park.[78] Existing connections to the University lured the earliest tenants; the first firm to lease

Figure 3.2. The General Electric facility in the Stanford Industrial Park was one example of an industrial structure whose architecture and landscaping reflected the influence of California modernism and allowed it to blend in almost seamlessly to the surrounding suburbs. Courtesy Stanford University Archives.

land was run by Terman's former students the Varian brothers. Although the University was not explicitly recruiting high-technology tenants at the outset, the presence of large facilities for Varian and similar firms set the tone for the development, and many other technology-related companies soon followed.

While the Park's tenants were private businesses, the presence of the federal government also was strongly felt in their operations. A significant portion of the tenants—particularly those who were newer companies, who numbered its Stanford faculty and former students among its founders—relied on government defense contracts to maintain and grow their profitability. A good number of the Park's tenants were federal contractors; many more benefited in a secondhand fashion from federal contracts by supplying electronic equipment to large aerospace manufacturers and other companies who were building the hardware and technology for the military. Hewlett-Packard, is another early tenant and a firm founded by Terman protégés, is an instructive example. Company lore tends to highlight its first client, the Walt Disney Company, who bought eight of its oscillators in the early 1940s to provide technologi-

Figure 3.3. The Stanford Industrial Park created new alliances between university and industry beginning in the late 1950s. Here, Stanford and Lockheed officials inspect the location of the park on an area map. Courtesy Stanford University Archives.

cally advanced sound for the movie *Fantasia*. But as Terman later recalled, military investments were more important: "In all the companies that supplied military equipment, new things were being developed, and the companies bought a lot of instruments to help them with new developments. It just turned out that these expensive things that Hewlett-Packard had developed just were right in where the line of great progress was."[79] In an era when there was virtually no consumer market for high-technology electronic equipment or computers, the direct or secondary support of fledgling companies like Hewlett-Packard by the military was essential in keeping the industry alive. The Stanford Industrial Park and its supporting services acted as one of the first business incubators for these kinds of companies, who at the time they moved into the Industrial Park were so little known that even Stanford administrators like Alf Brandin were "trying to find out something about Hewlett-Packard stock. Nobody even knew about them. That's how young they were."[80] Yet within a few short years of moving into the Industrial Park, Hewlett-Packard had grown in size and wealth to such a degree that one of its founders, David Packard, served as president of Stanford's Board of Trustees.

The "youth" of technology companies like Hewlett-Packard was part of their appeal as tenants of the Industrial Park. Stanford administrators kept tight control over who leased land there, and they looked for tenants who reflected the energy and innovation of the new high-technology industries. Even non-industrial clients had to meet this test. When presented with the possibility of a synagogue being located in the Park, a key Stanford administrator handling the Park "said this would be OK if they are a young and vigorous group, but not if they are old and orthodox."[81] "Young and vigorous" tenants were desirable not only for the economic potential of their companies but because they would bring their young, educated, professional employees to Stanford and Palo Alto. Published brochures and unpublished internal documents about the Park repeatedly refer to the Park's ability to "attract a better class of workers" as one of its chief assets.[82] Engineers and scientists, already lionized by the national political culture of the space age, were what David Packard called "a very desirable kind of resident" for the community.[83]

The Park looked and felt different from other industrial developments that had grown up throughout the Bay Area since 1940, and the way in which business executives and local elites responded to it reflected the national political and cultural transformations accompanying the rise of the Cold War science complex. Its industry was "smokeless," not dirty, and its workers were not only white-collar professionals but were portrayed as people of exceptional creative abilities. Discussions of workers in the Park often played off the prevailing stereotypes of scientists as quirky but brilliant. Discussing his Industrial Park facility, one Lockheed executive quipped: "we don't have any set working hours for our scientists. . . . If a man works better from midnight till morning it's all right with us. We're working with gifted individuals and we try to encourage them to have bright ideas. We don't care what time of day they have them."[84]

In mandating such stringent architectural standards and such high standards for its tenants, Stanford violated nearly every cardinal rule of economic development. "We didn't know what the hell we were doing," Alf Brandin admitted to a group of real estate developers in 1958. "If we knew how hard it was to get industry, that you've got to give tax exemptions, cheap labor and free buildings, we probably wouldn't have tried." But instead of struggling to find tenants, University officials found that industries were very interested in coming to the Park. "We were as tough as we could be," Brandin said, "and we couldn't discourage them."[85] However, advanced scientific industries' footloose nature and the shortage of scientific manpower caused these sectors to behave differently from other industries in making location choices. The old rules of economic development did not necessarily apply, and this was exceedingly clear in the area surrounding Stanford, which already enjoyed numerous economic and environmental advantages over other regions of the country.

Companies evaluating whether to locate in the Industrial Park were drawn by the proximity to defense installations, the many natural and community amenities, and the growing concentration of scientific minds working at Stanford and its spin-off companies. As the *San Francisco Chronicle* noted in 1961, "Brains Are Bait" for advanced scientific industry: "Certainly one of the greatest single attractions for the new—and highly desirable—smogless, light industries that make exotic products is brains. The electronics and missile industries as well as the less novel, more familiar varieties, must have a large pool of deep thinkers from which to draw new ideas, push ahead of competitors in the mad research scramble."[86] The desires of scientific workers to be near communities of other scientists and in places with the right amenities for them and their families gave the Stanford Industrial Park a huge advantage in luring industry, as it was located in the sort of community that offered all these advantages. The campuslike look and feel of the park presented an additional advantage for firms who were attempting to lure workers away from university jobs and into industrial research. By locating in the park, firms could potentially have their pick of some of the best "brains" in the country—not only faculty but Stanford graduates as well. The particularly Californian atmosphere, communicated through architecture, planning, and the internal culture of the entrepreneurial and innovative young companies that populated the park, also was a compelling asset in an era when the Golden State was the favored destination for so many migrants.[87]

Industrial parks elsewhere had already demonstrated the effectiveness that pleasant landscaping and high architectural standards could have on the ability of real estate developers to find tenants, and on the willingness of wealthy communities to accept industry in their midst. What the Stanford example demonstrated was the extremely positive effect of proximity to, and association with, a prominent research institution. Stanford administrators structured the development to maximize the connection between university and industry in a way that was mutually beneficial. The businesses that leased land in the Industrial Park gained access to Stanford faculty and laboratory facilities, as well as the cachet of the Stanford name. Lockheed Corporation, the giant Los Angeles–based aerospace company, announced that it was leasing an Industrial Park facility in 1956, noting that "proximity to the University and its outstanding laboratories will give Lockheed researchers an opportunity for advanced study; and that consulting opportunities in the Lockheed laboratories will be afforded the Stanford faculty."[88]

Among the opportunities enjoyed by Lockheed and other tenants was an Honors Cooperative program that offered company employees part-time enrollment toward advanced degrees in scientific disciplines. This unique offering added to Stanford's attraction as an industrial location and was a useful source of funds for academic programs. About four hundred employees from thirty-two companies were participating in the program by 1961, and enrollment later grew significantly.[89] "The program is fully self supporting through a combination of the tuition paid by the students and supplementary grants made by the participating companies," Terman noted in 1959. "This is also a good deal for the employer on the San Francisco Peninsula because it is such an attractive fringe benefit that, with this to offer, the employer is able to recruit the cream of the crop graduating from colleges all over the country in a market which is highly competitive for men."[90] At a moment in history when many American research universities remained wary of overly close ties with industry, Stanford administrators, led by Terman, embraced the concept of corporate education and the cross-pollination of research efforts.[91]

The Honors Cooperative program complemented another ingenious fund-raising tool of Terman's, the "Industrial Affiliates Program" of the Department of Aeronautical Engineering. Companies like Lockheed paid $10,000 annually for the privilege of being Industrial Associates. In return, they enjoyed an enhanced relationship with the researchers at Stanford and, again, the cachet of a close affiliation with the university.[92] Ancillary benefits like these increased tenants' allegiance to Stanford and resulted in additional revenue through corporate donations. High-technology companies, who benefited most from access to Stanford's faculty and research laboratories, were the most willing to give, and this in turn influenced the University's choice of tenants for the Park. Terman "pointed out to Brandin that we were getting more money here at Stanford from gifts from these technical companies [than] lease income from the land. . . . And Alf Brandin saw the point very quickly, and very soon thereafter, if you weren't a high-technology company, you had a hell of a time coaxing him to give you a lease."[93]

While the Stanford Industrial Park was distinctive in many regards, we must not forget that its success was due in good part to its being on the right side of larger economic and demographic trends. By the early 1960s, when the Park was filling up to capacity, the region's population had suburbanized to a degree that the ratio of population between the suburbs and the core cities (San Francisco and Oakland) was "well over" two to one, noted a survey by the Bay Area Council.[94] Regional decentralization was mirrored in business decentralization within suburban towns as well; a 1960 Council publication found that "even in suburban communities some dispersion of trade and service establishments is taking place in accordance with the trend in the entire Bay Area toward a broader distribution of economic activities."[95] The commuting patterns of Industrial Park employees attested to the shifting live-work patterns in the Bay Area. A 1962 survey showed that the majority of the Park's 10,500 employees did not live in the immediate area but commuted from communities south of Palo Alto (56 percent). Seven percent lived outside the "regional area" of the Peninsula altogether. Palo Alto residents made up 21 percent of the workforce. Employees overwhelmingly depended on cars to get to work:

> Few people use means other than the automobile—(little other means is offered). Nine men walk to work, four use the S.P. [commuter] train, and 8 use bicycles—a total of 1.6%. It should be observed that many companies do not encourage walking or public transportation. For example, Hewlett-Packard has no means for pedestrians to walk from public sidewalks to the entrances of their plant. Apparently it is assumed that all people will arrive by automobile or private motor vehicle.[96]

It is little wonder that alternative transportation was so limited given the design requirements of the Park, which despite their numerous requirements about setbacks and landscaping made no mention of sidewalks. Stanford's model industrial development was designed for the worker who commuted by car, even though the design of the park took pains to disguise its car dependence by placing the company parking lots behind the buildings.[97] The findings of the study also might have raised some warning signals about the ability of high-tech employees to find or afford housing in the immediate area. Because of developments like the Industrial Park, the Peninsula was on the leading edge of the trend toward living in one suburb and working in another. The residential and commuting patterns seen in the Park in 1962 also presaged the later housing shortages that would face the Bay Area, particularly Palo Alto, where by the end of the twentieth century few professionals could find available and affordable places to live.

The Park had its critics, some inside Stanford. During a 1959 meeting of the University's Advisory Committee on Land and Building Development (at which, significantly, committee member Fred Terman was not present), some administrators and faculty expressed concern that "the type of industry attracted to the Industrial Park [tended] to lend strong professional support to one part of the University's academic program, but not to other parts. The question was raised whether a more aggressive effort should not be made to attract regional governmental centers, professional society headquarters, and other leasees which would support a wider range of faculty interests." The committee members present generally agreed "it would be highly desirable to attract more diversified activities to Stanford lands, but that it is not immediately clear how to proceed."[98] While the committee made no further mention of diversification efforts after this meeting, the minutes reveal the tensions within the University about whose interests the Industrial Park was furthering.

The concerns that members of Stanford's liberal arts faculty might have had about the University's relentless focus on science-based economic development were drowned out by the avalanche of public attention, political power, and revenue that Stanford received as a result of the Park. By 1963 the Park was home to forty-two firms employing about twelve thousand workers.[99] By 1969 the number of tenants had swelled to sixty, and the number of employees to nearly eighteen thousand.[100] Between 1955 and 1968, the Industrial Park brought in over $13 million in net revenues, becoming by far the most lucrative of Stanford's land developments and a smashing economic success in terms of commercial real estate development.[101] In a very short time, Stanford's administrators had turned Palo Alto from a residential suburb and college town into an important center for innovative, advanced scientific industrial production.

A Model City

Almost from the very beginning, journalists, politicians, and business leaders hailed the Industrial Park and the other Stanford land developments as a national and international model for regional economic development. By the mid-1950s, the Stanford projects, and particularly the Industrial Park, were the subjects of numerous glowing national magazine features and newspaper articles. Although in the midst of the suburbs, these observers quickly took to referring to the Stanford developments as a new sort of city. The Stanford land program was "a model city" that "dwarfs ordinary town development schemes," enthused the *Saturday Evening Post* in 1955.[102] The *Los Angeles Times* reported in 1956:

> Parts of the 9,000-acre university landholdings are fast taking on the appearance of a fully integrated city. When completed it is expected that 45,000 people will live in homes on the land and thousands will be working at light industry or in business offices and buying at a shopping center. And, of course, there will be many gaining a higher education on the campus.[103]

The Park's greatest public relations coup came in 1958, within only a few years of its opening, when it was featured in an exhibit at the World's Fair in Brussels. "A color film showing the park and the life of its workers and enlarged color transparencies of its buildings are in the exhibit 'Industrial Parks USA' co-sponsored by the Society of Industrial Realtors and the Mobil Overseas Oil Co.," noted the *Stanford University Bulletin.* "Of the nine parks featured in the display, the co-sponsors considered the Stanford Park the most photogenic. The six-minute continuous loop film taken at Stanford is the closing element in the exhibit. In addition to the Industrial Park, the film shows scenes in local residence areas and at Stanford Shopping Center."[104]

After the World's Fair, the Park began to attract a steady stream of visitors from other countries and elsewhere in the United States who wanted to see for themselves this wonder of modern industrial development. Charles DeGaulle specifically asked to tour the Park during a visit to the United States in 1960; eight members of the Japanese Diet visited the Stanford developments shortly thereafter. Other foreign dignitaries followed.[105]

To the hundreds of other cities and regions in the United States who were seeking potent and fast-acting economic development strategies, Stanford University and its surrounding area seemed to have stumbled upon the perfect and easy solution: parklike industrial real estate, located near good housing and quality schools, whose tenants could take advantage of the resources of a world-class university. As other local economic-development authorities embarked upon their own schemes for industrial development—high-tech and otherwise—they often invoked Stanford as a model. Newspapers from Oregon and Idaho to Texas, Kansas, and Mississippi gave glowing reports of local initiatives inspired by the Stanford Industrial Park.[106]

The University's administrators were understandably pleased with this recognition and did what they could to provide technical assistance to other universities and communities. Lyle Nelson, Stanford's director of university relations, proudly wrote in 1962 that the Park was a "development which has become a national model for city-University cooperative action in attracting science-based research activities."[107] On the top of a 1963 newspaper clipping describing a Stanford-inspired research park at the University of Illinois, one excited University administrator wrote "Pace Setter!"[108]

While localities interested in advanced scientific development in general were drawn to the Stanford Industrial Park as a model, the development served as a particularly instructive example for universities and university towns who wanted to enter the real estate and economic development business. Representatives of four Southern California college towns—Pomona, Claremont, Le Verne, and Montclair—toured the facility in 1959. Pomona's city administrator commented that "Pomona Valley wants to look closely at Stanford because we feel that we have very nearly the same set of factors in Pomona Valley which led to Stanford's success, namely industrial sites in proximity to colleges and good residen-

tial areas."[109] Universities with land endowments were particularly interested in learning from Stanford. In Canada, the *Vancouver Sun* editorialized in 1964 that the University of British Columbia should develop its
lands not only for immediate profit, but also for the long-term benefits
to society: "A scientific-industrial complex on our own university endowment lands in the light of this experience takes on almost the appearance
of a necessity. Its immediate benefits are obvious. But beyond that, it
shapes as a doorway into a new social and economic age."[110]

Yet projects without overt ties to universities also looked to Stanford
for inspiration. In 1958 Bernard Hegeman, the president of the Brooklyn
Real Estate Board petitioned the New York City Planning Commission
to create an industrial park like the one flourishing in Palo Alto. "New
York City . . . can try to make fairly extensive areas available for large
plants which like to have all their working space on one level," he argued.
"Since no smoke or other noxious fumes will be permitted in an industrial park, there should be no fear on the part of the people living in
the area that the new development will be in any way objectionable. . . .
Stanford University . . . has such an industrial park on land which it owns
adjacent to the campus."[111] Hegeman was not alone in invoking the association between "clean" industry and the Stanford Industrial Park. Officials in neighboring Santa Clara, California, a few miles to the south of
Palo Alto, announced that an industrial park to be developed there in
1960 would be " 'similar to the Stanford Industrial Park' in that smoke,
noise, and odor will be restricted."[112]

The success of Stanford's land developments also influenced broader
trends in campus planning. The regents of the University of California,
for example, chose the lightly populated coastal mountains of Santa Cruz
as a site for a new campus in 1961 because they "want their new installations to be more like Stanford and less like UCLA." Building on an open
and unpopulated site, the regents announced, would "make possible
provision for faculty and staff housing and other features of a model
university community." Rather than being limited by existing surrounding development, like the urban UCLA campus, "the university
will be able to control the commercial, industrial, and residential districts
surrounding the campus—much as Stanford has done."[113] Stanford's experience showed others the value of having large open tracts of land at
a university's disposal; the "model city" in Palo Alto could not have come
about within the confines of an already-developed urban area.

The story of the University of California at Berkeley, across the Bay
from Stanford, is instructive in this regard. Berkeley enjoyed many of the
advantages Stanford did during the early Cold War period. It was the
home of huge federally sponsored scientific research projects and some
of the nation's finest physicists and engineers. It was located in a metro-

politan area that enjoyed a favorable climate and good natural amenities, and that was experiencing massive economic growth, much of it stemming from military investment. Like Stanford, the University was in a suburban area that was a desirable place for its faculty and other professionals to live. With all these conditions in place, it initially seems puzzling that Berkeley did not also become a center for high-tech industrial development.

In 1961 Berkeley city officials visited the Stanford Industrial Park to assess whether similar economic development could be possible in their university town; one local reporter sarcastically called the visit "a reverent Pilgrimage . . . to the Site of the Miracle of Palo Alto." The officials "returned home painfully aware of the differences" between the two towns. One of these was the issue recognized by the University of California regents in their choice of Santa Cruz: available land and population density. While technically suburban, the City of Berkeley was much larger and more densely populated than the towns of the Peninsula: "Palo Alto has an area of 22.27 square miles and a population of 53,000. Berkeley has an area of 17.87 square miles (almost half of it under water) and a population of 111,000, more than twice that of Palo Alto."[114] City and University officials did not have the freedom to develop land enjoyed by Stanford as a result of its unique land grant.

The other factor limiting industrial development of this kind in Berkeley was a very different political environment, both inside and outside the University of California. As a public institution, the University had fewer resources and much less entrepreneurial agility. The pro-business views of Stanford's administrators had made it eager to form alliances with industry in ways that were almost unprecedented at the time. The University at Berkeley, although led by the great champion of the "multiversity," Clark Kerr, did not provide the extension programs and special faculty exchanges that Stanford gave the tenants of its Industrial Park.[115]

Outside the University, the demographics of the town of Berkeley were a stumbling block to attracting this kind of high-tech development. "Palo Alto's population is almost completely Caucasian, whereas Berkeley's is 26 percent non-white," noted the article about the Berkeley officials' 1961 "pilgrimage." "Berkeley, in the immediate future, at least, would probably have a harder time providing the highly skilled and professional personnel needed by the new glamor [sic] industries."[116] While the reporter's frank observation reflected the racial politics of the time and the fact that few minorities then had professional careers in the sciences, he hit upon an important truth behind Stanford's success—the racial and economic homogeneity of Palo Alto. The professionals who worked in high-tech industry already lived near Stanford, or wanted to live there. Part of what made the "city of knowledge" on the Peninsula so desirable to professional workers and employers during this time of racial change and social upheaval was its whiteness.

Because of constraints like those experienced by Berkeley, many of the university communities that aspired to recreate the "miracle of Palo Alto" were not able to replicate Stanford's success. Yet the Stanford model had an enduring legacy on the economic development strategies of the 1960s in two respects. First, it helped make state and local leaders pay closer attention to the role research universities played in attracting businesses and educated workers. "A tremendous complex of clean industry has grown up around Stanford University because of its outstanding research facilities," Oregon governor Mark Hatfield exhorted an audience of his state's business leaders in 1961, "and this is where we should make improvements."[117]

Second, Stanford's real estate developments further solidified the association between science-based economic development and a low-rise, low-density environment in the minds of public policy makers and business leaders. Stanford's imitators quickly recognized that Stanford's ownership of a large parcel of undeveloped land had been essential to the success of the Industrial Park and the other real estate projects sponsored by the University. They also saw that the Park's cachet derived in part from its lush landscaping, its generous use of space, and its modern facilities. This design made electronics and computer manufacturing plants blend in well with a high-income suburban landscape and, perhaps even more importantly, attracted workers who were, by and large, well-educated professionals who added financial and social resources to the community.

By the mid-1960s the Stanford Industrial Park—a project developed under extraordinary conditions of university land ownership, massive regional economic growth, and location in an affluent suburb—had become the gold standard for science-based industrial development elsewhere in the country and the world. By 1965 economic-development officials and business leaders as far away as Scotland were concluding that "the establishment of 'industrial parks' on the Stanford University model would bring about the most profound interpenetration" of university and industry.[118]

The communities that appear to have most eagerly embraced the Stanford land developments as a model were often in economically struggling regions of the country and were sometimes rural or semi-rural. However, larger cities and equally prestigious research institutions also noted Stanford's success and, while usually refraining from an open acknowledgement of Stanford as a model, proceeded to develop industrial projects along very similar lines. Whether in cities or in rural areas, Stanford's imitators felt that they had to be similarly exclusive and suburban in look and feel in order to replicate the successes of Palo Alto. While rarely discussed, Stanford's imitators also noted the role that racial and economic homogeneity played in the success of the Industrial Park and the other developments. Placing a "city of knowledge" in a suburban, white, middle-class setting appeared to greatly reduce community opposition to these projects. Universities and economic development officials would take these lessons from their visits to Stanford and attempt to replicate the "miracle at Palo Alto" elsewhere around the country, with mixed results.[119]

"The Battle of the Hills"

While closely observing the features that contributed to Stanford's success, the steady stream of visitors to Palo Alto and the Industrial Park did not seem to have taken much notice of another outcome of these real-estate-development efforts: community controversy. Palo Alto residents did not unilaterally welcome the incursion of industry into their town, and the conflicts that emerged between community members and Stanford administrators over the course of the late 1950s and early 1960s demonstrated that building the city of knowledge could generate resentment and community antagonism, even in a homogeneous, low-density suburb.

By the late 1950s, it was clear to the elected leaders of Palo Alto and Menlo Park that their acquiescence to Stanford's land developments was paying off handsomely in increased tax revenue and enhanced economic visibility. The Industrial Park and the other Stanford land developments were a huge boon to the finances of the towns of Palo Alto and Menlo Park. Both the Shopping Center and the Industrial Park were on land that had been annexed by Palo Alto, and their presence caused a huge jump in the city's tax revenue. "Assessed valuation of property in Palo Alto has jumped almost $14 million to a record high of $95,742,760, city assessor Harold L. Marty has announced," the *San Francisco News* reported in 1956. "Prime reason for the increase is shopping center and industrial developments on Stanford-owned land. The new shopping center . . . for example, is assessed at more than $5 million." This jump in revenue caused tax rates to decrease, making Palo Alto an even more attractive place for residents and businesses.[120]

However, by the end of the decade, local officials also could not ignore the growing discontent among their constituents about the effects the new commercial and industrial activity was having on Palo Alto. Even during the relatively complacent 1950s, there had been scattered complaints from local businesses and residents. In 1953 Palo Alto's downtown merchants had been sufficiently distressed by the prospect of the Stanford Shopping Center to propose razing the existing downtown and building the shopping mall there instead.[121] In 1956 some residents of the unincorporated neighborhood of Roble Ridge, which bordered the back side of the Industrial Park, protested to the Palo Alto city council that the famous ninety-foot buffer zones of green space in the Park were not required on the back of facilities, thus bringing the buildings very close to their homes. In a rare incidence of the city wielding its zoning authority over Stanford, the council forced Park tenants to increase the buffer at the rear. The debate over this issue reveals the brewing tensions between local residents and the University regarding industrial development. One councilman "charged the university had been 'negligent' in its treatment of the public, and was 'selfishly developing its property from a dollars and cents angle.' "[122]

This situation was not improved by university administrators' approach to community relations. Stanford's leaders operated under the strong and ingrained belief that Palo Alto existed only because of Stanford, and they were reluctant to think of the city as anything but a college town whose cultural and economic center was the University. While their opinion had its root in fact, it caused Stanford to be rather impatient and heavy-handed in dealing with its neighbors and caused it public relations problems that might have been unnecessary had they treated Palo Altans with more respect in the first place.

The administrators had been well aware of community resistance from the beginning. As Stanford was beginning to crystallize its plans for creating an industrial park on its lands, university administrators participated in local community meetings where, as Alf Brandin noted "it was evident that certain factions in attendance were attempting to put in the minds of those present the fact that industrial property, as such, holds little or no advantage for the City of Palo Alto. . . . I took the opportunity of presenting the point of view that industrial property, as we are planning and developing, has a great many more advantages to the City of Palo Alto than otherwise."[123] University allies in local government and in the local Chamber of Commerce joined the University in trying to assure skittish Palo Alto residents that the Park would not bring the "noxious" by-products of the air and noise pollution usually associated with industrial development. Brandin noted later, "when it came to the industrial park, our problem was semantics. What were we producing out there? We tried to say it has got to be clean, no smoke, no heavy manufacturing. Light manufacturing that is clean and electronic."[124]

Despite official assurances, some residents—many of whom were Stanford alumni whose loyalties otherwise lay with the University—remained highly skeptical of the development. Brandin recalled: "I remember people in town saying we would build right to the sidewalk with a sea of asphalt parking lots—nothing but cars. They'd say, 'They can talk about all these pretty pictures and this sort of thing, but that's a lot of hogwash. Developers don't do that.' One of them was a classmate of mine and I said, 'I want to remind you of something. We can't sell this property, we've got a university we're trying to help finance and we've got a cultural center we are proud of. We're not going to desecrate our land for a buck. We have to keep it in tune with the university.' "[125]

Stanford administrators and Palo Alto officials may have grown impatient with some residents' continued reluctance to welcome industrial development to Palo Alto, but to a certain degree these residents had good reason to be fearful. High technology manufacturing was not always as "clean" as its proponents claimed it to be. By the early 1960s the volume of industrial activity in the Stanford Industrial Park made this fact clear to the surrounding neighborhoods. People who lived in subdivisions adjoining the Stanford Industrial Park experienced various sorts of pollution, from the irritating to the potentially lethal. In 1962 a group of residents petitioned President Sterling with complaints about early-morning noise coming from Varian Associates' Industrial Park facility:

> [T]hey use machines that make a high pitched whine. All last week we were awakened mornings—usually around 5:30. . . . And the noise and fumes from their stack continues unabated 24 hours a day. On certain days the acid odor is very strong and the acid fumes has [sic] damaged many of our trees and shrubs, our cars and much of our patio furniture. When we contact Varian directly we usually have a few days respite—then it all starts again.[126]

Stanford used its clout as a landlord to try and limit these sorts of disturbances. When Hewlett-Packard's nighttime lights began to create another community-relations problem at a time when the company had indicated a desire to expand its facilities in the Park, President Sterling's Advisory Committee on Land and Building Development wrote that it "strongly recommends that corrective measures be taken promptly to remedy this situation, particularly in view of the proposed Hewlett-Packard expansion in Industrial Park."[127]

While lights and noise were problems that could usually be remedied by "corrective measures" on the part of Stanford, the fact remained that the manufacturing processes at some Industrial Park plants never could keep the area completely clean. A more disturbing kind of pollution resulted from manufacturing processes that used radiation. One resident who lived adjacent to Lockheed's plant wrote the *Palo Alto Times* in 1960 that "it is disconcerting . . . to have a federal agent pick leaves from our shrubs once a month, to test them for radioactivity."[128] The artful landscaping and architecture of the Industrial Park could not disguise various

types of pollutants created by its tenants. Although Stanford had successfully made a place of industrial production look and feel like a college
campus, its neighbors could see firsthand that high-tech manufacturing
produced undesirable side effects that would rarely be found within the
confines of a real university.

The Palo Alto residents' fears for their health, alumni nostalgia about
Stanford's lands, the shaky and inequitable alliance between the university and the city's political leadership, and the dismissive manner in
which Stanford often dealt with community concerns all came to a head
in 1960, when the University proposed expanding the Industrial Park
toward the rolling foothills that were a near sacred part of Stanford's
property. The neighborhood opposition to this expansion led to a
fiercely fought ballot referendum campaign that President Sterling
called "the Battle of the Hills."[129]

Stanford's decision to expand the Park demonstrated how the runaway
economic success of the development had subtly changed the University's attitudes about careful planning. The University had embarked on
its first real estate developments after exhaustive study and planning and,
during the early- to mid-1950s, had tried its best to develop in a deliberate and conscientious manner that would reserve open space and preserve land values. As one resident noted in a letter to the editor of the
Palo Alto Times, the expansion of the Industrial Park in 1960 grew not
out of a similarly deliberative process but out of the demands of its tenants for more space.[130]

As word spread through community and alumni networks that the
Stanford foothills were allegedly going to be defaced by industrial development, indignant letters poured into President Sterling's office and
swamped the editorial offices of the *Palo Alto Times*. Sterling received
approximately four hundred letters of opposition and about fifty of support; all the correspondents lived in the immediate area, and most were
alumni.[131] One telegram to Sterling summed up the emotional nature of
this opposition: "Official request to annex Stanford foothill land to Palo
Alto in advance of scheduled Board of Trustees meeting today shocking.
Complete disregard to objective alumni and community public opinion
evident. Irresponsible attitude clearly shown. Apparent moral deterioration and decay and abandonment of high Stanford University standards
and principles is sickening."[132]

Nostalgia and environmentalism, not just objection to an industrial
presence in the suburbs, fueled Stanford's opponents in the Battle of
the Hills. As the above telegram shows, expanding into the "foothills"—
a topographical feature so closely associated in the alumnus's mind with
the beautiful campus landscape—was what made Stanford's plan so objectionable. The outcry generated by the connection between the devel-

opment and the Stanford foothills led Stanford administrators to abandon use of the term "foothill" altogether when describing the park. One university official protested: "there are only about 275 acres which could be used for industry—extremely unusual industry, too, but I won't go into that—and they have one little foothill in their midst."[133]

Stanford administrators had never responded very well to community conflict, but by 1960 the University's power had grown to a degree that it did not need to be overly solicitous of residents' concerns or of local political niceties. As a result, it behaved as somewhat of a bully, paying lip service to community concerns but privately rolling its eyes at the protesters. Donald Carlson, one of Sterling's assistants, left a vividly worded trail of correspondence from the Park expansion controversy. Responding to one alumna who had written an angry note accusing Stanford of all sorts of greed and selfishness, Carlson dryly replied: "I am so impressed by your knowledge of the University and its land problems that I feel compelled to address you a personal acknowledgement. The consideration, logic, and unselfish interest you have demonstrated surely must have given inspiration to the Trustees."[134]

Stanford administrators firmly believed that they had the public's best interests at heart in expanding the Industrial Park. The existing development had already brought huge tax benefits to the community and, by enriching Stanford's coffers, had enabled the University to raise its profile and that of the Peninsula in general. Many in Palo Alto and neighboring towns certainly would have agreed with these conclusions, and Stanford might not have faced such a large amount of opposition if it had had a more public decision-making process at the outset. But, as one resident put it, "there has been growing concern over Stanford's policy of presenting pre-packaged zoning requests. . . . They resemble closely the tactics of many a Land Developer asking for variances from planned uses."[135] President Sterling angrily challenged that accusation, asserting, "Stanford has made a conscientious effort to keep the communities surrounding the campus informed of our plans, an effort which could easily be documented."[136]

Outside Palo Alto, the press took some notice of the controversy but generally dismissed it. "Stanford University . . . is being niggled by a small but vociferous group," reported the *San Francisco Examiner*; sounding much like a Stanford administrator, the reporter referred to the "wild-eyed claims" of the protesters.[137] Yet within Palo Alto, residents were not placated, and the decision to expand the Stanford Industrial Park became a referendum on Palo Alto's November 1960 ballot. A "yes" vote would allow the expansion to go along as planned. Some of Stanford's staunchest allies were against the measure. Dorothy Varian, wife of Industrial Park tenant Russell Varian, wrote the *Palo Alto Times* urging a "no" vote on the referendum.[138]

Yet over the course of the year, Stanford managed to muster more public support from alumni and other members of the community. One letter to the *Palo Alto Times* turned the protester's nostalgia-infused laments about the loss of the foothills on its head: "I feel that an expression of gratitude is due Stanford for so generously permitting thousands of people to freely enjoy the rolling, tree-studded hills, the lakes, and views of the campus, with a minimum of restriction, for over sixty years. As a result of this privilege having been granted for so long a time, many have come to feel that they have 'rights' to the Stanford land and should have a voice in determining what use Stanford will make of it."[139] As the election neared, the *Times* itself spoke out in favor of the referendum, reminding Palo Alto residents of the debt they owed Stanford for keeping its lands open for so long: "Stanford's 9,000 acres have constituted a free park for the people of Palo Alto and surrounding communities. If these broad acres had been owned by other private interests, they long ago would have been converted to the houses, business places and industries where so many of us live and work—including those who oppose Stanford's industrial expansion."[140]

In the end, Stanford's arguments—and its successful marshaling of its own grassroots support—won the "Battle of the Hills." The referendum passed by a comfortable margin in November 1960, and Stanford proceeded to expand the Industrial Park. Although the community protesters lost this battle, their actions had an impact. The University had a new awareness of community sensitivity and public relations after this debacle. It scaled back future plans to build on the hills, and sought to defuse community suspicion by giving the development a softer title, the Stanford Research Park. "The term 'Industrial Park' serves as a real red flag," warned some administrators in a 1961 internal memorandum.[141] The mobilization of community opposition also signaled a changing power dynamic in Palo Alto and elsewhere on the Peninsula. No longer would development, even pleasantly landscaped development, be universally welcomed. The planning process could no longer occur behind the closed doors of town halls or university offices. Plans had to now win the seal of approval of grassroots "community" groups—and Stanford needed to mobilize its own base of support among Peninsula residents in order to execute further land development.

The lessons that Stanford learned about community politics were evident in its handling of another local controversy a year later. In 1961 Palo Alto officials began to consider expanding Oregon Avenue, a thoroughfare running through some of the town's most desirable residential areas, into an expressway intended in part to accommodate industrial

traffic to and from the research park. Residents opposing this plan immediately mobilized in opposition, but no sooner had they done this than
another group of Oregon Avenue residents, calling itself the Traffic Action Committee, rose up in support of the measure. The pro-expressway
movement might have had its grassroots partisans, but the Traffic Action
Committee was hardly a grassroots organization. Stanford development
chief "Alf's [Brandin's] hand was damned obvious" in the process, Donald Carlson noted privately to a colleague. "There is more politicking
here than meets even my jaundiced eye." But, he mused, intervention of
this sort wouldn't hurt:

> Because of our Industrial Park and all of the emotion the just-off Oregon Ave-
> nuers have stirred up about it, Stanford is a nasty word down in that area. We
> are not going to suddenly turn on any lights, show the truth and make them
> love us. So I don't see much harm in our taking a background role in the
> Traffic Action Committee. It could improve our relations with the Menlo peo-
> ple because the peripheral plan proposes to put a heck of a lot more truck
> traffic on the proposed Willow Freeway. . . . there are at least a half dozen coun-
> cilmen (including the mayor) who are anxious to get the thing turned around
> somehow and get some of that bond money applied to the city's traffic prob-
> lem where it hurts the most. So they are looking for public support.[142]

In the end, this strategy worked. While the community opponents of
the Oregon Expressway won on some points, managing to downsize the
original plans and redirect the route so that it would be slightly less dis-
ruptive to residential areas, university officials got the traffic artery the
research park needed. The "community" support that Stanford officials
worked to mobilize made the project politically saleable to local officials
and attested to the new power of the community-level activist in local
politics.

The political furor generated by Stanford's plans to expand the Industrial Park, while not successful in blocking the university's plans, was an
early and important instance of resident activism against uncontrolled
suburban growth. The intensity of community opposition reflected not
simply hostility toward Stanford's actions, but the encroachment Peninsula residents were facing on all sides. By 1960 persons who had lived
there for ten years or longer felt besieged by new subdivisions, highways,
office complexes, and shopping centers. In the Bay Area and across California, this rising concern about growth began to generate a host of
publications decrying the "slurban" landscape that had resulted from
rapid, decentralized, and haphazardly regulated growth. In many of
these early environmental tracts, the Santa Clara Valley became the
prime example of the excesses and environmental degradation resulting
from postwar suburbanization. This political movement gained steam

over the course of the 1960s and 1970s and spurred a host of open-space preservation and growth-control efforts in the region, making the Bay Area home to some of the environmental movement's most important early battles and precedent-setting land-use-planning measures.[143]

The great irony about the Battle of the Hills and other moments of community opposition faced by Stanford in its development plans was that the protests were coming from precisely the sort of educated professional residents whom these developments were designed to recruit. The "brains" that were essential components of Stanford's city of knowledge were fighting to keep their community as residential and unspoiled as possible—the natural response of people who had already made a significant financial and psychic investment in their new hometown. The complaints residents voiced to Stanford administrators were the same ones they held about real estate development in general. But Stanford was a known quantity and hence an easy target for their anger. In many ways, it was residents' (and particularly alumni's) love for and faith in Stanford that made them try to change its development plans. The real estate developers were strangers, Stanford was "family."

The community tensions generated by the Industrial Park reveal the pitfalls that could plague even the most successful city of knowledge and the uncontrollable elements that were present in even the most rigorously controlled urban development. Environmental passions, nostalgia for the "old" Stanford, concern about industrial development, and tension between residential and industrial interests were all factors underlying this community conflict. The Battle of the Hills revealed that even the place that had seemingly perfected the magic formula for a city of knowledge could not completely escape the messy realities of local politics.

Conclusion

Over the course of the 1950s and 1960s, Stanford administrators built what was arguably the prototypical city of knowledge, creating a desirable high-income, highly educated community of scientific men and women and serving as a catalyst for the most important concentration of advanced scientific industry in the world. The Stanford story is a vivid example of how the federal attention to science and scientists in the early Cold War set in motion forces that had a defining effect upon urban spatial and demographic patterns. The militarization of Northern California was a major reason behind population growth and the consequent increase in the value of Stanford's lands. Stanford's new wealth and political clout as a favored Cold War university drew many private-sector allies, particularly young high-tech enterprises that sought prestige and profit through alliances with Stanford laboratories and faculty. The Cold War gave Stanford the opportunity and the tools with which to create an ideal environment for scientific production, one which borrowed from American campus-planning traditions of low density, intensive landscaping, exclusivity, and enclosure.

In its active entry into real estate development, community planning, and economic affairs, Stanford University was also a trendsetter in creating partnerships between the American university and American industry. Stanford's great "educational example" of land development in the 1950s and 1960s created a community of scholars, as Fred Terman argued, that, rather than being cloistered away from the rest of society, was integral to the workings of modern industrial production.[144] The fact that the regional civic leadership shared Terman's entrepreneurial ideology helped to foster this close and mutually profitable affiliation between the university and local industry. In this respect, Stanford was ahead of its time, entering into partnerships with corporate America and its allies in ways that would become common by the close of the twentieth century, but were rare fifty years earlier. Even the University of California at Berkeley, whose chancellor conceived the idea of the "multiversity," did not have the close ties to industry—nor did it act as a force for regional economic development—as its neighbor to the south.

However, while Terman's entrepreneurial, capitalist university was becoming more and more involved in the wider world, it did not adapt its shape to fit existing industrial architecture. Instead, it took the pastoral, isolationist principles of campus planning, combined them with distinctively Western architectural and planning motifs, and created a new prototype for the shape and appearance of places of high-tech industrial production. While this approach to planning created an industrial space that, by outward appearances, fitted seamlessly into the surrounding upper-class suburbs, there was not always a smooth relationship between the development and its neighbors. The Stanford example illustrates the pitfalls inherent in suburban industrialization, even in the most successful of advanced scientific industrial developments. Placing industry in close proximity to upper-class residential areas created the potential for community conflict, especially at a political moment of increased environmental awareness. Yet although the stunning economic example of the Stanford Industrial Park enjoyed extensive and favorable worldwide publicity, the Battle of the Hills—and the fact that the "clean" industries of science might not be so clean after all—received little notice.

Other cities, states, and research universities took note of Stanford's stunning economic success and sought to imitate it with developments that mirrored the look and feel of Stanford's research park and the surrounding community. Stanford became a model for other universities to imitate—both in the way it managed its land and its relationship with private-sector tenants, and in the way it used the aesthetics of postwar Californian architectural styles to allow industrial activity to blend harmoniously into the surrounding residential landscape of affluent suburbia. Yet these other institutions did not have the great and unique advantages enjoyed by Stanford: location in an economically booming region with good climate and affluent, homogeneous population; a set of unusually entrepreneurial administrators; and sole ownership of large tracts of undeveloped, desirable land. Stanford University's unique position as a large landowner greatly affected its fortunes, as did its physical location in a supremely beautiful and temperate region. Stanford's imitators often did not have such a tabula rasa on which to build; replication of the Stanford model, then, would prove quite difficult to accomplish.

Built by complex and often contradictory relationships between public and private, federal and local, the Stanford story demonstrates that it is impossible to exclusively credit the development of high-tech regions either to the forces of the market or to the state. It is also incorrect to chalk the success of this exemplary high-tech region as the result of the actions of certain individuals or companies. The "Valley of the Heart's Delight" would never have become "Silicon Valley" without the leadership of people like Fred Terman or the innovations of high-tech entrepreneurs like Varian, Hewlett, and Packard, but we must not forget that these men were able to capitalize upon an extraordinary array of regional assets—not the least of which was a bucolic suburban location. As the next two chapters will show, other universities and regions also had visionary leaders, but they did not have similarly fortuitous regional, economic, demographic, and political conditions. Re-creating Stanford's quintessentially suburban model proved difficult elsewhere, and nearly impossible amid the radically different landscape of large and heterogeneous industrial cities.

4

Building "Brainsville": The University of Pennsylvania and Philadelphia

I N 1940, if a casual observer had been asked which large American metropolis—the San Francisco Bay Area or greater Philadelphia— would become the capital of the nation's high-tech industry sixty years later, they would have very likely answered "Philadelphia." Philadelphia was then the third-largest city in the country, and its region was headquarters to many leading electronic and advanced scientific firms. Because the U.S. financial sector was concentrated almost entirely on the Eastern Seaboard, Philadelphia firms and entrepreneurs had easy access to necessary private financing. The University of Pennsylvania, the region's most prestigious research institution, was home to one of the nation's finest engineering schools and to the nation's first supercomputer.

At midcentury the Philadelphia region and its leading university had innumerable financial, industrial, and technological advantages over the Bay Area. Yet Philadelphia failed to become a high-tech capital like Silicon Valley, and Penn—while remaining a top-tier research institution throughout the late twentieth century—did not become a physics and engineering powerhouse on the scale of Stanford. There are numerous reasons why this did not happen. One set of reasons had to do with the larger social and economic context. The Philadelphia region did not experience the benefits of massive federal military spending enjoyed by California during the Cold War, nor was its industrial infrastructure well adapted to the decentralization and downsizing trends of the post-industrial economy. The science-based industry that remained in or near Philadelphia was mostly health care and pharmaceuticals—rapidly growing and prosperous sectors, employing many white-collar scientists, but not direct beneficiaries of the Cold War defense complex to the same degree as electronics.

The second set of reasons were institutional and had to do with institutional resources, local politics, and the choices that university administrators and their allies made about how to approach science-based economic development. While similar to Stanford in that it was an independent institution with a growing national reputation as a center for scientific research, Penn did not have the abundant land or the bucolic environment of Stanford, and the demographic and racial makeup of its neighborhood was far from that of the San Francisco Peninsula. Rather than being located in a white, upper-middle-class suburb, Penn's campus stood in the middle of a nineteenth-century neighborhood rapidly turning from middle- and working-class white to working-class and poor black. Second, Penn's greatest research strengths lay in medicine, not physics and engineering. Although this made the university well positioned to win millions of dollars in federal health research money, it meant that there was a less logical connection between the resources of the university and the industries of the federal defense complex. In the early Cold War era, the big money went to electronics more often than to pharmaceuticals, making it more difficult for Penn to build connections with home-grown industries.

Despite these important distinctions, Penn administrators and their allies in local politics and industry embarked on a science-based economic development effort that drew heavily upon the industrial partnership and community planning models used in Palo Alto. These leaders conceived these forays into advanced scientific industrial development as an urban adaptation of the prototype developed by Stanford, but they did not seem to realize the extent to which Stanford's regional economic context and its suburban setting—particularly its absence of racial and class politics—were integral to its success.

Franklin's University and Its City

The University of Pennsylvania was an institution founded upon pragmatic principles. It sought to train students for careers in business and commerce, and, to these ends, made applied research a centerpiece of its activities from the start. Unlike suburban Stanford, however, Penn was an institution founded to serve the needs of a city, and one whose purpose and history reflected that of the great metropolis in which it was located. Benjamin Franklin, perhaps the original American scientific entrepreneur, was instrumental in establishing the University that would provide the city with what he called "a compleat Education of Youth."[1] The future University of Pennsylvania held its first classes in 1751 and received its charter of incorporation in 1755 as the College, Academy, and Charitable School of Philadelphia, known familiarly as the College of Philadelphia. While still of a modest size, the college quickly gained a reputation for academic strength in science and medicine. Just as rapidly, the college became the most prominent educational institution and ranked among one of the most important institution—of any sort—in the city. The participation of the University of Pennsylvania lent an aura of prestige to civic affairs, and its leaders easily mingled among Philadelphia's commercial and political elite.

In retrospect, it appears as though Franklin and his colleagues saw the creation of institutions of science and institutions of education as a two-pronged approach to refining and maturing scrappy, money-making Philadelphia. The city was rapidly on its way to becoming the second-largest English-speaking city in the world (aside from London), and it needed science and scientific education to help give it world-class culture. While science alone would not make Philadelphia a city of culture—the early nineteenth century witnessed a blossoming of the arts and other learned disciplines in Philadelphia that gave the city the moniker "America's Athens"—it is significant that scientific and medical learning was always something celebrated and nurtured by Philadelphia's ruling elite, not in the least part because scientific advancement had the potential to help businessmen make more money through technological innovation.

The University continued to thrive in the nineteenth century, even though Harvard, Yale, and Princeton still managed to lure away many of Philadelphia's brightest young men. The University's focus on practical and mechanical disciplines positioned it well to capitalize on the explosion of industrial activity in urban America after the Civil War—an explosion whose spiritual and economic nexus, it might be argued, was Philadelphia. Home of the nation's greatest railroads, site of the 1876 World Exposition that celebrated the technical and scientific wonders of the age, Philadelphia grew by leaps and bounds in wealth and global prestige, a phenomenon mirrored spatially by the miles of new neighborhoods sprawling out from the center of the city along new streetcar lines. Philadelphia was the place that built the great tools of the industrial world—where mechanical ingenuity was celebrated in small factories and massive wealth generated in huge railroad conglomerates.

While an urban university from the start, Penn's choices about campus expansion during this period reflected allegiance to the principles of campus isolation and exclusivity—and a commitment to escape from the worst elements of the nineteenth-century industrial city. In 1872, when the University decided to move from its older in-town location to a spacious new campus in the wealthy neighborhood on the western fringe, its supporters and patrons met the decision with widespread approval. West Philadelphia was still only spottily settled, and the migration of the University there was "viewed as an extension of elite Philadelphia and was welcomed to this setting."[2] The presence of the University of Pennsylvania campus meant that West Philadelphia had "arrived" as a desirable neighborhood. University administrators undoubtedly saw this as a winning situation as well. Not only did the institution need more room for buildings and dormitories, but it also needed to escape the less salubrious qualities of the growing city. By removing itself to the more verdant environs of West Philadelphia, the University could create an enclosed campus with the flexibility to expand in the future.

The move to West Philadelphia, combined with the growing prosperity of the Philadelphia region and its industrial leadership, ushered in an era of expansion and accomplishment for the university. Penn's original inclination toward the practical and scientific disciplines became more pronounced in this age of industrial capitalism. Much more so than its peer universities, Penn drew its administrative leadership and its trustees from the ranks of the emerging professional culture spawned by large-scale industrial production and specialization. Manufacturers and engineers began to help run the University, and the academic curriculum became geared toward applied science.[3] Penn's industrial-era leadership recognized the institution as a vehicle that could not only educate the next generation of business and technical leadership, but also produce scientific and technical innovations that would enhance the efficiency and profitability of Philadelphia businesses in the immediate term. While the late nineteenth-century Penn was quite different from the institution it became two to three generations later, its pragmatic focus upon using scientific and technical knowledge to support local economic development would endure fundamentally unchanged into the Cold War era.

During the early decades of the twentieth century, despite its growing record of scientific and technological excellence and its local prestige, Penn continued to have a difficult time competing with nationally prominent universities for students. Until the late 1940s, Penn was a regional school better known outside Philadelphia for its winning football teams than for its academics. Many in its undergraduate student body were commuters from the city and surrounding suburbs; the University's graduate programs remained relatively underdeveloped in comparison to their counterparts at Harvard, the University of Chicago, and Johns Hopkins, all pioneers in graduate education. Compounding Penn's difficulties in breaking out of the middle of the pack was the fact that the city around it was beginning to change. Philadelphia remained an industrial powerhouse through the 1920s, a position that continued to generate wealth for the city's elite and for its favored educational institution, the University of Pennsylvania, but one that also made the city increasingly crowded and polluted. The city's middle and upper classes began to move farther west into outer neighborhoods or suburban towns, gradually leaving the gracious Victorian mansions around the Penn campus to students and families of lesser means.

Citywide, the anti-urban sentiment of mid-nineteenth-century city fathers had endured into the twentieth-century, overlaid with an added layer of nostalgia for an idealized version of the vanished Revolutionary-era city. Two major urban planning efforts in early twentieth-century Philadelphia reflect this attitude: the bulldozing of packed row-house neighborhoods to the north of downtown to construct the monumental Benjamin Franklin Parkway; and the creation of Independence National Park. In a remarkable act of publicly financed collective amnesia, the latter project deemed all post-1830 structures in the area undesirable and tore them down, creating an inauthentically parklike area of eighteenth- and early nineteenth-century houses and buildings in the heart of the old city.[4] During this period, elite Philadelphians' consternation about the corrupt, dirty, and increasingly decrepit state of their city spurred discussions of whether Penn should move from its West Philadelphia location to still-rural Valley Forge, on the outskirts of the metropolitan area. These discussions were happening at the same time as the University was being forced to consider widening its admissions practices beyond the white male elite that made up the vast majority of its student body. The parallel nature of these debates gave the move to Valley Forge a somewhat sinister aspect. As one history of the University observed, "How better to exclude women, the children of recent immigrants, and others who would not have been in attendance a generation or two earlier than to move to the distant suburbs?"[5] And the move was hardly unprecedented; as one Penn official noted in 1963, looking back on the Valley Forge decision, "a move to the suburbs after the second World War would . . . have been in keeping with University tradition."[6]

Unlike fifty years earlier, however, Penn had grown to such a size by the late 1920s that moving its entire physical plant would have been incredibly expensive. Nonetheless, conversations about moving to Valley Forge persisted until the early 1950s, in good part because the possibility was a useful threat to hang over the head of recalcitrant city leaders. The University's political power in urban affairs stemmed from its importance as an employer and landowner, and from city leaders' deep-seated fears that it might leave. In order to keep Penn in the city, Philadelphia's leaders needed to do all they could to keep the city surrounding the campus in social and economic order.

From Computers to Medicine

By 1945 the University of Pennsylvania had a nearly 200-year history marked by scientific and technical innovation, a close alliance with commercial and industrial capitalism, and a long and mutually dependent relationship with the City of Philadelphia. It did not yet have a national reputation, despite having been the home of some notable scholars and scientists. Its campus remained relatively compact, crisscrossed with city streets and dotted with nonacademic residences and businesses. With the deindustrialization of American cities, the shifting role of university education in American society, and the massive investment by the military and other branches of the federal government in universities and other research institutions, all this changed.

World War II provided a rich opportunity for Penn to become a nationally prestigious research institution. Despite its inability as an institution to break into the very top ranks of universities, the medical and engineering schools at Penn—building on the University's long history of scientific innovation—had outstanding reputations. As a consequence, the upsurge in federal funding of scientific research and development resulted in a number of large contracts for Penn-affiliated researchers. The most famous of these was ENIAC, and its story demonstrates not only how Penn researchers played a key role in the history of the computer and electronics industry, but also demonstrates how regional market conditions, combined with the University's capacity and administrative structure, may have kept Penn from becoming nationally competitive in the computer field. For only five weeks after John Mauchly and Presper Eckert unveiled their supercomputer to great national acclaim, this celebration disintegrated into such a painful dispute between the project's researchers and university administrators that Mauchly and Eckert resigned their posts. The two engineers had made what was, in retrospect, the fatal mistake of not securing patent rights to their invention as they embarked on their research. Conceived as a national defense project, ENIAC was now a potentially valuable commercial commodity; both its inventors and the university that sponsored its creation wanted rights to its future profits. Dean Harold Pender of Penn's Moore School of Engineering demanded that the researchers give up their financial claims to the product and "certify you will devote your efforts first to the interests of the University of Pennsylvania and will during the interval of your employment here subjugate your personal commercial interests to the interest of the university."[7]

While Mauchly and Eckert—both scientific geniuses who lacked strong business sense—failed in not securing their rights at the outset, Penn also was to blame for the impasse in that it lacked any clear patent policy. This scenario that would be played out countless times during the early years of the Cold War, as both researchers and universities began to see the profit-making potential of their federally sponsored research efforts and tried, often clumsily, to keep the financial rewards for themselves. After many months of legal maneuvering, Mauchly and Eckert obtained limited rights to the patent and struck out with their own corporation, Eckert-Mauchly Computer Company, housed in a Philadelphia warehouse.

In the end, neither party in the ENIAC dispute would see great profits from this invention, for other university and industrial researchers quickly began to jump on the computer bandwagon and develop comparable machinery. Faced with bankruptcy after only a few years in business, Mauchly and Eckert sold their business to Philadelphia-based electronics firm Remington Rand, which later became Sperry Rand and then was renamed UNISYS. This company remains in the Philadelphia suburbs, many miles away from the campus of the university where ENIAC was born. Although the Moore School of Engineering had become a Mecca for computer engineers in the mid to late 1940s, other research institutions and companies eclipsed Penn after the departure of Mauchly, Eckert, and many of their loyalists; by the end of the decade "computer development was finished" at the University of Pennsylvania.[8] In an ironic moment that underscored how far Penn had fallen from its pioneering days in computing, in 1957 University president Gaylord P. Harnwell solicited the donation of a UNIVAC computer from Remington Rand, the University not being willing to allocate the resources to create or to buy one itself. The debacle with ENIAC prompted Penn to establish a relatively restrictive policy that limited researchers' abilities to reap commercial profits from their inventions. As a later internal memorandum regarding industrial research would note: "It is the responsibility of department heads to insure that work of this character is not permitted to become of such magnitude as to give an unduly commercial aspect to the activities of their department" and "it is essential that the results of such collaborative investigations be published and be made generally available in order that the community responsibility of the University be appropriately discharged."[9]

Penn's administrators felt quite strongly that commercial interests jeopardized the integrity of the basic research and education functions of the university, and in this opinion, they were hardly alone. But relative to some of their peer institutions, Penn's policy was more limiting and perhaps had something of a chilling effect on the relations between the university and its potential industrial partners in the region. It would be almost another twenty years before University administrators fully embraced partnerships with industry, and they would do this only after establishing quasi-independent research and development organizations that were distinct from the regular academic operations.

It is intriguing that a university with such a long history of close ties to industry did not choose to capitalize more upon the commercial implications of scientific research. Yet it is important to consider the economic context in which the University of Pennsylvania was operating during the war and immediate postwar years. The administrators' restrictions on commercial profit making sprang from their disdain for putting individual financial gain before the general scientific good, but they were shaped in part by the fact that there were not as many opportunities for mutually beneficial cooperation between the University and Philadelphia industry as there had been in the age of the great nineteenth-century industrialists.

The loss of ENIAC and the end of its brief moment of leadership in the computing field had by no means dampened Penn's reputation in other areas, and the University started to rank among the favored customers of federal agencies when it came to doling out contracts for basic and applied research projects. By the 1952–53 school year, the University was receiving $3 million in outside research funds, half of which was from federal agencies. Only two years later, the total had swelled to $5 million, two-thirds of which was federal money.[10] Defense funding, which had made up only 1.5 percent of the University's total annual income in 1941, accounted for 6.4 percent of its income in 1951.[11] With the research accomplishments and enhanced graduate programs generated by this federal funding, the University of Pennsylvania began to creep up in national rankings.

While the University was taking on a role that thrust it into a national spotlight more than ever before, the characteristics of the research grants awarded during the 1950s, taken as a group, clearly reflected its legacy as a powerhouse of medical and biological research. Most of the federal grants went to the medical sciences, and thus allowed the University's Medical School to build upon its many "firsts" in medicine with new innovations and discoveries. Over the course of the 1950s, as the overall rate of federal assistance to the University rose, the proportion of federal grants for the medical sciences increased at an even higher rate. While the Department of Defense and other military-related contracts generally awarded larger sums of money per grant, the Medical School had a greater number of small contracts with individual researchers. By the 1959–60 school year, the medical sciences received about 55 percent of the contract money and about 65 percent of the total number of contract projects conducted with outside assistance, the vast majority of which were in the form of direct grants from the federal government. Correspondingly, the federal agency contributing the largest share to Penn's total grant allocations was the U.S. Public Health Service (PHS), its grants making up 38 percent of the University's federal funds in 1959–60.[12]

The Medical School's prodigious ability to gather research dollars stemmed not only from Penn's solid reputation in the area but from the clout and entrepreneurship of its leaders, most notably Medical School dean I. S. Ravdin. "Rav" headed the School of Medical Sciences from the mid-1940s until the mid-1960s. Described by former colleagues as "charming, cunning, or ruthless by turns," Ravdin was savvy about surrounding himself with talented people and also cultivated a close, collegial relationship with University president Harnwell and others.[13] A prime example of a university administrator who knew to be acutely aware of the outside world, Ravdin hired a Washington public relations firm to brief him on legislative developments in Washington of relevance to the Medical School.[14]

Despite the Medical School's dominance, the Department of Defense still made a sizeable contribution to the University, contributing about 20 percent of the federal total that year, sending grants to departments such as chemistry, physics, biology, and the School of Engineering. In addition, the projects it funded at Penn were, in the tradition of ENIAC, large and of national significance, such as the over $2 million contract awarded in 1961 for a Materials Science Research Center (one of only three in the country).[15] Even grants and contracts awarded by the Department of Defense and the Advanced Research Projects Agency (ARPA) during the 1950s reflected an emphasis on the biological sciences. In a development later to be much regretted during the anti-Vietnam campus protests of the late 1960s, the University won a number of important chemical and biological weapons research contracts, including "Big Ben," which ran from 1952 to 1958. The size and scope of Big Ben led the university to establish a semi-independent research unit, the Institute for Cooperative Research (ICR), to house the project and attract similar contracts.[16]

The influx of federal dollars between 1950 and 1960 affected the University as a whole in two ways. First, the increased federal research support created a distinct change in the University's self-image. As its researchers began to land prominent national research projects and its administrators were invited to testify before Congress, serve on federal advisory boards, and be the government's guest at tours of military facilities, Penn came to see itself as a national, not a regional, institution.[17] Because of the institution's long and prestigious history, University administrators had functioned as a part of the City of Philadelphia's power elite. Now, the men who ran the University of Pennsylvania were not only important people locally but nationally as well. As the University increased its prestige, the undergraduate population became more geographically diverse. The graduate programs grew rapidly as a result of increased outside funding for graduate students and the hundreds of new, federally funded research projects that required additional manpower. Like many other universities thrust in the limelight during this decade, Penn and its leaders had never played these roles to such a degree before World War II.

Second, federal funding resulted in certain parts of the University becoming more important than others. As at Stanford and other institutions that were increasingly orienting themselves toward the chase for federal research dollars, Penn's administrators focused most of their time and attention on the care, maintenance, and expansion of the schools and centers that were gaining the most in federal research contracts. This strategy was designed so that the University could better compete with other top-ranked schools for both federal grants and private donations. In 1957 Penn administrators commissioned a University-wide survey aimed at determining the institution's most productive research areas and concluded that the University needed "to eliminate or assign lower priority status to educational functions which lie outside areas of strategic importance."[18]

As at other schools, a secondary effect of federal funding was an increased need for more laboratory and research space to house new research activity. By the end of the 1950s Penn had construction under way on a number of new classroom buildings and dormitories; most of the former were for departments and schools that were engaged in scientific research. Traditional methods of alumni and private fund-raising were used for land acquisition and construction in some of these projects. But, increasingly, the University was joining with Philadelphia redevelopment officials in strategies that used public funds to expand the campus.

Industrial Decline and Urban Renewal

Until the Great Depression, Philadelphia continued to live up to the moniker "Workshop of the World." In the neighborhoods to the north of downtown, large textile and carpet mills hummed; to the south, the shipyards were still hard at work, employing thousands. The miles and miles of neat row-house neighborhoods in Philadelphia made it perhaps the most affordable large city for working-class home buyers. While there were pockets of dire poverty, and while the rapid spread of the automobile was taxing Philadelphia's eighteenth- and nineteenth-century streets, the city was still among the largest and more prosperous in the country. Yet after the Great Depression and the World War, when Philadelphia's leaders and its citizens assumed that economic conditions would return to where they had been prior to 1929, the factories began to shrink their workforce or shut down altogether. Industries that had been based in the city for over a century started to move to more spacious quarters in the suburbs and then to other parts of the country and the world where land and labor did not come with the costs and bureaucratic headaches that existed in a large, highly regulated, unionized city like Philadelphia.[19]

Beginning about 1940, the demographic makeup of the city began to radically change with the arrival of thousands of African American migrants from the South. Economically and politically disenfranchised in the Jim Crow South, black migrants came north to Philadelphia from states like North Carolina and Virginia in search of the secure, unionized blue-collar jobs for which the city was justifiably famous. Yet they arrived in the city at almost precisely the same time as the factories and their jobs were leaving—moving to the non-unionized South or overseas, where land, labor, and raw materials were all cheaper. The influx of African Americans and the simultaneous decline in Philadelphia's economic base resulted in new concentrations of poor and underemployed minorities in the row-house neighborhoods of North and West Philadelphia. But unlike other cities such as Detroit and Chicago, deindustrialization was not the primary cause of black poverty in Philadelphia. Jobs in the manufacturing sector were scarce for African American workers not simply because factories were closing, but because of the racism inherent in hiring practices. Philadelphia's white workers fought to keep their unions white and practiced informal hiring through kinship and neighborhood networks, both of which excluded blacks. Discriminatory housing and mortgage-lending practices also restricted blacks to a limited number of neighborhoods, and as more migrants arrived these areas became increasingly crowded. By 1950 the black migration had contributed to Philadelphia's population swelling to nearly 2 million—its highwater mark—but it also meant that the median per capita income in the city declined.[20]

Philadelphia was not alone in these simultaneous economic and demographic changes. But Philadelphia was distinctive in that its industrial base relied on a wide variety of manufacturing activities rather than one dominant industry, like automobiles in Detroit or steel in Pittsburgh. As a consequence, the deindustrialization of Philadelphia was less perceptible than in other places, more like the air slowly leaking out of a tire rather than a sudden, shocking blowout. Philadelphia's industrial tire was nearly flat before local officials realized the magnitude of what had happened.

Although fundamental economic realignment was already under way by the late 1940s and early 1950s, the response of local politicians and other civic leaders focused more on the aesthetic and infrastructural shortcomings of Philadelphia, relaying the rather complacent presumption that Philadelphia would continue to be a dominant industrial center.[21] As it had been since the early 1920s, when city fathers decided to improve matters by creating the Benjamin Franklin Parkway, Philadelphia leaders were preoccupied with the idea of "blight" and tended to lump all evidence of economic deterioration and social change into that category. In 1946, concern about the deterioration of some older neighborhoods—many of which were the first points of entry for poor black migrants from the South—prompted Philadelphia to follow the example of other large northeastern cities and establish a Redevelopment Authority (RDA). In their first annual report, which described an instructive visit to the much-praised Stuyvestant Town development in New York City, the RDA officials noted that "In Philadelphia blight is largely due to age. This city was not poorly planned for its early years. When Philadelphia was planned no one could foresee the era of automobiles, the industrial development that lay ahead, the growth and congestion of the modern city, or the changes in urban living."[22] The chief problem, city officials reasoned, was that Philadelphia was suffering economically because it was built for nineteenth-century industry, not the modern needs of the automobile era. The implication of this type of infrastructural shortcoming was that blight could only be eliminated if neighborhoods were transformed completely—in the most radical cases, by tearing down nearly every building, redesigning the streetscape, and rebuilding from the ground up.

The ambitious urban renewal plans of the RDA came to fruition under the mayoral administrations of Joseph Clark and Richardson Dilworth. In 1952 decades of political corruption in the city government ended with the election of Democratic reformer Clark. A reform-minded representative of the Philadelphia elite, Mayor Clark entered office determined to rid city government of its reputation for cronyism and wastefulness, and set about hiring a set of like-minded, forward-thinking city administrators who would rise above partisanship and patronage. After Pennsylvania voters elected Clark to the U.S. Senate in 1956, Dilworth became his successor.

While reformers and liberals, both Clark and Dilworth were members of Philadelphia's native-born white establishment, and both had close ties to the local business community. They practiced their own sort of "enlightened" cronyism, for the most part hiring and dealing with other white men of similar backgrounds even while advocating for the uplift of the poor and downtrodden. While an old-boy network based on family and business ties was a long-standing institution in Philadelphia, the mid-twentieth-century's infatuation with experts of all sorts gave it a new twist. Just as the American public sector, the press, and society at large increasingly venerated the professions of scientist and engineer during this period, persons trained in the disciplines of city planning and scientific city management became key players in Philadelphia's urban politics. City planners and managers were the antithesis of corrupt and partisan machine functionaries; they were considered above politics and hence able to make decisions that were in truly in the public interest.[23]

In keeping with the capitalist orientation of Philadelphia, the reform-minded mayors made economic development and support of private enterprise a key function of city government. A healthy private sector, they argued, would spur badly needed investment in housing, create jobs, and promote neighborhood development. The city's reform and renewal efforts during the 1950s also drew much of their philosophical orientation from Philadelphia's nostalgia about its rich history as the birthplace of American democracy. As the construction of Independence National Park demonstrated, this nostalgia was selective and somewhat ahistorical, but it spurred a strong sense of civic duty and responsibility for the public good among Philadelphia's leadership. Clark's speeches were littered with references to the city's proud history, the legacy of tolerance bequeathed by William Penn, and the city's role as an example to the rest of the nation.[24] This ethos of civic duty considered itself liberal in its racial attitudes and decidedly pro-urban and cosmopolitan in its desire to enhance urban culture as well as social equity.

In sum, the Philadelphia brand of elite-expert rule incorporated a strong economic development thrust and an abiding belief in the power of Philadelphia to behave as a just and democratic place. Clark and Dilworth ranked their policy priorities accordingly. In a tidy prediction of where Philadelphia would focus its attention during the next decade, Clark said in 1953: "There are three constant dangers which threaten urban civilization in the United States today. The first is the strangulation of movement by traffic congestion, which may well kill further economic development. The second is the ineffectiveness of personnel in Government agencies and the vital necessity for improving its caliber, its dedication, its imagination and its ability, and the third is the danger that houses and roofes [sic] over our heads will not be available for enough of our people to raise the level of intelligence, and ability and education and to establish a floor beneath which nobody shall be permitted to sink; because if that is not done, my friends, democracy is not going to work."[25] Clark immediately took on the second task by giving Philadelphia a new, more democratic, City Charter. He turned to his key experts to handle the first and the third.

The iconic unelected "expert" in postwar Philadelphia was Edmund Bacon, director of the Philadelphia City Planning Commission (PCPC). Bacon took the power vested in him by Philadelphia's ruling elite and turned the PCPC into one of the most prominent, ambitious, and active agencies of the kind in the country. Bacon was a proponent of grand, holistic planning that incorporated transportation solutions for congested streets (freeways and widened arterial roadways), substandard housing (a mix of modern high-rises and rehabilitated row houses for all classes of people), outmoded commercial space (office towers with plenty of parking), and lack of green space (new parks and plazas).[26] The RDA was Bacon and the PCPC's ally in this effort. Over time, the RDA focused its attention on projects in and around the downtown that more explicitly intended to restore private-sector vitality and lure middle-class residents to the city.[27]

This shift in focus facilitated Bacon's greatest and most well-known triumph, the plan for Center City Philadelphia. First conceived in the 1950s and nearly completely implemented over the course of the 1960s, the plan was a mix of Le Corbusier–style modernism and one of the earliest examples of historical preservation and neighborhood gentrification. Striking new high-rises replaced some deteriorated commercial and residential blocks, but in other areas, dilapidated eighteenth- and nineteenth-century homes were meticulously restored. Society Hill, the part of Center City where residential redevelopment and restoration took place, became a prestigious in-town address. A few blocks away, soot-stained Victorian office buildings gave way to massive examples of the finest modern architecture.[28]

Philadelphia's dramatic residential and commercial renewal projects, and the other reform efforts of its mayors, won the city glowing national publicity in the 1950s and early 1960s. National news headlines proclaimed Philadelphia "The Great Exception" to corrupt and decaying city governments; the city was led by "Clean-Cut Reformers" who were "Making Our Cities Fit to Live In." The city was named an "All-American City" by *Look* magazine several years in a row during the mid-1950s. Sealing the image of Philadelphia as a city that was doing city planning right was a 1964 *Time* magazine cover featuring Ed Bacon titled "Urban Renewal: Remaking the American City."[29]

The federal urban renewal program gave city leaders a rich opportunity to address the elderly and "obsolete" infrastructure and the rising social problems of postwar central cities. Yet federal dollars of this kind were not unlimited, and they flowed to particular cities and parts of cities in priority of perceived need. The case of West Philadelphia provides a powerful example of how ideas of "need" were intensified in a university neighborhood where emergent institutions of modern science were existing cheek by jowl with the socioeconomic consequences of deindustrialization and suburbanization.

West Philadelphia became a microcosm of all of the economic and demographic changes affecting Philadelphia and of the local leadership's response to these problems. The presence of the University of Pennsylvania in the midst of this changing neighborhood made it into a high-profile target for government-sponsored renewal and rehabilitation. In 1940 the West Philadelphia census tracts were solidly blue collar; fewer than 10 percent of the adults in the area were classified as "professional workers." They were predominantly white. A good number of these residents were employed in manufacturing, and a few (primarily blacks and women) were employed as household workers or as service workers in businesses. As West Philadelphia was already working class at the outset of deindustrialization and suburbanization, and because of the gradual nature of the economic transformation in Philadelphia industries, there was little evidence of an economic downturn in West Philadelphia prior to 1960. The big change in West Philadelphia was the rapid transformation of certain neighborhoods from majority-white to majority-black in the 1940s and 1950s. In the areas to the north of the Penn campus, the total percentage of black residents doubled in the span of twenty years, jumping from 17.2 percent in 1940 to 34.3 percent in 1960. On the census-tract level, the change is even more dramatic: one tract went from under 30 percent black in 1940 to over 70 percent black in 1950, another jumped from 24 percent black in 1940 to 60 percent in 1950 and over 91 percent in 1960.[30]

Becoming a predominantly African American neighborhood did not mean West Philadelphia became a poor neighborhood; many who moved in were working families whose economic profiles differed little from the working-class whites who preceded them. Nonetheless, the African American migration into West Philadelphia gave even Penn's liberal academics pause. West Philadelphia was becoming more crowded, more heterogeneous, and, to some, seemingly more dangerous than before. The University that had moved to West Philadelphia eighty years before to escape the disorder of the city suddenly found itself in the middle of a very urban and somewhat uncontrollable space.

The demographic changes of postwar West Philadelphia, and the response of affluent and educated white leaders to these changes, reveal complicated and intersecting currents of race and class. Certainly, Penn administrators and city officials were much quicker to conclude that West Philadelphia was "blighted" after it had a significant black population; the presence of white working-class families had not elicited such distress. This response to the increasingly black face of West Philadelphia seemed to contradict the public stance of progressive and enlightened leaders, all of whom would have likely professed to have been quite broad-minded in their ideas about race relations and civil rights. Yet many of the problems singled out by university administrators and city officials in West Philadelphia had to do with the area becoming more *poor*, as the African Americans who moved there became increasingly economically disenfranchised as the result of racial discrimination in employment practices, and deindustrialization and economic decline in the city and region.

One irony of the Penn community's distress about a changing West Philadelphia was that some of the "blight" was the result of cheap boardinghouses, restaurants, and bars proliferating around the area to serve

Penn's students. In a speech in Philadelphia in the early 1960s, federal urban renewal chief William Slayton gently chided Penn and other urban universities for their inattention to the effects these businesses had on neighborhood ambience: "Because the university has been unwilling or unable to devote more resources to the provision of the full range of services needed by its students and faculty, the result has been the influx of commercial services, rooming houses, and other uses to meet the demands of the university community."[31] Nonetheless, the prevailing definition of "blight" among Philadelphia's political and business leadership hinged on a neighborhood's being a place of racial transition. Because of market conditions and racial discrimination, there was some logic to this connection; neighborhoods that were already in economic decline tended to be more open to black housing, and the lack of mortgage assistance in minority neighborhoods limited homeownership and maintenance and thus encouraged further physical decay.

As white families moved out to other neighborhoods and to the suburbs, and black families moved in, the city officials who ran the Redevelopment Authority added West Philadelphia—particularly, the area surrounding the University of Pennsylvania—to its list of "blighted" neighborhoods in need of redevelopment and renewal. By the mid-1950s, even as racial transition was still incomplete, urban renewal in West Philadelphia was moving toward the top of the list for federal funding. A chief reason for this prioritization was the fact that the university that lay in the midst of this changing neighborhood was growing in size, activity, and national prominence. Swelling enrollments enabled by the GI Bill and proliferating research activities enabled by federal military and other research contracts were resulting in universities across the nation bursting at the seams by the 1950s. But Penn's political role in city affairs also was an important factor. Penn's administrators during this period were an integral part of Philadelphia's elite and expert leadership, sharing its pro-economic-development philosophy and its sense of civic duty.

Understanding Penn's significance to the economic and cultural life of the city, Philadelphia officials were sympathetic to Penn's needs as early as 1947, when a confidential planning report assured Penn officials that "University expansion is of great interest and importance to the city, both economically and culturally. It is certainly to our advantage to have the University, a growing institution of increasing prominence and reputation, attracting visiting leaders in all fields, and extending the name and credit of the city in which it is located."[32] Penn needed more and better space, and Philadelphia's city leaders were going to find a way to get it for them.

In West Philadelphia, the Philadelphia reformers' brand of enlightened urbanism met with the abiding faith in the economic and cultural potential of scientific research and development, creating a new sort of urban renewal project. In the part of Philadelphia that bordered Penn, urban renewal became a federal funding stream used by university administrators and the local reformers in tandem with other federal support in order to build a particular type of city of knowledge, one that suited the political philosophy of Philadelphia's reform leadership and adapted many principles of the Stanford model to the landscape and culture of the industrial city. As Penn administrators and city officials portrayed it, this city of knowledge housed urban, liberal, well-educated white families who held relatively progressive ideas about race and the diversity of urban living.

Yet the planning and construction of this ostensibly progressive city of knowledge reflected the hubris, elitism, and racial biases of the city's and the University's leadership. It attempted to demographically and spatially reconfigure an urban neighborhood in a way that ignored its identity as a racially diverse, working-class community. Faced with a university neighborhood—and a city and region—undergoing dramatic and unnerving economic and social change, Philadelphia's leaders responded with a science-based economic development strategy aimed entirely at the white professionals and firms that were in the process of fleeing to the suburbs. They used university-centered real estate development to eliminate poor and black areas and create a physical barrier between the white, professional community of scholars and the working-class, black West Philadelphia. While professing their racial tolerance and asserting that they were acting in the best interests of the city and all of its people, Penn administrators worked diligently to replace the disorderly urban landscape with an idealized community of scientific production. Postwar Philadelphia was becoming increasingly low-income and minority; in the new city of knowledge—in contrast to the changing composition of the city surrounding it—the workers and residents were almost entirely educated and white.

Building University City

All the talk of transforming West Philadelphia's neighborhoods through urban renewal resulted in little action until the end of the 1950s. By the end of the decade, however, there were two key developments on the federal level that had a resounding effect upon Penn and its neighborhood. First was the addition of Section 112 to the federal Housing Act in 1959 that allowed cities to use federal urban renewal dollars for university-related construction. The city's 1950 plans for West Philadelphia did not include public support for the construction of any campus buildings for Penn or the other educational institutions in the area, but instead sought to "integrate the schools with the requisite residential and commercial facilities surrounding them and . . . make the Area a better place in which to study, work, and live."[33] After the enactment of Section 112, Philadelphia's urban renewal plans incorporated extensive campus construction and consequently shifted the emphasis of West Philadelphia redevelopment much more toward the universities and other educational institutions.

Second, the post-Sputnik upsurge in federal funding began to reach the University of Pennsylvania. Penn, now well established as a federal grantee, began to land some very large and very prestigious federal research projects and dramatically increase overall research dollars. Chief among these was a $2 million grant for a Materials Science Center, only one of four awarded in the country. The total federal grants for the fiscal year ending in July 1961 were an astonishing $19 million, up nearly 400 percent from only six years before.[34] This dramatic upswing also reflected the increasing political clout of Penn administrators in Washington. Penn fared well in having charismatic and persuasive administrators like Gaylord Harnwell and I. S. Ravdin, whose warm correspondence with federal officials during this period attested to the close relationship the University had cultivated with its federal grantors.[35] Savvy political lobbying and continual communications about the federal funding situation allowed Penn's administrators to increase its standing as a favored institution over the course of the late 1950s and 1960s.[36]

Now, more than ever before, maintaining and enhancing Penn's function as a national research institution became a primary rationale for urban renewal in West Philadelphia. Section 112 freed up a significant amount of federal money to create the necessary infrastructure to make this happen on Penn's campus. The passage of Section 112 was a major reason that, after a number of years of informal participation in Philadelphia's urban renewal effort, Penn and some of its fellow educational and medical institutions created the West Philadelphia Corporation (WPC), a nonprofit community and economic development organization. Ostensibly, the WPC was led by a coalition of West Philadelphia–based educational and medical complexes—Penn, the Drexel Institute of Technology, the Philadelphia College of Pharmacy and Science, the Philadelphia College of Osteopathy, and Presbyterian Hospital—but from its founding it was a Penn-dominated group. President Harnwell chaired its board; the director hired to run the WPC, a city planner named Leo Molinaro, dealt almost exclusively with Harnwell and his fellow administrators. It was, for all intents and purposes, a branch of the University in the guise of an independent nonprofit organization.[37]

   The WPC was less a program agency than a coordinator and cheerleader for the urban renewal and economic development efforts in West
Philadelphia. It married neighborhood-based urban redevelopment efforts with a larger regional economic development vision that saw Philadelphia's future hinging on the presence of advanced scientific industry.
Leaders at Penn and the WPC saw federal urban renewal funds and federal research grants and contracts as tools that could revitalize West Philadelphia, but as one official noted in 1959, "it will take private capital
for the kind of massive redevelopment needed," and the recruitment of
research-based business was essential for success.[38]

   While Philadelphia's leadership had been emphasizing regional economic development for some time, their activities focused more on re-
storing the sorts of industries that had once been the heart of the metropolitan economy. The WPC served as a potent tool for Penn to get its
message out and to create a central role for itself in regional economic
development. And its well-publicized efforts prompted a distinct shift in
tone in the rest of the Philadelphia region's economic development and
urban renewal projects—away from old industries and toward the new.
The savvy public relations tactics of the WPC, and its genuine interest in
refocusing Philadelphia's economic development strategies toward scientific industry, deflected public attention from the other motives of
West Philadelphia's urban renewal. West Philadelphia was not open, undeveloped space like the Stanford landholdings. The new city of knowledge could rise only after the current neighborhood fabric disappeared;
university administrators' goal of making West Philadelphia more white
and professional required the destruction of the homes and businesses
of poor blacks. This aspect of redevelopment went unsaid in the relentlessly sunny publicity materials produced by the WPC. The WPC-led discussions about the gleaming modern research facilities soon to rise in
West Philadelphia made no mention of the people and businesses displaced by their construction.

   Yet it seems that University administrators must have realized that community discontent about these planned developments would become evident sooner rather than later. By the end of the 1950s, Philadelphia was
like other large cities in that urban renewal had generated considerable
protest and resentment in the black community. African Americans' out-
rage was justified; discriminatory housing practices and poverty had
channeled African Americans into the most dilapidated and over-
crowded parts of the city, and these areas became the prime targets of
anti-blight and urban renewal campaigns. From the outset, the most
prominent elements of Philadelphia's renewal program—Center City,
Society Hill—benefited better-off, white citizens, often at the expense of
poor blacks. RDA executive director Francis Lammer stated in 1951 that

his "Philosophy of Redevelopment" was that "redevelopment should be undertaken as a program of bold, not limited, proportions; that such activity affects and *should benefit all the people of all income groups*; that the problem presenting the most difficulty is that of furnishing good dwelling accommodations to persons of *middle income*; that this therefore must be attacked and solved if the program is to have its broadest applications and if it is also to have social significance" (emphasis added).[39]

Arguing that urban renewal served to help the city as an organic whole enabled Philadelphia officials to rationalize turning predominantly low-income and minority neighborhoods into developments that housed middle-class whites or became nonresidential altogether. The RDA helped recruit new middle-class residents into renewal areas using the same sort of public relations tactics later employed in West Philadelphia by the WPC. One "wife of a businessman who left a well-established community" to move to a North Philadelphia urban renewal site proclaimed in a 1953 RDA report that "we're carving out a brand new community here. We like to think of ourselves as modern-day pioneers."[40]

Although guardedly optimistic at first, the low-income and black residents of urban renewal areas soon began to become suspicious of the city's plans for their "betterment." There were lags of months and even years between demolition of old structures and construction of new; families were hastily displaced from their homes, and the structures razed, but nothing was built as a replacement. Community resistance began to spring up every time the RDA announced a new project affecting an existing residential area. By the end of the 1950s, there was widespread criticism of Philadelphia's urban renewal program tactics that displaced poor and minority residents without finding them adequate replacement housing and left wide swaths of open urban space where demolition had occurred but new construction had not yet begun.

The controversy that urban renewal had engendered in Philadelphia by 1959 indicates another motivation in Penn's sponsorship of the WPC. This organization allowed Penn and its fellow institutions to distance themselves from the front lines of potential neighborhood protest. The WPC—not Penn—was the implementing agency for urban renewal, even though Penn administrators had almost total control over its decisions. Had Penn considered its real estate developments entirely nondisruptive and noncontroversial, it might not have seen a need for the creation of a proxy organization like the WPC. University administrators likely knew that the development choices they were about to make would not always be popular or fair, and that controversy might be mitigated by having "community-based" organization like the WPC—rather than an institutional behemoth like Penn—as the public face of urban renewal in West Philadelphia.

4.1. The University of Pennsylvania's urban environment was dramatically different from that of Stanford. This aerial view of West Philadelphia from 1959 shows university-driven urban renewal in its early stages, with vacant lots appearing to the north of Penn's campus (top of photograph). From the Collections of the University of Pennsylvania Archives.

Within a year of beginning its operations, the WPC unveiled a comprehensive plan for West Philadelphia to the press and the public. In a mode similar to Edmund Bacon's sweeping vision of Center City, the plan incorporated campus expansion, additional commercial research facilities, retail, and renovated and new housing. The plan encompassed WPC's 83-acre territory, which stretched across the part of West Philadelphia most dominated by the University, from the banks of the Schuylkill to Fifty-second Street, encompassing not only middle-class faculty neighborhoods and student apartments but also census tracts with some of the most dramatic racial transition.[41]

Announcing this plan, the WPC and its colleagues in the Philadelphia Redevelopment Authority decided to dub the area "University City" to distinguish it from the rest of West Philadelphia and emphasize its association with the area's higher-education and medical complexes. What was left unsaid in this renaming process was that the new designation also attempted to disassociate the university community from its poor and African American neighbors. To middle-class whites and white-collar businesses, "West Philadelphia" connoted a place that was increasingly unattractive, poor, and black. Calling the neighborhood around Penn and other educational institutions "University City" was an important first step in re-creating the area as a place that was well planned, well educated, and—by implication—white. The name has endured to this day with few people aware that, unlike other Philadelphia neighborhood titles that emerged more organically, this was a brand name (or, as Harnwell and Molinaro often called it, a "concept") dreamed up by city planners.[42]

Philadelphia newspapers, most already solidly in the University of Pennsylvania's corner, greeted the WPC's plans for University City in terms well suited for an era enraptured by science. The *Philadelphia Inquirer* wrote that it was "a precedent-shattering concept—awesome in size and breath-taking in scope. The country—indeed, the world—never has seen anything like it. . . . University City is progress at its best. It is a bold plan to help the Nation generally, and the Delaware Valley particularly, meet urgent responsibilities in the fields of education and medicine. It is a new kind of approach to urban redevelopment whereby established institutions of higher learning seek to fulfill important roles of good citizenship and civic duty."[43] The Philadelphia *Evening Bulletin* echoed, in more moderate tones, that the University City plan would "provide an educational and research city within a city—a much-needed redevelopment of an area which has been pretty largely sliding downhill for years."[44]

Penn administrators and the WPC also framed their task in grand historical terms. Harnwell wrote: "the University City Idea is based on a commitment to the pursuit and production of knowledge and the application of knowledge to all areas of life for individual and community good. Obviously, this idea is not original with us. In Western Civilization, it emerged in the Renaissance, gathered force in the Industrial and American Revolutions, and is now at the center of the Scientific Revolution. . . . University City is strategically located in the very heart of one of the largest industrial and educational complexes in the world. The implication of this reality for University City is that it provides an unusual opportunity for education and industry to find common cause through research and development."[45]

Because Penn's leadership had the clout to win the WPC such favorable press as well as a seat at the table in boardrooms and business clubs throughout the Philadelphia region, WPC director Leo Molinaro quickly became the person with whom local and federal urban renewal agencies dealt in West Philadelphia. Molinaro and the WPC became intimately involved with local and federal urban renewal and, in turn, with regional economic development. Echoing its past role as the brain center for nineteenth-century industrial Philadelphia, Penn was once again in the economic development business. As Harnwell wrote in 1961, "we are also cognizant of the role University City must play in the total fabric of the municipal economy. . . . University City must be a vital center for the Delaware Valley, educating leadership for industry and government, the arts and sciences."[46]

While the WPC's stated goals were numerous, its effort to build a city of knowledge in Philadelphia fell into one of two broader categories.[47] The first goal, upon which most of the WPC's earliest efforts centered, was making University City a neighborhood of well-educated professional families with young children. Unlike some other research universities located in bucolic college towns or shiny new suburbs, Penn had for some time been forced to "sell" its location to potential employees. In doing so, it had developed a strategy—now implemented through the work of the WPC—that ingeniously capitalized on Penn's urbanity as an asset rather than a drawback. Penn and WPC administrators created a particular vision of University City designed to appeal to professionals' liberal and tolerant instincts, and slickly packaged to reassure white, educated families that this was a great place to live.

An inherent message in the University City plan and in the promotional materials that explained it was that University City was not only the antithesis of "blight" (poor minorities replaced with educated, well-scrubbed faculty families) but that it was also a far cry from the antiseptic and homogeneous suburbia derided in the work of suburban critics like William H. Whyte and John Keats. As the WPC's 1962 *Annual Report* argued, the institutions behind the WPC had a "vision of bringing about a true community of scholars within the larger urban community . . . [but] do not, however, wish to create a single-class community, sterilized of all the cultural, ethnic, and racial differences that make urban society dynamic."[48] The educated professionals to whom the WPC was trying to make West Philadelphia attractive were more cosmopolitan and more tolerant of diversity than others of their class. They were people who, under the right conditions, wanted to live in a university "city," not simply a university neighborhood or college town. The moment was right for this kind of sales pitch; one year earlier, Jane Jacobs's *The Death and Life of Great American Cities* had challenged the hegemony of modernism and the near deification of the city planner. Jacobs's lyrical arguments resounded powerfully with urban liberals who were the University's target audience.[49]

Another concurrent social change that certainly would have increased faculty families' openness to the idea of moving to University City was the civil rights movement. Northern urban liberals were the whites who were most visibly involved and openly sympathetic toward Southern blacks' civil rights battles during the early 1960s. Although Philadelphia was far from a racially tolerant place, some of the families to whom the WPC was appealing liked the idea of sending their children to integrated

schools (provided were of a high quality) and living in integrated neighborhoods (provided that they were clean and safe).[50] The *conditional* ac-
ceptance of integration was another way for the WPC and its member
institutions to mask the inherently unjust nature of the urban renewal
process, in which the houses and businesses of low-income minorities
gave way to a carefully planned and controlled urban landscape for
higher-income people and higher-revenue economic activity.

In its first few years of operation, the WPC acted primarily as a highly
sophisticated neighborhood association, focusing on projects that would
"stabilize and maintain environmental and social values." These included
what WPC materials termed "vigilante duty against attempts to down-
grade neighborhood standards" as well as campaigns for more parks and
playgrounds, and better schools.[51] Concerned about a "rapidly deteriorating Market Street that has become an unbroken row of junkyards,
second hand furniture stores, tap rooms, and very modest business
places," Harnwell, Molinaro, and others began to press Philadelphia
urban renewal authorities to rezone and to expedite demolition projects
under way along Market.[52]

Elsewhere in University City, private funds raised under the auspices
of the WPC bolstered publicly funded efforts to build new, attractive
housing for faculty families and individuals associated with Penn and the
other institutions. The purchase and renovation of older homes by faculty families and other professionals was vigorously tracked by the WPC
in its monthly newsletter, which included a regular column that noted
these new residents and heartily welcomed them to the neighborhood.[53]
Other, nonprofessional and nonwhite families may have been moving to
the area as well, but they never got this kind of welcome note. Slick brochures continued to pour out of the WPC, featuring stories of young,
artsy academic families who lived in University City and loved it.[54]

There was also the all-important task of making neighborhood public
schools competitive with those in the suburbs. The thrust of this effort
incorporated the WPC appeal to urban liberalism as well as the era's
belief in the paramount importance of scientific and mathematic education. "As more scientific, medical and professional specialists are attracted to University City," a 1964 WPC paper argued, "those with children will demand higher quality education in the elementary and
secondary schools of the area. These families not only bring a new di-
mension of demand for education, they also provide a rich resource for
the support of high quality education in our public schools."[55]

The WPC dubbed the neighborhood elementary and secondary
schools "university-related schools" that emphasized science and math
and drew upon the resources of Penn and other institutions to
strengthen their curricula. These schools were hailed not only for their

excellence but also for their diversity. Lea Elementary, which served an increasingly diverse neighborhood population of white faculty children and middle- and working-class blacks, was referred to in one WPC publication as a place where "roll call reads like a United Nations roster."[56] A more ambitious element of the university-related schools program was the decision by the mid-1960s to construct a new high school, University City High School, on urban renewal land a few blocks from Penn's campus. "The focus of the school is to be science and mathematics," noted Harnwell in 1966. "It is planned to open enrollment not only to neighborhood students but to students throughout the city who are seeking a special preparation in science."[57] Through these strategies—and due to a natural inclination on the part of some urban liberals to choose West Philadelphia over the suburbs—more faculty and professional families moved to West Philadelphia during the 1960s. In 1959 only 600 families of institutional personnel, less than 10 percent of total employees, lived in the University City area. According to the WPC, within only two short years of its activities, that number had doubled, to 1,200 families. By 1966, it was estimated that over 2,000 families, over 30 percent of the total employees, lived there.[58]

Nonetheless, the fact that more academic families were choosing West Philadelphia over other areas did not mean that University City was truly becoming the "community of scholars" its leaders desired. Nor was Philadelphia managing to attract significantly larger numbers of scientists and engineers. In 1965 the Philadelphia Federal Reserve Bank reported that the city had a lower-than-average proportion of scientists with Ph.D.s (even when one included medical Ph.D.s) despite Philadelphia's many hospitals and medical research facilities.[59] This continued deficit pointed toward the need for larger, regionally based economic development and revitalization strategies that would complement neighborhood-based redevelopment in University City. To create a "city of knowledge," Penn and the WPC not only needed to enhance and maintain the existing academic community, but had to implement more far-reaching approaches to keep the University, the City of Philadelphia, and the metropolitan region at the forefront of new space-age research and industry.

Scientific Industry Comes to West Philadelphia

The ambitious economic development goals of Penn and the WPC were born partly out of desperation. The desertion of the Philadelphia region by its core manufacturers that had begun in the 1940s slowed a bit in the first half of the 1960s, but not enough to keep the region—particularly Philadelphia—from a net loss of jobs. Of the sixteen largest U.S. metropolitan areas, Philadelphia ranked fourteenth (ahead of only Pittsburgh and Buffalo) in growth of nonfarm employment between 1959 and 1964. Between 1955 and 1964, private employment in the City of Philadelphia declined 12 percent.[60]

The prognostications of Philadelphia planners in the early 1950s—that economic trends could be reversed simply through better roads and better planning—seemed overly optimistic one decade later. However, Philadelphia leaders continued to argue that the massive investments in urban renewal *were* paying off economically. As the RDA asserted in 1959: "It becomes more apparent each year that: Urban renewal is good business."[61] It is undeniable that the new freeways and commercial rehabilitation projects downtown, and the positive national attention they generated, were an economic boon for the city. Yet these steps also had great costs, disrupting neighborhood life and displacing thousands of families. And urban renewal was not stemming the tide of deterioration and economic distress in low-income and minority neighborhoods, nor was it slowing the stream of people and jobs to the suburbs.[62]

Philadelphia needed a powerful injection of economic activity to bring it back to its old position of economic leadership, and local officials and civic leaders increasingly turned to the solutions put forth by the WPC and its plan for University City. National and regional publications were full of positive statistics. "Some observers believe that a major remedy for these adverse trends is the stimulation of university and college oriented research and development industry in the area," noted one magazine article in 1966, as "this industry is the heaviest accelerator of further industrial growth—stimulating about twelve jobs in other industries for every job in research and development."[63]

Just as city officials were beginning to recognize the key role high-technology and advanced medical industries could play in the regional economy, Penn was beginning to more actively explore the ways it could use its reputation as a research institution and as a significant federal grantee to create closer and mutually profitable ties with industry. The lessons of Stanford University's success were not lost on Penn administrators. "There is ample evidence that a most significant new relationship is emerging between economic development and higher education," a WPC report noted in 1964. "Industry's need for specialized information has led industrial leaders directly to the doors of our educational institutions."[64] As a more clear distinction between basic and applied research began to emerge in the 1960s—universities generally becoming less and less involved with applied research—Penn, like other universities, began to explore the creation of a semidetached, private entity that would be able to carry on applied research without conflicting with the interests of academic departments, but would provide an outlet for university researchers and other scientists to apply their findings commercially.

Philadelphia needed advanced scientific industry; Penn needed a way to further enhance its reputation, and attract and retain faculty, through commercial ties. These needs were answered by the economic centerpiece of the WPC's University City plan, the University City Science Center (known as the Science Center or UCSC). The project was Philadelphia's version of the Stanford Industrial Park, a bold plan of advanced scientific industrial development housed in the heart of West Philadelphia, just to the north of Penn's campus. Both high-tech firms and quasi-independent research departments of Penn and its medical affiliates would have a home at the UCSC; it was to be a place where scientific innovation literally existed next door to the commercial application of technology.

This model of university-industry partnership hearkened back to Stanford's example. But at Penn, the Science Center not only helped the University strengthen its ties to industry, it also distanced it from increasingly controversial military research projects. "Private companies will be able to hire professors for applied research through the institute," one contemporary account noted, "and its creation will take the University of Pennsylvania off the hook by providing a nearby place for professors to undertake classified research."[65] In this respect the UCSC was something of a hybrid of Stanford's Industrial Park and the Stanford Research Institute, an institution that served in part to move politically sensitive research projects outside University laboratories.

Planned along the main commercial artery of Market Street, which was considered the epicenter of "blight" in the University City area, the UCSC would serve both urban redevelopment and economic development functions by replacing run-down houses and shops with gleaming modern facilities full of jobs for scientists and engineers. Although left unmentioned in the documents about the development, the UCSC's placement along Market Street also conveniently eliminated a decrepit strip of houses and storefronts, and created a massive physical barrier between black neighborhoods to the north and the Penn campus to the south. Combined with the WPC's work to recruit professional and academic families to West Philadelphia, the Science Center was the key to making the neighborhood into what one newspaper account termed "Brainsville, U.S.A.,"[66] and hence turn Philadelphia into a magnet for scientific research and development like the San Francisco Peninsula or Boston.

Penn employed a variety of glossy marketing materials to promote the Science Center project during its early stages. It was, said one brochure, going to be the "core and symbol of a new concept—a giant structure in which industry, business and government can advance their specialized research goals, spurred and abetted by close association with University City's vast existing pool of advanced scientific, technological manpower and equipment. . . . Here, private researchers will be stimulated by the cross-fertilization of many minds and disciplines. Here, too, from the laboratories, classrooms and clinics of five famous educational institutions, private enterprise will recruit the young scientists and engineers who will pioneer the breakthroughs of tomorrow."[67]

But the leaders of this effort at Penn and at the WPC made it clear that they could only be boosters and did not have the resources to implement the project alone. Molinaro wrote in 1961: "The West Philadelphia Corporation will strive to create general interest in the community for such a highly desirable project. . . . It must be noted, however, that the project will be realized only through the efforts of the Redevelopment Authority of Philadelphia, the City Planning Commission, and the Philadelphia Industrial Development Corporation. . . . Through this cooperative effort will result a multi-million dollar project which will house substantial tax-paying research and development industries."[68] The project would also be expected to bring lots of jobs—good, white-collar jobs—to West Philadelphia; one newspaper reported that it was "expected to draw industries that rely heavily on scientific brains such as are available in the college community" and employ as many as seven thousand of these "brains."[69]

Harnwell and Molinaro knew that the time was right for public investment in this sort of project, and true to form, local and federal agencies were eager to cooperate. The UCSC was cleverly structured so that it would be eligible for federal dollars under Section 112 yet would be distinct enough from its parent institutions that its commercial operations could flourish independent of academic concerns. The Philadelphia City Council approved the project as an urban redevelopment area in August 1961, and the RDA approved it in December 1961, dubbing it Unit #3. By 1962 the project had over $5.5 million in federal urban renewal funds at its disposal, and land development began in 1963. The U.S. Department of Commerce granted a regular stream of economic development grants to the UCSC and its tenants. Later, when Science Center buildings opened, federal grants from other agencies such as the National Institutes of Health and NASA gave a hefty financial boost to the researchers.[70]

The UCSC echoed Stanford's development not only in its model of university-industry partnership, but in its physical design. Penn administrators and their allies knew they needed to redesign West Philadelphia's urban spaces to attract the coveted science-based industrial facilities and research laboratories that were being lured to suburban "Brainsvilles" like Stanford. The planners first envisioned the facility as a single high-rise tower, similar to the sleek modernist structures built as part of the urban renewal projects in Philadelphia's Center City. Yet the center proposal was soon modified to become a sprawling low-rise complex that ran several blocks across the heart of West Philadelphia, immediately to the north of Penn's campus.[71] Although a higher-density development than the Stanford Industrial Park, the Center paid similarly close attention to architectural detail and the inclusion of green spaces, and tried to attract an exclusive group of tenants engaged in scientific research.

The shift in design seems to have been prompted in part by the response of potential tenants to the idea of the high-rise tower. A 1963 survey of 52 firms conducted by science-center administrators found that one half of the respondents had problems moving into a multi-story structure, and cited concerns ranging from security to ventilation problems and floor load capacity. Interestingly, however, 30 of the 52 firms currently resided in traditional office buildings, and 17 of the 52 said they would have no problem locating in a multi-story facility.[72] The response of the firms reflects the legitimate logistical concerns that encouraged location of high-tech industry in low-rise facilities, but it also perhaps indicates the degree to which Stanford's success (and the success of other privately developed research parks) had resonated in the industrial community. The Science Center's transformation from a single large high-rise to a set of low-level buildings responded to the desires of potential firms for structures more well suited to their research activities, but it also revealed a desire on the part of the UCSC's planners to make the project a parklike, or campuslike, environment.

Yet by making the Science Center a physically more sprawling and more central part of the neighborhood landscape, Penn officials also were better able to use the facility as a tool to further prevent the spread of low-income African American settlement. Although unspoken in official planning documents, continued concerns about separating University City from black and poor West Philadelphia undoubtedly influenced the choice of location of the facility. A development to the north of Penn's campus acted as a barrier between the university community and some of West Philadelphia's poorest and most heavily African American census tracts.[73]

Had the Science Center been designed purely as a response to tenant needs, a significant portion of the space could have been kept in high-rise form, a design with which 30 percent of the surveyed firms seemed quite content. This also would have reduced the need for the Center to take up so much urban space and would have limited the displacement of existing residents and buildings. The choice to make the Science Center a sprawling and landscaped space with multiple buildings seems to have responded to three things: the external influence of the research park aesthetic; the city's desire to make this a high-visibility project for Philadelphia and its region; and the institutional interest in getting rid of "blight" and low-income neighborhoods.

Cognizant of the neighborhood protests that might arise from such a large redevelopment project, Penn officials played down the role UCSC played in slum clearance and seemed to visibly cringe when local newspapers cheerfully noted that the project would "wipe out many sub-standard buildings and residences."[74] Molinaro warned Harnwell that such articles would "give us some serious public relations problems. It is important that we do not discuss this matter publicly."[75]

The UCSC stood as a powerful example of how urban renewal grants, federal economic development funds, and federal research and development dollars were used together at the local level to create a project that simultaneously aimed to accomplish neighborhood-level urban redevelopment, regional economic development, and national intellectual competitiveness. Its savvy creators were aware of the many levels upon which the UCSC functioned. At the ceremony announcing the project in 1961, Harnwell asserted:

> It is quite clear that American industry, education, and government are entering an era of two outstanding characteristics. The first is the increasing importance of science, technology, and research associated with them, and the second is the impact of the urbanized pattern of American living. These two dynamic forces—research and urbanization—provide two primary resources for fulfilling our potential for leadership and for meeting the international challenge that requires new knowledge, new skills, governmental interventions, and industrial innovations.[76]

By the middle of the 1960s, the Science Center had become the centerpiece not only of Penn's efforts in University City but of Philadelphia's city- and regionwide efforts to raise its economic standing and secure a place for itself in the space-age economy. The project was hailed as "Greater Philadelphia's most imaginative and promising answer to the demand for 'scientific and technological competence' "[77] And the efforts of Penn and the WPC to make the University City neighborhood attractive to research professionals and their families was considered key to making the UCSC—and its promise of economic revitalization—work.

As the 1960s progressed, the increasing importance of research and development to the Philadelphia region's economic growth goals made these strategies nearly consonant with those of the University of Pennsylvania. The Philadelphia Federal Reserve Bank could have been speaking on behalf of the University when it noted in 1965: "Brain-power is the only source of research and development. It is the source of vitality for a research institute. The more outstanding the brains, the richer the region. A community's investment in developing and nurturing top-flight talent is an investment in its own economic growth as well as the nation's."[78]

By the late 1960s, Penn was well positioned as the key institution upon which Philadelphia's city of knowledge depended. Philadelphia, after years of trying to vainly revive its industrial past, was not ready to support new strategies to lure the growth industries of the post-industrial age. Other forces, however, would shadow Penn's and Philadelphia's efforts to transform West Philadelphia into another Palo Alto.

Controversy and Protest

The glowing editorials and glossy promotional materials about the University City Science Center and other WPC efforts during the 1960s did not acknowledge another new development in West Philadelphia—increasing levels of community controversy and dissatisfaction with these projects. These difficulties emanated both from within the University community and from the neighborhoods of West Philadelphia.[79]

Despite the WPC's descriptions of happy resident families and the steady stream of new home buyers in the University City area, most faculty and staff continued to live outside the neighborhood and, in many cases, outside city limits. The difficulties inherent in turning West Philadelphia into a desirable white-collar area were illustrated in one chain of correspondence from 1963. A faculty wife, Betty Jacob, spearheaded an effort to develop a high-rise housing complex for faculty families and was angrily disappointed by the plans the WPC produced. "I don't know whose philosophy is determining land use for the area but it certainly is not a realistic reflection of the requirements that Penn needs if they are serious about establishing a balanced community for the faculty with . . . 'competitive amenities' with the suburbs." She warned ominously that she and another faculty member were "going up to Columbia next week to see what we can work out there and I am inclined to think that if Penn has not more imagination about the human factors in their 'integrated development plan' they will find other places outbidding them for faculty."[80]

Yet Betty Jacob's complaints paled in comparison to the growing chorus of dissent coming from the African American community in West Philadelphia. While University City was being marketed to academic and professional families as a place of progressive racial integration, its urban redevelopment efforts were causing painful—and class-conscious—racial conflict.[81] The fact that University City—which was probably one of the more racially progressive neighborhoods in 1960s Philadelphia—was the site for such bitter community protest reflected the disjointed way in which Penn and the WPC dealt with West Philadelphia's black population. It also reflected the class distinctions University City's middle-class white residents drew when considering integration with their black neighbors. White professional families seemed to have little problem with minorities of their class and background, but had little tolerance for working-class black culture and values. The builders of West Philadelphia's city of knowledge adhered to this distinction as well; certain kinds of integration were to be celebrated, but the presence of large numbers of poor blacks was incompatible with the "new" community of scientific production. Many African American residents of University City found this attitude duplicitous and disrespectful of a community that, in a relatively short period, had grown up in West Philadelphia and was now being scattered and destroyed.

Because of these vastly different opinions on what West Philadelphia was and should be, University City became home to some of the fiercest urban renewal conflicts of the 1960s. Most of these battles centered around plans for Unit #3, the designated urban renewal area for the University City Science Center and the science-focused University City High School. The "ring of blight" that Penn and Philadelphia officials designed the UCSC to eliminate happened to be the center of African American commercial and residential activity for this part of the city. The RDA estimated that of the 574 families living in Unit #3, 467 were nonwhite.[82]

As citizens became more suspicious of the urban renewal plans, the WPC went to great pains to emphasize that it was incorporating citizen participation into its redevelopment plans for University City. In 1962 the WPC noted rather wearily: "As of this writing, more than one hundred meetings of citizens in University City have been held in the past twelve months on questions of boundaries, costs, relocation, clearance, and reuse proposals. It is anticipated that many more such sessions will be held. In no case has public debate been cut short. In fact, quite the contrary has occurred."[83]

Initially, Penn and its partners in the WPC viewed community involvement as a boon to their efforts—that is, if they were the right sorts of community groups. White, middle-class neighborhood groups were seen as helpful assets to the process; one UCSC administrator noted that West Philadelphia was lucky in having "the presence of strong, alert, and articulate neighborhood associations with demonstrated capacity to get results in community improvement."[84]

As time went on, and community awareness of the scope of the plans for Unit #3 increased, another type of citizens' group emerged—made up not of like-minded homeowners but of African American residents fearful and angry that they would lose their homes and businesses. Making this situation more complicated and controversial was the fact that black residents generally had been living and working in the area for only a short time and tended to rent more often than own their homes. West Philadelphia's swift racial transition began in earnest after 1940; the overwhelming majority of the African Americans who lived in the area in the early 1960s had lived in their current homes less than five years and had lived in Philadelphia for less than a generation. The relatively recent arrival of these West Philadelphia residents made their housing and employment situations even more precarious; having had little time to establish themselves financially in the city, eviction from their homes by urban renewal projects could plunge them into deep poverty.

Only a few years into the project, the combination of citizen discontent and bureaucratic red tape were serving to considerably slow down land acquisition and construction in Unit #3. Philadelphia officials, already politically scarred by the repeated community protests in other areas of the city and by accompanying charges of racism in urban renewal, appear to have dragged their heels in obtaining the necessary federal funds for the project. Penn administrators, desperate to keep the University City effort moving, tried to appeal to city officials' economic development desires. Harnwell pleaded with the RDA chief, Gustave Amsterdam, to respond to "those realities of urban growth outside our boundaries, even outside our state boundaries, which constantly threaten to erode our position in the great competition to secure industrial research and development investments and personnel. It is in the face of these unrelenting pressures that we are asking for a schedule that will give us a firm basis in our negotiations with prospective Science Center tenants."[85]

By 1966 protest had reached what Harnwell called "a high point" in Unit #3, much to Penn and UCSC officials' distress. Discontent had spilled out of community meetings and onto the pages of local newspapers, which diligently reported the emerging showdown between disenfranchised blacks and the powerful universities and hospitals. The press attention delayed federal approval of new funds for the UCSC project, stopping it in its tracks. While Harnwell politely noted that the UCSC "value[d] their participation," university and city officials were becoming increasingly impatient with the African American protesters' concerns.[86]

In a manner that echoed Stanford officials' protests during the Battle of the Hills that the Industrial Park site contained virtually no hills, the WPC's Leo Molinaro grumbled: "this area has never had any 'neighborhood' identification, nor organization. It was, from the beginning, marginal in use and occupancy."[87] This interpretation was dramatically at odds with many black residents' conception of their neighborhood as a place with strong community ties and an important history. University officials tried to counter the bad publicity by arguing that "only 7 acres

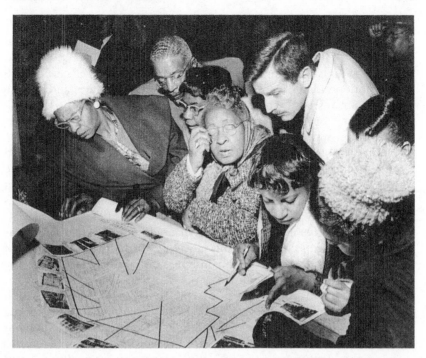

Figure 4.2. Residents of University City look over a map of University City area at a community meeting held in February 1962. Courtesy Urban Archives, Temple University, Philadelphia, Pennsylvania.

of the total 106 acres in the project area are involved in the controversy and only 31 homeowners within that 7 acres have figured in the protest that has caused the delay." They attributed the controversy to "a handful of militant individuals—none of whom live any place close to the area—[who] convinced these homeowners they should make a vigorous protest at the eleventh hour before land acquisition began."[88] In an internal memorandum, an exasperated Molinaro could barely contain his disdain for the protestors, arguing that "the self-appointed leaders" resided outside the project boundaries and that the "spurious" interest of such leaders was "that of a speculator holding property and not of a resident who is protesting displacement."[89]

The problems posed by what Molinaro termed a "few homeowners" and "speculators" were not insurmountable; Penn was a powerful institution and had the city and the federal government on its side. But the protests were escalated in the late 1960s by the addition of a new group of protesters to the anti-UCSC cause—Penn undergraduates. These students (who were a relatively small group within a generally moderate-to-conservative undergraduate population) were drawn to the battle because of their opposition to the more insalubrious aspects of Penn's contract research for the Department of Defense and related federal entities.[90]

The students' fight against Penn's military research began in 1965 when undergraduate activists found out about the chemical and biological weapons research that was quietly being undertaken at the University's Institute for Cooperative Research. Projects "Summit" and "Spicerack," under way at Penn since the late 1950s, were singled out by the student protesters because of their connection to the development and deployment of Agent Orange in the Vietnam War. Harnwell moved the programs into the Science Center in 1967, hoping to defuse the conflict by housing the programs in a more independent institution. But it was a testament to how wide the understanding was at the time that the UCSC was merely another extension of Penn that neither the students nor their allies in the faculty considered this move to be ridding the University of this type of research. Faced with continued opposition, Harnwell terminated the contracts later that year.[91]

Emboldened by their efforts to change the University's research agenda, the student protesters turned their attention to the ongoing struggles of the African Americans in Unit #3 against the development of the UCSC. The students saw Penn's role in the development of this project as a further example of its thuggishness as an institution, and they found the University's plans for Unit #3 as unjust and inhumane as the nation's actions in Vietnam. The students went to the community meetings, wrote scathing articles in the student newspaper, and culminated their protest with sit-ins at President Harnwell's office.

In response, the University established what it awkwardly termed the "Quadripartite Committee on University/Community Development" to provide a forum for students, community members, city officials, and the University administration to reach mutually agreeable decisions on the continued implementation of the Science Center project. These efforts were enough to mollify HUD and get the federal urban renewal funds flowing once again to Unit #3. By March 1967, according to the WPC, 43 percent of all the property owners in Unit #3 had accepted the RDA's offer to buy their buildings and reimburse all moving and incidental costs.[92]

Yet all these efforts had little discernible effect on the design and scope of the Science Center; the project proceeded as planned, albeit more slowly and without some of the potentially more controversial research projects under its wing. A chief reason for the ultimate lack of influence years of protest on the long-term outcome of the project was that the Penn students lost interest in the cause by the end of the decade. The participation of the students had forced the University power structure

Figure 4.3. The bleak landscape created by urban renewal in parts of West Philadelphia lasted for years, as the grand visions of university administrators and
planners were downsized and delayed. This photograph from 1968 shows a lot
cleared for University City development. Courtesy Urban Archives, Temple University, Philadelphia, Pennsylvania.

to respond to concerns about the human costs of the UCSC project.
Without this pressure group, Penn and the city soon ceased to pay much
attention to resident concerns. In fact, by the early 1970s, there were
very few residents left in Unit #3; demolition and new construction had
forced most to move, and the Science Center was achieving a degree of
critical mass that made its eventual completion more of an inevitability.

The controversy surrounding Unit #3, and Penn and the WPC's response to it, was a telling moment in the history of Philadelphia's city
of knowledge. Penn administrators and their allies were understandably
frustrated at the strong objections raised about the demolition of what
seemed to them a neighborhood that had disintegrated within the span
of less than twenty years into an ugly place of cheap rooming houses
and low-grade shops. University leaders also saw the UCSC as a tool for
removing the more controversial elements of its federal grant program
from the core activities of the University.

In Unit #3, Harnwell, Molinaro, and the other leaders of the University City effort saw no evidence of "a well-knit, viable neighborhood struc-

ture that would warrant preserving the area for residential uses" like they found in the faculty-dominated neighborhoods to the west of campus. Local and federal officials seemed to agree with them on this, Molinaro argued, as recent HHFA rulings had "released the Redevelopment Authority from any compulsion to retain a specified portion of a project as residential." The purpose of the UCSC was to "strengthen Philadelphia's economy," not provide better homes for low-income people, and "the most obvious use [of the area] is for additional industrial research facilities."[93]

To some degree, the University's and the WPC's assessment of the neighborhood was correct. Unit #3 was not a "community" in the sense that other parts of black Philadelphia (and black West Philadelphia) were. But their wholesale dismissal of the neighborhood as a place of value for its current residents was myopic and conveyed the racism inherent in the entire University City project. The administrators' response to community protest demonstrated that there was no place for the poor African American residents of Unit #3 in West Philadelphia's city of knowledge. Despite the liberal rhetoric of the WPC's attempts to recruit professional families, the University City was no different from many other urban renewal projects elsewhere in the country in that it used this federal program as a tool to keep areas of black poverty from further dominating certain parts of the city.[94]

The liberals who ran the City of Philadelphia and the University of Pennsylvania were not overtly discriminatory. But their actions appear to have been based on a fundamental (and unproven) assumption: that racial and socioeconomic heterogeneity was damaging to economic development, particularly science-based economic development. These leaders' goals were institutional expansion and economic development, but the means they used to accomplish these goals included racial gerrymandering. The well-mannered elite reformers of midcentury Philadelphia were horrified that their opponents labeled them racists, and they clearly felt that they did not act out of deliberate antipathy toward blacks. But the ugly truth of urban renewal—in Philadelphia and elsewhere—was that areas targeted as most in need of "economic development" were those most likely to be nonwhite. Discrimination and lack of opportunity shunted Philadelphia's African Americans into the least desirable areas; therefore the presence of blacks was a powerful indicator that a neighborhood *had* slid downhill economically.

The story of West Philadelphia also demonstrates how class biases intersected with racial prejudices in the creation of the city of knowledge. Poor people—who in this case were African American—had no place in this new kind of community. Science may have been meritocratic, but in the pre–Civil Rights Act, pre-affirmative-action United States, people of color almost never obtained the opportunities to join this elite. The residents recruited to University City were of a certain income level, extremely well educated, and almost all white. The persons displaced by University City renewal projects were almost all poor and black. The thousands of jobs created by the Science Center and its spin-off developments were for scientists, engineers, and mostly white-collar professionals. Blue-collar minorities had to look for work elsewhere, and these sorts of job opportunities were diminishing by the day in the Philadelphia region.[95]

In 1967 Jean Paul Mather, the president of the University City Science Center, resigned. Recruited to Philadelphia after he spearheaded a successful research park effort at Purdue University, Mather left the job citing great frustration with the task of building a community of scientific production in an urban setting. The Philadelphia *Evening Bulletin* editorialized that Mather "had relatively few problems in building a research park in a cornfield. . . . He met with frustration after frustration, however, trying to develop a much more ambitious version of that center on built-up land." Not only was Mather working against the preferences of industry for open, undeveloped land, but he also "found himself ensnared in the complexities and confrontations of urban renewal." Nonetheless, despite Mather's frustrations with the UCSC project, the *Bulletin* concluded optimistically that Mather "saw it through what will probably prove to have been its most trying years."[96]

Unfortunately for the UCSC and the Philadelphia regional economy, Mather's prediction did not come true. Over the course of the next three decades, the UCSC gained jobs and important grant monies, but University City did not become a center for science-based industry on the scale of those in Palo Alto or Route 128. This is not to assert that the UCSC and University City were total failures. By 1976 the UCSC was a $30 million complex of sixty firms, and was home to four thousand jobs.[97] Yet this success paled in comparison to that of Stanford and Silicon Valley. The university also fell short in its mission to turn West Philadelphia into a vibrant college-town-within-a-city and to lure large numbers of professionals and young families back from the suburbs. By the end of the 1990s, West Philadelphia was home to a significant number of faculty and students, but continued to struggle with crime and poverty. University High School and Lea Elementary, the much-heralded educational experiments sponsored by the WPC, had become just two more troubled urban public schools. While Penn continued to take an active role in bolstering both institutions, the faculty and white-collar professionals who lived in West Philadelphia tended to send their children to better-quality magnet schools and private schools elsewhere.[98]

Over the course of the 1970s, 1980s, and 1990s, other obstacles to creating a city of knowledge in Philadelphia became more apparent. In a high-tech economy fueled by individual entrepreneurship and new start-up firms, Philadelphia had a tax and regulatory environment highly unfriendly to new companies. Not only did Philadelphia have an ever-increasing wage tax that made it more costly for employees to work in the city than in the suburbs, but it also taxed businesses on their gross, not net, receipts. The latter tax served as a giant disincentive for start-up firms—who often had large initial capital outlays and little to no profit in their early years—to locate within city limits.[99] Another discouragement to entrepreneurship in Philadelphia in general and in University City in particular was the limited availability of capital for new entrepreneurial, high-tech ventures. The Philadelphia financial community tended to fund large institutions and corporations, not small and unpredictable new companies. By 1986 the Philadelphia metropolitan area only had 14 percent of its available venture capital invested in young companies, while the national average was 24 percent.[100]

Conclusion

Penn did not become another Stanford for some obvious reasons. The decline of manufacturing and great shift of jobs of population to newer suburbs and to the Sunbelt, were huge stumbling blocks to the ambitious economic development goals of the University and its city. The Philadelphia region not only was losing jobs and population, but it also lacked a significant defense contracting industry—the presence of which had been key to Stanford's becoming an engine of regional economic development in the Bay Area. While Stanford sat amid a region enjoying all the positive economic effects of postwar transformations, Penn did not.

However, the choices Penn and Philadelphia made in their approach to building a city of knowledge were not inconsequential to eventual outcomes. Penn, while an institution with historically close ties to industry, did not embrace entrepreneurial opportunities to the same degree that Stanford did during the immediate postwar period. The ENIAC debacle was one example of how Penn's delayed reaction to the commercial possibilities of its technology led to missed opportunities for leadership in science and engineering and for profitable partnerships with industry. While this was not altogether a bad thing—university-industry alliances ran the risk of compromising free intellectual inquiry—it helps explain why Penn was not able to serve as a catalyst for regional economic development to the same degree as Stanford. While the latter provided its engineers and scientists with the opportunity to make money off their innovations, and to translate their work into a commercial marketplace, Penn administrators had a more limited vision of how its faculty and students might profit from their basic research. This more conservative institutional approach helps explain why Penn, despite its world-class reputation in medicine and its tremendous success in winning federal medical research funds, did not create university-industry partnerships with the region's pharmaceutical and health care industries along lines similar to the ones Stanford created with electronics firms.

Philadelphia's handling of urban renewal and redevelopment, while winning national accolades, also was a factor hampering the success of high-tech economic-development strategies. Redevelopment projects, designed in large part to make the city more palatable for middle-class white residents and professional firms, displaced and antagonized low-income minority residents and showed little regard for existing neighborhood cohesion. While this occurred in nearly every city touched by urban renewal, in Philadelphia it gained additional strength from city officials' being guided by an idealized vision of the intellectual and industrial capital the city had been in the past, not the heterogeneous and troubled metropolis it had become. The Philadelphia leadership's wish to replace an "undesirable" new minority population with a "desirable" one of educated professionals was made most clear in the case of West Philadelphia, resulting in fierce community resistance that greatly slowed the economic development process.

Yet, despite their missteps, the University City projects of the 1950s and 1960s sought to preserve the economic and cultural life of the central city, and fought fiercely to slow the exodus of professional people and high-tech jobs to the suburbs. Penn and Philadelphia wanted to keep professional people and scientific industries centralized, and tried to work against the prevailing trend of scientific suburbanization. In the decades since, the university tried to develop more equitable university-community partnerships and sought to bridge the gaps between town and gown, and race and class.[101] In other metropolitan areas that sought to build cities of knowledge during this period, the fight to "save" the city was not as focused. Atlanta, the subject of the next chapter, was a metropolitan area that used university-centered economic development not to rescue the city, but to help build a deliberately decentralized metropolitan economy. This led to a regional economy that ultimately was more successful than Philadelphia in attracting new firms, but created a landscape of industrial sprawl and deeply entrenched residential racial segregation.

5

Selling the New South: Georgia Tech and Atlanta

UNLIKE Stanford and the University of Pennsylvania, the Georgia Institute of Technology was a minor player in the boom in federal support of university research during the first two decades of the Cold War. A state-supported university founded in the late nineteenth century to foster the industrialization of the South, by the 1950s Georgia Tech was a modest place with engineering and science programs that were among the strongest in that part of the country, but that were by no means the national research powerhouses of Stanford and Penn. Likewise, prior to the 1970s, the Atlanta region was a place that, while prosperous and incredibly fast-growing, was hardly a nationally or internationally significant metropolitan area like Philadelphia long had been and the San Francisco region was becoming.

Yet despite these outward dissimilarities, the same cultural impulses and policy choices that fueled the creation of cities of knowledge at Stanford and Penn were in evidence at Georgia Tech and in Atlanta during the 1950s, 1960s, and well into the 1970s. State and local politicians and business leaders quickly recognized that the Cold War science complex could be a potent tool for economic development and began to place new emphasis on the resources of Georgia Tech and on making the Atlanta region more attractive to highly mobile scientific industry and scientific workers. Atlanta was home to other universities—include the private Emory University and the public Georgia State University—but local leaders fixed their attention on Tech because it alone seemed to have the strong engineering and science programs that could bring high technology to Atlanta.[1] Georgia Tech administrators looked admiringly at the example of Fred Terman's Stanford and consciously imitated its "steeples of excellence" strategy, going so far as to hire a Terman protégé, Joseph Pettit, as the institute's president in order to transform itself from a respectable regional institution into a nationally-recognized hub of scientific innovation. And Atlanta's civic leadership—a group that included a preponderance of real estate developers—built attractively landscaped suburban research parks and aggressively marketed the pleasant white-collar neighborhoods of the metropolitan area to lure men of science to the region. Their efforts were not in vain, for although Atlanta did not amass a high-tech district of the type later found in other Southern places

like North Carolina's Research Triangle and Austin, Texas, it became
home to a number of significant high-tech companies and, more generally, a large white-collar employment base made up of workers from all
parts of the nation and the globe.

On one level, the example of Georgia Tech and Atlanta functions as
another instance of the way in which other metropolitan areas sought to
imitate Stanford's success, and the challenges encountered in replicating
such a suburban model in a dense urban setting. As in Philadelphia,
Atlanta's efforts to build a city of knowledge capitalized upon the scientific prowess of an institution located in an aging central-city neighborhood. Local leaders used federal urban renewal dollars to enhance and
expand Georgia Tech's urban campus and to create physical barriers
between the loci of scientific activity and the surrounding working-class,
and increasingly African American, neighborhoods. Atlanta's and Georgia Tech's story also is a prime example of the way in which scientific
activity became a key element of state- and local economic development
campaigns, and how urban and regional development strategies of the
era were structured to attract scientific employers and scientific professionals. And this example also shows the complicated interactions between public and private, politics and markets, in the growth of high-tech
regions. In focusing on a public institution less favored by the largesse of
the Cold War science complex, this case study provides something that
the previous two did not: a portrait of an educational institution dependent on the whims of state legislators for its financing, and even more
closely allied with state-run economic development efforts as a result.
This illustrates further complexities and nuances in the relationship between institution and state during the Cold War period.

However, the significance of this city of knowledge goes beyond its
role as another example of a would-be Silicon Valley. What the Atlanta
example also shows us is how the suburbanization of science relates to
the *Southernization* of science. As earlier chapters have discussed, patterns
of defense spending during the Cold War had a distinct regional tilt,
sending the vast majority of defense contracts to the South and West
both as a result of practical and political considerations. In the case of
the Southern states, the powerful positions held by Southern Democrats
in the Congress and Senate during this period resulted in a windfall of
defense- and space-related projects. By looking at these Congressional
politics in the context of concurrent state- and local-level urban and metropolitan economic development, we begin to understand how this regional favoritism translated into suburban favoritism.

The case of Atlanta indicates that the way in which Southern cities were
growing during this era—and the economic development approaches
embraced by state and local leaders in the South—made it much more

easy, and logical, for high-tech activity to be suburban rather than urban. Atlanta was like many of its Southern peers in that its greatest growth spurt occurred in the age of the automobile, the freeway, and the subdivision. Unlike Philadelphia, where city planning professionals dominated local politics, Atlanta (and its Southern sisters) had a relatively weak city planning tradition as well as a highly fragmented local governance structure that served to hasten suburban growth and encourage low-density development. And unlike Philadelphia leaders, who sought science-based urban redevelopment strategies that fostered urbane and ethnically diverse living and working environments, Atlanta elites treated science-based economic development as largely a thing apart from its urban renewal efforts. Urban redevelopment in Atlanta focused on transportation infrastructure and entertainment and retail facilities; science-based economic development was part of a regionwide strategy to attract white-collar firms and workers. The leaders of Cold War–era Atlanta made little effort to recruit scientific firms to the city itself, but instead steered industries and workers to the affluent and all-white areas of the region's northern suburbs.

The Atlanta example also vividly demonstrates the way in which race and class affected the development of cities of knowledge. The era of Sputnik and university science was also the time of the greatest battles, and greatest victories, of the civil rights movement; in Southern cities like Atlanta, politics was defined and consumed by the African American struggle for equality and by white responses to it that ranged from some of the most virulent strains of segregationist rhetoric to more moderate and pro-integration views. The presence of a community of scientific industry and scientific workers became one way Atlanta's more racially progressive white leaders could show the rest of the country that their city was a place without the messy racial troubles of other Southern towns. Yet the rhetoric and politics surrounding racial issues during this era can obscure the important class divisions shaping local and regional economic development strategies. Atlanta was run by a white elite that drew little of its political support from the white working class. Working-class whites, threatened by a changing economy and racial order, had little stake in the vision of science-based economic development put forth by Atlanta's leaders, and the choices that local leaders made about the geography of high-tech industry reflected these class divisions.

The Cold War legislative politics that steered such a preponderance of defense investments to the Southern states meant that these investments went to a region whose leaders were often intensely pro-growth and pro-suburb and where politics reflected deep divisions of both race and class. In their quest for economic development, Southern leaders sought to position themselves as racially progressive—and what was more progressive than space-age science?—while doing little themselves to change deeply engrained racial hierarchies. In Atlanta, this resulted in an energetic campaign to position the metropolis as a place of social progress and thus an ideal home for progressive scientific industry. The homes they created for science were not in the increasingly black central city, or in white working-class neighborhoods, but in office parks at the affluent suburban fringe.

The New Industrial South

Understanding Atlanta as a would-be city of knowledge requires understanding the distinctive character of Atlanta itself, created over the course of more than a century by its white middle-class political leaders and businessmen, and the role of the Georgia Institute of Technology within it. The city's Cold War campaign to attract advanced scientific industry was in keeping with a long tradition of enthusiastic city boosterism and the recruitment of outside industrial enterprise. From the time of its founding in 1837, the city's leaders had engaged in one effort after another to turn a small railroad town in the agricultural South into a world-renowned industrial metropolis.[2]

These various campaigns consistently attempted to emphasize Atlanta's distinctiveness as an energetic, modern industrial city with little in common with the sleepy, premodern rural South, and as a city that was far too busy making money to dwell too much on racial hatreds that paralyzed the rest of the region. Again and again, Atlanta's leaders invoked Gen. William T. Sherman's 1864 burning of Atlanta—and the city's rapid rebuilding on top of the ashes and rubble—as the defining example of Atlanta's willingness to leave the past behind and embrace the new. General Sherman himself was in the audience when Atlanta newspaper editor and orator Henry Grady remarked to an 1886 New York gathering: "we have raised a brave and beautiful city, somehow or other we have caught the sunshine in the bricks and mortar of our homes, and have builded therein not one ignoble prejudice or memory."[3]

Despite the rosy picture painted by Grady and other white boosters, racial discrimination was alive and well in Atlanta, as it was throughout the post–Reconstruction South. Blacks and whites lived rigidly separate lives, segregated by neighborhood and often separated by wide differences in class. As was the case in many other turn-of-the-century Southern cities, working-class whites did not share the elite desire for outward racial harmony. Instead, the white working class saw African Americans as their direct competition for jobs and housing and resorted to violence as a way of expressing their desire for economic superiority. A horrific four-day race riot in 1906 laid waste to the heart of black Atlanta and killed and wounded many people, most of whom were black. Atlanta was hardly an oasis of tolerance; like so many other industrial-era cities, race and class resentments simmered barely below the surface of civic life.[4]

At the same time that Atlanta was attempting to become the ultimate symbol of what Grady famously labeled the "New South"[5]—industrial, metropolitan, and progressive—the State of Georgia founded a new educational institution that channeled these hopes for industrial growth into applied research and training. Established in 1885 with state funds raised by the sale of federal lands under the Morrill Act, the Georgia Institute of Technology was the first institution of this kind in the South. Its mission from the start was dedicated to the development of new technologies for industrialization and more sophisticated and productive modes of agriculture. In its early years the institution had a technical curriculum based entirely on practice; students learned math and the hard sciences by working in model factories. These facilities were going commercial concerns, producing finished goods for sale made from Southern raw materials.[6]

Yet Georgia Tech was much less an urban-identified institution than the University of Pennsylvania. While located in Atlanta (the state capital) on land donated by the city, Georgia Tech was a state institution subject to the whims of state legislators and not particularly obligated to serve the economic development needs of the city.[7] Sometimes, particularly in the early years, these economic needs intersected. Both Atlanta and Georgia had an interest in expanding opportunities for higher education and training a larger supply of professional engineers and technicians. However, although Georgia Tech proudly identified itself with the hustle and bustle of the city surrounding it—as one speaker put it on Georgia Tech's opening day, "the rapid strides which [Atlantans] made in wealth and prosperity gave her more the appearance of one of our western or northern cities than of a southern metropolis"[8]—its relationship with the city remained somewhat distant. Money was always in short supply, and Tech's annual reports were often filled with pleas for additional money for various academic and administrative functions.[9] In order to stay solvent, the school dared not stray far from its original mission—to serve the state's interests rather than greater and more intangible academic ends. Tech was an urban institution in location, but its status as a state institution gave it a somewhat ambiguous political identity.

Georgia Tech, despite its aspirations to be a great training ground for Southern industry, was still a small and somewhat struggling institution during the early decades of the twentieth century. Its model factory was closed before the turn of the century, and Tech busied itself with low-tech research and engineering projects that dealt with the chief economic activities of the parts of Georgia outside Atlanta: agriculture, mining, forestry. Attempts to expand its repertoire were often frustrated by a lack of funding. In 1919 the state legislature authorized the establishment of an Engineering Experiment Station (EES) at the school to carry on more advanced research efforts. Yet the State did not authorize any funds to run the Station until 1934, when it (rather grudgingly) allocated $5,000 to the EES "to study engineering problems of commercial, economic, and social interest to Georgia and the South."[10]

Although falling short of its original ambition to train a new class of Southern technical professionals, Tech was becoming a favored destination for college-bound sons of Atlanta's white business class. This development was one with important effects on the institution's future role, as Georgia Tech alumni went on to key leadership roles in city government and local business. Tech football games became important events on the social calendar of Atlanta's white elite, encouraged by school ties and, particularly after winning the Rose Bowl in 1929, a consistently good football team.[11]

While Georgia Tech remained small and somewhat limited in research capacity during the early twentieth century, Atlanta continued to grow. By the 1920s the city was the national center of the cotton and textile industries, whose factories ringed downtown and swelled the city population with new workers. As Atlanta prospered, the unique composition of the city's power structure became more clearly defined. While Atlanta's white city fathers may have been rather disingenuous in their professions of racial tolerance, their business-mindedness was genuine. Private-sector growth was good for Atlanta, reasoned these leaders, and thus the business community became an active, vocal partner with elected officials in running the city. The prevailing influence of commercial interests, along with a Southern legacy of relatively laissez-faire governmental structures, prevented Atlanta from developing a strong and independent political infrastructure. The result of this power structure was that Atlanta was relentlessly pro-growth in its public policy choices and equated success with "bigness"—more industry, larger population, and a greater physical area.[12]

One effort that exemplified this approach toward growth, and would set the tone for regional economic development campaigns to follow, was the "Forward Atlanta" campaign run by the Atlanta Chamber of Commerce between 1925 and 1929. This $1 million initiative sought to sell the city to out-of-state manufacturers and was an early example of the local industrial marketing strategies that would become so common in the postwar years. Just as the city's most important manufacturer, the Coca-Cola Company, had built a national brand in the early twentieth century through advertising and promotion, Atlanta civic leaders worked to build a "brand" for the city that emphasized how different it was from Southern stereotypes. The campaign highlighted the area's "great labor force" (which in this context connoted white, non-unionized labor) and low taxes.[13] "Forward Atlanta" claimed that 762 companies moved to Atlanta as a result of the campaign, a later assessment estimated that the campaign brought 17,000 jobs and over $29 million to the local economy.[14] By 1928 the Chamber of Commerce crowed that Atlanta "truly lives up to her name, THE GATE CITY OF THE SOUTH . . . a gateway to a trade area embracing a territory where the purchase possibilities and the building and industrial expansion are commanding the attention of the Nation."[15]

Just as the Forward Atlanta campaign measured its success by the number of new firms it attracted to the city and region, city planning efforts during this period often adhered to a similar "bigger is better" philosophy in encouraging the spatial expansion of the city into leafy suburban neighborhoods. Atlanta's leaders not only wanted the city to grow "up"—building modern downtown skyscrapers—but celebrated its growing "out" into upper-middle-class suburbs connected to the center of the city through modern roads and parkways. This development was achieved not through massive public planning and infrastructure projects, but through private-sector development by entrepreneurs who were already important figures in the city's power structure. At the request of one of these developers, Joel Hurt, the ubiquitous Frederick Law Olmsted visited Atlanta in 1890 and created a plan for a new subdivision of curvilinear roads and parks that later became the neighborhood of Druid Hills.[16] The fact that a private developer sponsored Olmsted's work, while hardly a unique development, was an important indication of the central role private-sector interests played in Atlanta's city planning efforts—and the influence they would continue to have even when planning and infrastructure projects were publicly sponsored.

The region's historic role as a transportation hub also had a tremendous influence on elite Atlantans' approaches to urban growth. Not located near seaport or riverport, the city's prominence and prosperity had resulted from its place as a railroad terminus and transfer point. In the era of Forward Atlanta, the railroad continued to be the predominant mode of commercial transportation, although truck traffic was gaining a small foothold, and the city had made the small but important step of opening a municipal airport to the south of downtown in 1929. As a leading transportation center, Atlanta was defined by movement—of goods and of people—into the center and away from it. Transportation made Atlanta deeply aware of, and interdependent with, the rest of the South and perhaps contributed to a mindset among its white leaders that measured economic success on a regional, not just a local, basis.

Even as campaigns like Forward Atlanta trumpeted Atlanta's economic progress, Atlanta's legacy of racial discrimination and segregation deeply dictated the way in which the city was allowed to grow. The planning area in which the city government itself was most active was zoning, a new technique widely adopted by American municipalities during this period as a way to regulate and separate commercial and industrial activities from residential areas. Yet in Atlanta, zoning became a mechanism to control development not just by use, but also by race. As the city's population, particularly its black population, grew larger and more densely settled, leaders put a number of local ordinances in place that restricted the areas in which blacks could live. Between 1913 and 1931, a number of these segregation ordinances designated first residential blocks, then entire neighborhoods, by race. A 1922 ordinance zoned the residential areas of the city into white and black single-family and multi-family housing sections.[17] These kinds of restrictions never made it into the promotional literature of campaigns like Forward Atlanta, but had a decisive effect on the socioeconomic fortunes of the city's African American residents.

By the 1940s many of the key ingredients that shaped Atlanta's science-based economic-development efforts of the Cold War years were in place. Atlanta's business-dominated civic elite had already proven itself an aggressive and successful promoter of industrial development and had already exhibited a mindset that closely associated the city's success with that of the larger metropolitan region and, to some degree, the entire "New South." Georgia Tech was a quiet but significant part of regional economic development strategies. Privately sponsored real estate development built up the downtown business district in concert with building new suburban areas for the white middle class, and constructed ample roadways running between the two. Government-led planning efforts often focused on maintaining clear distinctions between commercial and residential, and between blacks and whites.

Yet two key ingredients were missing, both of which would be supplied by the Cold War–fueled economic expansion of the postwar years. The first was size. In 1940 Atlanta was still quite a small city; its population numbered about half a million people—similar in size and economic structure to Birmingham, Alabama.[18] The postwar years would witness an explosion in population and industrial activity, and a consequent spatial expansion of the metropolis that was barely controlled by formalized planning. The second change that the Cold War years would bring was the rising influence of federal spending, and of Congressional politics, on the state and local economy. As a growing metropolis at the center of a regional boom created by the Cold War military-industrial complex, Atlanta was ideally situated to create a new, Southern version of the city of knowledge.

Table 5.1

Metropolitan Atlanta Employment Growth, Selected Sectors, 1939–53

	1939	1953 (estimate)	Increase, 1939–53
Manufacturing Employment	27,692	79,400	187 %
Percent of total (U.S. percent of total)	15.2 % (16.5 %)	26.2% (26.2 %)	
Number of plants	845	1,650	95 %
Wholesaling/Retailing Employment	40,067	82,700	107 %
Percent of total	45.5 %	36.7 %	
Total Employment	182,759	303,300	74 %

Source: Industrial Bureau of the Atlanta Chamber of Commerce, "Employment in Atlanta Metropolitan Area (Cobb, Fulton, DeKalb Counties)," 10 February 1954, FF 8, Box 1, Atlanta Bureau of Planning Files, City Range A-7, AHC.

Postwar Growth and Postwar Power

World War II set Atlanta's massive growth spurt in motion. Like the Bay Area, Atlanta found itself on the winning side of national political and economic trends during and after the war. The movement of people and jobs away from aging Northeastern and Midwestern industrial cities—the trend that had dealt such a blow to Philadelphia—transformed the Atlanta region. The region's low taxes, cheap land, and cheap labor lured hundreds of manufacturing facilities to the area over the course of the thirty years after the end of World War II. While a good deal of this growth was due to the expansion of home-grown companies, many out-of-town corporations established facilities in Atlanta in the immediate postwar years (shown in Table 5.2), bringing an influx of executives and other employees who were not native Atlantans or even Southerners. William B. Hartsfield, who served (with one short interruption) as mayor of Atlanta from 1936 to 1961, crowed in 1947 that "Atlanta has reached the big city stage. It has all of the favorable advantages for future growth. All over the Nation people are looking towards Atlanta as the southern city most likely to expand."[19]

The racial demographics of the Atlanta region also changed during the postwar decades of growth. The shift of industry to the Sunbelt coincided with the mechanization of agriculture in the Southern countryside. Dwindling farm jobs, combined with the extreme racial inequality of the pre-civil-rights South, set off the migration of rural African Americans to Northern cities and precipitated dramatically the demographic shifts of places like Philadelphia.[20] Atlanta became a destination city for thousands of Georgia's rural blacks who crowded into older neighborhoods in the central city and precipitated a housing crisis similar to that experienced in West Philadelphia. The migration of these African Ameri-

Table 5.2

New and Out-of-Town Businesses Moving to Metropolitan Atlanta, 1946–53

Year	No. of New Firms	No. of Firms Moving from Elsewhere	Total New Jobs	Estimated Annual Payroll
1946	170	193	4,603	$11,968,000
1947	131	160	3,531	$7,100,000
1948	101	127	2,533	$6,350,000
1949	82	151	2,895	$7,884,000
1950	91	153	3,802	$11,000,000
1951	39	160	2,810	$8,500,000
1952	78	130	2,130	$7,200,000
1953 (est.)	78	130	2,775	$8,500,000
TOTAL	770	1204	25,079	$68,502,000

Source: Atlanta Chamber of Commerce Industrial Bureau, "New Industries and Out-Of-Town Businesses Established in Atlanta, Georgia, 1946–1953 Inclusive," 10 February 1954, FF8, Box 1, Atlanta Bureau of Planning Files, City Range A-7, AHC.

cans to Atlanta was different from what was experienced in Northern cities in that there was already a sizeable black working-class population in the city, and those who came to Atlanta moved from not very far away. The city's nonwhite population growth prior to 1960 (the years that witnessed the greatest amount of northern migration by black Southerners) reflected a "reshuffling of the SMSA's nonwhite population rather than an influx from outside of the area." Atlanta's new black residents moved into the city limits from rural areas immediately outside the city. Yet these places were at the same time being re-categorized as part of the statistical metropolitan area because of the surge of postwar suburbanization. Thus, the city became more heavily African American, while the new suburbs (formerly rural towns) became more white.[21]

Federal expenditures—and the Congressional politics that steered military dollars to the South—were instrumental to Atlanta's postwar expansion. Already on the advantaged side of demographic and economic trends, the metropolitan area was in a particularly privileged position in terms of military spending. The South saw its share of military contracts rise from 7.6 percent in 1951 to 25.4 percent in 1970, a phenomenon that had much to do with the powerful positions held by Southerners in the Congressional leadership during these decades, and these legislators' relentless efforts to win defense contracts for their home districts.[22] Two Georgians, Sen. Richard B. Russell and Rep. Carl Vinson, chaired the Senate and House Armed Services Committees during many of the years in which Cold War defense spending was at its peak.[23] Russell's efforts to bring military spending to Georgia demonstrated the potent lure the economic promise of the Cold War defense complex exerted

Figure 5.1. The Lockheed aircraft facility to the northwest of Atlanta was a major metropolitan employer during the early years of the Cold War. This photograph is from 1951, the year that wartime producer Bell Bomber turned this facility over to the Lockheed Corporation. Tracy O'Neal Photographic Collection, Special Collections, Pullen Library, Georgia State University.

upon even the most conservative of states-righters.[24] Russell's and Vinson's political clout brought fifteen new military installations to the state by 1960.[25]

Like California, the presence of military facilities in turn made the state a magnet for defense contracting industries. During World War II, the upsurge in defense production gave a large boost to Atlanta's existing industrial base and brought large new facilities to the area. The most important of these was the Bell Bomber airplane manufacturing plant, which opened in Marietta, in the northwest part of the metropolitan area. After the war, Lockheed took over the plant, becoming the state's largest industrial employer by the end of the 1950s.[26] While providing primarily blue-collar employment opportunities, Lockheed's presence had a significant effect on the metropolitan economy. It pushed the average manufacturing wages in suburban Cobb County, where Marietta was located, above the U.S. national average.[27] The company brought psychic benefits to the region and its boosters as well; hardly any city economic development publication of the period failed to mention Lockheed and its products. Atlanta-area newspapers and periodicals celebrated the work of Lockheed and reminded their readers of the defense industry's relevance to the local and national economy.[28]

Market trends and federal expenditures presented opportunities for regional growth in nearly every Southern city during and after World War II. What set Atlanta apart was the caliber and energy of its white elites during this period, and the way in which these leaders took advantage of these opportunities and aggressively marketed the region to outside investors. Atlanta's leadership—which was entirely white and made up primarily of downtown business owners and elected officials—took advantage of private-sector needs for more efficient transportation networks and cheaper labor, and of federal public-sector resources like highway and urban renewal funds, and turned itself into a magnet for new jobs and new residents.

Mayor Hartsfield was the central figure in the campaign to grow Atlanta and sell it to the rest of the world. While a politician and not a businessman, he was an extraordinarily business-friendly official and became the personification of Atlanta's midcentury economic development efforts. "We roll out a red carpet for every damn Yankee who comes in here with two strong hands and some money," Hartsfield once remarked. "We break our necks to sell him."[29] Hartsfield had a knack for identifying promising trends and was an early and relentless advocate of Atlanta's airport, envisioning the great economic promise of what he called "the ocean of the air" when the city's airfield was little more than a dirt landing strip.[30] A member of one of Atlanta's old-line white families, Hartsfield had lifelong relationships with the city's most powerful business leaders and sought to strengthen home-grown industries as well as recruit the new. One childhood friend was Coca-Cola Company president Robert Woodruff, and Hartsfield was tireless in promoting the interests of the company, the City of Atlanta's biggest manufacturer. During the 1950s France was threatening to boycott the import of Coca-Cola, charging that it was "deleterious to the health." Hartsfield, vacationing in England at the time, called Woodruff and "suggested that he fly over to Paris carrying several cases of Coca-Cola, which he would drink on all public occasions. The French could look upon him and see that he was still in glowing health after a lifetime of drinking Coke."[31]

Like Hartsfield and Woodruff, many in Atlanta's power elite had grown up together, attended the same schools (including Georgia Tech), and sometimes were kin by blood or marriage. In this respect, the city was more like the small town it used to be than the national metropolis it was becoming. The ideological cohesion between public and private in Atlanta made it easier to implement the large-scale changes to the built environment made possible under the federal highway and urban renewal programs. In contrast to the consensus among the members of the business community and the elected city leadership, possible opposing forces—working-class whites, middle-class blacks, working-class blacks—were fractured along class and race lines and could do little to challenge such a cohesive group.[32]

The way in which Atlanta grew not only reflected this union of public and private, but it also was shaped by the kinds of business in which these leaders were engaged. While Atlanta prided itself on being a factory town, the key members of its power structure were not manufacturers but were in the retail and real estate development businesses. Robert Woodruff was an important exception to the general rule that Atlanta's decision makers at midcentury were people who were interested in property and the maintenance of land values. Retailers were interested in locating in places where consumers wanted to shop; real estate developers were looking for locations with the best values and the highest profit potential. A glowing 1954 *Newsweek* article about Atlanta declared that the industrial real estate developer—"the ID man"—was the quintessential Atlanta business figure. "An ID man devotes himself to mastering area analysis and business-site selection—the kind of markets, the costs and availability of labor, raw materials, transportation, legislation, financing, water (stream flow and chemical analysis), power, vulnerability to enemy attack, community characteristics, management reaction, and even such details as how many female welders there are between the ages of 25 and 30." One outstanding example of the Atlanta ID man was "an independent industrial real-estate broker, a big, powerfully built man who has located 33 industries in his own Peachtree Industrial Boulevard," a suburban industrial park.[33] The prominence of "ID men"—and all kinds of real estate developers—in Atlanta's power structure was immensely influential upon the economic development and planning choices made in the region during the postwar period.

From the 1940s on, the strategy adopted by these leaders was what might be termed "bifurcated boosterism." On the one hand, Atlanta's civic leaders were intensely interested in maintaining the economic viability of Atlanta's downtown, a concern they saw as dependent upon keeping Atlanta's population majority white. The other side of this bifurcated boosterism stemmed in part from the dominance of the "ID man" in city politics, as well as from the deeply entrenched divisions of race and class in Atlanta. Atlanta's leaders viewed economic development as a truly *metropolitan* enterprise, one in which success was measured not simply by bringing people and businesses to the city itself, but also by the number of firms and people moving to the Atlanta suburbs. To that end, the city's leadership worked aggressively to create an extensive suburban infrastructure of office parks, highways, and residential neighborhoods.

This two-fronted approach to development was evident in one of the early organizations leading these postwar efforts, the Central Atlanta Improvement Association (CAIA). Founded in 1941, the CAIA was a private group made up of large downtown property owners interested in maintaining capital investment in the area even as Atlanta decentralized; it often took leadership on issues like transportation policy and slum clearance before the elected local government did. Significantly, it was the CAIA—not the city—that won funding from the U.S. Bureau of Public Roads and the Georgia Department of Transportation to commission a comprehensive traffic plan in 1946 from Chicago's Lochner Company. Just as the city had been the hub of multiple railroad lines during the previous century, the Lochner Plan "envisioned Atlanta as the central city in an interstate highway system linking the major cities of the Southeast."[34] The plan also provided recommendations for slum clearance and public housing that revealed the CAIA's concern about the encroachment of more dilapidated (mostly black) residential areas upon downtown. The vision of Atlanta's city leadership, which was implicitly endorsed by the federal government through its funding of the Lochner Plan, was that poor and minority neighborhoods could be separated from downtown not only through physical distance but also through the erection of arterial highways as barriers and containing mechanisms. While many of these roadways would not be erected for another decade, the transportation network laid out by the Lochner Plan neatly delineated border areas between black and white, rich and poor neighborhoods as well as getting rid of particularly troublesome spots near the central business district.[35]

Beyond downtown, Atlanta's early focus on redeveloping its transportation networks stemmed from the central role transportation industries played in its regional economy. Although less glamorous an economic development coup than winning new automobile manufacturing plants and the like, distribution facilities had long been the bread and butter of Atlanta's regional economy. After the war, as truck transportation became more central to the distribution of goods across the country and more American manufacturers became national in their market reach, Atlanta's civic leaders lobbied the federal and state governments for funds to expand their regional roadway system. The State of Georgia, because of its relative poverty and desperate need for an improved transportation infrastructure, was remarkably successful in getting federal subsidies for roads even before the age of the interstate; in 1951 federal funds made up 11.7 percent of total dollars spent on highways in Georgia. By contrast, a wealthier and more populous state like Pennsylvania received only 5 percent of its highway funds from the federal government.[36] Atlanta's leaders became vocal advocates for a federal highway

Figure 5.2. Atlanta's enthusiasm for freeway-building made it among the first of the U.S. metropolitan areas to build freeways radiating from downtown, as shown in this 1955 photograph. This roadway led to the northern suburbs, home to many affluent neighborhoods and, later, many high-technology firms. Tracy O'Neal Photographic Collection, Special Collections, Pullen Library, Georgia State University.

program, and there was a frenzy of road building in the region well before the enactment of the federal Interstate Highway Act in 1956.[37] Atlanta's civic leaders took full advantage of the federal government's inclination to fund its highways and played an active role in mapping out a metropolitan highway system that enabled a smooth flow of traffic between downtown Atlanta, the emerging manufacturing centers in its suburbs, and the rest of the Southeast.[38]

In 1947, in response to the metropolitan area's outward growth, the Georgia state legislature established the Atlanta Metropolitan Planning Commission (MPC), whose membership consisted of representatives from the City of Atlanta, Fulton County (in which Atlanta and key suburbs were located), and suburban DeKalb County. The organization billed itself as "perhaps the first metropolitan planning body in the U.S. supported from the start entirely by public funds and given the sole job of long-range planning."[39] Like the Philadelphia City Planning Commission, the MPC recruited "a brilliant young Harvard-trained planner," Philip Hammer, to be the chief architect of the MPC's plan for the region. While Atlanta held only four of the fourteen seats on the board, contemporary observers considered the MPC another product of the civic-minded city elite, like the CAIA.[40] In 1952 Hammer and the MPC released a widely publicized regional planning report titled *Up Ahead* that argued that Atlanta was ideally situated to become a great city of the future. "Crowded, congested cities could be on their way out," announced the report. "In their place we could have a new type of city in the future—wide, green, open and well-planned. Its people would be on wheels and wings, moving swiftly and surely from suburb to suburb, from rim to core and back again. The forces toward this New City are clear. Today's urban growth is taking place on the flanks."[41]

Unlike other, larger metropolitan areas, Atlanta was not hemmed in by outdated infrastructure, argued the report. "Few cities have as favorable a 'background for planning' as Metropolitan Atlanta in 1952. No physical barriers stand in the way of outward expansion—no ocean or lake or mountain or large river. Rails and highways move in from all sides. The land is rolling but generally not rough. Its ridges give fine home sites and serve as dividing lines between land uses." The federal government's industrial dispersion program was one key to making this "New City" a reality. The report's authors used very similar language to federal pamphlets and reports as they described the problem: "Our target value to a potential enemy—and our chances of survival if we do get bombed—can depend on how well we scatter our plants and facilities." Despite this implicit endorsement of federal dispersion strategy, the report made it clear that industrial dispersion was something Atlanta's leadership supported regardless of defense needs or federal incentives. The industrial development proposal made in *Up Ahead* was that new industrial facilities be located in eight large parklike developments. Seven of the eight were not only outside Atlanta's city limits, but were about ten to fifteen miles away, along the path of a proposed perimeter highway. The one facility located in Atlanta was in the far northwest of the city. "Today when we talk about the 'city,' " wrote the MPC, "we usually have in mind the 'metropolitan area.' In our own case, the real Atlanta is the Atlanta you see from the air—spreading across the countryside with little regard for political boundaries."[42]

As we have seen in earlier chapters, the regional leadership's willingness to decentralize reflected the accepted wisdom of the time. Yet the way in which Atlanta's leaders talked about creating extensive highway systems and supporting industrial facilities at the outskirts of the metropolitan area, while maintaining a strong downtown business center, re-

veal a metropolitan mindset that was distinct from that of older industrial-era capitals. These leaders defined "Atlanta" as the city *and* its
suburbs, not just the city alone. An economic success for this broadly-
defined "Atlanta" was something that brought jobs, people, and positive
economic growth to *any part* of the metropolitan area, not just the city.
The open attitude city leaders took to industrial location acted as a magnet for the coveted "footloose" industries that were the target of so many
state and local marketing campaigns of the era. As one MPC report
noted, "perhaps the most significant point about the many types of industrial plants likely to move here is that they will not rely heavily on peculiar
locational requirements such as mineral deposits and other natural resources. As long as they have access to the regional transportation network, they will be able to locate almost anywhere in the multi-county
region."[43] One 1949 *Business Week* article about the city informed its readers: "Finding facilities for new business has never been much of a problem for Atlanta. The chamber [of commerce]'s reply to queries from
prospects is: 'If we don't have the kind of building you want, we will help
you get one built—and fast. We have better than 2,000 acres of industrial
sites to play with.' "[44]

Yet white leaders' complex and inconsistent ideas about race and class
had a subtle but strong influence on the Atlanta metropolitan mindset.
The first published version of *Up Ahead* betrayed the underlying presumption that, as metropolitan Atlanta grew, it would maintain traditional patterns of residential separation. Its master plan for the area specified certain neighborhoods as "Negro expansion areas," concluding
brightly that there were good open areas to the south and west of the
city, adjacent to existing black neighborhoods, where African Americans
could move as the city expanded. While the MPC backed away from this
plan after it caused a political uproar in the city's black community, it
fell short of retracting and reprinting the entire report, instead merely
inserting a letter of correction in the report's front cover.[45]

The MPC could hardly be faulted for assuming that race-based planning was a politically acceptable strategy for the Atlanta region, as the
City of Atlanta had just spent a decade trying to expand its borders in
order to keep the city majority-white. Mayor Hartsfield had begin in 1941
to campaign for the annexation of a large area of white suburbs, including Buckhead, an affluent white area that was home to many of the city's
business leaders. The pressure to annex intensified in 1946, when federal
courts struck down Georgia's all-white primary as unconstitutional and
a huge number of black voters joined Atlanta's voter rolls.[46] The new
political clout of black Atlantans forced politicians like Hartsfield to
court their vote for the very first time, but as he was doing so Hartsfield
intensified his campaign with whites to maintain a racial majority

through annexation. Although the mayor was increasingly positioning himself as a racial progressive, in private communication to his fellow white elites he was blunt about the reasons for annexation:

> With the Federal government insisting on the recognition of negroes in local affairs, the time is not far distant when they will become a potent political force in Atlanta if our white citizens are just going to move out and give it to them. This is not intended to stir race prejudice because all of us want to deal fairly with them, but do you want to hand them political control of Atlanta, either as a majority or a powerful minority vote?[47]

What went unremarked by Hartsfield in these communications was the fact that the annexation of Buckhead was not simply racial gerrymandering, but a strategy to increase the city's population of the *affluent* whites from whom Hartsfield drew the vast majority of his political support. There were other predominantly white neighborhoods bordering Atlanta, but they were home to blue-collar workers whose lukewarm support for Hartsfield diminished further every time he spoke out in favor of integration or civil rights. As Hartsfield mused in some internal notes from the same period, "it is not until we get to the area to the north and northeast we find the place where the citizens have moved."[48] In 1952 the measure finally passed, annexing Buckhead and other wealthy suburbs and adding 171,000 mostly white people to the tax rolls.

At the time city and regional leaders were implementing strategies that restricted the political clout of Atlanta's black population and enforced residential segregation, these same leaders were going to great lengths to convince Northern audiences that it was not racist or backward. The new twist on this old message, which had been proclaimed by leading Atlantans since Henry Grady's time, was to acknowledge that Atlanta *had* had some racial difficulties in the past but that it was now remarkable in that it had moved on from them. In 1955 Mayor Hartsfield coined the ultimate sound bite to describe this "new" Atlanta: it was the city "too busy to hate."[49]

The city worked diligently to burnish its reputation throughout the 1950s and distance itself from the image of the hot, lazy, and backward South. Atlanta was industrial, it was busy; it was not unpleasantly racist. As a *Newsweek* article reminded readers, "Atlanta was never part of the plantation South. It was never a population of planters—Atlantans were different people: railroad construction workers, carpenters, storekeepers, hard-bitten mountain people come down from northeast Georgia, and a trickle of New Englanders."[50] Yet the not-so-subtle message conveyed by the Atlanta region's marketing campaign of the 1950s was that it was a place where the modern businessman could get his work done and still have the opportunity to behave like an antebellum aristocrat.

"Give the Yankees a few years," one Atlantan remarked to *Newsweek*, "and they plant a magnolia tree, sit under it, drink mint juleps, and now and then wear a thin black tie to the office."[51] Neither the Atlanta city fathers nor the new professional migrants to the metropolitan area wanted to be seen as racist, but they also did not want all of Atlanta's many changes to upset a social order of separation by race and by class. The desire to maintain this segregation fueled dramatic decentralization and de-densification of the metropolitan area. By 1957 population density was 4.4 people per square mile, down from 6.7 in 1930 and 9.3 in 1900.[52]

While Atlanta's leadership was unusually aggressive and creative in its regional economic development efforts, in many respects its experience during the postwar years was typical of large Southern cities. The benefi-ciary of national economic, political, and demographic trends, the urban South grew and decentralized with such rapidity that what had been small cities surrounded by an assortment of small agricultural towns turned into single, large urban agglomerations. These transformations occurred without significant consolidation of the multiple municipal and county governments now swallowed up within its borders, creating competition among suburban governments for their share of the eco-nomic development pie. Growth was often so rapid that, even if the civic leadership had been amenable to regional governance measures and more careful planning, it is unlikely that much could have been done to halt the outward spread that turned small towns into suburban subdivi-sions.[53] As it was, the leaders of Southern cities tended to be much like Atlanta's in their political priorities: welcoming economic growth in all its forms, doing what it could to counter the South's image as a backward region, yet simultaneously structuring regional development strategies in ways that retained long-entrenched divisions of race and class. This resulted in a political environment that was unusually hospitable to the decentralization of industrial activity, particularly the kind of industrial activity—like scientific research—that relied heavily on a white-collar, highly educated workforce.

It is interesting, and somewhat curious, that despite plunging such extensive energies into industrial growth in the 1940s and 1950s, Atlan-ta's civic elite did little to single out scientific R&D as a target for its economic development efforts. Because of the power of the Georgia Congressional delegation in the defense appropriations process, the At-lanta region was well positioned to lobby for defense projects. In these early years, however, Atlanta seemed to limit its vision of defense-related economic activity to large manufacturing facilities like Lockheed's Mari-etta facility; there was little discussion of scientists in white lab coats and gleaming research parks. To be sure, in the pre-Sputnik era of lower funding levels for basic and university-related research, the connection between R&D and economic development was less readily apparent. Yet

Atlanta officials—intensely interested in increasing the city's white professional class, proud of their successes in creating a modern and efficient regional infrastructure, and having a promising public research institution in their midst—did not fix upon science as an economic development strategy in these first fifteen years of postwar growth and development. Exploring the development of Georgia Tech during this period helps explain why this was the case.

Expansion and Entrepreneurship at Georgia Tech

As the Atlanta metropolitan area grew and diversified during the 1940s and 1950s, Georgia Tech grew as well, albeit on a somewhat smaller scale. The school was in a very different league than the growing research powerhouses of Stanford and Penn, but it was gradually building an infrastructure that could enable it to compete for new federal R&D contracts. It created a Ph.D. program in 1946 and awarded its first doctorate in 1950. While Tech won only a fraction of the war-related research contracts enjoyed by larger research universities, federal wartime R&D contracts revitalized the school's moribund science and engineering programs, particularly the EES. By the 1943–44 academic year, 58 percent of the EES budget came from federal and industrial contracts. Although the EES's total budget of less than $240,000 remained tiny compared to the multi-million-dollar expenditures the government made nationally, the influx of federal R&D funds was "a harbinger of things to come."[54]

As it enlarged its research capacity, the school gradually became more engaged with Atlanta's economic development efforts. Yet Georgia Tech's status as a state-funded institution continued to shape the dimensions of this engagement. The state officials who funded Tech were important political allies in Atlanta's efforts to recruit industry, build highways, and develop infrastructure at the suburban periphery. They remained largely uninterested in issues of central-city development. Atlanta mayor Ivan Allen (a Tech graduate, former Chamber of Commerce president, and Hartsfield's successor) later noted that "most state politicians still seemed more concerned with building roads in obscure rural counties than helping Atlanta solve its awesome housing and transportation problems."[55] A late-1950s magazine article observed that although 21.5 percent of the state's tax base was in the Atlanta region, only 4.6 percent of that revenue flowed back to the metropolitan area from the state. As the author noted, "states' righters aren't always cities' righters."[56]

The arrival of new federal money added further complexity to the relationship between Georgia Tech and these various layers of government. The influx of R&D funding enlarged Tech's research mission, heightened its regional and national reputation, and reduced its heavy dependence on state funds. It also created significant pressure to up-grade and expand the school's urban campus, beginning even before the end of the Second World War. In October 1944 the school's Board of Regents approved a campus redevelopment plan that established a process for buying adjacent land for new campus buildings.[57] In the same year, Georgia Tech installed a new president, Blake Van Leer, a leader committed to transforming Tech into a nationally competitive research institution. Van Leer recognized that one of the greatest obstacles to Tech's growth was the relatively paltry level of state funding for new campus construction, and he began to doggedly lobby the Georgia legislature for additional money for the school.

Van Leer announced that the school had reached a crisis point because of the lack of state resources to repair dilapidated buildings and build new ones. "It is exceedingly difficult to understand," he wrote, "why the State of Georgia should spend more per student per year upon a girl in Milledgeville ($330.00 per year), a lawyer at Athens ($197.00 per year), a Negro at Fort Valley ($307.00 per year) than it does upon an engineering student in Atlanta ($112.00 per year), especially when the cost of engineering education is known to be higher."[58] The postwar surge in the size of the student body made problems much worse. In 1948 Van Leer wrote that Tech could simply not cope with the tremendous influx of students: "The situation is bad. During the year July 1, 1947 to June 30, 1948, Georgia Tech received a total of 10,274 students. The full-time day students on the campus reached a maximum of 5,402. The physical plant is equipped to serve about 2,600."[59] Lack of money from the state legislature continued to be a prevailing theme of Tech's annual reports throughout the early 1950s.[60]

Increased R&D grants from the federal government, primarily the Department of Defense, became the solution to Georgia Tech's financial woes. In an effort to separate out the profits of new research activities from the mercurial patterns of state spending, administrators established a quasi-independent research entity, the Georgia Tech Research Institute (GTRI), within the EES. "An independently chartered, nonprofit corporation, this institution would serve as a contracting agency for the Experiment Station and handle all 'profits' that came from such research in the form of overhead (indirect costs). As administrator of all external contracts, the GTRI would be able to accrue and redistribute funds as well as carry over projects from one fiscal year to another."[61] The GTRI was a not-for-profit corporation, and all of its revenues went back to Georgia Tech. This arrangement worked well, as the Korean War brought a new surge of research dollars. By the 1951–52 fiscal year, the EES budget had skyrocketed to over $1.3 million. Eighty percent of this budget came from military research conducted for the federal government.[62] Similarly, the income of the GTRI, through which all outside EES contracts flowed, rose steadily throughout the 1950s; by 1958, it had topped $2 million.[63]

Tech's entry into the world of military R&D placed it in new kinds of relationships with the private as well as the public sectors. In the mid-1950s the EES established an "Industrial Associate Program" that seemed remarkably similar to the model developed by Fred Terman at Stanford. Corporations could pay $15,000 over a three-year period to fund EES research; in exchange, the firms would have some control over how money was used and would get the research advice and counsel of EES staff.[64]

In 1957 the arrival of a new president, Edwin Harrison, further improved the outlook for Georgia Tech. Like Wallace Sterling at Stanford and Gaylord Harnwell at Penn, Harrison took an entrepreneurial and energetic approach to administration, and he was particularly encouraging of the expanding research activities at the EES. By 1959 the EES employed approximately 350 full-time researchers and about the same number of part-time staff (many of whom were graduate students).[65] Harrison also instituted more selective admissions standards and established new merit-based scholarships that "would not only improve the freshman class at Georgia Tech but would also stimulate higher standards within the Institute." Tech also broadened its required core curriculum to include more liberal arts requirements like English. These and other measures instituted under Harrison brought a more diverse and high-achieving student body to the institution and further broadened its reputation beyond being merely a solid technical school.[66]

As Georgia Tech expanded its research capacity, it expanded its campus, taking advantage of new federal funds for this purpose and building new alliances with city officials in the process. In 1950 Atlanta designated the Hemphill Avenue area, adjacent to Tech, its first official urban redevelopment project.[67] Over the course of the rest of the 1950s, Tech continued to buy parcels of land, but it did so in a gradual and piecemeal way. The dynamics of race and class were somewhat different than in West Philadelphia; nearly three-fourths of the neighborhood population was white and predominantly working class.[68] In contrast to Penn's drafting of large-scale renewal plans before community consultation, Tech officials bought out homeowners one by one, going to visit them personally in their homes and trying to make the process as polite as possible.[69] Some residents were vocal in their objections. "We just want to be left alone with our little homes which most of us have worked a lifetime to buy," said one white homeowner in a 1951 community hearing. "We do not object to a buffer for Tech. Cut down on the project, but do not ruin us."[70] The careful handling of the process reflected the complex city politics of the era, as white elites sought to keep the city majority-white (and thus perhaps were reluctant to displace white residents) but understood that their racial progressivism gave them little support in the white working-class community. These politics were magnified in Tech's surrounding neighborhood, as it was the home of restaurant owner and future governor Lester Maddox, a virulent segregationist who was the political icon of Georgia's white working class during this period. Maddox's restaurant was directly in the path of Tech's proposed expansion.[71]

Over the course of the 1950s, as urban renewal and highway projects elsewhere in Atlanta displaced the black population out of some central neighborhoods, the areas surrounding Tech, particularly to the south and west of campus, became increasingly black. In the MPC's *Up Ahead* in 1952, the Tech campus was identified as an isolated "good" neighborhood amid areas classified as only "adequate" or "blighted."[72] Racial change in the area undoubtedly made Georgia Tech and the city more inclined to embark on comprehensive urban renewal. By the end of the 1950s an internal city memorandum concluded that the mixed racial composition and "sub-standard" housing of the area made it ideal for redevelopment.[73]

The sensitive racial politics of Tech's surrounding neighborhood was one reason Atlanta's city officials were willing to put Georgia Tech's redevelopment plans on the list for urban renewal funding. Another reason was the possibility that space-starved Tech might move to roomier quarters in the suburbs. Harrison wrote in letter to Mayor Allen in 1962, "I am sure that you have heard recently some of the comments suggesting that Georgia Tech move out of the heart of Atlanta to a less congested and confining area and completely relocate its campus. You realize that this represents a fantastic outlay of money, and I feel it would tend to sever the very close association which Tech has always had with Atlanta."[74]

While the school's surrounding neighborhood had become an official Atlanta urban renewal project in the late 1950s, it was not until Section 112 had been authorized that Atlanta agreed to make Tech's development a top urban renewal priority.[75] In June 1962 Georgia Tech published a report with a new campus plan that was far more comprehensive and extensive that any that had come before. The plan created a 42-acre campus and a host of new modern buildings to house research laboratories, classrooms, and dormitories, and closed a number of streets and one cross-town roadway.[76] In 1964 Harrison presented Georgia Tech's comprehensive redevelopment plan, based on the1962 report, to city officials. In his presentation, he emphasized the positive effects of replacing dilapidated housing with modern institutional buildings. "Tech's renewal and development program will remove the centers of blight and will provide a stabilizing influence, not only for the immediate area, but for the total neighborhood." Most importantly, as one of Harrison's note cards for the meeting reminded him to mention, as a result of Section 112 funds, the project could be done at "NO COST TO CITY."[77]

Was Tech's urban renewal program a deliberate attempt to stave off racial change? It seemed hardly a coincidence that the area of most intensive expansion was on the west side of the campus, in the direction of areas undergoing racial transition. Not only was it less politically sensitive to redevelop blocks that were home to a relatively disenfranchised population, but new campus buildings also could create a physical barrier to further expansion of black neighborhoods, by turning these areas from residential to institutional use. However, while racial considerations bubbled under the surface throughout all these deliberations and decisions, it appears that the greater influence was the metropolitan mindset about economic development that pervaded decision making about regional planning. We also can see the urban renewal in and around Georgia Tech as a manifestation of Atlanta's "bifurcated boosterism," where the attention paid to infrastructure and redevelopment projects in the central city was distinct and separate from the efforts to attract national corporations and new white-collar migrants to the region.

A comparison with the University of Pennsylvania highlights this difference in approach. The story of Tech's expansion into its surrounding neighborhood parallels that of Penn's: persuasive school administrators, racially changing neighborhoods, and ample federal funds being made available through Section 112. Yet Atlanta officials and Tech administrators had redevelopment goals that fell far short of the ambitious vision of University City. The urban renewal projects of the 1950s and 1960s did not aim to persuade Tech faculty to live in the neighborhood; nor, to any great degree, did they try to convince science-based industry to locate there. While Penn's University City project was more about preventing racial transition that university administrators or city officials were willing to admit, the UCSC was a genuine attempt to inject a new kind of economic activity into the moribund Philadelphia economy. Even though Georgia Tech was an institution that made regional economic development central to its research mission, little was done to encourage high-tech investment in the surrounding neighborhood.

The choice Harrison and other Tech administrators made not to pursue such development seems odd in light of the support the idea had from some "expert" quarters. In 1963 the Georgia Tech Alumni Association commissioned a report by Arthur D. Little titled "Georgia Tech: Impetus to Economic Growth." The report examined Tech's potential to generate high-tech economic development and suggested that Tech model itself after Stanford by building a research park. "Participation [in a research park effort] would be a concrete demonstration of Tech's commitment to the growth of the community and the expansion of Georgia's business and industry," the report argued. The report also indicated that conversations about building a suburban research facility were under way, and forcefully emphasized that this kind of development should adjoin Tech's campus rather than locate in the suburbs. "We believe that the proposal to build new physical facilities in the suburbs . . . would amount to a wasteful duplication of services and facilities which the station can now provide," the report noted. "We therefore urge that the so-called industrial development research center at an off-campus site be given no further consideration."[78] Georgia Tech administrators seem not to have taken the Little report into serious consideration, however. In the comprehensive campus plan released the following year, no mention was made of a research-park development next to the campus; the "comprehensive" development incorporated institutional facilities and nothing more.

In 1965 city planner Philip Hammer again raised the subject of an urban research park by writing a report that suggested the city build an industrial research center near Tech. Harrison's comments on the report were somewhat dismissive. "Although I do not think it possible that the Georgia Institute of Technology could participate directly in the establishment of a research and development center, we could certainly cooperate with those interested in the research and development activities," wrote Harrison. "I shall be glad to have someone at Tech talk with possible prospects about the services which Georgia Tech offers and from which they could profit."[79]

In fact, while the Little report and the Hammer report were urging that Tech redevelop its neighborhood into a high-tech center, Tech had already started to establish a presence in the suburbs. The EES had moved its Ceramics Branch to Chamblee, to the northeast of the city, and its Industrial Development Branch to West Peachtree Road. These facilities located where they were because surplus land had been available to the state, but their presence seemed like a tangible expression of Tech's ambivalence about strengthening the surrounding neighborhood.[80] Yet the lack of action in developing the neighborhood into a high-tech industrial center was not solely the fault of Georgia Tech. While Atlanta officials clearly valued Tech as an important contributor to the Atlanta economy, both civic leaders and Tech administrators did not consider it essential that its spin-off companies, or their workers, live near Tech.

In the Atlantan vision of the city of knowledge, the people and companies who made up such a community did not necessarily have to live and work in close proximity to the research institution—Georgia Tech—at the community's heart. This distinction becomes clearer when we explore the course that regional economic development took in Atlanta during the 1960s and into the 1970s. As federal R&D expenditures rose and Congressional attention turned toward science-based strategies for regional economic development, Atlanta officials increasingly focused upon science—and Tech-generated research—as a component of its regional economic development strategy. While the effort to grow science and technology was only one prong of this strategy, civic leaders firmly believed that the metropolitan area could be home to a "community of scholars" or a "Brainsville." However, their actions made it clear that they also felt this kind of development would be most at home in the affluent white suburbs.

Selling Atlanta in the Space Age

By 1960 the Atlanta region had made a name for itself as a national distribution center and industrial hub, and its landscape was changing from a small, contained Southern city to a sprawling collection of urban neighborhoods, suburban subdivisions, and industrial facilities, all linked by a comprehensive web of highways. While a good portion of the new firms arriving in the 1950s had located within city limits, the Atlanta region suburbanized its industrial and retail base earlier and faster than other metropolises.[81] Atlanta's leadership proudly pointed to this decentralization as evidence of the region's success. In a 1959 report, the MPC enthused that "the people, the homes, the shops, and the factories are spreading further out over the countryside" and proudly pointed out, "the number of local government jurisdictions encompassed by the Standard Metropolitan Area is now 51."[82] The region's population had grown nearly 40 percent between 1950 and 1960, and in 1959 it surpassed 1 million.[83] In yet another display of Atlanta's identification of metropolitan "bigness" with success, Hartsfield and the rest of the city's leadership designated the moment that the population of city and suburbs was expected to pass a million—just after 9:00 A.M. on 10 October 1959—as "M Day."[84] Hartsfield, the Chamber of Commerce, and the local newspapers all came together in turning the day into a celebration. The mayor presented a key to the city to the person who they projected to be the millionth resident. In a coincidence that must have delighted Atlanta leaders, the man was a Yankee—a branch manager newly arrived to the area from the Northeast.[85]

Despite so many positive growth trends, the Atlanta metropolitan area was not gaining the kinds of jobs that might have been expected in a region with a booming defense industry. Unlike Northern California, in the early postwar years, Atlanta and its suburbs did not become a magnet for firms employing large numbers of white-collar engineers and scientists. "At present," EES director J. E. Boyd observed in 1961, "Georgia . . . has no "electronics row" as do Massachusetts and California, with the thousands of high wage jobs such as the industry produces. . . . Tech's electrical engineering and physics graduates and young experienced researchers still must, for the most part, seek employment elsewhere."[86] The industries that came to Atlanta were attracted by its transportation facilities and its cheap labor, not for the trained scientists at Georgia Tech.

In Atlanta and Georgia the new jobs that had arrived since World War II were largely blue-collar and low paying. Both General Motors and Ford Motor Company had opened large plants in the Atlanta metropolitan area after the end of the war. Lockheed, after converting the wartime Bell Bomber facility into a giant aerospace production complex, also brought thousands of jobs to the region. The vast majority of the jobs in these factories were blue-collar positions on the assembly line. By the mid-sixties these firms offered the highest-paying manufacturing jobs in the state, but these wages, while good for Georgia, were still less than the national average for transportation industries.[87] The vast majority of Georgia's manufacturing jobs were not in heavy manufacturing at all but in the region's old standby, the textile industry, which employed over 30 percent of the workforce.[88] Georgia's 1965 per-capita income of $2,159 was nearly six hundred dollars lower than the national average.[89] Even though Atlanta's industrial growth was diverse and strong, it tended to generate more blue-collar jobs than white-collar ones. This trend was reflective of elsewhere in the South, where unionization (particularly in the textile industry) was a rarity and costs and standards of living were much lower than in the Northeast and Midwest.[90]

By the end of the 1950s, Atlanta's leadership had grown concerned about the need to attract more white-collar professionals and advanced scientific industries to the area. It seemed clear that the Atlanta region could not survive on factories alone; manufacturing employment in Georgia peaked in 1956 and declined over the rest of the decade.[91] The post-Sputnik expansion of federal R&D programs and the space program increased local leaders' worries. Not surprisingly, Southern states won a disproportionate number of these new facilities and contracts, particularly from NASA, but the Atlanta area (and Georgia in general) lagged behind places like Florida, Alabama, and Texas. A 1961 Tech report found that Georgia had but "one lone electronics plant with 100 or more employees, while every other state in the Southeast has at least one plant in the 1,000 and over category."[92] A later report remarked: "since there are great variations in learning ability, there will always be a demand for unskilled or semiskilled jobs; these low-wage industries, therefore, form an essential part of the state's economy. Georgia's need is to balance these low-wage jobs with a better proportion of high-wage, high-skill jobs."[93]

The fact that Atlanta was not keeping up with its neighbors deeply wounded the pride of the civic elite. "Atlanta could glance over either shoulder and see a group of 'sister' cities closing the gap and almost at her heels in their bid for Southeastern supremacy," noted one observer.[94] It was a problem that might have far-reaching implications if it were not fixed, they reasoned. The elevated sense these leaders had of Atlanta's importance to the national economy was reflected in one article in the Chamber of Commerce's new house publication, *Atlanta* magazine, which warned that national security might be jeopardized if Atlanta did not continue to grow: "its great potential and promise will not have been fulfilled and it will have played a major and shameful role in the decline of the United States as a world power."[95]

The desire for a larger white-collar employment base and the increasing importance of advanced scientific industry to the Southern economy led to a shift in Atlanta's economic-development and marketing strategies. By the early 1960s, Atlanta's leaders were turning their attention to luring not simply *any* industry but particularly *knowledge-based* industry. While this was by no means a wholesale departure from earlier practice—the city continued to lobby for manufacturing facilities of any sort—there was now recognition that science could bring just the sort of jobs, and residents, that were most desired by the white elites who ran Atlanta. Just as Atlanta had been well positioned to take advantage of the boom in highway and air commerce, its placement in relation to the emerging space and defense-related industries made it a logical choice for high-tech development, reasoned Atlanta officials. "In addition to the many physical features and services present in the local area, Metropolitan Atlanta is well situated with regard to R&D as a result of its favorable location within the so-called 'space crescent,' " noted a 1962 MPC report.[96] "As rocket boosters get bigger and less transportable and as space missions get longer and more complicated, a vast industrial migration to the Crescent is inevitable," *Business Week* had observed earlier that year. "It will bring a fever of activity in ancillary industries, utilities, retailing, and personal services for the companies and the people who settle in the region."[97]

In order to properly take advantage of the new scientific boom—and attempt to surpass other parts of the South in becoming a center for such industry—Atlanta's leaders began to work on improving two of the essential ingredients for this kind of economic development: a respected research institution that could serve as a magnet for scientists and engineers; and neighborhoods that offered competitive amenities for professional scientists and their families. The first part of this strategy centered on Georgia Tech, which became more closely allied with Atlanta politicians and business organizations and took a principal role in the campaign to market Atlanta as the next high-tech capital.

The State of Georgia also recognized that Tech was crucial to winning a larger share of federal research projects—not only because of its scientific research activities, but also because of its ability to survey and analyze statewide industrial trends. In 1960 the state legislature passed a resolution that officially expanded the original economic development mission of the EES and decreed that "it shall further be the duty of said Station to render assistance to national programs of science, technology, and preparedness."[98] The EES began to function as a training ground and business incubator for private spin-off enterprises. One of the first of these spin-offs was Scientific Associates, which later became a multi-million-dollar private research corporation called Scientific Atlanta.[99] Research grants and contracts also had economic value in and of themselves. One Tech administrator noted in 1961: "One can regard this support as a significant stimulus in the Georgia economy, for each of the more than three million dollars which came from outside the State during the last fiscal year will be spent several times within the State."[100] As part of their industrial development activities, Tech researchers also began to provide technical and marketing assistance to economically struggling small towns. Some of these happened to be places on the outskirts of Atlanta that, in a matter of a few years, would become its suburbs. Reflecting the metropolitan mindset articulated in the MPC's reports, Tech-sponsored marketing materials promoted these towns as particularly ideal places for industrial development because they were close, but not *too* close, to the city. A 1960s brochure promoted the Douglas County Electric Membership Corporation as being "On the Atlanta fringe . . . close enough for convenience, far enough for privacy."[101]

As Atlanta's leaders began to reorient their economic development appeals and increase the region's appeal to scientific industry, the Chamber of Commerce commissioned a series of reports from the industrial-development experts at Georgia Tech that, for the first time, examined the Atlanta region apart from the rest of the state, and expanded the scope of its industrial surveys beyond cotton, timber, and textiles to publish reports on emerging industries like electronics and computers. The Chamber had revived the 1920s title Forward Atlanta to apply to its new economic-development campaign, and through its new magazine, *Atlanta*, as well as other publications, was taking a lead role in selling Atlanta to the outside world.[102] While the reports Tech produced for the Chamber were serious in tone and contained extensive statistical research, they were upbeat in their conclusions and did not deviate far from the business community's message of regional prosperity and economic potential. The reports were useful marketing tools for Georgia

Tech, as well, as they all highlighted the central role the institute would play in building a regional high-tech economy.

The reports made some familiar conclusions. Researchers noted that Georgia Tech's presence meant that there was a good supply of trained professionals in the area—many of whom usually had to leave Atlanta in search of work. "Evidence of the abundance of these highly trained people in the area is shown by the experience of one of the largest manufacturers of electronics equipment in the country in recently locating a major engineering facility in Atlanta," noted one of these publications. "One of the vice presidents of the firm stated that the company had received far more applications for the Atlanta facility than it had required or expected." Lower production costs and excellent transportation networks as assets also made Atlanta ideal for this kind of investment.[103] A report on the aerospace industry demonstrated acute awareness of the central role trained personnel played in wooing this industry, and the importance of local amenities to scientific professionals: "Since brainpower is always scarce, companies in the aerospace industry find themselves in the position of constantly (1) competing for technical people and (2) attempting to make the best use of those they have. . . . Competitive advantages tend to fall to those companies located where people want to live."[104]

Another component of Atlanta's strategy was a concerted effort to bring press attention to the research activities underway at Georgia Tech. While newspapers and magazines in the post-Sputnik era were eager to write about science and scientists, the degree of attention given the various activities of the EES reflects a deliberate effort to show a wider audience its capabilities.[105] Tech was portrayed as Georgia's secret weapon in the race for industrial success. One local newspaper reporter noted in 1962: "the research done at Tech can often mean the difference between an industry's gaining knowledge for an important breakthrough, or its continuing in the old—often marginal or submarginal—rut." A Tech official reminded the newspaper, "people who buy research from universities are buying brainpower."[106] Another example of the breathlessly adulatory press Tech received in the local press was a 1965 feature story on the EES's work in making heat-resistant missile reentry cones for the space program. The article extolled the virtues of "Tech men" and emphasized the positive effect their work had on the local economy.[107]

Such articles boosted Tech's reputation and made Atlantans and Southerners aware of its growing reputation regionally and nationally. Other economic development reports, published by the MPC as well as by the Chamber, continued to spread the message of Atlanta's fitness for high-tech development.[108] Yet Atlanta's leaders knew that, whatever its other assets, the region had one continuing deterrent to outside investment: racial segregation. Despite being a city "too busy too hate" 1950s Atlanta still had many segregated public facilities and segregated public schools. Corporate middle managers might have been able to swallow living in a place with officially sanctioned segregation, but not highly educated and socially progressive scientists and engineers.

Public schools—and school quality—were at the heart of this situation. A 1961 economic development report published by the EES was unequivocal in its assessment of why Georgia lagged behind other states in luring high-tech firms: "A specific deterrent to the development of an electronics industry has been the uncertainties [*sic*] surrounding Georgia's school situation. Not of particular concern to some industries, the question of open schools is a primary one in fields like electronics, where scientists and engineers place a high premium on the availability of high quality schools."[109] In order to lure educated professionals to Atlanta, city leaders had to show them that a violent integration process would not disrupt their children's schooling.

In the late 1950s and early 1960s, racial violence was exploding all over the South as segregationist politicians and citizens resisted court-ordered desegregation mandates. The 1957 integration crisis at Little Rock, Arkansas' Central High School, and the numerous acts of violence against peaceful civil rights protesters in Alabama were events that gave the South global notoriety as a backward and hate-filled region. Hartsfield looked at Southern cities consumed by violence, and condemned them, not for their racial intolerance, but for their willful damage to the bottom line. Desegregation mandates were not going to go away, and resisting them was bad for business. In an interview with *Look* magazine, Chamber of Commerce president Ivan Allen "showed *Look* a study of business stagnation in Little Rock since 1957. 'We won't let this happen here.' "[110]

By 1961, the final year of his mayoralty, William B. Hartsfield was quite vocal about his dissatisfaction with continued segregation. "Not long ago, a group of [white business leaders] asked Mayor Hartsfield when they might expect the jet port to become international," noted an article in *Fortune* in September of that year. "His answer was blunt: 'Not until Atlanta becomes an internationally minded city. What do you plan to do with [the] Brazilian millionaire who flies in with some money to invest but happens to be black? Send him to the Negro YMCA? Think about it, friends.' "[111] In a dogged effort not to be another Little Rock or Birmingham, Hartsfield decided to make the desegregation of Atlanta's public schools—which was scheduled to start in the fall of 1961—a national news event. Reporters who flocked to Atlanta on the eve of the first day of desegregated public schooling in the fall of 1961 were shocked at their welcome: "old hands who had been harassed and badgered by city officials on the integration beat from Little Rock to New Orleans were awed by Atlanta's anxious effort to cater to the working press."[112] The first day of school went off successfully, in large part because hardly any students were integrated. Hartsfield had decided to take an extremely gradualist approach to integration, and only grades 11 and 12 were being integrated that fall. Only *nine* black students in these grades, citywide, would be attending white schools (despite the fact that 133 students had applied for such transfers).[113]

In his farewell address, Mayor Hartsfield seemed to breathe an audible sigh of relief that Atlanta had avoided the racial conflagrations of other parts of the South: "Many sections of our southland have tried to stop the inexorable clock of time and progress, but without success and at great cost to themselves. Atlanta's mature and friendly approach to the problems of racial change has earned for us the respect of the nation."[114] Elsewhere in the address, Hartsfield drew an explicit connection between Atlanta's successful desegregation and the nation's battles with the Soviets for intellectual and ideological supremacy: "To have adopted any other course than racial progress and harmony would have been doubly tragic for us, and a serious blow to our National Government in its fight to stave off world Communism."[115]

Some national reporters saw past the elaborate publicity campaign orchestrated around school desegregation. "This southern city's reputation for being progressive in racial matters is not entirely warranted," warned the Philadelphia *Evening Bulletin*.[116] Yet skeptical voices were few and far between, and national news and business publications continued to write glowing articles about Atlanta as "an oasis of tolerance," "no longer a 'Southern city,' " and a place that had "the 'sleepy sand' of yesterday rubbed out of its eyes."[117] Despite the extensive effort civic leaders put into presenting a particular image of school desegregation to the public, afterward they affected a folksy, business-as-usual attitude toward the entire process. "Hell," Mayor Allen remarked to *Time* in 1962, "the law was on the books, and it was here and we got it done, that's all."[118] Allen's matter-of-fact rhetoric masked the fact that the desegregation scheme created such hurdles for black students to transfer to white schools that only 9 of the 133 applicants actually won transfers. Atlanta had to be prodded by the courts and the NAACP to speed up what one black newspaper called an "eyedropper" desegregation plan.[119]

Hartsfield and the rest of the Atlanta elite were correct in their assessment that resisting integration would cost the metropolitan area a great deal of economic and political capital. Yet desegregating the Atlanta public schools—as much of an "eyedropper" process as it was—had its costs to the city. The affluent whites that city leaders had worked to hard to keep in the city through annexation, as well as the more modest-income whites who had fiercely resisted neighborhood and school integration, left for the suburbs in droves. Between 1960 and 1963, the years when integration went into effect, the Atlanta metropolitan area went from being twenty-first in the nation in the rate of new (suburban) home construction, to being sixth—outranked only by the much larger metropolitan areas of Los Angeles, New York, San Francisco, Washington, and Chicago.[120]

City leaders noted the increased exodus to the suburbs with alarm. In 1966, in an effort to remedy the situation, they launched a new annexation campaign to bring the new, affluent suburb of Sandy Springs into the Atlanta city limits. Mayor Allen and Mayor Emeritus Hartsfield, aided by a new Chamber of Commerce group calling itself "Team for Tomorrow," campaigned fiercely for the measure, which appeared as a ballot referendum in the spring of 1966.[121] The campaign had the same racial dynamic seen in the Buckhead annexation—keeping the city majority-white—but it also had a more overt class component than the earlier effort. The civil rights movement had unleashed not only the political power of African Americans, but also the reactionary anger of many working-class Southern whites. By annexing Sandy Springs, Atlanta could keep more of the "good" whites—affluent moderates and progressives—in the voting population and keep the influence of the "bad," segregationist whites at a minimum.

The growing rift between urban and suburban Atlanta was made clear to Atlanta's old-line leaders when the Sandy Springs annexation measure was defeated by 2 to 1 in the spring of 1966. Hartsfield did not give up his campaign to expand the city boundaries, however. Well into his retirement he kept waging the battle for the city to expand further into the white suburbs on the north, "where," as he wrote in a 1969 letter, "you will find the best and most homogeneous white citizenship which the town badly needs."[122] Hartsfield's words reflected the residual class snobbery and racism of Atlanta's power structure—even as the city was only a few years away from having a black mayor—and they also reflected a growing resentment against a population that used the amenities of the city but did not pay for them. "They enjoy big league sports while you and I pay for the stadium," he wrote. "They use our Civic Center and send their children to the zoo while you and I pay the bill."[123]

As in many other large American cities, the white flight and urban crises—increasing poverty, urban violence, and physical deterioration—of the 1960s prompted a number of new downtown redevelopment efforts in Atlanta. As in the earlier part of the century, white business owners led the effort, although unlike the 1920s Forward Atlanta campaign and the CAIA of the 1940s, these projects were largely funded by public money. In Atlanta, this phase of downtown renewal devoted much of its energy to the creation of entertainment and convention venues to bring suburban residents and businesspeople back to downtown. The "ID men" and private real estate developers who had played such an important role in Atlanta politics continued to take central roles in this downtown redevelopment. The leading figure of the early 1970s was Georgia Tech graduate and architect/developer Henry Portman, who spearheaded a new breed of retail-office space downtown and built showplaces like the Atlanta Merchandise Mart and Peachtree Center. In Atlanta's soaring Hyatt Regency Hotel, Portman designed the first multistory hotel atrium—a design imitated endlessly in hotels worldwide during the 1980s and 1990s. Yet Portman's designs reflected a presumption that downtown environments needed to be separated from the urban streetscape in order to be attractive—and seem sufficiently "safe"—to white suburbanites. "He likes to build 'em by the block full," wrote the *Saturday Evening Post* of Portman in 1974, "communities of skyscrapers tied together by aerial bridges and malls with fountains and trees, complexes where people can live and work and shop and go out to dinner, to the theater or to a museum—all without ever setting a foot in an automobile or bus or subway."[124]

Despite a new focus on Atlanta's downtown, and even in the face of abundant evidence that untrammeled suburbanization was hurting the central city, Atlanta's leaders continued to market the region to outsiders as a place where residents could take advantage of these new urban amenities while remaining safely in the suburbs. In fact, the failure of annexation in 1966 appeared to redouble city boosters' efforts to pretend city limits didn't exist and sell Atlanta as a multi-municipal *metropolis* that was both urban and suburban. "The growth and development of the strong central city has far outstripped the artificial city limits established by rural legislators long ago," Mayor Allen told *Business Week* in 1967. "The city of Atlanta is intensely interested in the development of the city and the metropolitan area."[125] Atlanta had "a rare kind of environment," wrote the Chamber of Commerce in 1972, "combining the advantages of big city interests, attitudes and economic opportunities with the pleasures of small town living."[126] Atlanta boosters also continued to market the suburbs as an ideal place to work. If they could not have actual, political annexation, they could still continue to claim most of the metropolitan area as being part of "Atlanta."

One urban asset that could increase the economic and social connection between city and suburb, city leaders recognized, was Georgia Tech. The school was, by the late 1960s, a growing research center with a sleek, modern campus in the city and satellite departments and affiliates in the suburbs. It already was proving its usefulness to state and local economic development efforts through its survey research, and to local industry through its technical assistance programs. And, by the late 1960s, national and international events prompted political shifts that placed Georgia Tech—still a small, state-run school with a relatively modest research budget—in a more competitive position within the federal science complex. However, in this phase of science-based economic development, the goals of state and local, public and private, and Tech administrators and others all seemed to be at odds with one another when it came to deciding *where* such development should be. The general agreement that high-tech industry should move to the suburbs began to be challenged, first by state officials who felt that academia and industry should remain in close physical proximity to each other, and then by a new, black-led city power structure that urgently needed new tax dollars and economic vitality to remain in Atlanta's city limits.

Research Parks, Office Parks, and Another Stanford?

In 1965 the Georgia university system welcomed a new chancellor, George L. Simpson, who arrived in Atlanta after having spent nearly all his professional life at the University of North Carolina, from where he had gone on to serve as the first director of the Research Triangle Foundation. Although run by the private sector, this entity was the outgrowth of a late-1950s economic development campaign by North Carolina governor Luther Hodges that focused on using the R&D assets of the state's three research universities and bringing new high-tech industry to the state. While a research park was not part of the project's original vision, the centerpiece of the effort became the Research Triangle Park (RTP). By the mid-1960s the RTP had established itself as the chief Southern challenger to Silicon Valley and Route 128, home to a major IBM facility as well as the National Institution of Environmental Health Sciences. The appointment of what one press account called "the brains of the project" signaled the state government's interest in replicating such a project in Georgia, drawing upon either the resources of Georgia Tech or the flagship institution of the state system, the University of Georgia in Athens.[127] In coming to Georgia, Simpson brought with him a clear understanding of the importance of research universities in creating economies of scientific industry, and a commitment to the kind of high-caliber graduate research and education that elevated institutional reputations and produced successful spin-off companies.[128]

By the late 1960s, there were enough research-oriented companies scattered around the metropolitan area to indicate that science-based economic-development efforts were bearing some fruit. Atlanta's status as a regional business center brought research-related firms to the region; a 1969 survey found that "eighteen major computer and related hardware manufacturing companies have regional, branch or local offices in Atlanta."[129] But much of this gathering of industry appears to have resulted from Georgia Tech's success in spinning off high-tech companies. In 1969 an EES report identified 29 Tech spin-offs, having over $23 million annual sales and nearly 1,400 employees. This record of success paled in comparison to other universities—"estimates indicate that about 35 companies have been formed by faculty and staff members from the University of Michigan in Ann Arbor and that about 166 firms located in the Boston area can be traced to MIT"—but for a relatively small institution, the tally was impressive.[130]

Spin-off companies, alliances with industry—Georgia Tech appeared to be taking several cues from Fred Terman, an impression the school reinforced in 1969 by hiring one of Terman's associates, Joseph Pettit, as president. Pettit was the former dean of engineering at Stanford, who came to Tech determined to build up its graduate research programs in the same way Terman had transformed Stanford.[131] Tech's good fortune in hiring someone from such a prestigious research institution was a consequence of larger trends in the national research picture, trends that the EES already was capitalizing upon. The fierce antiwar protests on American campuses during the late 1960s had frequently targeted the research projects being conducted for the military. Penn students' protests against the "Summit" and "Spicerack" chemical-weapons projects was one example of this, and Stanford's campus had also been rocked in the late 1960s by protests over the covert research conducted at SRI. More conservative and pro-military areas of the country, like the South, did not experience these convulsive campus protests. Southern schools and universities maintained close ties to the military; at Tech, compulsory ROTC endured until 1965 and was abolished not out of antiwar sentiment but because of administrative changes. Pettit explicitly chose to come to Atlanta to escape these battles over military research. "Georgia Tech," he later said, "was my kind of place."[132]

As more universities chose to dissociate themselves from more politically sensitive research projects, the military increasingly turned to places like Georgia Tech in awarding grants and contracts. However, the other consequence of antiwar sentiment, combined with the increasingly tight federal budgets of the late 1960s, was that federal R&D spending was in a decline. The GTRI—the profit-making arm of the EES—reported a 3.5 percent decrease in its gross research income between the 1967–68 and 1969–70 school years.[133] Research income increased in subsequent years, however, reaching nearly $4 million in 1971; about 75 percent of this total came from federal grants.[134] As a result of these national trends, Georgia Tech's research capacity did not increase dramatically, but unlike many other research institutions it held steady, thereby increasing the school's relative share of overall research spending compared to its peers. The composition of research at Tech began to diverge from its contemporaries, as Tech took on more of the secret military research that other universities rejected.

Georgia Tech was making promising strides toward increasing research capacity and fostering spin-off industry, a process helped along by the attention of George Simpson and the leadership of Joseph Pettit. Yet the vast majority of these firms located at least ten miles away from the institution that had spawned them, many along the white-collar industrial corridor sprawling out to the northeast of the city. They might have chosen to locate in this area because the EES High Temperature Materials Branch was in Chamblee, but it seems that they simply followed prevailing industrial trends. Unlike Stanford or Penn, Georgia Tech did not become actively involved in real estate development, even though many of its graduates founded or worked for the firms that made up Atlanta's nascent high-tech economy. Instead, private real estate developers—metropolitan Atlanta's most prolific and influential city planners—led what efforts there were to create research parks in the Atlanta suburbs.

Not surprisingly, given the racial and economic patterns of residence in metropolitan Atlanta, these parks stretched out to the north and northeast of the city, along a corridor of affluent white city neighborhoods and suburban subdivisions, from Buckhead to Sandy Springs and beyond.[135]   Peachtree Industrial Boulevard, the suburban extension of the main thoroughfare running north from downtown through some of Atlanta's richest neighborhoods, became a center for white-collar industrial and office parks. Many of the real estate developers who were part of Atlanta's civic elite had developments on Peachtree and marketed these facilities as ideal locations for white-collar firms who desired leafy exclusivity, proximity to executives' homes, and an escape from urban problems. A 1966 *Fortune* article described a "dazzling, 140-acre project" that was typical of those on the Boulevard:

> Executive Park is a group of handsome new buildings occupied almost exclusively by national corporations and surrounded by a lushly landscaped setting. The project competes directly with the new, high-rise office space in downtown Atlanta and, so far, it has competed very successfully. Executive Park meets a clear need. Most national companies that set up regional headquarters in Atlanta do not have to be in the city. Their market is really the whole Southeast, and any location close to Atlanta will suffice.[136]

Even though this was not explicitly a research park, J. Michael Gearon, the young developer of Executive Park, seemed to have taken Fred Terman's development methods to heart. "To insure that contractors would not denude the landscape, Gearon penalized them $1,000 for every tree they knocked down," wrote *Business Week*.[137]

Some of the real estate developers building research parks at the out-skirts of the city tried, and failed, to get Tech more actively involved in their efforts. Their failure revealed a changed attitude at Tech about the value of urban development. In 1969, prior to Pettit's arrival, developer and Georgia Tech alumnus Paul Duke offered President Arthur G. Han-sen "a gift of a minimum of 200 acres of land to the Georgia Tech Foun-dation for industrial and research development use." Although Duke had been inspired to make the offer by the Alumni Association–spon-sored Little report of six years earlier, he did not follow the report's conclusions that a Tech-sponsored research park be located in the city. The acreage in question was seventeen miles away from Tech, in the heart of Atlanta's new office-park belt: "this land will front on the Peachtree Industrial Boulevard adjacent to the Norcross area."[138] Duke proposed that Tech establish a research park on the site that would be an "Industrial and Research Center for Georgia," and also indicated that, if Georgia Tech did not take him up on his offer, another research institu-tion would.[139]

The proposal seems to have piqued Hansen's interest, and his subordi-nates set about researching the experience of the RTP to see how a simi-lar development might fare. An undated memorandum from Hansen's files rued that Tech and Atlanta were embarking on such an effort quite late—"it is unfortunate that this venture could not have been initiated one or two decades ago in order to have taken advantage of the major growth of science and technology following the initial launch of Sput-nik"—but stated that it was worthwhile nonetheless.[140] Yet Tech adminis-trators, needing approval from university system officials and the state legislature for any endeavor so large in scope, dragged their feet in giving Duke an answer. In a 1970 note, Duke strove to reassure Hansen of his commitment: "the Research Park is the biggest commitment of my life-time. My total physical and financial capacities will be involved in making every effort to create a successful venture, regardless of how many years it takes."[141]

In making this offer, Paul Duke had set up a difficult political dynamic for Hansen, because George Simpson was against locating such a facility in the distant suburbs. Simpson may have headed an effort to build a typically low-rise, landscaped research park, but Paul Duke's proposal for a similarly designed suburban facility appears not to have met Simpson's standards. Ten years of urban deterioration in Atlanta, and an extensive city commitment to urban renewal projects, made Simpson interested in keeping any new high-tech development in the city. In an unsigned memorandum to Hansen, a Simpson associate told the president that

the chancellor would prefer the research park be in a nearby urban renewal area, not Norcross.[142] Duke went ahead with his development in
the suburbs, but without the direct participation of Georgia Tech. The
development, called Technology Park, ended up in a slightly different
location, but one still twelve miles away from Tech and in the northern
arc of suburban development. By 1982 the Park was "home to some forty
companies employing 2,500 people."[143] Many Georgia Tech alumni
worked in the park, but unlike its model, the Stanford Industrial Park,
it operated independently of the academic and research operations at
Georgia Tech.

The changing administrative dynamics within the state university system were followed a few years afterward by tremendous changes in local
politics. In 1973 Maynard Jackson was elected Atlanta's first black mayor
and ended the era of the old white civic power structure. An equally
business-minded ruling class rose in its place, but prominent black politicians and business leaders had a seat at the table as well as whites. Atlanta's new black political leaders did not have the same metropolitan mindset of the old white elite. They paid closer attention to the problems
of inner-city neighborhoods and their minority residents, and focused
economic development efforts on further building up Atlanta's downtown. While Jackson strove to maintain Atlanta's old political alliances—
he remarked in 1974 that "Atlanta can't prosper without city hall and
business 'in bed' together"[144]—he focused the city's energies on building
retail capacity and downtown entertainment facilities, not on fostering
high-tech development near Georgia Tech.

If other Southern states were to serve as Atlanta's example in this regard, however, building high-tech capacity during the 1970s seemed to be
much more the responsibility of state, rather than local, government. RTP
continued to flourish with active state support, and a new high-tech region
was emerging near Austin, Texas—the result of concerted state investment in the University of Texas flagship campus and medical schools. In
the early 1980s, these efforts resulted in a giant economic payoff for the
region and the state when the semiconductor giants Sematech and Micro-
electronics and Computer Technology Corporation (MCC) chose to locate in Austin after a nationwide site selection process. Sematch and MCC
set in motion a technology boom in Austin that, unlike Silicon Valley, did
not have a significant dependence on defense. By the late 1980s, Austin
had made a name for itself as a "technopolis" highly competitive with
those in California and Massachusetts, analyzed by planners and economists as another model for science-based and university-centered economic development.[145]

Conclusion

Why didn't Atlanta become a Southern high-tech capital like Research Triangle Park or Austin? Like the Bay Area, Atlanta was a beneficiary of postwar economic, demographic, and political trends. It was in an area of the country that was growing rapidly, in a state whose Congressional leaders led the defense appropriations process, and in a region where there were few physical or political barriers to decentralized growth. Policy choices and market forces provided multiple reasons for scientific industry to find it more useful and profitable to locate in low-density landscapes and upper-middle-class communities, and metropolitan Atlanta provided an abundance of these kinds of environments. In fact, the way in which Atlanta grew—extremely decentralized and car dependent, and extremely segregated by race and class—could be seen as an ideal landscape for the city of knowledge. The underlying race and class bias of so many of Atlanta's economic-development strategies—from zoning restrictions to highway placement, downtown redevelopment, and piecemeal desegregation—are indefensible. However, the race and class stratification of Atlanta did not have any apparent effect upon its ability to recruit scientific industry, and this fact speaks volumes about the presumptions and prejudices underlying the idea of the city of knowledge, in Atlanta and elsewhere.

In Philadelphia the effort to create a city of knowledge foundered because of difficulties inherent in adapting the idea of an isolated scientific utopia for white middle-class families in the dense, disorderly setting of the postwar industrial city. But Atlanta's failure is not one that we can attribute solely to the fact that Tech was located in a struggling central-city neighborhood. In Silicon Valley, the city of knowledge succeeded not simply because of Stanford's suburban location (although that had a huge amount to do with it) but because the university and its administrators had the *power*—deriving in large part from Stanford's great land endowment—to turn their vision of a community of science into a reality. This power often allowed the school to dominate local political affairs and to enjoy a close, clubby relationship with Bay Area power brokers. Becoming a truly successful city of knowledge, it seems, derived not simply from building research parks but also from having a politically powerful research institution at the center.

State institutions could occupy these positions of power, as the examples of the Research Triangle and Austin demonstrate, but only in cases where state governments took an active and early interest in building up university-centered agglomerations of high-tech industry. As we have seen throughout this story, such commitment did not ensure success, but it does appear to have been an essential ingredient. The state officials who controlled Georgia Tech's funding were interested in building up scientific industry, but for a long time approached this as a statewide endeavor rather than one specific to the Atlanta metropolitan area. The often-tortured politics between state government and Atlanta officials in this era of great social and political change—the integrationist approach of Hartsfield and Allen ran counter to the opinions of a great many in the Georgia legislature as well as most of its governors and members of Congress during this era—left little time for the two parties to engage in cooperative economic development strategies.

The increased federal funding Tech won in the Cold War era gave its administrators more autonomy, and they engaged with the city in urban renewal strategies and provided its business leaders with extensive economic research. Yet they did not wield the power in local affairs that might have prompted Atlanta's civic leadership to create more holistic, Tech-focused strategies rather than leaving it to the private developers among them to build isolated research parks along Peachtree Industrial Boulevard. And, by the time the institution was beginning to spin off high-tech firms and keep more of its alumni in the region, any momentum to develop a more comprehensive research park infrastructure was stalled by dissention among state and local leaders about whether this industrial activity should be located in the city or in the suburbs. Even though Georgia Tech sought to make itself more like Stanford by hiring Joseph Pettit and enlarging its research base, it did not have the size, capacity, or powerful leadership to become the center of another Silicon Valley.

The story of Atlanta does, however, show how the institutional and demographic conditions of the Southern region of the United States during the Cold War contributed to the fact that the U.S. high-tech industry tends to be suburban rather than urban. When advanced scientific industry arrived in the South, on the heels of the abundant defense contracts flowing to these states as the result of their powerful Congressional delegations, it found metropolitan areas that were very raw and new, that had gained most of their size in the age of the automobile, a place where suburban industrial parks were plentiful and cheap. It found metropolitan areas, like Atlanta, where growth control measures applied only to the spread of neighborhoods that were poor or black, and where public monies were being poured into roads and subdivisions at the far fringes of the suburbs. Science was moving to the South—and inestimably enriching and diversifying the economy of the South—and because of the way the urban South was growing during this period, this regional shift became linked to a suburban shift as well.

Part Three

LEGACY

Conclusion _____

The Next Silicon Valley

T HE city of knowledge outlasted both the Cold War science complex and the Levittown-style suburban subdivision. These cities endure as centers of high-tech innovation and productivity, magnets for the professional class, with powerful research universities as their intellectual centers. While labeled "high-tech regions," most of the late twentieth century's most successful examples maintained the carefully assembled formula of people, firms, institutions, and spatial design that characterized the scientific communities of the early Cold War. These places have been profoundly important to the way in which we live and work, influencing not only the regional economies in which they are located but national and global economies as well. Now it does not seem the least bit odd for white-collar workers to travel for miles from the suburb in which they live to the suburb in which they work, and for these workers to spend the day in the low-rise buildings of the corporate campus rather than a downtown skyscraper. The city of knowledge—housing industries and people that are pacesetters for productivity and, particularly in boom times, the center of market attention—has played an important role in making these suburban patterns of industry a desirable norm rather than the exception.[1]

As this book has shown, the geography of high technology was no accident. Nor was it a simple process, but the result of a complex combination of fundamental economic shifts, changing geopolitics, demographic transformations, and individual and institutional actions. The second half of the twentieth century in the United States was a time when cities and regions (and institutions and industries) that had once been at the top of the economic heap lost ground to new places, people, and industries in the hierarchy of wealth and influence. Philadelphia went from the "Workshop of the World" to a city in crisis. Atlanta went from a small regional capital to a giant megalopolis, home to multinational companies and host of the Olympic Games, but often considered the quintessential example of suburban "sprawl." Stanford University went from a rich man's folly to being the institution perfectly situated to reap the benefits of postwar suburbanization and Cold War military spending.

This reordering was not only the result of being in the right place at the right time, but was also the result of individuals and institutions taking advantage of favorable conditions and directing the resources created by Cold War spending to local economic ends. The story of the city of knowledge is one in which the federal government once again employed the politics of private-sector *persuasion*, rather than centralized planning, to develop these communities of science. The story attests to the power of *imitation* in regional economic development, as states and localities and universities scrambled to create cities of knowledge that duplicated the demographic composition, architecture and planning, and economic potency of research parks in general and the Stanford land developments in particular. The history of the city of knowledge also demonstrates that the defense complex's *regionalization* contributed to its suburbanization, as the bulk of federal funds flowed to parts of the country where state and local land-use laws and planning practices worked in favor of highly decentralized industrial development. Finally, it underscores the fundamental importance of *implementation* to policy outcomes, showing that federal policy provided frameworks whose full implications were only realized when *local* actors—particularly nongovernmental ones—adapted these policies to preexisting social conditions and economic needs.

The power of cities of knowledge as economic-development engines is such that efforts to create them continue even during deep high-tech recessions, including one that spanned the period during which this book was written. The story of the city of knowledge may not explain why the high-tech sector is so susceptible to boom-and-bust economic cycles, but it does help explain why high-tech continues to obsess industrial development officials, regardless of economic climate. And it does provide some lessons for those who are trying to build the "next Silicon Valley" in a post–Cold War, post-dot-com world. These lessons have bearing not only on discussions of the how and why of high-tech development, but on debates about urban and regional planning as well.

Lesson One: You need a lot of money. The Cold War had a decisive effect on economic development and the shape of urban space because it provided a giant influx of capital. The city of knowledge came to be because of massive federal defense investments during the first two decades of the Cold War. This money enriched elite research universities, allowing them to vastly enlarge their academic scope and physical size, and it prompted an explosion of industrial research and high-tech production.

In the last three decades of the twentieth century, the source of capital changed, but the importance of having regionally concentrated investment did not diminish. Federal R&D funding declined after 1965, but as it receded the consumer market for high-tech products grew.[2] Beginning in the 1970s and accelerating rapidly in the 1980s and exponentially in the 1990s, sophisticated technologies that once only had military applications became tools used by millions. Silicon chips, personal computers, and the Internet turned technology into a mass-market commodity. The fact that these technologies only got cheaper as they got more efficient and powerful enhanced their marketability and their attractiveness to both business and consumer. In this new era of commercial technology, defense contracts were replaced by a new kind of private financing, venture capital, which became increasingly important to advanced scientific industry.[3] Because venture capital went where the innovation was, it concentrated in many of the same regional economies favored by military spending, so that at the close of the twentieth century the map of high-tech activity in the United States still bore a striking correspondence with the list of top university recipients of federal R&D in 1960. Building a city of knowledge in an area outside this list is not impossible, but clearly would require a comparably massive and flexible source of public or private financing that would empower local institutions and industries.

Lesson Two: You need a powerful university. Successful cities of knowledge have had universities at their center with (1) the resources and willingness to embrace corporate partnerships and (2) the political clout and institutional ability to play a leading role in local economic development. Stanford's administrators, Fred Terman chief among them, recognized the value of close relationships with industry and the commercial relevance of the products and people of the university laboratory. Stanford also enjoyed a privileged position as a giant landowner and the most important institutional actor in local politics. This position was further enhanced by relatively placid town-gown relations and—"Battle of the Hills" aside—a lack of truly significant community opposition to its actions. Penn, while having close relationships with the local power structure and playing an influential role in local politics, did not structure its research policies in a way that was particularly attractive to researchers or entrepreneurs, nor could it overcome the race and class politics generated by its attempt to create a city of knowledge in a dense, impoverished urban neighborhood. Georgia Tech lacked both the political clout and the blank slate on which to build, factors that help explain why—despite its favored location in the Sunbelt—it achieved only modest success in its efforts to recruit high-tech industry.

University-industry alliances became increasingly important to the cities of knowledge as federal support was reduced. From 1970 on, corporate America became a significant presence on many university campuses, as the latter traded access to research and scientists for financial donations for facilities construction, fellowships, and new research initiatives. If the close relationship universities had with the military had worried some academics in the early Cold War years, after 1970 the new closeness between universities and industry gave some observers even more concern for the future of free intellectual inquiry.[4] The debate over the merits of the "corporate university" of the late twentieth century highlights an inherent tension in the role of these institutions in the city of knowledge, as they act both as an intellectual anchor and as a catalyst of commercial profit. Nonetheless, the embrace of corporate partnerships was what gave certain universities an early advantage in the competition for scientific industry, and the engagement of the powerful university in economic development continues to be essential for the city of knowledge to flourish.

Since 1970, universities have also gone further in heeding Henry Commager's call and developing a "philosophy" around social engagement. From West Philadelphia to Upper Manhattan to Chicago's South Side, universities have sought to mend the rift between town and gown that resulted from the campus expansions and urban redevelopment of the 1950s and 1960s. Many set up community partnership programs that engage in a range of activities, from tutoring in local schools to large-scale institutional investments in local retail and residential developments. Academic, political, and business leaders continue to work together on a range of broader urban reinvestment strategies that, similar to those of the 1950s and 1960s, seek to leverage university resources in order to increase the size of the urban professional class and build a knowledge-intensive job base. Local leaders still believe that these assets "[remain] one of the greatest untapped urban revitalization opportunities in the country."[5]

The cases in this book indicate that leveraging university assets for economic development is a more complicated proposition than it may seem. The ability of a university to establish a power base—either to build a city of knowledge or to engage in urban redevelopment more generally—depends greatly on the institutional assets and administrative characteristics of the university. It may also have a lot to do with whether an institution is private or public. Independent institutions are less likely to become tied up in state-level power struggles; their financing and mission is not contingent on the political priorities of state executives and state legislatures. The ability of a public university to become an anchor for regional high-tech development depends on the engagement of the state government in the process, and the financial largesse of the state toward these institutions.

Lesson Three: You need control over land in the right location. The local interests and institutions that successfully developed clusters of high-tech industry were places that had control over the development of large parcels of land in locations that were desirable to middle-class professionals. Stanford owned thousands of acres amid one of the fastest-growing and most affluent areas of the country. Boston real estate developers Cabot, Cabot, & Forbes bought up property along a new suburban ring road, Route 128, within easy commuting distance of Harvard and MIT and close to upper-middle-class suburban subdivisions. Having land was important, but location was preeminent: Penn gained control over a large adjoining parcel of land through urban renewal, yet this land was in the distinctly "undesirable" environs of West Philadelphia.

For cities of knowledge, "desirability" was defined by a high degree of homogeneity, a certain level of cultural vibrancy, and architecture and design that created a physical separation from the rest of the urban landscape. For most of the late twentieth century, this combination of qualities existed solely in the suburbs. The correspondence between what suburbs offered, and what cities of knowledge needed, makes it tricky to distinguish racial homogeneity from class homogeneity, for until very recently these suburbs were nearly entirely white. And, as demonstrated in Philadelphia and Atlanta, the populations excluded from and displaced by these developments were often African American. The turbulent racial politics of the 1960s, particularly in the South, were an often unacknowledged, but incredibly significant, influence on the ideas and actions of public officials and university administrators. But, in thinking about the long-term development of these places, it is perhaps more accurate to think of the defining criterion as one having more to do with *class*—which in this case was usually synonymous with education levels—than with race.

Cities of knowledge are places cultivated for a rather rarefied stratum of the professional class: the professor, scientist, and engineer. Demographic changes since 1970 have further reinforced these class distinctions while making race—at least in high-tech capitals—matter less and less. In the 1970s, 1980s, and 1990s, immigration reforms and a shortage of domestic technical expertise led to Indian and Chinese engineers becoming a major presence in U.S. high-tech regions, Silicon Valley in particular. By the end of the century, high-tech America still operated on Vannevar Bush–style meritocratic elitism, but this group of elites now included more women, more minorities, and more immigrants. Education and training, not gender or skin color, determines entry into the city of knowledge. The new diversity of population does not bridge economic status, however. Cities of knowledge continue to remain in or near the most affluent—and expensive—places in America. Blue-collar, lower-skilled workers participate in high-tech production, but still remain a hidden and marginalized part of the workforce. Since 1970, more and more of these elements of the manufacturing process have left the United States for Asia and Latin America, where workforce and capital costs are much lower. As white-collar immigrants came to work in American cities of knowledge, more of the blue-collar work associated with these sectors left the country.[6]

The city of knowledge has worked because it provides an exclusive environment. This reality may make some uncomfortable, but the growth of high technology in the United States has never been a democratic or egalitarian process. It is a system that worked because it concentrated money, power, and privilege among certain groups, certain institutions, and certain places. As planners and policy makers look toward creating the "next Silicon Valley," they must accommodate the fact that success has always been contingent on creating an exclusive environment. Successful cities of knowledge have resulted from institutions or organizations having control of land in an economically homogeneous place where firms and workers want to live and work.

Lesson Four: You need to make high-tech development the end, not the means. The successful cities of knowledge were the places that applied all of their energies to the task of building university research capacity, generating industrial research and production, and attracting white-collar scientists and engineers. The places that used science-based economic development as a tool by which to "save the city" or present the right public image on racial issues were less successful. However, the ability of a place to make high-tech development its end goal depends very much on its circumstances. Stanford was blessed with so many institutional and geographic advantages that its administrators could have the luxury of focusing their energies on creating a community of science. Penn and Georgia Tech, even if they had taken a similarly single-minded approach, would have had to overcome the political distractions and economic limitations created by their urban locations. Such difficulties were compounded by the fact that these institutions, like so many others in similar situations, tried to apply science-based economic development as a solution to urban problems of race and poverty. In Philadelphia building "Brainsville" was an intensely place-based urban economic development strategy, one that foundered politically because it intensified deep divisions of race and class. In Atlanta this type of development was part of a larger campaign to make the region seem more racially progressive and, hence, more attractive to national and global business.

Like the issue of "desirability," this lesson is a rather uncomfortable one for people who care about the welfare of cities and the people who live in them. But it is something that helps explain why the line between success and failure often corresponds with suburban or urban locations. It also explains why there are exceptions to the rule. The case of Boston and Route 128 attests to the importance of the "ends not means" approach: Harvard and MIT, the two urban universities, did not concern themselves solely with revitalizing Cambridge, but let research parks grow on the outskirts of the metropolis. Would Philadelphia have become another East Coast high-tech capital had Penn focused its energies on a science center in the outer suburbs rather than in West Philadelphia? The counterfactual is impossible to prove, but it seems clear from these cases that the race and class politics that come along with an urban location create damaging distractions for builders of cities of knowledge. This does not mean that universities should cast aside their obligations to build and support surrounding communities; it just means that these institutions need to have a clear understanding of the trade-offs between economic goals and social ones.

The future development of the city of knowledge presents something of a conundrum for business leaders and policy makers. The idea of a planned community of scientific production has proved to be wildly successful in (and perhaps a catalyst for) generating unprecedented levels of innovation and economic productivity.[7] The state and local development officials who looked at the Stanford Industrial Park as part of a magic formula for economic growth were right: this university-centered economy of science and technology has profoundly affected the way the industrialized world works. While media hype overinflated a number of so-called technology revolutions, it is indisputable that the inventions of Silicon Valley and its imitators have changed the way lives are lived and work is performed.

The city of knowledge and its component parts must be given a good amount of credit for fostering the extraordinary level of high-technology productivity and growth experienced in the United States during the final decades of the twentieth century. The carefully planned idea of the live-work community for scientific production appears to have been the perfect "habitat for innovation and entrepreneurship" in the post–Cold War Information Age.[8] By concentrating scientific professionals and scientific industries and institutions in a carefully planned and generally pleasant and safe environment, the successful city of knowledge functioned as a glorified college campus, allowing for the free and often informal exchange of ideas, fostering new innovations, creating new kinds of ways of living and working. Companies abandoned old corporate hierarchies and adapted a loose and ostensibly democratic working style. High-tech companies might have still had tie-wearing "organization men" at their head, but they had room within their ranks for members of the 1960s counterculture, 1970s computer hobbyists, and 1990s techies in shorts and sandals. In many cases the tie-wearers disappeared altogether, and the iconoclasts writing code one year would be CEOs of publicly-traded companies the next.[9]

However, while this model seems to have been very good for productivity, it has had negative social, environmental, and economic consequences. Space-eating research parks and residential areas have meant that there simply has not been enough room in cities of knowledge to accommodate all who want to live and work in them. The economic exclusivity of these communities has had ripple effects upon their surrounding metropolitan areas. High land costs forced people and industries to move elsewhere; as these high-tech centers were already located on the fringe of the metropolis, new housing and jobs tended to move outward rather than inward, ending up even farther away from the central city. This has led to long commutes and precipitated transportation gridlock in many major metropolitan areas. While this is a phenomenon that also affects places without cities of knowledge, some of the most traffic-congested metropolitan areas in the nation at the close of the twentieth century also happened to be centers of high technology. The San Francisco Bay area had an average of 59 hours of annual traffic delay per eligible driver in 1997; Seattle had 69 hours, and Washington, D.C. had 76.[10] Decentralized development and transportation gridlock has alerted city and regional leaders of the long-developing environmental crisis at their fringe, as surrounding farmland was consumed by new development.[11] American suburbs now have many of the same problems that faced the city of 1950—overcrowding, pollution, deteriorating infrastructure, overloaded public services—and that prompted some city planners to become such enthusiastic proponents of dispersion and decentralization.

The problems that the city of knowledge, and the American city in general, face at the beginning of the twenty-first century call for a rethinking of the design of these kinds of communities. And the lessons of this story provide some clues about how this might be done in a way that preserves the ability of high-tech capitals to innovate, produce, and contribute to healthy economic growth. First, science moved to the suburbs not because they were *suburbs* but because they were "*desirable.*" This is an important distinction: the suburb of 1950 and 1960 provided the environment in which professionals and firms of this type wanted to live, and public subsidies made it economically advantageous for them to live there. A half-century later, the definition of "desirability" is less restricted, for metropolises are quite different than they were in the heyday of Cold War science. The multiracial meritocracy that U.S. high-tech capitals have become is a reflection of the change in suburban demographics. Increasing numbers of African Americans, Latinos, and Asians are moving to the suburbs, and increasing numbers of middle-class whites are moving back to central cities. Residential styles and preferences also have shifted dramatically. Architects and developers have begun to create higher-density subdivisions and communities that free their residents from going everywhere by car. While it is clear that quality-of-life factors continue to have immense importance for industries and professional workers who are inherently "footloose," the amenities that were important to the scientist of 1950 are not necessarily the same as those important to the computer engineer of today.[12]

Does this mean that it is time for science to return to the city? Not necessarily. As these landscape and demographics change, finding a fixed definition of "city" and "suburb" becomes more elusive. After years of scholarly arguments about the economic and social interdependence of cities and suburbs, state and local political leaders are finally beginning to regard metropolitan areas as one regional unit and to implement land use and tax policies that encourage regional cooperation and equity.[13] Perhaps it is also time to approach the city of knowledge as an entity that is not necessarily suburban or urban, and to instead capitalize on the changing political and social landscape of the city in order to make the next Silicon Valley more inclusive and more environmentally sustainable.

The second clue that history provides about where to go from here is the central role of the *American research university* in these processes—as land developer, entrepreneur, and political actor. The burst of high-tech activity at the end of the 1990s, and the continual economic struggles of many large central cities, prompted renewed attention to university-centered economic development strategies. Urban universities that stayed on the sidelines during the early Cold War are now more actively engaging in local revitalization efforts. But the danger remains—particularly for urban institutions—of reinventing a not-very-efficient wheel, and perpetuating an imitative economic growth model that does not respond to the realities and limitations inherent in high-tech development. The story of cities of knowledge shows that there was no magic formula for success; the ability of a place to become a center of high-tech industry had to do with a host of things, many of them determined at the local level. Building a city of knowledge never has been, nor will be, a one-size-fits-all process.

Therefore, this book cannot end with a prescription for high-tech growth, but with a call for policy makers and business leaders to remember the lessons of history and the importance of place and space. These lessons show us that the association of high technology with low-rise, manicured research parks and office complexes is not something that arose out of pure economic necessity, but resulted from public policy and individual choice. While amenities still matter in the design and location of these facilities, the adherence to this architecture is something that rose out of public persuasion and deliberate imitation, and is now perpetuated out of habit.

To many of the scholars, administrators, politicians, and business leaders who created and implemented the city of knowledge during the early Cold War years, the university was not merely the center of this enclosed community where educated people of science could live, work, and thrive creatively. Their words and actions also conveyed understanding of the secondary definition of city of knowledge, operating somewhat in tension with the first, that a scholarly community should use its scientific knowledge to improve society in general and urban life in particular. The design of the city of knowledge was not only intended to give scientists an ideal environment in which to live and work, but it also was seen as an ideal hybrid of urban and suburban life, and put forth as a model for other communities to imitate. Perhaps the future development of the city of knowledge will build upon this idea of a hybridization of urban and suburban life, and reconstitute the community of high-tech production in ways that better reflect the democratization of technology.

Universities cannot do this alone, however. As this book has shown, both public and private institutions have the power to determine where the economy grows. High-tech industries and high-tech workers are certainly swayed by the amenities offered by suburbs, but it is fifty years of public policy, not just consumer preference, that have made the high-tech sector as overwhelmingly suburban as it is today. If high-tech industries—and, more generally, all of the white-collar, suburbanized sectors of the post-industrial economy—are going to move to more dense and less exclusive settings, public policy must provide similarly powerful incentives to persuade them to do so. In this era of urbanized suburbs and suburbanized cities, this densification may no longer mean a return to the old central city. Yet the forces that moved science to the suburbs in the first place have now largely dissipated, and it is time for new models for the city of knowledge that reflect the diversity and dynamism of the twenty-first-century American metropolis.

Notes

Abbreviations

AHC   Atlanta History Center, Atlanta, Georgia

BAN   Bancroft Archives, University of California, Berkeley, California

ELBP   Edward L. Bowles Papers, Library of Congress, Washington, D.C.

EUSC   Emory University Special Collections, Atlanta, Georgia

FETP   Frederick Emmons Terman Papers, Stanford University Archives, Stanford, California

GTA   Georgia Institute of Technology Archives, Atlanta, Georgia

LMP   Lewis Mumford Papers, Rare Book and Manuscript Library, University of Pennsylvania, Philadelphia, Pennsylvania

LOC   Library of Congress, Washington, D.C.

NARA   National Archives at College Park, College Park, Maryland

PCA   Philadelphia City Archives, Philadelphia, Pennsylvania

RBML   Rare Book and Manuscript Library, University of Pennsylvania, Philadelphia, Pennsylvania

SFHC   San Francisco History Center, San Francisco Public Library, San Francisco, California

SUA   Stanford University Archives, Stanford, California

UPA   University of Pennsylvania Archives, Philadelphia, Pennsylvania

VBP   Vannevar Bush Papers, Library of Congress, Washington, D.C.

WBHP   William Berry Hartsfield Papers, Emory University Special Collections, Atlanta, Georgia

Introduction: Discovering the City of Knowledge

1. I draw the term "science region" from Robert Kargon, Stuart W. Leslie, and Erica Schoenberger, "Far Beyond Big Science: Science Regions and the Organization of Research and Development," in *Big Science: The Growth of Large-Scale Research*, ed. Peter Galison and Bruce Hevly (Stanford, Calif.: Stanford University Press, 1992), 339. Also see Ann Markusen, Peter Hall, and Amy Glasmeier, *High Tech America: The What, How, Where, and Why of the Sunrise Industries* (Boston, Mass.: Allen and Unwin, 1986); Peter Hall and Ann Markusen, *Silicon Landscapes* (Boston, Mass.: Allen and Unwin, 1985). A useful review of this literature and analysis of the dynamic relationship between technology and economic development is Edward J. Malecki, *Technology and Economic Development: The Dynamics of Local, Regional, and National Change* (Essex, England: Longman Scientific and Technical Publishers, 1991).

2. For example, the Potomac Conference, an organization of business and political leaders founded by the Greater Washington Board of Trade, convened

a conference in June 2003 addressing "the necessary ingredients for encouraging and growing successful technology partnerships among area businesses, universities and federal labs" ("Governors Warner, Ehrlich, Mayor Williams, Top Business, Academic Leaders Develop Strategy to Increase Technology Commercialization, Transform DC Region into Number One Tech Center in U.S.—Potomac Conference Convenes Region's Leaders to Develop Coordinated Plan," Press Release, http://www.bot.org/html/news/press/press_060302PotomacConference.asp, [accessed 4 September 2003]. The 2003–2004 New York State budget proposals of Republican governor George Pataki devoted a large portion of the more than $2 billion in economic development funds to high-tech projects, including $160 million to support a new computer-chip research-and-development facility ("Governor Unveils High-Tech Economic Development Plan," Press Release, New York State Office of Science, Technology, and Academic Research, http://www.nystar.state.ny.us/pr/devplan.htm, 4 September 2003]. Also see Mike Clenindin, "Shanghai Aims to Become China's Silicon Valley," *Electrical Engineering Times*, online edition (www.eetimes.com), 10 August 2001.

3. "Research-intensive scientific industry," "science-based industry," and "high technology" and "high-tech" will be terms used interchangeably. While the term "high-tech" was not in common usage during the early Cold War years, this book employs the term because of its familiarity to twenty-first-century readers. These terms follow the American Electronic Association's 2002 definition of "high-tech industry" in including 45 SIC classifications that fall into three general categories: high-technology manufacturing, communications services, and software- and computer-related services. See www.aeanet.org/Publications/IDMK_definition.asp (16 October 2002). I also use the term "advanced scientific industry"—a more common modifier during the 1950s and 1960s—to refer to this sector.

4. Other major studies of the transformation of research universities during the Cold War have focused on the "inside game." Feeding into larger scholarly debates about the role of scientists and other experts in postwar American politics, these authors have often reached differing conclusions about agency and influence in this process. Some have emphasized how federal policies imposed new and sweeping changes on university science that university administrators had little choice but to accept; others have countered by showing how university administrators were eager to take advantage of a lucrative opportunity and reconceived and reorganized their institutions accordingly. University-centered studies include Rebecca Lowen, *Creating the Cold War University: The Transformation of Stanford* (Berkeley and Los Angeles: University of California Press, 1997); Roger L. Geiger, *Research and Relevant Knowledge: American Research Universities since World War II* (New York: Oxford University Press, 1993); Stuart W. Leslie, *The Cold War and American Science: The Military-Industrial-Academic Complex at MIT and Stanford* (New York: Columbia University Press, 1993); Richard M. Freeland, *Academia's Golden Age: Universities in Massachusetts, 1945–1970* (New York: Oxford University Press, 1992). Works addressing the rise of the scientific expert include Jessica Wang, *American Science in an Age of Anxiety: Scientists, Anticommunism, and the Cold War* (Chapel Hill: University of North Carolina Press, 1999); Daniel J. Kevles, *The Physicists: The History of a Scientific Community in Modern America* (Cambridge, Mass.: Harvard University Press, 1995); Brian Balogh, *Chain Reaction: Ex-*

pert Debate and Public Participation in American Commercial Nuclear Power, 1945–1975 (New York: Cambridge University Press, 1991). For a useful review of the debate, see Balogh, *Chain Reaction,* 1–20.

5. In an era of shifting urban form, definitive classifications of "city" and "suburb" are elusive. This study—while ultimately arguing for a reconsideration of common presumptions about, and definitions of, the two types of settlement—defines "city" in the U.S. context following the 2000 U.S. Census Bureau definition of an "Urbanized Area Central Place," which is "an incorporated place or census designated place with the most population within an U[rban] A[rea]" (U.S. Department of Commerce, Bureau of the Census, *Census 2000 Geographic Terms and Concepts* [Washington, D.C.: U.S. Government Printing Office, 2002], A-23). A "suburb" is a settlement in an urban area that is (or has been at one point during its development) economically and culturally dependent on the core city. While a suburb is often located outside the political boundaries of the city, it can also refer to a neighborhood within city limits that shares spatial and demographic characteristics with suburbs. A useful definition is found in the *Columbia Encyclopedia*: "a community in an outlying section of a city or, more commonly, a nearby, politically separate municipality with social and economic ties to the central city" (*The Columbia Encyclopedia,* 7th ed. [New York: Columbia University Press, 2001]). There have long been many types of suburbs; the "affluent suburbs" that I argue are the primary homes for high-tech industry are places that I define as (1) having per capita incomes above the urban area average; (2) predominantly white-collar; (3) almost entirely Caucasian; and (4) predominantly residential prior to the arrival of high-tech industry.

6. John Seely-Brown, Foreword, *Understanding Silicon Valley: The Anatomy of an Entrepreneurial Region,* ed. Martin Kenney (Stanford, Calif.: Stanford University Press, 2000), xii. Also see John Seely Brown and Paul Duguid, "Mysteries of the Region: Knowledge Dynamics in Silicon Valley," in *The Silicon Valley Edge: A Habitat for Innovation and Entrepreneurship,* ed. Chong-Moon Lee, William F. Miller, Marguerite Gong Hancock, and Henry S. Rowen (Stanford, Calif.: Stanford University Press, 2000), 16–45; David P. Angel, "High-Technology Agglomeration and the Labor Market: The Case of Silicon Valley," and Stephen S. Cohen and Gary Fields, "Social Capital and Capital Gains: An Examination of Social Capital in Silicon Valley," both in Kenney, *Understanding Silicon Valley;* AnnaLee Saxenian, *Regional Advantage: Culture and Competition in Silicon Valley and Route 128* (Cambridge, Mass.: Harvard University Press, 1994); Markusen, Hall, and Glasmeier, *High Tech America;* Hall and Markusen, *Silicon Landscapes.*

7. These districts often have "silicon" in their names, ranging from "Silicon Desert" outside Phoenix, Arizona, to "Silicon Parkways" in both suburban New Jersey and suburban Connecticut. For a compendium of place names—from the well established to the colloquial—and their origins, see "Techvenue.com: Geographical 'Pet' Names," http://techvenue.com/siliconia.htm#top (9 June 2003). International examples range from the government of India's Software Technology Parks initiative, established in 1991, that played a central role in the development of high technology industry around Bangalore and Hyderabad (see "Infrastructure Special: Karnataka," *India Business Insight,* 28 April 2003) to the technology centers south of Dublin, north of Tel Aviv, and outside cities on the

Russian steppes ("Siberia's Silicon Valley," *Business 2.0,* April 2001; Eric Hellweg, "New Power Centers," *Business 2.0,* January 2000).

8. Max Weber's seminal essay "The Nature of the City" (1905), posits that a diversified and autonomous market economy is one of the fundamental characteristics that defines a city (Weber, *The City,* trans. and ed. by Don Martindale and Gertrud Neuwirth [Glencoe, Ill.: Free Press, 1958], 65–89). New work in urban history has demonstrated that postwar suburbs have long been more industrial and diverse than popular stereotypes, and that landscapes often derided as unplanned "suburban sprawl" were actually the products of deliberate planning. See in particular Robert O. Self, *American Babylon: Race and the Struggle for Postwar Oakland* (Princeton, N.J.: Princeton University Press, 2003), Greg Hise, *Magnetic Los Angeles: Planning the Twentieth-Century Metropolis* (Baltimore, Md.: Johns Hopkins University Press, 1997). Also see the *Journal of Urban History* special issue on these changing definitions (27:3 [2001]). For further discussion of the "new" cities and suburbs of the twenty-first century, see *Redefining Urban and Suburban America: Evidence from the 2000 Census,* ed. Bruce J. Katz and Robert E. Lang (Washington, D.C.: Brookings Institution Press, 2003). High technology regions also often are examples of what Robert E. Lang has dubbed "edgeless cities"—unbounded groupings of office space at the fringe of metropolitan areas (Lang, *Edgeless Cites: Exploring the Elusive Metropolis* [Washington, D.C.: Brookings Institution Press, 2003]).

9. In doing so, this study seeks to add to a growing literature on the domestic effects of the Cold War, and contribute new historical perspectives on the relationship between defense spending and economic policy. The role of economic and political concerns in national security strategy has generated a significant number of analyses by political scientists, including most recently David M. Hart, *Forged Consensus: Science, Technology, and Economic Policy in the United States, 1921–1953* (Princeton, N.J.: Princeton University Press, 1998). Also see *The Political Economy of Military Spending in the United States,* ed. Alex Mintz (London: Routledge, 1992); Mintz's introduction contains a useful short review of this literature to 1992 (1–14). Historians also have made important contributions to the understanding of the economic politics of the Cold War defense complex, notably Bruce Schulman, *From Cotton Belt to Sunbelt: Federal Policy, Economic Development, and the Transformation of the South, 1938–1980* (New York: Oxford University Press, 1991). The growing body of historical monographs on the domestic effects of the Cold War also include thoughtful studies of civil defense policy such as Laura McEnamey, *Civil Defense Begins at Home: Militarization Meets Everyday Life in the Fifties* (Princeton, N.J.: Princeton University Press, 2000) and Andrew D. Grossman, *Neither Dead Nor Red: Civil Defense and American Political Development During the Early Cold War* (New York: Routledge, 2001); and examinations of the effect of Cold War politics on political movements like civil rights, as explored in Mary Dudziak, *Cold War Civil Rights: Race and the Image of American Democracy* (Princeton, N.J.: Princeton University Press, 2000).

10. For the regional favoritism of military spending, see Schulman, *From Cotton Belt to Sunbelt;* Roger Lotchin, *Fortress California 1910–1961: From Warfare to Welfare* (Urbana: University of Illinois Press, 1992). For its economic consequences, see Ann Markusen, Peter Hall, Scott Campbell, and Sabrina District, *The Rise of the*

Gunbelt: The Military Remapping of Industrial America (New York: Oxford University Press, 1991); Anthony DiFilippo, *From Industry to Arms: The Political Economy of High Technology* (New York: Greenwood Press, 1990). Institutional influences are discussed in Cohen and Fields, "Social Capital and Capital Gains"; Christophe Lecuyer, "Making Silicon Valley: Engineering Culture, Innovation, and Industrial Growth, 1930–1970," Ph.D. diss., Stanford University, 1999; Robert Preer, *The Emergence of Technopolis: Knowledge-Intensive Technologies and Regional Development* (New York: Praeger Publishers, 1992). "Metropolitan-military complex" is a term used by Roger W. Lotchin in *Fortress California* as well as in *The Martial Metropolis: U.S. Cities in War and Peace*, ed. Lotchin (New York: Praeger Publishers, 1984).

11. American tax policy has been the pivotal "persuader" of this type. See Christopher Howard, *The Hidden Welfare State: Tax Expenditures and Social Policy in the United States* (Princeton, N.J., Princeton University Press, 1997); Thomas Hanchett, "U.S. Tax Policy and the Shopping-Center Boom of the 1950s and 1960s," *The American Historical Review* 101: 4 (October 1996), 1082–110.

12. Analyses of this connection can be found in *The Architecture of Science*, ed. Peter Galison and Emily Thompson (Cambridge, Mass.: MIT Press, 1999), whose essays explore the influence of scientific culture on architectural modernism and the way scientific function determined form. Examples of this architecture and discussion are found in Goodwin Steinberg, *From the Ground Up: Building Silicon Valley* (Stanford, Calif.: Stanford University Press, 2002).

13. See Thomas J. Sugrue, *Origins of the Urban Crisis: Race and Inequality in Postwar Detroit* (Princeton, N.J.: Princeton University Press, 1993); Douglas S. Massey and Nancy A. Denton, *American Apartheid: Segregation and the Making of the Underclass* (Cambridge, Mass.: Harvard University Press, 1993); *Urban Policy in Twentieth-Century America*, ed. Arnold R. Hirsch and Raymond A. Mohl (New Brunswick, N.J.: Rutgers University Press, 1993); Jon C. Teaford, *The Rough Road to Renaissance: Urban Revitalization in America, 1940–1985* (Baltimore, Md.: Johns Hopkins University Press, 1990); Carl Abbott, *The New Urban America: Growth and Politics in Sunbelt Cities*, rev. ed. (Chapel Hill: University of North Carolina Press, 1987); Kenneth T. Jackson, *The Crabgrass Frontier: The Suburbanization of the United States* (New York: Oxford University Press, 1985).

14. These local-level studies were inspired in part by, and seek to build upon, Arnold Hirsch's masterful *Making the Second Ghetto: Race and Housing in Chicago, 1940–1960* (New York: Cambridge University Press, 1983), which explored the urban renewal efforts of white business interests and institutions—notably the University of Chicago—in the largely black and poor South Side. While Hirsch documented how this university and its allies used urban renewal to attempt to halt the spread of poor black neighborhoods, these cases show how local actors worked not only to *prevent* social and economic change but also to *create* a new kind of settlement.

15. The Route 128–Silicon Valley comparison has been analyzed most thoroughly by Saxenian, *Regional Advantage*.

16. For discussion of the different national science and technology policy structures to the end of the twentieth century, see Daniel Lee Kleinman, *Politics on the Endless Frontier: Postwar Research Policy in the United States* (Durham, N.C.: Duke University Press, 1995), 158–71. For broader welfare state comparisons, see

Gösta Esping-Andersen, *The Three Worlds of Welfare Capitalism* (Princeton, N.J.: Princeton University Press, 1990), 221–29.

17. Market-driven tales of the triumphs of individual entrepreneurs tend to dominate popular narratives about the American high-tech industry. Similarly, the entrepreneur-centric mythology of high technology presumes that the market alone—not the government—determined the industry's geography. Examples of the entrepreneur-centered narratives include Michael Lewis, *The New New Thing* (New York: W.W. Norton, 2000); David A. Kaplan, *The Silicon Boys and Their Valley of Dreams* (New York: William Morrow and Company, 1999); Michael Malone, *The Big Score: The Billion-Dollar Story of Silicon Valley* (Garden City, N.Y.: Doubleday and Co., 1985). While many popular books and innumerable magazine and newspaper articles have been devoted to the rise of the Silicon Valley entrepreneur and the American high-tech corporation, these business journalists and popular chroniclers have paid little to no attention to the fact that these people and firms are almost always suburban in location. The low-density, decentralized, and economically homogeneous landscape of these places is mentioned in passing, as descriptive detail rather than the subject of investigative analysis.

18. Julian Zelizer rightly characterizes the postwar decades as ones of unprecedented state building (*Taxing America: Wilbur D. Mills, Congress, and the State, 1945–1975* [New York: Cambridge University Press, 1998]).

19. The complex interaction of multiple public and private interests traced in this discussion is a constantly shifting, multilateral policy-formation process that goes beyond what E. E. Schattschneider famously labeled the "iron triangle" of executive branch, legislative branch, and interest groups. Instead, it stands as a good example of Hugh Heclo's alternative conception of policy formation as "clouds of issue networks [that] overlay the once stable political reference points with new forces that complicate calculations, decrease predictability, and impose considerable strains on those charged with government leadership" ("Issue Networks and the Executive Establishment," in Anthony King, ed., *The New American Political System* [1st ed.] [Washington, D.C.: American Enterprise Institute, 1978]). An important review and analysis of the political science literature that addresses this topic is Paul Burstein, "Policy Domains: Organization, Culture, and Policy Outcomes," *Annual Review of Sociology* 17 (1991), 327–50. This study not only follows Heclo in arguing that policy making is a complex back-and-forth among multiple actors, but its examination of the intersections between urban spatial structure and Cold War spending patterns reinforces Burstein's observation that "public policy is also critically affected—indeed, created and given meaning—by culture" (346).

20. While the political debates of the end of the twentieth century focused on the more traditional and narrow definition of "welfare," limiting its definition to means-tested benefits like AFDC, new scholarship has approached welfare from what Esping-Andersen calls the "broader view" in which "issues of employment, wages, and overall macro-economic steering are considered integral components in the welfare-state complex" (*The Three Worlds of Welfare Capitalism* 2). This book hopes to build on these reconsiderations. They include Jennifer Klein, *For All These Rights: Business, Labor, and the Shaping of America's Public-Private Welfare State* (Princeton, N.J.: Princeton University Press, 2003); Jacob Hacker, *The Divided*

Welfare State: The Battle Over Public and Private Benefits in the United States (New York: Cambridge University Press, 2002); Michael B. Katz, *The Price of Citizenship: Redefining the American Welfare State* (New York: Metropolitan Books, 2001); Howard, *The Hidden Welfare State*.

21. See Hise, *Magnetic Los Angeles;* Self, *American Babylon*. For discussion of the West's influence on postwar urban landscapes, see John M. Findlay, *Magic Lands: Western Cityscapes and American Culture After 1940* (Berkeley and Los Angeles: University of California Press, 1992).

22. Daniel Bell, *The Coming of Post-Industrial Society: A Venture in Social Forecasting* (New York: Basic Books, 1973), 344. In *The Work of Nations: Preparing Ourselves for Twenty-First-Century Capitalism* (New York: Knopf, 1992), Robert B. Reich refers to these highly trained managerial and technical professionals as "symbolic-analytic workers."

Chapter 1
Cold War Politics

1. "Farewell Radio and Television Address to the American People," 17 January 1961, in *Dwight D. Eisenhower, Containing the Public Messages, Speeches, and Statements of the President, 1953–61* (Washington, D.C.: U.S. Government Printing Office, 1961).

2. Roger Geiger, *To Advance Knowledge: The Growth of American Research Universities, 1900–1940* (New York: Oxford University Press, 1986), 256. For further discussion of the origins of the National Research Council and federal involvement in prewar science, see pages 94–100 and 255–64.

3. Freeland, *Academia's Golden Age*, 84; see also Lowen, *Creating the Cold War University*.

4. For discussion of federal involvement in science prior to World War II, see Geiger, *To Advance Knowledge*, as well as Kevles, *The Physicists;* Walter A. McDougall, *The Heavens and the Earth: A Political History of the Space Age* (Baltimore, Md.: Johns Hopkins University Press, 1985); A. Hunter Dupree, *Science in the Federal Government: A History of Policies and Activities to 1940* (New York: Harper and Row, 1957).

5. The collaboration between the American university and American industry is long-standing and predates comparable relationships in other counties. Not only were important research institutions (Johns Hopkins University, University of Chicago) founded with generous donations from nineteenth-century industrialists, but the expansion of scientific disciplines in already established universities during this period was intended to respond to the needs of industrial capitalism. For further discussion of the prewar interaction between science and capitalism and the institutional growth of "expert" knowledge, see Olivier Zunz, *Why the American Century?* (Chicago: University of Chicago Press, 1998).

6. For discussion of prewar federal research policy, see Hart, *Forged Consensus*, 30–116. Industrial research was one element of the "managerial capitalism" explored by Alfred E. Chandler (*The Visible Hand: The Managerial Revolution in American Business* [Cambridge, Mass.: Harvard University Press, 1977]). Following Chandler, other studies have delved into the role of industrial research and the

importance of science to American commerce, including: David A. Hounshell and John Kenly Smith, Jr., *Science and Corporate Strategy: DuPont R&D, 1902–1980* (New York: Cambridge University Press, 1988); Leonard S. Reich, *The Making of American Industrial Research: Science and Business at GE and Bell, 1876–1926* (New York: Cambridge University Press, 1986); David Mowery, "The Emergence and Growth of Industrial Research in American Manufacturing, 1899–1945," Ph.D. diss., Stanford University, 1981.

7. Lowen, *Creating the Cold War University,* 18–26. For more on prewar university research practices, see Kevles, *The Physicists;* Galison and Hevly, *Big Science.* For a useful case study, see Richard S. Combes and William J. Todd, "From Henry Grady to the Georgia Research Alliance: A Case Study of Science-Based Development in Georgia," in *Science-Based Economic Development: Case Studies Around the World,* ed. Susan U. Raymond, *Annals of the New York Academy of Sciences* 798 (1996), 59–77.

8. Over the course of the war, the OSRD would fund "about 200 unpublicized weapons and secret modifications to military equipment" (Henry Gemmill, "Secret Weapons: Finding and Financing Them a $135 Million Job of Government OSRD," *Wall Street Journal,* 17 July 1945). The OSRD's short-lived predecessor agency was the National Defense Research Council, which performed similar duties.

9. Robert C. Wood, "Scientists and Politics: The Rise of an Apolitical Elite," in *Scientists and National Policy-Making,* ed. by Robert Gilpin and Christopher Wright (New York: Columbia University Press, 1964), 41–72.

10. Alsop and Alsop, *We Accuse! The Story of the Miscarriage of American Justice in the Case of J. Robert Oppenheimer* (New York: Simon and Schuster, 1954), 6.

11. Wang explores the political rifts in the scientific community and the wide range of scientific opinion about the validity and morality of the Cold War effort in *American Science in an Age of Anxiety.*

12. Eisenhower, Memorandum for Directors and Chiefs of War Department General and Special Staff Divisions and Bureaus, and the Commanding Generals of the Major Commands, 30 April 1946, FF6, Box 44, ELBP.

13. Truman, Address to Congress, 6 September 1945, quoted in *Appendix to Report from the Subcommittee on War Mobilization to the Committee on Military Affairs, United States Senate Pursuant to S. Res. 107 (78th Congress) and S. Res. 146 (79th Congress) Authorizing a Study of the Possibilities of Better Mobilizing the National Resources of the United States* (Washington, D.C.: U.S. Government Printing Office, December 1945), 1.

14. Allan Needell calls this new breed of scientists "science-statesman" ("From Military Research to Big Science: Lloyd Berkner and Science-Statesmanship in the Postwar Era," in *Big Science,* 290–311). Also see Wang, *American Science in an Age of Anxiety;* Kevles, *The Physicists;* Balogh, *Chain Reaction.*

15. For discussion, see Keith W. Olson, "The G.I. Bill and Higher Education: Success and Surprise," *American Quarterly* 25:5 (December 1973), 596–610.

16. Along with his many accomplishments in the political arena, Bush is celebrated among technology experts as "the father of hypertext" for a prescient 1945 article proposing "Memex," a device that would allow an easily configurable and logically linked system of electronic files (Bush, "As We May Think," *Atlantic Monthly,* July 1945).

17. Hoover's response to the Great Depression—in which he rejected the interventionist stimulus and public works strategies later adopted by his successor, Franklin Roosevelt—leaves him often characterized as more conservative than he actually was. While no liberal, Hoover was hardly a free-market conservative either, instead advocating associationalist strategies in which government agencies served to advise, inform, and provide incentives to private industry. See David M. Kennedy, *Freedom from Fear: The American People in Depression and War, 1929–1945* (New York: Oxford University Press, 1999), esp. 11–12, 43–50. Also see Ellis W. Hawley, "Herbert Hoover, the Commerce Secretariat, and the Vision of an 'Associative State,' 1921–1928," *Journal of American History* 61 (1974), 116–40.

18. Bush, *Science, The Endless Frontier* (Washington, D.C.: U.S. Government Printing Office, 1945), vi. In making this argument, Bush picked up not only on Hoover's imagery but on a powerful rhetorical strand of the "frontier" most famously articulated by historian Frederick Jackson Turner ("The Significance of the Frontier in American History" reprinted in *The Frontier in American History* [New York: Henry Holt and Co., 1921] 1893). Turner argued that the Western frontier was the major force shaping American civilization; the repeated process of creating a new culture from the "wilderness" of the West had been pivotal to the formation of a particularly American character—individualistic, rugged, and entrepreneurial. Turner's thesis subsequently has been revised, attacked, or amended, but the association of the concept of a "frontier" with the creation of some sort of collective cultural identity has been an enduring one in American popular culture ever since. The association of the culture-forming frontier with the West makes Bush's use of the idiom prescient, as much of the exploration of the frontier of scientific innovation would take place in the Western states, particularly California. See Martin Ridge, "The American West: From Frontier to Region," in Walter Nugent and Martin Ridge, eds., *The American West: The Reader* (Bloomington: Indiana University Press, 1999), 29.

19. G. Paschal Zachary, *Endless Frontier: Vannevar Bush, Engineer of the American Century* (New York: Free Press, 1997), 33. Bush was again picking up on earlier, widely circulated ideas. Economist Thorstein Veblen, most famous for coining the terms "leisure class" and "conspicuous consumption" also had prophesized in 1921 that "engineers would one day rule the U.S. economy" (Veblen paraphrased in Lewis, *The New New Thing*, 30). The meritocratic elitism expressed by Bush increasingly came to be incorporated into the design and function of American institutions. Standardized testing for university admissions (ostensibly accepting applicants on merit rather than wealth, race, or ethnicity) was one manifestation of this trend. See Nicholas Lemann, *The Big Test: The Secret History of the American Meritocracy* (New York: Farrar, Straus, and Giroux, 1999).

20. Vannevar Bush, "Science, Strength, and Stability," Address at Alumni Day Symposium on The Technology of International Peace, MIT, 8 June 1946, 5. Box 129, Vannevar Bush Papers, Library of Congress (henceforth VBP).

21. For detailed discussion of Kilgore's legislative efforts and analysis of the two very different political ideologies that underpinned the proposals put forward by Kilgore and by Bush, see Kleinman, *Politics on the Endless Frontier*, 74–99. Jewett remark is quoted on page 82. Also see Geiger, *Research and Relevant Knowledge*, 13–29.

244

NOTES TO CHAPTER ONE

22. *Preliminary Report on Science Legislation from the Subcommittee on War Mobilization to the Committee on Military Affairs, United States Senate Pursuant to S. Res. 107 (78th Congress) and S. Res. 146 (79th Congress) Authorizing a Study of the Possibilities of Better Mobilizing the National Resources of the United States* (Washington, D.C.: U.S. Government Printing Office, 1945) 3–4.

23. For further discussion of the civil rights battles of this period, see Gilbert C. Fite, *Richard B. Russell: Senator from Georgia* (Chapel Hill: University of North Carolina Press, 1991), 224–42; Robert Caro, *The Years of Lyndon Johnson: Master of the Senate* (New York: Alfred A. Knopf, 2002), 203–22.

24. See Richard Fried, *Nightmare in Red: The McCarthy Era in Perspective* (New York: Oxford University Press, 1990).

25. For further discussion and analysis of these political battles, see Neil Smith, *American Empire: Roosevelt's Geographer and the Prelude to Globalization* (Berkeley and Los Angeles: University of California Press, 2003), 427–35.

26. John Steelman, *Science and Public Policy: A Report to the president* (Washington, D.C.: U.S. Government Printing Office, 1947), 27. The American Association for the Advancement of Science, perhaps the most prominent professional association for scientists, had sounded a similar note in the proceedings of its 1944 meeting when it called for "scientific statesmanship" (quoted in L. K. Frank, "Research After the War: National Policy," *Science* 101 [27 April 1945], 433–34). The Association formally endorsed the idea of a National Science Foundation at the end of 1946 (*AAAS Resolution: Inter-Society Committee for a National Science Foundation*, December 29, 1946, http://archives.aaas.org/docs/resolutions.php?doc_id=231, August 18, 2003).

27. *Appendix to Report from the Subcommittee on War Mobilization*, 2.

28. *Appendix to Report from the Subcommittee on War Mobilization*, 12.

29. Statement of Edwin H. Land, *Hearings Before the Committee on Interstate and Foreign Commerce, House of Representatives, Eightieth Congress, First Session, on H.R. 942, H.R. 1815, H.R. 1830, H.R. 1834, and H.R. 2027, Bills Relating to the National Science Foundation, 6 and 7 March 1947* (Washington, D.C.: U.S. Government Printing Office, 1947), 143.

30. George H. Gallup, *The Gallup Poll, Public Opinion 1935–1971, Vol. 1* (New York: Random House, 1972), 534–35, 595–96.

31. *Economic Report of the President to Congress* (Washington, D.C.: U.S. Government Printing Office, 1950).

32. F. Russell Bichowsky, *Industrial Research* (Brooklyn: Chemical Publishing Co., 1942), iii.

33. Scott McCartney, *ENIAC: The Triumphs and Tragedies of the World's First Computer* (New York: Walker and Co., 1999). For further discussion of gender and the early "computer," see Jennifer Light, "When Computers Were Women," *Technology and Culture* 40: 3 (1999), 455–83.

34. Kleinman, *Politics on the Endless Frontier*, 179; RAND Corporation, "50 Years of Service to the Nation," www.rand.org/history (18 August 2003); Martin J. Collins, *Cold War Laboratory: RAND, the Air Force, and the American State, 1945–1950* (Washington, D.C.: Smithsonian Institution Press, 2002).

35. As Kleinman notes, the institutional exclusivity of the process was one thing that Kilgore sought to remedy with his science legislation. Instead, the

version of the NSF that eventually passed served to reinforce the power of top institutions. For discussion of the role of Harvard and MIT scientists and administrators in the process, see Kevles, *The Physicists*; Leslie, *The Cold War and American Science*; and G. Paschal Zachary's biography of MIT alumnus and Harvard administrator Bush, *Endless Frontier: Vannevar Bush, Engineer of the American Century* (New York: Free Press, 1997).

36. The Washington staff person hired for the position was Thomas J. Spragens, at the time an official with the Foreign Economics Administration who was planning a civil service career; after taking this post, Spragens spent the rest of his life as an academic administrator and college president. Stanford's investment in Spragens quickly paid off; in 1946 the University secured ownership of a nearby military surplus property, Dibble General Hospital, and turned the facility into much-needed student and family housing. Edwin Kiester, Jr., *Donald B. Tresidder, Stanford's Overlooked Treasure: A Biography of the University's Fourth President* (Stanford, Calif.: Stanford Historical Society, 1992), 70–74.

37. Alf Brandin, interview by Robert Moulton, 9 August 1985, "Remembering Wallace Sterling," Stanford Oral History Project, SUA.

38. As Neil Smith observes, "it left the political direction of science policy in the hands of science elites, who could reject any challenge as politically motivated" (*American Empire*, 434). For further discussion, see Smith as well as Hart, *Forged Consensus*, 174–205; Kleinman, *Politics on the New Frontier*, 101–44.

39. "92 Atom-Bomb Targets for Russia in U.S.," *U.S. News and World Report*, 7 October 1949, 16–17.

40. Vannevar Bush, draft of report to the president on "OSRD in the War," undated, probably October 1945, Box 139, VBP.

41. The debate and passage of the National Security Act was a critical moment in the negotiations around the extent of centralized state control in general, and military control in particular, that marked the early Cold War decades. As Michael J. Hogan demonstrates, the National Security Act was passed only after a long debate about the "specter of the garrison state" posed by such a far-reaching security, and the administrative structure outlined by the final legislation reflected these concerns by retaining a good deal of civilian control of these new institutions (*A Cross of Iron: Harry S. Truman and the Origins of the National Security State, 1945–1954* [New York: Cambridge University Press, 1998], 23–68).

42. Arthur M. Hill, "Before—Not After," *Reserve Officer Magazine*, October 1948.

43. *P.L. 413, the Armed Services Procurement Act of 1947*, Senate Report No. 571 (80th Congress), 13. Quoted in John Steelman, Letter to Robert W. Jones, March 28, 1949, FF 300.4, Box 12, Entry 30, RG 304, NARA. The provision of P.L. 413 to which the report referred was section 2(c)(16).

44. Referred to in Department of Defense Directive 5220.3 on Industrial Dispersion Policy, 11 September 1951, reprinted in Armed Services Committee, U.S. Senate, *Hearings Before a Subcommittee of the Armed Services Committee on S. 500, S. 1383, and S. 1875*, 86th Congress, 1st Session, 13–31, July 1959 (Washington, 1959), 219.

45. Joint Economic Committee, *The Need for Industrial Dispersal* (Washington, D.C.: U.S. Government Printing Office, 1951), 3.

46. E.O. 10172, *Federal Register* 15 (17 October 1950), 6929.

47. Joint Economic Committee, *The Need for Industrial Dispersal*, 3.

48. National Security Resources Board quoted in "Factory Dispersal for National Security and Rational Town Planning," *The American City* 53:9 (September 1948), 5.

49. Ebenezer Howard, *Garden Cities of To-Morrow* (Cambridge, Mass.: MIT Press, 1965), first published in 1898 under the title *To-morrow: A Peaceful Path to Real Reform*.

50. Catherine Bauer Wurster quoted in Hise, *Magnetic Los Angeles*, 45.

51. Clarence Stein, Memo, June 20, 1940, FF "FWA Defense Housing Reports, 1940–41," Box 103, (John) Carmody Papers, Franklin Delano Roosevelt Presidential Library, quoted in Hise 49–50.

52. Augur, "The Dispersal of Cities—A Feasible Program," *The Bulletin of the Atomic Scientists* 4:10 (October 1948), 315.

53. "Architects Discuss Atomic-Age Building Implications," *The American City* 64:4 (April 1949), 97. Other leading proponents of dispersion were Lewis Mumford and his former protg Catherine Bauer Wurster.

54. " 'Fringe' Cities: Answer to A-Bomb: Blueprints Call for Spreading of Big Centers," *U.S. News and World Report*, 7 October 1949, 18–19.

55. "CIO Urges Regional Development and Urban Decentralization," *The American City* 65:1 (January 1950), 101.

56. Paul Opperman, Address to Businessman's Conference on Urban Problems, 20 November 1950, excerpted in *The American City* 66:1 (January 1951), 7. In his study of postwar growth and politics in Oakland, California, Robert Self describes how the city's business establishment spearheaded a decentralized, "industrial garden" strategy of economic growth (Self, *American Babylon*, chap. 1).

57. "New Book Urges Dispersion," *The American City* 64:6 (June 1949), 131.

58. "Dispersion of Large Cities," *Journal of the Franklin Institute* 248:1 (July 1949), 103.

59. See Sugrue, *The Origins of the Urban Crisis*. Bennett Harrison and Barry Bluestone examine the "sunset" of certain industries and the "sunrise" of others, and the technological and economic reasons behind these changes, in *The Deindustrialization of America* (New York: Basic Books, 1982). For further discussion of changing transportation technology, see Mark Rose, *Interstate: Express Highway Politics, 1939–1989* (Knoxville: University of Tennessee Press, 1990 [rev. ed.]); Martin V. Melosi, "Cities, Technical Systems, and the Environment," *Environmental History Review* 14 (Spring–Summer 1990), 45–64. Traditional industrial-location theory emphasizes the importance of transportation, land, and labor costs in location decisions. Alfred Weber's seminal work, *Theory of the Location of Industry* (Chicago: University of Chicago Press, 1929) finds transportation to be the leading factor with labor costs and agglomeration forces also bearing on location. For discussion of air-conditioning and additional reasons Americans moved to the Sunbelt, see Jackson, *The Crabgrass Frontier*, as well as the collected *Essays on Sunbelt Cities and Recent Urban America*, ed. Robert B. Fairbanks and Kathleen Underwood (College Station: Texas A&M University Press, 1990).

60. The increased African American presence in Northern cities resulted in violent white resistance and in the increased political conservatism of working-

class whites (who, after Ronald Reagan's decisive 1980 presidential victory derived significant support from white ethnics, would be famously categorized as "Reagan Democrats"). White violence is described in Sugrue, *Origins of the Urban Crisis*, 231–58; Hirsch, *Making the Second Ghetto*, 171–211. School desegregation and busing were a galvanizing force for the growth of working-class white conservatism, as discussed in Jonathan Rieder, *Canarsie: The Jews and Italians of Brooklyn Against Liberalism* (Cambridge, Mass.: Harvard University Press, 1985). The economic and social consequences of the isolation of poor blacks in central-city neighborhoods after white wealth and jobs had fled to the suburbs is chronicled in William Julius Wilson, *When Work Disappears: The World of the New Urban Poor* (New York: Knopf, 1996) and Massey and Denton, *American Apartheid*.

61. For discussion of highway programs and financing, and the spatial consequences for cities, see Rose, *Interstate*, 29–84; Jackson, *Crabgrass Frontier*, 246–71. For in-depth discussion of tax incentives for suburban commercial construction (a topic explored further in the next chapter), see Hanchett, "U.S. Tax Policy and the Shopping Center Booms of the 1950s and 1960s." The suburban bias of infrastructure provision is discussed in Myron Orfield, *Metropolitics* (Washington, D.C.: Brookings Institution Press, 1997).

62. For discussion of prewar efforts related to affordable housing and neighborhood redevelopment, see Gail Radford, *Modern Housing for America: Policy Struggles in the New Deal Era* (Chicago: University of Chicago Press, 1996). For discussion of reform in Philadelphia, see John F. Bauman, *Public Housing, Race, and Renewal: Urban Planning in Philadelphia, 1920–1974* (Philadephia: University of Pennsylvania Press, 1987).

63. Philadelphia Redevelopment Authority, *1946 Annual Report* (Philadelphia, 1946), 5, Redevelopment Authority file, A-448, RG 60–2.2, PCA.

64. N. S. Keith, Memorandum to Raymond Foley, 15 February 1951, Box 2, HHFA Administrator's Files, RG 207, NARA.

65. An important recent monograph discussing these various political currents is Hogan, *Cross of Iron*.

66. Ralph L. Garrett, "Summary of Studies of Public Attitudes Toward and Information about Civil Defense, Research Report No. 8, Department of Defense, Office of Civil Defense, August 1963. Box 2, RG 397, Entry 6, NARA.

67. A particularly useful analysis of the development and implementation of the civil defense program—which treats it with the seriousness it deserves and properly contextualizes it within postwar American political development—is Grossman, *Neither Dead Nor Red*.

68. 24 February 1951, Gallup, *The Gallup Poll*, 967–68.

69. Harry S. Truman, Memorandum and Statement of Policy on the Need for Industrial Dispersion, 10 August 1951, *Public Papers of the Presidents of the United States, January 1 to December 31, 1951* (Washington, D.C.: U.S. Government Printing Office, 1965), no. 189. Further quotes, as indicated, are from the same source.

70. National Security Resources Board, *Is Your Plant a Target?* (Washington, D.C.: U.S. Government Printing Office, 1951).

71. Paraphrase of *Washington Post* editorial, 30 August 1951, in internal "Daily News Summary," Office of Public Information, Office of Secretary of Defense, RG 330, Entry 137, Box 568, NARA.

72. Department of Commerce, Office of Industry and Commerce, "Industrial Dispersion Guidebook for Communities" (Washington, D.C.: U.S. Government Printing Office, 1952).

73. DOD Directive 3005.3, 7 December 1954 and DOD Directive 4005.13, 27 March 1958 reprinted in Armed Services Committee, U.S. Senate, *Hearings Before a Subcommittee of the Armed Services Committee, U.S. Senate on S. 500, S. 1383, and S. 1875*, 86th Congress, 1st Session, 13–31 July 1959 (Washington, 1959), 252–53, and 255–57. Quotation on p. 257.

74. "Revised National Dispersion Policy," *Area Development Bulletin*, December 1955–January 1956, 4. Box 1, Accession 66A2584, RG 378, NARA.

75. Statement of Dr. Arthur S. Flemming, Director, Office of Defense Mobilization, at a Hearing on Operations and Policies of the Civil Defense Program Before the Subcommittee on Civil Defense of the Committee on Armed Services, United States Senate, 84th Congress, 1st Session, 22 February 1955.

76. "Applying Dispersion Criteria to Rapid Tax Amortization Applications," *Area Development Bulletin*, October–November 1956, Box 1, Accession 66A2584, RG 378, NARA. This tax policy complemented a policy of "accelerated depreciation" written into the tax code in 1954, under which commercial and industrial enterprises could rapidly write off the costs of new construction, a policy that, as Thomas Hanchett argues, prompted a rapid increase in the development of shopping centers and large retail developments on the suburban periphery. See Hanchett, "U.S. Tax Policy and the Shopping-Center Boom of the 1950s and 1960s," *The American Historical Review* 101:4 (October 1996), 1082–110.

77. One example of this lower-level bureaucratic reinforcement is a Defense Department memorandum reminding its regional directors that industrial dispersion remained a criterion for contract awards. V. Couch, Assistant Director for Industrial Participation, Office of Civil Defense, Draft Memorandum for all Regional Directors, Office of Civil Defense on Industrial Participation-Continuing Assignments and Projects, 21 June 1963, Box 5, RG 397, Entry 6, NARA.

78. Electronics Division, Business and Defense Services Administration, U.S. Department of Commerce, Memorandum on "The Electronics Industry—Factors in Selecting Plant Locations—Methods for Approaching Industry," 23 August 1956, Box 3, Accession 66A2584, RG 378, NARA. Calculating dispersion's "success" or "failure" is difficult not only because of the policy and market context in which it was implemented but also (and most signicantly) because of a lack of further narrative or statistical data on dispersion's effects in federal records. The federal government did not gather (or retain in its archives) firm-level data that indicated the degree to which contractors decentralized as a consequence of dispersion-related incentives. What is clear from federal reports like this one, however, is that federal officials believed that dispersion was a factor in location decisions of electronics companies and other smaller and more footloose suppliers of scientific equipment.

79. National Science Foundation, *Funds for Research and Development in Industry, 1957* (Washington, D.C.: U.S. Government Printing Office, 1957), 7, 12.

80. Oliver J. Greenway [Vice President of International Resistance Co, Philadelphia], "Dispersal Is More than Defense Against Disaster," *SIGNAL* (official

journal of the Armed Forces Communications and Electronics Association), May–June 1955, Box 3, Accession 66A2584, RG 378, NARA.

81. Lizabeth Cohen, *A Consumers' Republic: The Politics of Mass Consumption in Postwar America* (New York: Knopf, 2003). For an illustration of the relation of changing modes of consumption and shopping patterns to metropolitan decentralization, see Stephanie Dyer, "Markets in the Meadows: Department Stores and Shopping Centers in the Decentralization of Philadelphia, 1920–1980," Ph.D. diss., University of Pennsylvania, 2000.

82. "Revised National Dispersion Policy."

83. Greenway, "Dispersal Is More than Defense Against Disaster."

84. National Science Foundation, *Annual Report, 1950–51*, 2.

85. National Science Foundation, *Federal Funds for Research and Development and Other Scientific Activities* (Washington, D.C.: U.S. Government Printing Office, 1972), 3.

86. Freeland, *Academia's Golden Age*, 91.

87. "Dangerous Neglect," *Time* 65 (18 April 1955), 54.

88. "Research and Development in the Government," a report to the Congress by the Commission on Organization of the Executive Branch of the Government, May 1955, p. xii, quoted in *Federal Budgeting for Research and Development: Hearings Before the Subcommittee on Reorganization and International Organizations or the Committee on Government Operations*, United States Senate, July 26 and 27, 1961 (Washington, D.C.: U.S. Government Printing Office, 1961), 99.

89. McDougall, *The Heavens and the Earth*, 142.

90. Robert C. Cowen, "President Talks on Research," *The Christian Science Monitor*, 15 May 1959.

91. *Scientific Progress, the Universities, and the Federal Government*, Statement by the President's Scientific Advisory Committee, 15 November 1960 (Washington: U.S. Government Printing Office, 1960), 11.

92. "Science and the State," *Time*, 25 May 1959; John T. Wilson, *Academic Science, Higher Education and the Federal Government, 1950–1983* (Chicago: University of Chicago Press, 1983), 45.

93. These figures include expenditures within government agencies, in associated federally funded R&D centers, and grants to industry, universities, and nonprofit institutions. U.S. Census Bureau, *Statistical Abstract of the United States 1970* (Washington, D.C.: U.S. Government Printing Office, 1970), 519.

94. *Scientific Progress, the Universities, and the Federal Government*, 5.

95. Ibid., 5.

96. Ibid., 14.

97. Barbara Barksdale Clowse, *Brainpower for the Cold War: The Sputnik Crisis and National Defense Education Act of 1958* (Westport, Conn.: Greenwood Press, 1981), 105.

98. "Why the White House Worries," *Business Week*, 27 January 1962, 82–83. Clowse notes the preponderance of articles on this topic that came out in large-circulation periodicals in the fall and winter of 1957–58, including: "US Change of Mind," *Life*, 3 March 1958, 91 and 96; "The Changing Mood in America," *US News and World Report*, 20 Dec 1957, 42–59; and "The New Mood" *Time*, 3 March 1958, 39.

99. Wilson, *Academic Science, Higher Education and the Federal Government*, 45.

100. Quoted in ibid., 43.

101. Health, Education, and Welfare Secretary Wilbur E. Cohen, 1968, quoted in Clowse, *Brainpower for the Cold War*, 147. The NDEA was a great boon, but it also stirred great controversy, as one of its provisions was that recipients sign not only a loyalty oath to the U.S. government but an affidavit "disclaiming membership or belief in the aims of subversive organizations" (Wilson, *Academic Science, Higher Education and the Federal Government*, 46). Aghast at this requirement, which brought back ugly memories of the still recent McCarthy era, many scholars refused to sign the oath, and a number of prominent institutions refused to accept any NDEA money until the provision was dropped. In 1961, the loyalty oath was modified and diluted into a more palatable form, thus quieting the controversy. The NDEA loyalty oath controversy was but the first in a long series of public and private struggles between the federal government and the academy, as scholars and universities tried to keep institutions that were increasingly dependent on federal money independent from political control. For further discussion and analysis of the implications to the twenty-first century university, see David A. Hollinger, "Money and Academic Freedom a Half-Century after McCarthyism: Universities Amid the Force Fields of Capital," in *Unfettered Expression: Freedom in American Intellectual Life*, ed. Peggie J. Hollingsworth (Ann Arbor: University of Michigan Press, 2001), 161–84, and Michael B. Katz, *Reconstructing American Education* (Cambridge, Mass.: Harvard University Press, 1987), chap. 6.

102. Terman, "Engineering and Scientific Manpower for the Cold War—The Next Decade," paper presented at the President's Scientific Advisory Council's Manpower Panel, 21 April 1962, FF 66, Box 1, Series X, SC160, SUA. Also see President's Science Advisory Committee, *Meeting Manpower Needs in Science and Technology, Report Number One: Graduate Training in Engineering, Mathematics, and Physical Sciences*, 12 December 1962 (Washington, D.C.: U.S. Government Printing Office, 1962), 1.

103. Testimony of Earl D. Hilburn, Deputy Assistant Administrator for Industry Affairs, NASA, *Government and Science: Distribution of Federal Research Funds; Indirect Costs re Federal Grants*, Hearing before the Subcommittee on Science, Research, and Development of the Committee on Science and Astronautics, U.S. House of Representatives, 88th Congress, Second Session, May 5, 1964, 34.

104. Higher Education Facilities Act of 1963, PL 88–204.

105. National Institutes of Health cited in Herbert H. Rosenberg, Letter to University of Pennsylvania President Gaylord P. Harnwell, 2 April 1962, FF "United States Government—HEW, 1960–65," Box 149, UPA 4, UPA.

106. Testimony of William H Steward, Asst. to Spec. Asst. to the Secretary of Health, Education, and Welfare, 6 May 1964, in *Government and Science: Distribution of Federal Research Funds; Indirect Costs re Federal Grants*, Hearing before the Subcommittee on Science, Research, and Development of the Committee on Science and Astronautics, U.S. House of Representatives, 88th Congress, Second Session (Washington, D.C.: Government Printing Office, 1964), 112.

107. "Health Facility Construction," *Health, Education, and Welfare Indicators*, September 1962, FF "Health Facilities Construction," Box 1, Accession 68A5470, RG 40, NARA.

108. This was authorized under Section 203 (k) of the Federal Property and Administrative Services Act of 1949. Description of program and eligibility found in Stephen L. Simonian, Regional Representative, Division of Surplus Property Utilization, Department of HEW, Letter to Gaylord P. Harnwell, 23 March 1965, FF "United States Government—HEW, 1960–65," Box 149, UPA 4, UPA.

109. James Killian, *Sputniks, Scienctists, and Eisenhower: A Memoir of the First Special Assistant to the President for Science and Technology* (Cambridge, Mass.: MIT Press, 1977), 39.

110. *Satellites, Science, and the Public* (Ann Arbor: Survey Research Center, Institute for Social Research, University of Michigan, 1959), 32.

111. *Scientific and Technical Manpower: Supply, Demand, and Utilization*, staff study prepared for the Committee on Science and Astronautics, U.S. House of Representatives, 87th Congress, 2nd Session, September 13, 1962 (Washington, D.C.: U.S. Government Printing Office, 1963), 5. Discussions of the lack of racial and gender diversity in science and technology during the 1950s and 1960s rarely acknowledged that women and minorities were given scant opportunities to pursue scientific careers and in fact were often discouraged from doing so. See Margaret W. Rossiter, *Women Scientists in America: Before Affirmative Action, 1940–1972* (Baltimore, Md.: Johns Hopkins University Press, 1995); Vivian O. Sammons, *Blacks in Science and Medicine* (New York: Hemisphere Publishing Corp., 1990); Willie Pearson Jr., and H. Kenneth Bechtel, eds., *Blacks, Science, and American Education* (New Brunswick, N.J.: Rutgers University Press, 1989). College enrollments (and graduation rates) in general were much higher for men than for women (*Higher Education in the Sciences in the United States*, Report of the Subcommittee on Science, Research, and Development of the Committee on Science and Astronautics, U.S. House of Representatives, 89th Congress, 1st Session, Prepared by the National Science Foundation, Serial I [Washington, D.C.: U.S. Government Printing Office, 1965], 17).

112. U.S Congress, Senate, Committee on Foreign Relations, Inquiry into Satellite and Missile Programs, *Hearing before the Preparedness Investigating Subcommittee of the Committee on Armed Services*, 85th Congress, 1st session, November 1957, quoted in Clowse, *Brainpower for the Cold War*, 60.

113. Kevles, *The Physicists*, 383.

114. William H. Whyte, *The Organization Man* (New York: Simon & Schuster, 1956), 214.

115. This was particularly true of the space program. See James Kauffman, *Selling Outer Space: Kennedy, the Media, and Funding for Project Apollo, 1961–63* (Tuscaloosa: University of Alabama Press, 1994).

116. The honored scientists were Linus Pauling, I. I. Rabi, Edward Teller, Joshua Lederberg, Donald Glaser, Robert Woodward, Charles Stark Draper, William Shockley, Emilio Segre, John Enders, Charles Townes, George Beadle, James Van Allen, Edward Purcell, and Willard Libby. "Men of the Year," *Time* 77:1 (2 January 1961), 40–46.

117. Robert C. Wood, "Scientists and Politics: The Rise of an Apolitical Elite," 58, 60.

118. *Science Education in the Schools of the United States*, Report of the National Science Foundation to the Subcommittee on Science, Research, and Develop-

ment of the Committee on Science and Astronautics, U.S. House of Representatives, 89th Congress, 1st Session, Serial D (Washington, D.C.: U.S. Government Printing Office, 1965), 20.

119. Freeland, *Academia's Golden Age*, 91; Murphy, *Science, Geopolitics, and Federal Spending*, 9–10. The National Science Foundation published annual reports ranking top university grantees; see for example National Science Foundation, *Federal Support of Research and Development at Universities and Colleges and Selected Nonprofit Institutions, Fiscal Year 1968*, NSF 69–33, 15–17.

120. U.S. Congress, House Committee on Armed Services, *Hearings on Military Posture and H.R. 4016*, 89th Congress, 1st Session, 1965, 159, cited by Thomas P. Murphy, "Political Economy and Geographic Distribution of Federal Funds for R&D: The Midwest Case," in Murphy, *Science, Geopolitics, and Federal Spending*, 64.

121. As Schulman has shown, certain powerful legislators, particularly those from under-industrialized Southern and Southwestern states, were aggressive in courting the location of federal research facilities and military bases in their districts (*From Cotton Belt to Sunbelt*, esp. 135–73). Lyndon Johnson, for example, was particularly successful in winning defense and space agency contracts (as well as other large expenditures like highways) for Texas while he led the U.S. Senate. But Johnson and others seem to have paid little attention to regional equity in university research programs during this period, although Johnson would become a strong advocate for more equitable distribution of research dollars after he became president. For further examination of Johnson's activities in this regard and the tactics of persuasion that became known as the "Johnson treatment," see the third installment of Caro's comprehensive Johnson biography, *Master of the Senate*, esp. 589–90.

122. The particular effect that World War II and the Cold War had upon California metropolitan areas is richly explored in Lotchin, *Fortress California*. Also see Gerald D. Nash, *The American West Transformed: The Impact of the Second World War* (Bloomington: Indiana University Press, 1985).

123. Text of Address by Dr. J. Herbert Holloman at the Governor's Conference, Miami Beach, FL, July 22, 1963. FF "Civilian Technology," Box 1, Accession 68A5470 (Office of Science and Technology, Science and Technology Research File, 1962–1970), RG 40, NARA. Also see Paul J. Grogan, Statement before the Special Subcommittee on Scientific Manpower Utilization of the Senate Committee on Labor and Public Welfare, 26 January 1967, Box 2, Accession 76–4, RG 40, NARA.

124. *Obligations for Research and Development, and R&D Plant, by Geographic Divisions and States, by Selected Federal Agencies, Fiscal Years 1961–1964*, Report to the Subcommittee on Science, Research, and Development of the Committee on Science and Astronautics, U.S. House of Representatives, 88th Congress, 2nd Session (Washington: GPO, 1964), 11. The fact that the Subcommittee requested this report from the NSF attests to growing political concern about the distribution of R&D money.

125. Introduction, *Government and Science: Distribution of Federal Research Funds; Indirect Costs re Federal Grants. Hearing before the Subcommittee on Science, Research, and Development of the Committee on Science and Astronautics*, U.S. House of Representatives, 88th Congress, Second Session, May–June 1964 (Washington, D.C.: Government Printing Office, 1964), 1.

126. Daniel S. Greenberg, "R&D Boom: House Report Sees Harm to Higher Education," *Science* 150 (22 October 1965), 464–66.

127. *Government and Science*, 15.

128. Quoted in "Monopoly in Federal Research?" Editorial, *Philadelphia Evening Bulletin*, 2 July 1965.

Chapter 2
"Multiversities," Cities, and Suburbs

1. Clark Kerr, *The Uses of the University* (Cambridge, Mass.: Harvard University Press, 1963: New York: Harper & Row, 1966), 49.

2. Ibid., 89.

3. Ibid., 41, 125.

4. Henry Steele Commager, "Is Ivy Necessary?" *Saturday Review*, 17 September 1960, 89, quoted in Martin Klotsche, *The Urban University and the Future of Our Cities* (New York: Harper and Row, 1966), 22.

5. Paul V. Turner writes that "the romantic notion of a college in nature, removed from the corrupting forces of the city, became an American ideal" (*Campus: An American Planning Tradition* [Cambridge, Mass.: MIT Press, 1984], 3 and 4).

6. Ibid., 101.

7. Thomas Bender calls this "a major deviation from the central theme of the history of universities" (Introduction to *The University and the City: From Medieval Origins to the Present*, ed. Bender [New York: Oxford University Press, 1988], 3).

8. For discussion of the rise of machine politics in the context of nineteenth-century political economy, see Amy Bridges, *A City in the Republic: Antebellum New York and the Origins of Machine Politics* (New York: Cambridge University Press, 1984). For a revisionist perspective on late nineteenth-century municipal corruption, see Jon C. Teaford, *The Unheralded Triumph: City Government in America, 1870–1900* (Baltimore, Md.: Johns Hopkins University Press, 1984).

9. Turner, *Campus*, 4. For comparisons to Europe, see Herman van der Wusten, "A Warehouse of Precious Goods: The University in Its Urban Context," in *The Urban University and Its Identity: Roots, Location, Roles*, ed. Herman van der Wusten (Dordecht: Kluwer Academic Publishers, 1998), 1–13.

10. John O. Merrill, Skidmore, Owings and Merrill, "The Urban Campus," *Urban Land* 25:11 (November 1966), 3–4.

11. Robert E. Boley, "Industrial Districts Restudied: An Analysis of Characteristics" Urban Land Institute Technical Bulletin no. 41 (Washington, D.C., 1961), 18.

12. "Industrial Park: What It Is, What It Isn't," *Nation's Business* 57 (September 1969), 72. The separation of industry from residential areas was a primary goal of the first systematic zoning initiatives, which local officials implemented in many major U.S. cities beginning in the 1910s and 1920s. For discussion of the early zoning movement, see M. Christine Boyer, *Dreaming the Rational City: The Myth of American City Planning* (Cambridge, Mass.: Harvard University Press, 1983).

13. Robert Kargon, Stuart Leslie, and Erica Schoenberger, "Far Beyond Big Science: Science Regions and the Organization of Research and Development," in *Big Science: The Growth of Large-Scale Research*, 338.

14. Ibid.

15. Schulman, *From Cotton Belt to Sunbelt*; Lotchin, *Fortress California*.

16. "Manufacturing Employment in Metropolitan Areas, 1947–1954" *Area Development Bulletin,* October–November 1956, Box 1, Accession 66A2584, RG 378, NARA.

17. George I. Whitlanch and Winfred G. Dodson, *Industrial Sites: Their Selection and Development* (Atlanta: Industrial Development Division, Engineering Experiment Station, Georgia Institute of Technology, 1968), 29.

18. William Bredo, *Industrial Estates: Tool for Industrialization* (Menlo Park, Calif.: Stanford Research Institute, 1960), 11.

19. Bredo, *Industrial Estates,* 12.

20. The "representational" prewar districts profiled by the Urban Land Institute in its survey by Robert E. Boley, *Industrial Districts: Principles in Practice* (Washington, D.C.: Urban Land Institute, 1962) all were products of these sorts of private consortia.

21. For discussion of accelerated depreciation in particular, see Hanchett, "U.S. Tax Policy and the Shopping Center Boom." For discussion of tax policies more generally, see Howard, *The Hidden Welfare State.*

22. Congressional Budget Office, *Real Estate Tax Shelter Subsidies and Direct Subsidy Alternatives* (Washington, D.C., 1977), 22. The Tax Reform Act of 1969 substantially reduced allowable rates of accelerated depreciation for commercial and industrial buildings, but continued to allow these measures for rental housing.

23. For further analysis and examples of how these various tax structures encouraged suburbanization, see Self, *American Babylon,* chapter 3.

24. *A Report on the Dartmouth College Conference on Industrial Parks,* prepared by William Lee Baldwin, sponsored by Arthur D. Little, Inc., and the State of New Hampshire, June 1958, 27, quoted in Robert E. Boley, "Industrial Districts Restudied: An Analysis of Characteristics," Urban Land Institute Technical Bulletin No. 41 (Washingtony D.C., 1961), 10.

25. "Is There a Trend to Suburban Sites for Office Buildings?" *Area Development Bulletin* (published by the Office of Area Development, U.S. Department of Commerce), December 1957–January 1958, 4. The statistic cited in this report regarding the pace of central business-district construction was reported originally in "Trends in Office Location," *Tax Policy,* September–October 1957.

26. As Peter S. Reed argues, the wartime experience also popularized modernist architecture and created highly replicable forms of it, like the ubiquitous wartime Quonset Hut ("Enlisting Modernism," in *World War II and the American Dream: How Wartime Building Changed a Nation,* ed. Donald Albrecht [Washington, D.C.: National Building Museum, 1995], 2–41).

27. For discussion, see Peter Galison and Caroline A. Jones, "Factory, Laboratory, Studio: Dispersing Sites of Production," in *The Architecture of Science,* ed. Galison and Thompson, 497–540.

28. Operating without retrofits could severely compromise production. The Eckert-Mauchly Computer Company, founded in the late 1940s by the developers of the nation's first supercomputer, faced severe competitive disadvantages partly as a result of the challenge of fabricating computers in an un-air-conditioned warehouse in Philadelphia. McCartney, *ENIAC.*

29. Charles Haines, "Planning the Scientific Laboratory" (1950), reprinted in *Buildings for Research: An Architectural Record Publication* (New York: F. W. Dodge, Inc., 1958).

30. T. K. Pasma, *Characteristics of 63 Modern Industrial Plants*, (Washington, D.C.: U.S. Department of Commerce, 1966), cited in Whitlanch and Dodson, *Industrial Sites*, 29.

31. Paul A. Groves, "Towards a Typology of Intrametropolitan Manufacturing Location: A Case Study of the San Francisco Bay Area," University of Hull Occasional Papers in Geography no. 16, 1971, 71.

32. Klotsche, *The Urban University and the Future of our Cities*, 85, paraphrasing John Fischer, "Money Bait," *Harper's Magazine*, September 1961, 12.

33. A case in point, which will be discussed more extensively in chapter 3, is Stanford University's Industrial Park, which charged significantly higher rents to its tenants in exchange for a carefully landscaped and regulated industrial park that had the cachet of Stanford's name.

34. George A Dudley, "Problems of a Physical Environment," Remarks to New York State Symposium on "Research and the Community," 1 May 1961, Sterling Forest, New York, FF "State Science and Technology Conference," Box 1, Accession 76–4, RG 40, NARA.

35. As early as the 1960 Census, there was evidence that scientific and technical workers were markedly more mobile than other professionals. See Jack Ladinsky, "Occupational Determinants of Geographic Mobility among Professional Workers," *American Sociological Review* 32:2 (April 1967), 253–64. William H. Whyte also points out that higher education levels correlated with higher rates of mobility (*The Organization Man* 269–70).

36. Cited (in reference to Silicon Valley's success in luring high-paid technical workers) in Sir Peter Hall, "The Geography of the Fifth Kondratieff," in *Silicon Landscapes*, ed. Hall and Markusen, 14.

37. For comprehensive discussion of the different types of research parks—university owned, university marketed, or publicly developed—see Michael I. Luger and Harvey A. Goldstein, *Technology in the Garden: Research Parks and Regional Economic Development* (Chapel Hill: University of North Carolina Press, 1991).

38. Henry Bund, "Economic Problems," Remarks to New York State Symposium on "Research and the Community," 1 May 1961, Sterling Forest, New York, 59–60, FF "State Science and Technology Conference," Box 1, Accession 76–4, RG 40, NARA.

39. George Philips, "Laboratory Location," *Frontier*, Summer 1961, quoted in Atlanta Regional Metropolitan Planning Commission, "Economic Potentials: R&D, The Outlook for Research and Development in Metropolitan Atlanta," December 1962, 30–31.

40. George A. Dudley, "Problems of a Physical Environment."

41. Victor J. Danilov, "The Seduction of Science," *Industrial Research*, May 1965, 39–40.

42. Speech to Industrial Council of the Urban Land Institute, 28 January 1965, quoted in R. John Griefen, "A Research Park Does Not Live by Research Alone," *Urban Land* 24:3 (March 1965), 7.

43. Electronics Division, Business and Defense Services Administration, U.S. Department of Commerce, Memorandum on "The Electronics Industry—Factors in Selecting Plant Locations—Methods for Approaching Industry," 23 August 1956, Box 3, Accession 66A2584, RG 378, NARA.

44. For example, both Bredo, *Industrial Estates,* and Boley, *Industrial Districts,* feature Route 128 research parks as models of this type of industrial development.

45. Zachary Robinson and Oscar Hernandez, "Neighborhood Bully: Harvard, the Community, and Urban Development," in *How Harvard Rules,* ed. by John Trumpbour (Boston: South End Press, 1989), 190–91.

46. Arthur D. Little, Inc., *Georgia Tech: Impetus to Economic Growth,* Report to Georgia Tech National Alumni Association, November 1963.

47. Saxenian, *Regional Advantage,* 12.

48. While town-gown controversies were hardly absent in Cambridge, their relative importance to the affairs of the universities is indicated by the fact that Morton and Phyllis Keller's biography of twentieth-century Harvard, *Making Harvard Modern: The Rise of America's University* (New York: Oxford University Press, 2001), devotes less than a page to political controversies over the school's land management and development (333). One issue that may have affected this is that—unlike some other urban universities—Cambridge was working-class white.

49. Alan M. Voorhees, "Urban Growth Characteristics," *Urban Land* 20:11 (December 1961), 6.

50. Greg Hise notes that the real estate developers' "creed might be stated simply as 'Stay just ahead of the pack.'. . . In this milieu, innovation begins with a close study of what competitors have done" (Hise, *Magnetic Los Angeles,* 31).

51. Griefen, "A Research Park Does Not Live by Research Alone," 4.

52. Kerr, *The Uses of the University,* 90.

53. Teaford, *Rough Road to Renaissance,* 11.

54. For various perspectives on democracy, efficiency, and cronyism in machine politics, see Bruce M. Stave et al., "A Reassessment of the Urban Political Boss: An Exchange of Views," *The History Teacher* 21 (May 1988): 293–312. For further discussion of how public tax and housing policies excluded nonwhites and contributed to urban deterioration, see Sugrue, *Origins of the Urban Crisis;* Massey and Denton, *American Apartheid;* Jackson, *Crabgrass Frontier.*

55. Teaford, *Rough Road to Renaissance,* 147–48.

56. Mumford, letter to F. J. Osborn, 10 August 1958, in *The Letters of Lewis Mumford and Frederic J. Osborn: A Transatlantic Dialogue 1938–1970,* ed. Michael R. Hughes (Bath, England: Adams and Dart, 1971), 283.

57. Fred Hechinger, "Campus vs. Slums," *New York Times,* 1 October 1961, quoted in Klotsche, *The Urban University and the Future of Our Cities,* 64.

58. The University of Pennsylvania, for example, had warned for decades that it might leave its West Philadelphia campus for suburban Valley Forge, and its crosstown neighbor, Temple University, even went so far as to purchase a large tract of suburban land on which to relocate its campus. George E. Thomas and David B. Brownlee, *Building America's First University: An Historical and Architectural Guide to the University of Pennsylvania* (Philadelphia: University of Pennsylvania Press, 2000), 99–103.

59. A number of these complaints were lodged in reauthorization hearings; see United States Senate, Committee on Banking and Currency, *Hearings Before a Subcommittee of the Committee on Banking and Currency, 84th Congress, 1st Session,* May 1955 (Washington, D.C.: Government Printing Office, 1955); United States Senate, Committee on Banking and Currency, *Hearings Before a Subcommittee of*

the Committee on Banking and Currency, 85th Congress, 2nd Session, May 1958 (Washington, D.C.: Government Printing Office, 1958); United States Senate, Committee on Banking and Currency, *Hearings Before the Committee on Banking and Currency,* January 1959 (Washington, D.C.: Government Printing Office, 1959).

60. Incorporated in S. 3399, 1958.

61. United States Senate, Committee on Banking and Currency, *Comment on Title V, Section 502, Housing Act of 1959, Report of the Committee on Banking and Currency Together with Individual Views to Accompany S. 57,* 3 February 1959, 42.

62. Klotsche, *The Urban University and the Future of Our Cities,* 75–76.

63. Quoted in West Philadelphia Corporation, 1962 *Annual Report,* UPA.

64. Slayton, "The University, the City, and Urban Renewal," in *The University, The City, and Urban Renewal: Report of a Regional Conference Sponsored by the American Council on Education and the West Philadelphia Corporation,* 25 March 1963 (Washington, D.C.: American Council on Education, 1963), 4.

65. Ibid., 9.

66. "The University and Exploration of Space," speech given to the National Academy of Sciences, October 1965, reprinted in *Science* 150 (26 November 1965), 1129–33. NASA also sponsored conferences and other events exploring the applicability of new technology to the problems of urban life, and the university role in such technology transfer. See National Aeronautics and Space Administration, *Conference on Space, Science, and Urban Life,* Proceedings of a conference held at Oakland, California, March 28–30, 1963, supported by the Ford Foundation and the National Aeronautics and Space Administration in cooperation with the University of California and the City of Oakland (Washington, D.C.: U.S. Government Printing Office, 1963). One outcome of this interest in university leadership in urban affairs was the short-lived Urban Observatory program, first proposed by MIT's Robert Wood (who later served as undersecretary of the Department of Housing and Urban Development) in 1962 and implemented in 1965 with the support of the National League of Cities ("Can Science Cure Urban Ills?" *Nation's Cities,* July 1965, 8–9, 27).

67. Levi, "The Influence of Environment on Urban Institutions," *Educational Record,* April 1961, 137, quoted in Klotsche, *The Urban University and the Future of Our Cities,* 69.

68. Klotsche, *The Urban University and the Future of Our Cities,* 70.

69. U.S. Department of Health, Education, and Welfare, *Casebook on Campus Planning and Institutional Development: Ten Institutions, How They Did It* comp. John B. Rork and Leslie F. Robbins (Washington, D.C.: U.S. Government Printing Office, 1962).

70. Public awareness of these inequalities increased in the early 1960s as the result of best-selling books on the subject, notably Michael Harrington's *The Other America: Poverty in the United States* (New York: Macmillan, 1962). As Thomas J. Sugrue has demonstrated, while there has always been a significant poverty population in the U.S., the spatial isolation and segregation of the poor that resulted from these mid-twentieth-century economic changes was unprecedented ("The Structures of Urban Poverty: The Reorganization of Space and Work in Three Periods of American History," in *The "Underclass" Debate: Views from History,* ed. Michael B. Katz (Princeton, N.J.: Princeton University Press, 1993), 85–117.

71. Ted M. Levine, "Keys to Sound Promotion," part of Special Report on "How to Woo and Win Industry" *Nation's Business* 56 (November 1968), 100.

72. "Virtually every [industrial development council] uses some form of purchased advertising or printing to find prospects and to convince them of the relative merits of their locality," Levine's 1968 article reminded corporate leaders ("Keys to Sound Promotion").

73. For further exploration and incisive analysis of how and why Southern states used these marketing tools, see James C. Cobb, *The Selling of the South: The Southern Crusade for Industrial Development, 1936–1990* (Urbana: University of Illinois Press, 1993). Slogans compiled in survey of late-1940s advertisements in national business magazines conducted by Industrial Survey Associates, *San Francisco Bay Area: Its People, Prospects, and Problems*, A Report Prepared for the San Francisco Bay Area Council, advance review edition (March 1948), 24–26, SFHC.

74. Bredo, *Industrial Estates*, 14.

75. Jacob J. Kaufman and Helmut J. Golatz, *The Industrial Development Corporation: Its Objectives, Functions, and Problems*, Bulletin no. 62, Bureau of Business Research, College of Business Administration, Pennsylvania State University, April 1960, 3.

76. "The Big Plant-Site Scramble," *Duns Review and Modern Industry* 83:2 (March 1964), 104–5 et seq. Estimate of number of local economic development agencies from the same source.

77. "The Big Plant-Site Scramble."

78. Eugene Lichtenstein, "Higher and Higher Go the Bids for Industry," *Fortune* 69 (April 1964), 118.

79. *Economic Report of the President 1960* (Washington, D.C.: Government Printing Office, 1961), 57.

80. Of course, civil rights pressures were never absent from these debates. As Alice O'Connor observes, approaching inequality as a product of market forces, rather than discrimination, reflected policy-makers' belief that "growth and tight labor markets would diminish the need for more overt, politically risky, antidiscrimination policies" (*Poverty Knowledge: Social Science, Social Policy, and the Poor in Twentieth-Century U.S. History* [Princeton, N.J.: Princeton University Press, 2001], 20).

81. Roger Biles, *Crusading Liberal: Paul H. Douglas of Illinois* (DeKalb: Northern Illinois University Press, 2002). Douglas, an economist by training who long was an advocate of working people and the unemployed, describes his political career and evolving ideology in his memoir *In the Fullness of Time: The Memoirs of Paul H. Douglas* (New York: Harcourt Brace Jovanovich, 1972).

82. Biles, *Crusading Liberal*, 135. Douglas's political chances were probably further diminished by his contemporaneous crusade to cut wasteful military spending—spending that happened to benefit contractors located in Southerners' home districts.

83. Eisenhower, State of the Union Address, January 1956, quoted in Conley H. Dillon, *The Area Redevelopment Administration: New Patterns in Developmental Administration* (College Park: University of Maryland Press, 1964), 5.

84. For discussion of the legislative debates over area redevelopment in the 1950s, see Roger Davidson, *Coalition-Building for Depressed Areas Bills: 1955–1965,*

Inter-University Case Program no. 103 (Indianapolis, Ind.: Bobbs-Merrill, 1966) and Sar A. Levitan, *Federal Aid to Depressed Areas: An Evaluation of the Area Redevelopment Administration* (Baltimore, Md.: Johns Hopkins University Press, 1964), 1–29. For discussion of depressed–areas legislation in the context of Eisenhower-era approaches to employment policy, see Margaret Weir, *Politics and Jobs: The Boundaries of Employment Policy in the United States* (Princeton, N.J.: Princeton University Press, 1992), 64–67.

85. *Economic Report of the President 1960*; Arthur M. Schlesinger Jr., *A Thousand Days: John F. Kennedy in the White House* (Boston, Mass.: Houghton Mifflin Company, 1965), 1002–12.

86. The ARA became law on 1 May 1961. In 1965 it was renamed the Economic Development Administration and continues to be an operating division of the Commerce Department.

87. The ARA established a "Central City Action Program" in 1964, targeting funds to distressed urban neighborhoods (ARA, *Annual Report 1964* [Washington, D.C.: GPO, 1964], 26). While the ARA performed an important service in shoring up the economic fortunes of struggling rural towns through infrastructure investments and business assistance, it could be argued that such support inadvertently hastened suburban sprawl in building up centers of economic activity at the periphery of metropolitan areas, so that development "leapfrogged" past existing metropolitan boundaries and interstitial open space into these growing municipalities.

88. "Some Schools Accused of Hogging Research," *Philadelphia Evening Bulletin,* 7 June 1967.

89. H. W. Williams, Deputy Administrator of the ARA, Memorandum to Hyman H Bookbinder, Spec. Asst. to Sec. of Commerce, on "Regional Impact of R&D Contracts," 26 September 1962, FF "Research & Development Contracts," Box 5, Accession 65A2307, RG 378, NARA.

90. *Economic Report of the President 1962* (Washington, D.C.: Government Printing Office, 1963), xxv. This was not the first time the federal government had attempted science-based economic development; in April 1950, when Commerce still had responsibility for small business policy, the agency proposed a program in which it would "act as marriage broker or catalyst between small industry and the research facilities already in existence." The program was, as one administrator later observed, "well conceived," but seems to have never come to fruition (R. A. Bowman, Letter to J. Herbert Holloman, 4 August 1965 attaching April 1950 proposal summary. FF "STSA—Internal Memoranda," Box 1, Accession 76–4, RG 40, NARA).

91. The strategy of building out university capacity as well as industrial capacity was not unique to the United States but was a hallmark of similar economic development efforts in Western Europe during this period. "The spread of university facilities to enlighten the peripheries and lift up their unexceptionable towns has been a part of the established economic development doctrine around the world," writes Herman van der Wusten ("A Warehouse of Precious Goods," in *The Urban University and Its Identity,* ed. vander Wusten, 6).

92. Dr. Charles Tiebout, Letter to Gerald Greenstein, 5 February 1965, FF "STSA—Holloman Testimony," Box 1, Accession 76–4, RG 40, NARA.

93. PL 89–192, 89th Congress, S 949, 14 September 1965, FF "State Federal Technical Services Act," Box 1, Accession 76–4, RG 40, NARA. Also see Roy L. Morgan, Director of Office of Field Services, DOC, Memorandum to All Field Officers, 10 March 1965, FF "State Federal Technical Services Act," Box 1, Accession 76–4, RG 40, NARA.

94. Quoted in Luther J. Carter, "Technical Services Act: Industry to Benefit from New State Programs Paralleling Farm Extension Service," *Science* 149, 24 September 1965, 1485–86, 1547–50. Carter also notes that Johnson called the bill "the 'sleeper' of the 89th Congress."

95. Paul J. Grogan, "New Concepts in the Development of the Universities as Technological Centers," Remarks to the 74th Annual Meeting of the American Society for Engineering Education, Pullman, Wash., 23 June 1966, Box 2, Accession 76–4, RG 40, NARA.

96. The work of University of North Carolina regionalist Howard W. Odum was an important influence on this line of thinking; his hypothesis that scientific development could stimulate overall economic development played an important role in the development of a model "city of knowledge," Research Triangle Park. "Over time, economic development officials nationwide and in other parts of the world have come to treat Odum's hypothesis as an axiom," note Michael Luger and Harvey Goldstein (*Technology in the Garden*, 56–57).

97. ARA, *Annual Report 1963*, 15.

98. Summary of Remarks of Richard Holton, Assistant Secretary of Commerce for Economic Affairs, *Summary of Proceedings of the State Science and Technology Conference*, Department of Commerce, Washington, D.C., February 3–4, 1964, 6, FF "State Science and Technology Conference," Box 1, Accession 76–4, RG 40, NARA.

99. Paul J. Grogan, "The State Technical Services Program at the National Level," Address Delivered at the Special Libraries Association Convention, New York City, 30 May 1967, 11–12, Box 2, Accession 76–4, RG 40, NARA.

100. Mead's assessment was prophetic; in twenty-first-century high-technology capitals like Silicon Valley, unskilled work is overwhelmingly performed by immigrants from Latin America and Asia (Mead, "Building Communities for the Builders of Tomorrow," Remarks to New York State Symposium on "Research and the Community," 1 May 1961, Sterling Forest, New York, FF "State Science and Technology Conference," Box 1, Accession 76–4, RG 40, NARA).

101. Bund, "Economic Problems," 66.

102. "Relationship of National Interests to Regional Technical Resources," Appendix to Summary of Proposed State Technical Services Act of 1965, undated, FF "State Federal Technical Services Act," Box 1, Accession 76–4, RG 40, NARA.

103. Technology Audit Corporation, "A Proposal to Stimulate Entrepreneurial Activity in Certain Depressed Communities," December 1962, FF "Technology Audit Corporation," Box 5, Accession 65A2307, RG 378, NARA.

104. Department of Commerce, Fact Sheet on Proposed State Technical Services Act, undated, FF 2 (Contract and Grant Matters), Box 13, Series III, SC160, SUA.

105. Danilov, "The Seduction of Science," 39–40.

106. David Riesman, "The Suburban Sadness," in *The Suburban Community*, ed. William M. Dobriner (New York: G. P. Putnam's Sons, 1958).

107. *Business Week*, 20 April 1968, 28.

108. George Herbert [President of Triangle Research Institute], *Summary of Proceedings of the State Science and Technology Conference*, Department of Commerce, Washington, D.C., February 3–4, 1964, 11, FF "State Science and Technology Conference," Box 1, Accession 76–4, RG 40, NARA.

109. Grogan, "The State Technical Services Act—Underlying Assumptions and Organizational Structure," Remarks before the Committee on Science, Engineering, and Regional Development, National Academy of Sciences Building, Washington D.C., 15 June 1967, 8, Box 2, Accession 76–4, RG 40, NARA.

110. James F. Mahar and Dean C. Coddington, "Scientific Complex: Proceed with Caution," *Harvard Business Review* 43 (January 1965), 140–8 et seq.

111. Griefen, "A Research Park Does Not Live by Research Alone," 4.

112. Herbert, *Summary of Proceedings of the State Science and Technology Conference*, 12.

113. Stanford Research Institute quoted in Danilov, "The Seduction of Science," 40.

Chapter 3
From the Farm to the Valley: Stanford University
and the San Francisco Peninsula

1. Nearly every book about the history of the University mentions this perhaps apocryphal story. See for example Edith R. Mirrieless, *Stanford: The Story of a University* (New York: G. P. Putnam's Sons, 1959), 23–24.

2. Oscar Lewis, *The Big Four: The Story of Huntington, Stanford, Hopkins, and Crocker, and of the Building of the Central Pacific* (New York: Alfred A. Knopf, 1951).

3. *The Founding Grant with Amendments, Legislation, and Court Decrees* (Stanford, Calif.: Stanford University, reprinted 1971), 4 (Section 1).

4. Pamela Gullard and Nancy Lund, *History of Palo Alto: The Early Years* (San Francisco: Scottwall Associates, 1989), chap. 8.

5. The *New York Commercial Advertiser*, for example, labeled the endeavor "an empty shell" and "a rich man's folly" (1885, quoted in Margo Davis and Roxanne Nilan, *The Stanford Album: A Photographic History, 1885–1945* [Stanford, Calif.: Stanford University Press, 1989], 13). Despite the popular perception of Stanford as a heartless Gilded Age industrialist, the generosity of this gift demonstrates the size of his civic conscience. Like another famous politician associated with Stanford University, Herbert Hoover, Stanford was more progressive than commonly portrayed, having been a dedicated abolitionist and a supporter of populist causes like worker-owned cooperatives. See Lee Altenberg, "Beyond Capitalism: Leland Stanford's Forgotten Vision," *Sandstone and Tile* 14:1 (Winter 1990), 8–20, Stanford Historical Society, Stanford, Calif.

6. The literature on the Progressive Era and social reform is too extensive to address here, but a particularly important recent monograph is Daniel Rodgers, *Atlantic Crossings: Social Politics in Progressive Age* (Cambridge, Mass.: Harvard University Press, Belknap Press, 1998), which traces the connections between North

American and European reformers. Also useful is Rodgers's review essay, "In Search of Progressivism," *Reviews in American History* 10 (1982), 113–32.

7. While framed an exercise in civic betterment and working-class uplift, new city parks were often designed with a more elite audience in mind. New York's Central Park, the most famous of these projects, was situated in Uptown Manhattan—a location that, at the time of the park's construction, was well beyond walking distance from the crowded downtown slums, but an easy carriage ride from upper-middle-class neighborhoods. See Roy Rosensweig and Elizabeth Blackmar, *The Park and the People: A History of Central Park* (Ithaca, N.Y.: Cornell University Press, 1992).

8. For discussion of "natural" landscapes and industrial agriculture, see Steven Stoll, *The Fruits of Natural Advantage: Making the Industrial Countryside in California* (Berkeley and Los Angeles: University of California Press, 1998). A significant number of the Valley's working-class residents were (and are) Mexican; see Steven J. Pitti, *The Devil in Silicon Valley: Northern California, Race, and Mexican Americans* (Princeton, N.J.: Princeton University Press, 2003). For further discussion of politics and capital in Gilded Age San Francisco, see Philip J. Ethington, *The Public City: The Political Construction of Urban Life in San Francisco, 1850–1900* (Berkeley and Los Angeles: University of California Press, 1994); Gray Brechin, *Imperial San Francisco: Urban Power, Earthly Ruin* (Berkeley and Los Angeles: University of California Press, 1999).

9. As Stephanie Pincetl writes, "unspoiled nature could bring serenity and wisdom to people" (*Transforming California: A Political History of Land Use and Development* [Baltimore, Md.: Johns Hopkins University Press, 1999], 12).

10. Olmsted's biography—from an upbringing in preindustrial New England and life as a gentleman farmer on Staten Island, to crusading journalist and publisher, government official, and urban landscape planner—reads like nineteenth-century American history told in miniature; see Witold Rybcynski, *A Clearing in the Distance: Frederick Law Olmsted and America in the Nineteenth Century* (New York: Scribner, 1999).

11. The Mall in Washington was one of the most enduring examples of the City Beautiful era, one that created a startling physical and social contrast with the neighborhoods surrounding it; see Howard Gillette, *Between Justice and Beauty: Race, Planning, and the Failure of Urban Policy in Washington, D.C.* (Baltimore, Md.: Johns Hopkins University Press, 1995). Also see William H. Wilson, *The City Beautiful Movement* (Baltimore, Md.: Johns Hopkins University Press, 1989).

12. *San Francisco Examiner*, 28 April 1887, quoted in Paul V. Turner, "The Collaborative Design of Stanford University," in Marcia E. Vetrocq, and Karen Weitze, *The Founders and the Architects: The Design of Stanford University* (Stanford, Calif.: Department of Art, Stanford University, 1976), 58.

13. The architect hired by Stanford to execute this part of the vision was Henry Hobson Richardson, as preeminent in his field as Olmsted was in landscape design. Richardson died shortly after receiving this commission, and his associate Charles Coolidge executed the project (Richard Joncas, David J. Neuman, and Paul V. Turner, *Stanford University: The Campus Guide* [New York: Princeton Architectural Press, 1999], 2). Also see Turner, "The Collaborative Design," 13, 45. Also see Davis and Nilan, *The Stanford Album*, 13–14.

14. It is no small coincidence that Olmsted's work would give the United States the suburban design aesthetic of curvilinear roads and cul-de-sacs and single-use zoning. Suburban design also emphasized construction that reflected regional architectural and ethnic heritage and anticipated the romantic Mission Revival architecture of early twentieth-century Southern California. In the late twentieth century, this country also witnessed the rise of the gated community, an enclosed suburban residential development that was literally walled and gated off from its neighbors. Stanford's campus reflects all these elements, perhaps making it a suburb well ahead of its time. See Rybcynski as well as Robert Fishman, *Bourgeois Utopias: The Rise and Fall of Suburbia* (New York: Basic Books, 1987). For discussion of the cultural impulses and historical reinterpretations behind Mission Revival architecture in California, see Roberto Lint Sagarena, "Building California's Past: Mission Revival Architecture and Regional Identity," *The Journal of Urban History* 28:4 (May 2002), 429–44.

15. Katherine Ames Taylor, *The Romance of Stanford* (San Francisco, Calif.: H. S. Crocker Co. for the Stanford Alumni Association, 1927), 5.

16. Introduction to ibid.

17. Timothy J. Sturgeon, "How Silicon Valley Came to Be," in *Understanding Silicon Valley*, 15–47.

18. Industrial Survey Associates, *San Francisco Bay Area: Its People, Prospects, and Problems, A Report Prepared for the San Francisco Bay Area Council,* advance review edition (March 1948), SFHC.

19. Jacques F. Levy, *San Francisco Bay Region Industrial Study,* Final Confidential Report to the Executive Committee and the Technical Advisory Committee, The San Francisco Bay Area Council, 28 January 1946, 18, SFHC.

20. Richard Walker, "Industry Builds the City: The Suburbanization of Manufacturing in the San Francisco Bay Area, 1850–1940," *Journal of Historical Geography* 27:1 (2001), 36–57.

21. San Francisco Bay Area Council, *Economic Guide to the Bay Area* (1961), 4–5, SFHC.

22. Warren A. Beck and Ynez D. Haase, *Historical Atlas of California* (Norman: University of Oklahoma Press, 1974), 74.

23. Roger Lotchin "World War II and Urban California: City Planning and the Transformation Hypothesis," published in the *Pacific Historical Review* (1993), reprinted in *The Urban West*, ed. with introduction by Gordon Morris Bakken and Brenda Farrington (New York: Garland Publishing, Inc., 2000), 119–48.

24. Pincetl, *Transforming California,* 74.

25. Herbert Hoover and Leland Stanford had much in common. Like Leland Stanford, Hoover was a businessman who entered politics late in life and is commonly portrayed as a somewhat heartless friend of big business, but he had a history of affiliation with progressive interests that belie this image. He served among the progressive administrators of the Wilson Administration and, as commerce secretary, instituted programs (such as a housing improvement initiative) that drew heavily upon progressive reform ideas. As Kennedy notes, these experiences infused Hoover's thinking about the obligations of public and private to work together toward a larger civic good (*Freedom from Fear,* 11). Also see *Understanding Herbert Hoover: Ten Perspectives*, edited with an introduction by Lee Nash

(Stanford, Calif.: Hoover Institution Press, 1987); Gary Dean Best, *The Politics of American Individualism: Herbert Hoover in Transition, 1918–1921* (Westport, Conn.: Greenwood Press, 1975); Hawley, "Herbert Hoover, the Commerce Secretariat, and the Vision of an 'Associative State,' 1921–1928."

26. Industrial Survey Associates, *San Francisco Bay Area: Its People, Prospects, and Problems, A Report Prepared for the San Francisco Bay Area Council*, advance review edition (March 1948), 30, SFHC.

27. San Francisco Bay Area Council, Industrial Development Meeting, Minutes, 13 August 1947. FF "S.F. Bay Area Council," SFHC.

28. San Francisco Bay Area Council, *Program and Objectives* (December 1945), SFHC. The six firms pledging financial support to the Council in its first year were Bank of America, American Trust, Standard Oil of California, Pacific Gas and Electric, U.S. Steel, and Bechtel Corporation.

29. Among other things, the Bay Area Council played a role in the much reviled efforts to build freeways across the City of San Francisco (only one, the late and unlamented Embarcadero Freeway, came into being) and in urban renewal projects that erased deeply rooted ethnic neighborhoods within the City. For a contemporary account of the San Francisco "freeway revolt," see Samuel E. Wood, "The Freeway Revolt and What It Means," in *The California Revolution*, ed. Carey McWilliams (New York: Grossman Publishers, 1968), 100–109. Also see Charles Wollenberg, *Golden Gate Metropolis: Perspectives on Bay Area History* (Berkeley: Institute of Governmental Studies, University of California, Berkeley, 1985), 255–90.

30. Levy, *San Francisco Bay Region Industrial Study*, 43.

31. See for example Oscar Lewis, *Within the Golden Gate: A Survey of the History, Resources, and Points of Interest of the Bay Region Designed to Acquaint Visitors with its Past Accomplishments and Its Future Promise* (San Francisco: San Francisco Bay Area Council, 1947), FF "SF Bay Area Council," SFHC.

32. Tresidder, Address to Fire Underwriters of the Pacific, 6 March 1945, FF 11, Box 40, SC 151, SUA.

33. Kiester, *Donald B. Tresidder*.

34. Quoted in Saxenian, *Regional Advantage*, 22.

35. The fact that Silicon Valley was the result of the combination of forces, and not simply the work of Terman alone, has been argued skillfully by Kargon, Leslie, and Schoenberger, "Far Beyond Big Science," as well as Stuart W. Leslie, "The Biggest 'Angel' of them All: The Military and the Making of Silicon Valley," in Kenney, *Understanding Silicon Valley*, 48–67.

36. U.S. Department of Commerce, Bureau of the Census, *Census of Population: 1960, Volume I, Characteristics of the Population, Part 6, California* (Washington, D.C.: U.S. Government Printing Office, 1961), table 5.

37. Terman, Letter to Paul Davis, 29 December 1943, FF2, Box 1, Series I, SC 160, SUA. Quoted in Stuart W. Leslie, *The Cold War and American Science*, 44.

38. Keister, *Donald Tresidder*, 70–74.

39. "Stanford Looks Ahead," Address (audience unknown), San Francisco, 14 October 1942, FF 1, Box 40, SC 151, SUA.

NOTES TO CHAPTER THREE

40. As early as 1948, in fact, the Engineering School received more of its funding from DOD and AEC than it did from the University (Lowen, *Creating the Cold War University*, 118).

41. Stanford fostered innovation among its students and faculty, and in return it reaped the benefits of commercially marketed inventions. One of these was the Klystron microwave tube invented in the 1930s and licensed to Sperry Gyroscope Company. Stanford had a steady stream of income from this invention well into the 1950s. In FY 1955 the total royalties paid to Stanford by Sperry were over $83,000; in FY 1956 they were nearly $90,000 (Thomas W. Ford, Memorandum to Alf E. Brandin, 15 November 1955, 5, FF 5, Box 12, Series III, SC 160, SUA; undated and unsigned memorandum [presumably by same author], 29, FF 5, Box 12, Series III, SC 160, SUA.). For extensive discussion of the Klystron and Stanford's sometimes difficult relationship with Sperry, see Lowen, *Creating the Cold War University*, 37–42.

42. "Deck the Halls with Ivy," *Newsweek*, 20 February 1961, 59.

43. "The First Fifty Years of Electronics Research," *The Tall Tree* 1:9 (May 1958), 3, FF Palo Alto History, SC 486, 90–052, SUA.

44. The most comprehensive case study to date on Stanford's land developments and their implications on urban design is John Findlay's chapter on the Stanford Industrial Park in *Magic Lands: Western Cityscapes and American Culture after 1940* (Berkeley and Los Angeles: University of California Press, 1992). This section owes much to Findlay's insights, particularly his argument that Stanford's developments created a new urban paradigm, but it differs in its use of sources and in its thematic emphasis.

45. Stanford Oral History Project, Transcript of interview with Alf Brandin, ca. 1980, 30–31, SUA.

46. The University was a 501(c)(3) organization subject to Unrelated Business Income Tax (UBIT). It paid $700,000 in property taxes by 1968. "Why Develop Stanford Lands?" undated and unsigned memorandum (probably 1968), FF 9, SC486, 95–174, SUA. For explication of the origins and applicability of UBIT, and its evolution into a less onerous tax for some institutions, see Evelyn Brody and Joseph Cordes, *The Unrelated Business Income Tax: All Bark and No Bite?* (Washington, D.C.: Urban Institute, 1999).

47. Arthur L. Norberg, Charles Susskind, and Roger Hahn, *Frederick Emmons Terman* [transcript of interviews, 1971–78], The Bancroft Library, History of Science and Technology Program, University of California, Berkeley (Berkeley: University of California, 1984), 127.

48. E. Howard Brooks, "Remembering Wallace Sterling," transcript of taped session, 9 August 1985, Stanford Oral History Project, SUA, 19.

49. Kiester, *Donald B. Tresidder*, 76.

50. Lewis Mumford, "Memorandum on Planning II," Subject File 1226 (VP Finance), SUA.

51. Findlay, *Magic Lands*, 125.

52. The British Parliament enacted the New Towns Act in 1946 but bureaucratic tangles and fiscal constraints bogged down the program by the 1950s; the program endured into the 1970s but other urban development strategies super-

seded it. See Gordon E. Cherry, *Cities and Plans: The Shaping of Urban Britain in the Nineteenth and Twentieth Centuries* (London: Edward Arnold, 1988) and Meryl Aldridge, *The British New Towns: A Programme Without a Policy* (London: Routledge and Kegan Paul, 1979).

53. E. Elmore Hutchinson, *Report on Land Use Survey of Stanford University Properties*, 5 June 1951, 3–4, FF 9, Box A29, SC 216, SUA.

54. Hutchinson, *Report on Land Use Survey of Stanford University Properties*, 20–21.

55. Skidmore, Owings, and Merrill, "Master Plan for Stanford Lands, 1953," SC 486, Accession 96–176, Box 1, SUA.

56. For discussion of this shift in California, see Pincetl, *Transforming California*; for discussion of its influence on grassroots movements and public policy nationally, see Samuel P. Hays, *Beauty, Health, and Permanence: Environmental Politics in the United States, 1955–1985* (New York: Cambridge University Press, 1987).

57. President's Advisory Committee on Land and Building Development, *Report on Master Plan* [for Stanford Lands, 1953], 1 June 1954, FF 7, Box 35, Series III, SC 160, SUA.

58. President's Advisory Committee on Land and Building Development, *Report on Master Plan*, 5.

59. Alf E. Brandin, Letter to Dr. Julio Bortolazzo, 25 May 1961, FF 10, Box A29, SC 216, SUA.

60. President's Advisory Committee on Land and Building Development, *Report on Master Plan*, 8.

61. Stanford Planning Office, *Land Development Annual Report*, Year Ended 31 August 1968, FF 9, Box 1, SC 486, 95–174, SUA.

62. Board of Trustees statement, 1954, quoted in Stanford University, "Land Development Fact Sheet," 2 April 1960, FF 11, Box A29, SC 216, SUA.

63. *Palo Alto Times*, 17 September 1953.

64. "Annexation of Stanford Lands Hailed as Great Development," *Palo Alto Times*, 1 October 1953.

65. Richard Stannard, "Regional Trade Center Is Just One of Stanford's Land Use Plans," *Palo Alto Times*, 26 February 1953.

66. Pincetl, *Transforming California*.

67. The center was a huge generator of rental income for Stanford in the 1950s and 1960s, producing over $8.8 million in profits for the University between 1955 and 1968. Stanford Planning Office, Land Development Annual Report, Year Ended 31 August 1968, FF 9, SC486, 95–174, Box 1, SUA.

68. Mary Madison, "Around the Beats: Packard Seems Torn Two Ways on Issue," *Palo Alto Times*, 3 November 1959.

69. "Stanford Will Break Ground in Tract Plan," *San Mateo* [Calif.] *Times and News Leader*, 6 March 1957. The Skidmore, Owings, and Merrill plan had proposed that houses be four to an acre and cost an average of $25,000.

70. Advertisement for Stanford Hills development placed by Peninsula Pacific Construction Co. in *Menlo Park* [Calif.] *Recorder*, 29 October 1959.

71. "Stanford to Build First Apartments," *San Mateo* [Calif.] *Times & News Leader*, 10 September 1959. Ironically, despite the upscale nature of this development, the idea of multi-unit housing of any kind raised the ire of Stanford's

neighbors, many of whom were living in homes built in the first phase of Stanford's land development. Palo Alto had become such a carefully regulated and exclusive place by this point that even luxury apartments seemed to have posed a threat to residents' housing values. Stanford seems to have eventually placated these worried neighbors by emphasizing the high-quality, educated tenants the development sought to attract (Mary Madison, "Around the Beats").

72. Findlay, *Magic Lands*, 129–34.

73. Alexander Bodi, "Memo from the Editor: They're Different Now," *Palo Alto Times*, 17 February 1960.

74. City of Palo Alto, "Basic Planning Policy and Objectives of Planning Program," 4 August 1954, FF 14, Box A22, SC 216, SUA. The report went on to note that industrial development in general was "basic from a 'good living' point of view. . . . More and more people should have the opportunity to work near their homes and thereby have greater opportunity to participate in community affairs and the relaxing leisure time activities available in this area."

75. Frank Meissner, "Quiet! Industrial Zone," *Redwood City* [Calif.] *Tribune*, 30 June 1962.

76. "Council Reverses Decision of 90-foot Buffer Strip," *Palo Alto Times*, 29 August 1956; "Stanford Bringing Old Vision to Life," *Los Angeles Times*, 25 March 1956.

77. "For Electronic Research and Development," *Architectural Record* (1954), reprinted in *Buildings for Research: An Architectural Record Publication* (New York: F. W. Dodge, Inc., 1958), 123–25.

78. Meissner, "Quiet! Industrial Zone."

79. See http://www.hp.com/hpinfo/abouthp/histnfacts, (accessed 25 August 2003); Norberg, Susskind, and Hahn, *Frederick Emmons Terman*. While it is true that Disney was the company's first client, Terman was right in observing that the defense industry provided the bread-and-butter contracts for Hewlett-Packard and other Stanford spin-offs.

80. Brandin Oral History.

81. Frederick Glover, note to Alf Brandin, 8 March 1957, FF 5, Box A16, SC 216, SUA.

82. Alf Brandin quoted in Tom Patterson, "Stanford Project Gets Cream of Crop," clipping from unidentified 1956 southern California newspaper in Stanford Lands file, SUA.

83. Packard, quoted in the *Palo Alto Times*, 17 February 1960, cited in Findlay, *Magic Lands*, 132.

84. Robert K. Sanford, " 'Think Tanks' Contain Far-Out Ideas," *Kansas City Times*, 21 June 1961.

85. Mel Wax, "Stanford Park—Weird Success," *San Francisco Chronicle*, 16 November 1958.

86. "Brains Are Bait," *San Francisco Chronicle*, 18 June 1961.

87. The California climate was a factor often emphasized by Stanford administrators, Park tenants, and the press (see for example "Stanford Bringing Old Vision to Life," *Los Angeles Times*, 25 March 1956). The actual climatic advantages of this sunny and temperate region were further magnified by the prominence of the state in American popular culture during this period when television and

radio airwaves were dominated by quintessentially California icons like the Mouseketeers, Gidget, and the Beach Boys. See Kirse Granat May, *Golden State, Golden Youth: The California Image in Popular Culture, 1955–66* (Chapel Hill: University of North Carolina Press, 2002).

88. Lockheed Corporation, press release, 24 January 1956, FF 5, Box A16, SC 216, SUA.

89. Saxenian, *Regional Advantage*, 23.

90. Terman, "Education for Growth Industries," Paper prepared for San Francisco Regional Technical Meeting of the American Iron and Steel Institute, 6 November 1959, FF 60, Box 1, Series X, SC 160, SUA.

91. In *Research and Relevant Knowledge*, Geiger notes the "cloistered mentality that . . . flourished in the 1960s" in regards to many federally-dependent universities' attitudes towards support from corporate America. This attitude began to break down in the wake of campus protests and diminished federal R&D allocations in the late 1960s (273). Also see Hollinger, "Money and Academic Freedom a Half-Century after McCarthyism."

92. Various memoranda, FF1, Box 38, Series III, SC 160, SUA.

93. Norberg, Susskind, and Hahn, *Frederick Emmons Terman*, 127.

94. San Francisco Bay Area Council, *Economic Guide to the Bay Area* (San Francisco, 1961), SFHC.

95. Mel Scott, *The San Francisco Bay Area: A Metropolis in Perspective*, quoted in *Trends* (San Francisco Bay Area Council Newsletter) 53 (March 1960), SFHC.

96. Stanford Industrial Park Employers in cooperation with Civil Engineering Department of Stanford University, "Residence and Commute Patterns: Employees, Stanford Industrial Park," June 1962, Box 2, 90–052, SC 486, SUA.

97. The office parks and industrial "campuses" that became the prevailing form of suburban commercial development by the end of the twentieth century demonstrate the influence of many of Stanford's design requirements, among them the lack of sidewalks. This of course particularly disadvantages low-income workers who may not have access to a private car and must take public transportation to work. See Margaret Pugh, *Barriers to Work: The Spatial Divide Between Jobs and Welfare Recipients in Metropolitan Areas* (Washington, D.C.: Brookings Institution Center on Urban and Metropolitan Policy, 1998).

98. Advisory Committee on Land and Building Development, Minutes, 10 November 1959, FF 2, Box 35, Series III, SC 160, SUA.

99. Terman, Letter to Irvine Sprague (Deputy Director of Finance State of California), 5 December 1963, FF 5 (NASA), Box A21, SC216, SUA.

100. Stanford Planning Office memorandum, FF9, Box 1, SC486, 95–174, SUA.

101. Stanford Planning Office, *Land Development Annual Report*, Year Ended 31 August 1968.

102. Falcon O. Baker, "City on the Campus," *Saturday Evening Post*, 31 December 1955 quoted in "Stanford Building a Model City to Cost 20 Millions," *Corona* [Calif.] *Independent*, 3 January 1956.

103. "Stanford Bringing Old Vision to Life," *Los Angeles Times*, 25 March 1956.

104. *Stanford University Bulletin*, 15 May 1958, FF "Palo Alto History," SC 486, 90–052, SUA.

105. Meissner, "Quiet! Industrial Zone." It should be noted that PACE (Plan of Action for a Challenging Era) was the acronym for Stanford's major fundraising campaign during this period. The notation on the article, however, reads "Pace" rather than "PACE," indicating that this writer is referring not to fundraising but to Stanford's influence on other research park developments.

106. "Chamber Unit Has a Research Probe," *Lawrence* (Kan.) *Journal-World*, 12 December 1961; "Four Studies for Future Growth Urged on Chamber of Commerce," *Corvallis* (Ore.) *Gazette-Times*, 6 March 1962; "Research Parks Meet Need," Editorial, *Lubbock* (Tex.) *Avalanche-Journal*, 9 April 1963; "Bringing Research Center to City Is Object of Plan Launched Here," *Meridian* (Miss.) *Star*, 20 February 1964; Quayne Kenyon, "City Encourages Start of Light Industry Center," *Idaho State Journal* (Pocatello, Idaho), 21 August 1964; Stanford Lands Scrapbooks VI and VII, 1961–62 and 1962–65, Subject Files 1300/9, SUA.

107. Letter to Editor of *Palo Alto Times*, 31 May 1962, FF 14 (City of Palo Alto), Box A22, SC 216, SUA.

108. "Midwest to Get Research Center," *New York Times*, 13 March 1963.

109. "4 Cities to Study Industrial Project," *Pomona* [Calif.] *Progress-Bulletin*, 16 October 1959.

110. "Canadians Envy Stanford Firms," Editorial, *Vancouver Sun*, Reprinted in *Palo Alto Times*, 27 June 1964.

111. James L. Holton, "Hegeman to Ask Approval of Industrial Park Plan," *New York World-Telegram and Sun*, 11 April 1958.

112. "SP plans to build industrial park—'like Stanford's'," *Palo Alto Times*, 9 March 1960.

113. "U.C. Santa Cruz Campus to Follow Stanford Style," *Oakland Tribune*, 19 March 1961.

114. "Pilgrimage Held to 'Miracle of Palo Alto' Site," *Berkeley Review*, 20 July 1961.

115. The fiscal and administrative constraints experienced at Berkeley and the rest of the University of California system during this period were illuminated in the upper-level political battles spurred by the student conflicts of the mid-1960s; see Matthew Dallek, *The Right Moment: Ronald Reagan's First Victory and the Decisive Turning Point in American Politics* (New York: Free Press, 2000), 81–102.

116. "Pilgrimage Held to 'Miracle of Palo Alto' Site."

117. "Governor Hatfield Tells Rotary: 'We Need 20,000 New Jobs Each Year!' " *Silverton* (Ore.) *Appeal Tribune*, 22 June 1961.

118. "Industry-University Links Needed," *The Scotsman*, 12 July 1965.

119. As Luger and Goldstein have observed, the fact that other institutions were imitators, not innovators, in the development of the university-run research park presented a built-in disadvantage. "The success of the Stanford Research Park, both as a real estate venture and as an instrument of economic development, is due less to planning foresight than to fortuitous timing and the ability of university officials to be flexible in their development efforts," they write. "Stanford University happened to have a critical mass of inventive individuals who needed space near the university at a time that electronics and other high-technology industries were about to burgeon. And, because Stanford's park was among the first to be established, there was little competition by other leading

research universities for these innovative businesses." Luger and Goldstein, *Technology in the Garden*, 154.

120. "Property Value in Palo Alto Soars," *San Francisco News*, 11 July 1956.

121. "Big Downtown Project Proposed for Palo Alto," *Palo Alto Times*, 4 April 1953.

122. "Council Reverses Decision on 90-foot Buffer Strip," *Palo Alto Times*, 29 August 29, 1956.

123. Alf E. Brandin, Memorandum to Wallace Sterling, 9 August 1954, FF 14, Box A22, SC 216, SUA.

124. Brandin Oral History 42.

125. Ibid.

126. Petition, 2 December 1962, FF 5, Box A16, SC 216, SUA.

127. Advisory Committee on Land and Building Development, Minutes, 15 March 1960, FF3, Box 35, Series III, SC 160, SUA.

128. Mary G. Steers, Letter to the Editor, *Palo Alto Times*, undated (Spring 1960), FF8, Box A29, SC 216, SUA.

129. Sterling, Letter to John Francis Neylan, 11 April 1960, FF8, Box A29, SC216, SUA.

130. Victor Thompson, " 'New Look' gives concern," Letter to the Editor, *Palo Alto Times*, 11 March 1960.

131. Correspondence records, President's Office, March 196, FF 11, Box A29, SC 216, SUA.

132. Edward J. Georgia, Telegram to Board of Trustees, 17 March 1960, FF 11, Box A29, SC 216, SUA.

133. Donald T. Carlson, Letter to Robert V. Brown, 1 April 1960. FF 11, Box A29, SC 216, SUA.

134. Donald T. Carlson, Assistant to the President, Letter to Mrs. Robert Scapple, 24 March 1960, FF11, Box A29, SC 216, SUA.

135. Morgan Stedman, text of presentation for meeting with Sterling, 14 March 1960, FF11, Box A29, SC 216, SUA.

136. "Sterling Answers Alumni," *Palo Alto Times*, 24 February 1960, FF11, Box A29, SC 216, SUA.

137. "Groups Clash over Use of Stanford Land," *San Francisco Examiner*, 18 March 1960.

138. Letter to the Editor, *Palo Alto Times*, November 1960 (specific date not given), Stanford Lands Scrapbook V, 1960–61, Subject File 1300/9, SUA.

139. Esther B. Clark, M.D., Letter to the Editor, *Palo Alto Times*, 28 March 1960, FF 11, Box A29, SC 216, SUA.

140. Editorial, *Palo Alto Times*, November 1960 (specific date unavailable), Stanford Lands Scrapbook V, 1960–61, Subject File 1300/9, SUA.

141. Jack L. Shepard, Memorandum to Tom Ford (Director of Land Development), 5 May 1961, FF10, Box A29, SC216, SUA.

142. Donald T. Carlson, Memorandum to Frederic O. Glover, 20 September 1961, FF 14, Box A22, SC216, SUA.

143. By the early 1960s, the rampant growth of the Bay Area had spurred the creation of the growth control organization California Tomorrow which, in the tradition of John Muir, published periodicals that sought to convince Californians of the terrible environmental toll of development. A representative exam-

ple is Samuel E. Wood and Alfred E. Heller, *California Going, Going. . .* (Sacramento: California Tomorrow, 1962). Historians of the modern environmental movement are now beginning to take a concerted look at the intersections between postwar suburbanization and environmentalism; see for example Adam Rome, *The Bulldozer in the Countryside: Suburban Sprawl and the Rise of American Environmentalism* (New York: Cambridge University Press, 2001); Peter Siskind, "Growth and Its Discontents: Localism, Protest and the Politics of Development on the Postwar Northeast Corridor," Ph.D. diss., University of Pennsylvania, 2002.

144. Terman, "The Newly Emerging Community of Technical Scholars," in *Colorado and the New Technological Revolution, Proceedings of the University-Industry Liaison Conference*, April 1964, 43–53; FF 4, Box 2, Series X, SC160, SUA.

Chapter 4
Building "Brainsville": The University of Pennsylvania and Philadelphia

1. Quoted in Russell F. Weigley, ed., *Philadelphia: A 300 Year History* (New York: W.W. Norton and Co., 1982), 83.

2. Thomas and Brownlee, *Building America's First University*, 52.

3. Ibid., 63.

4. David B. Brownlee, *Building the City Beautiful: The Benjamin Franklin Parkway and the Philadelphia Museum of Art* (Philadelphia: Philadelphia Museum of Art, 1989). As in other cities, early twentieth-century urban redevelopment projects in Philadelphia were often an architectural expression of the Progressive desire to "clean up" an increasingly disorderly urban environment. In Philadelphia's case, Progressive reformers found municipal corruption the most distressing manifestation of this disorder, a perspective expressed in Lincoln Steffen's 1903 essay "Philadelphia: Corrupt but Contented" (*McClure's Magazine* 21 [July 1903], 249–63). While no large American city escaped the excesses of machine politics in the late nineteenth century, Philadelphia was notable in the extent of corruption and its longevity.

5. Thomas and Brownlee, *Building America's First University*, 103.

6. "The U[niversity] of P[ennsylvania] Story, How an Institution Determines Its Development Aims and Needs" (notes for remarks and slide presentation at AEC/WPC [West Philadelphia Corporation] Conference on Institutional Development), 25 March 1963, FF2, Section A, UPJ 9.4, UPA.

7. Letter to Eckert and Mauchly, 22 March 1946, quoted in McCartney, *ENIAC*, 132.

8. McCartney, *ENIAC*, 134.

9. University of Pennsylvania, *Understandings with Commercial Organizations*, undated, FF 1, Box 2, UPA 5.7, UPA.

10. Committee on the Advancement of Research, Undated Report, FF 6, Box 1, UPA 5.7, UPA.

11. Mackenzie S. Carlson, " 'Come to Where the Knowledge Is': A History of the University City Science Center," unpublished research paper, 3 September 1999, UPA, 1–2.

12. Donald S. Murray, Director of the Office of Project Research and Grants, Summary Memorandum on Contract Grants, July 1960, UPA 5.7, Box 1, FF 33, UPA.

13. David Y. Cooper and Marshall A. Ledger, *Innovation and Tradition at the University of Pennsylvania School of Medicine: An Anecdotal Journey* (Philadelphia: University of Pennsylvania Press, 1990), 255.

14. See for example Luke Quinn, Letter to I. S. Ravdin, 17 September 1963, Box 168, UPA 4, UPA.

15. "New Light in the Search for Improved Materials: A Presentation to the Union Carbide Corporation," May 1961, FF "Research—ARPA II, 1960–65," Box 143, UPA 4, UPA.

16. The ICR later became the home for projects like "Caramu," begun in 1956 to estimate the casualties that might be produced from exposure to chemical agents; "Oro," which predicted the degree of toxicity of chemical and biological weapons agents under certain weather conditions; "White Wing," which focused on biological warfare; and projects "Summit" and "Spicerack," later the most controversial of them all, which studied air-delivered chemicals like Agent Orange. See Jonathan Goldstein, "Vietnam Research on Campus: The Summit/Spicerack Controversy at the University of Pennsylvania, 1965–67," *Peace and Change* 11: 2 (1986), 31.

17. Penn administrators did not necessarily jump at every opportunity to participate in national policy-related events. The ones they declined tended to be more ceremonial than substantive. President Harnwell was invited, but declined to attend, one of the Air Force Systems Command's Aeronautical Systems Division's Annual Conference of College Representatives, where military officials gave administrators tours of their facilities and used the event to "point up some of the many career opportunities available to your graduates." (Bertram M. Rose, Letter to Gaylord P. Harnwell, FF "United States Government 1960–65," Box 149, UPA 4, UPA). Harnwell was also invited to join the air force's Air University Board of Visitors made up of business and educational leaders; he declined this as well (John K. Hester, Memorandum to Harnwell, FF "United States Government 1960–65," Box 149, UPA 4, UPA).

18. Richard D. Stine, *Trends and Targets: A Study of the Financing of the University of Pennsylvania and Recommendations for Future Action* (April 1968), FF 8, Box 55, Section A, UPA 5.7, UPA, 16. The passage quoted here is Stine's assessment of the findings of the 1957 university-wide survey. The disciplinary favoritism displayed by Penn echoed Fred Terman's strategy of building "steeples of excellence" at Stanford.

19. Carolyn Adams, David Bartelt, David Elesh, Ira Goldstein, Nancy Kleniewski, and William Yancey, *Philadelphia: Neighborhoods, Division, and Conflict in a Postindustrial City.* Philadelphia: Temple University Press, 1991). Employers' aversion to the high costs of unionized labor continues today; in many cases firms will publicly cite high taxes as their reason for leaving urbanized areas, but as one analyst recently observed, "a CEO is unlikely to state publicly that he or she is moving the company to flee organized labor; it is more politically acceptable to say that taxes are too high" (Natalie Cohen, "Business Location Decision-Making and the Cities: Bringing Companies Back," working paper prepared for the Brookings Institution Center on Urban and Metropolitan Policy [Washington DC, April 2000]).

20. U.S. Department of Commerce, Bureau of the Census, *Census of Population: 1950. Vol. 3: Census Tract Statistics, Chapter 42: Philadelphia, Pa., and Adjacent Area* (Washington, D.C.: GPO, 1952).

21. Suburbanization, though disquieting, was also barely acknowledged as a problem. For example, none of the archived speeches Mayor Joseph Clark (1952–56) gave during his first year in office are explicitly about the problem suburbanization posed to cities, although a number of the topics he addresses are clearly partial outgrowths of a population shift toward the suburbs, including traffic control, voter participation, and the city's fiscal stability. RG 60–2.2, Box A-448, PCA.

22. Redevelopment Authority of Philadelphia, *Annual Report 1946* (Philadelphia, Pa., January 1947), 4. Box A-571, RG 161, PCA.

23. In the post–civil rights era to come, this seemingly benign oligarchic style of governing would give way to a broader democracy that focused more on social justice and economic equity than grand planning schemes. Richard M. Bernard, ed., *Snowbelt Cities: Metropolitan Politics in the Northeast and Midwest since World War II* (Bloomington: Indiana University Press, 1990). Of course, this new pluralism could have disastrous consequences; see for example Ken Auletta's tale of New York City's financial collapse in *The Streets Were Paved with Gold* (New York: Random House, 1975).

24. Clark, FF "Speeches and Statements," Box A-448, RG 60–2.2, PCA.

25. Transcript of Speech to the Advisory Committee to the Philadelphia Housing Authority Luncheon, 17 April 1953, FF "Speeches and Statements," Box A-448, RG 60–2.2, PCA.

26. Madeleine L. Cohen, "Postwar City Planning in Philadelphia: Edmund N. Bacon and the Design of Washington Square East," Ph.D. diss., University of Pennsylvania, 1991.

27. Philadelphia Redevelopment Authority, *Annual Report 1949* (January 1950), A-448, RG 60–2.2, PCA; Adams et al., *Philadelphia*, 100–123.

28. Cohen, "Postwar City Planning in Philadelphia." For discussion of Society Hill, see Neil Smith, *The New Urban Frontier: Gentrification and the Revanchist City* (New York: Routledge, 1996), 119–39.

29. "Philadelphia, The Great Exception," *New Republic* 125 (19 November 1951), 15; "Clean-Cut Reformers in Philadelphia," *New Republic* 133 (24 October 1955), 7–9; "Making Our Cities Fit to Live In," *The Reporter* 16 (21 February 1957), 30–34. Ed Bacon was on the cover of the 6 November 1964 issue of *Time*.

30. U.S. Department of Commerce, Bureau of the Census, *Sixteenth Census of the United States, 1940: Population and Housing: Statistics for Census Tracts, Philadelphia, Pa.* (Washington, D.C.: GPO, 1942); U.S. Department of Commerce, Bureau of the Census, *Census of Population: 1950. Vol. 3; Census Tract statistics, Chapter 42: Philadelphia, Pa., and Adjacent Area* (Washington, D.C.: GPO, 1952); U.S. Department of Commerce, Bureau of the Census, *U.S. Censuses of Population and Housing: 1960. Census Tracts, Philadelphia, Pa.-N.J. Standard Metropolitan Statistical Area*, Final report PHC(1)-1–116 [Volume 15, part 116] (Washington, D.C.: GPO, 1962).

31. William L. Slayton, "The University, the City, and Urban Renewal," in *The University, The City, and Urban Renewal: Report of a Regional Conference Sponsored by*

the American Council on Education and the West Philadelphia Corporation (Washington, D.C.: American Council on Education, 1963), 4.

32. Philadelphia City Planning Commission, Confidential report on the Philadelphia Trolley Corporation, 10 Sept. 1947, FF "Development Program (Committee on Physical Development) II 1945–50," Box 29, UPA 4, UPA, quoted in Adam B. Klarfeld, "Private Taking, Public Good? Penn's Expansion in West Philadelphia from 1945 to 1975," Senior thesis in History, University of Pennsylvania, April 1999, 19.

33. Philadelphia City Planning Commission, *University Redevelopment Area Plan*, September 1950, FF2, Section C, Box 55, UPJ9, UPA.

34. F. Haydn Morgan (Director of Project Research and Grants, University of Pennsylvania), "Penn Given $19 Million in 548 Contracts, U.S., Foundations and Industry All Sponsor Projects," *Philadelphia Sunday Bulletin* (Special section on research in Philadelphia), 4 June 1961; Committee on Advancement of Research, University of Pennsylvania, *1954–55 Annual Report*, UPA.

35. See Maj. Gen. John Willems, Letter to Harnwell, 3 March 1960, FF "United States Government (Army)—I," Box 155, GA110, UPA4, UPA; Robert B. Livingston, Letter to Harnwell, 12 June 1963, FF "Research, Sponsored—National Science Foundation, 1960–65," Box 143, UPA 4, UPA.

36. An example of this correspondence is Luke Quinn, Letter to Ravdin, 17 September 1963.

37. *University City News*, 14 September 1962, 9, FF "News Bureau Files, University City Project, Clippings III," UPF 8.5, UPA; also see various administrative documents, Box 152, UPA 4, UPA.

38. John L. Moore (Penn's Vice President for Business Affairs and then serving as Acting Director of the WPC), quoted in "Private Capital Is Sought to Build 'University City' in West Phila.," *Evening Bulletin*, 15 September 1959.

39. Francis J. Lammer, Introduction, *1951 Annual Report* (Philadelphia: January 1952), RG 161, PCA.

40. Philadelphia Redevelopment Authority, *1953 Annual Report* (Philadelphia: January 1954), 21, RG 161, PCA.

41. *University City News*, 14 Sept. 1962, 9, FF "University City Project Clippings III," UPF 8.5, UPA.

42. The earliest mention of this term is by John L. Moore in "Private Capital Is Sought to Build 'University City' in West Phila." Penn and its allies were not alone in using neighborhood renaming as a public-relations tool; other urban universities did this as well. Washington University, for example, renamed the part of St. Louis in which it was located "University City."

43. "University City: Dream to Reality," Editorial, *Philadelphia Inquirer*, 16 October 1960.

44. "The New University City," Editorial, *Evening Bulletin*, 13 October 1960.

45. Harnwell, Introductory Message to 1964 WPC *Annual Report*, Box 152, UPA 4, UPA.

46. President's Message, West Philadelphia Corporation *Annual Report*, October 1961, Box 154, UPA 4, UPA.

47. President Harnwell described the WPC's goals to a national high-tech business audience in "University City: Rebirth of a Community," *Challenge* (Magazine

of the Missile and Space Division of the General Electric Company) 2:1 (Spring 1963), 31–32.

48. Box 152, UPA 4, UPA. The "community of scholars" catchphrase caught on quickly with the sympathetic local press; see Daniel F. O'Leary, "Community of Scholars Planned for West Phila." *Sunday Bulletin*, 5 March 1961.

49. Jacobs, *The Death and Life of Great American Cities* (New York: Random House, 1961).

50. Arnold Hirsch shows how these impulses affected residence patterns in the University of Chicago's Hyde Park neighborhood in *Making the Second Ghetto*.

51. West Philadelphia Corporation, *Annual Report*, October 1961, Box 154, UPA 4, UPA.

52. Suggested Remarks for Greater Philadelphia Movement Meeting (unsigned; prepared for Harnwell or for Molinaro), 22 May 1963, FF "Community Relations-West Philadelphia Corporation," Box 154, UPA 4, UPA.

53. WPC newsletter files, Box 188, UPA 4, UPA.

54. West Philadelphia Corporation, *Elaborations on Living in University City,* FF "Community Relations—West Phila. Corp. 1960–65 V," Box 152, UPA 4, UPA.

55. West Philadelphia Corporation, "A Progress Report on University City, Philadelphia," September 1964, Box 152, UPA 4, UPA.

56. West Philadelphia Corporation, *Elaborations on Living in University City.*

57. Harnwell, Remarks to Luncheon Meeting of the West Philadelphia Corporation, 19 September 1966, FF "Community Relations—West Philadelphia Corporation," Box 188, UPA 4, UPA.

58. West Philadelphia Corporation, *Annual Report* 1962, Box 152, UPA 4, UPA; Harnwell, Remarks to Luncheon Meeting; Suggested Remarks for Greater Philadelphia Movement Meeting.

59. "Scientific Talent in the Third Federal Reserve District," Philadelphia Federal Reserve Bank *Business Review,* August 1965, 15, quoted in William H. Wilcox, "Research and Development and Local Universities and Colleges," *Delaware Valley Announcer,* April 1966.

60. Pennsylvania Economy League, "Philadelphia Labor Market Area Trends in Private Employment," *Citizens' Business*, 24 January 1966, quoted in Wilcox, "Research and Development at Local Universities and Colleges."

61. *Annual Report* (October 1959), FF "Redevelopment Authority," A-448, RG 60–2.2, PCA.

62. Between 1950 and 1970, the heyday of urban redevelopment in Philadelphia, the city's share of the regional population shrank from 56.4 percent to 40.4 percent, and its share of regional employment declined from 67.5 percent to 51.2 percent (Adams et al., *Philadelphia*, 17).

63. Wilcox, "Research and Development at Local Universities and Colleges," citing Jack Alterman, "Interindustry Employment Requirements," *Monthly Labor Review,* July 1965, 844.

64. West Philadelphia Corporation, "A Progress Report on University City, Philadelphia," September 1964, Box 152, UPA 4, UPA.

65. James Ridgeway, *The Closed Corporation: American Universities in Crisis* (New York: Ballentine Books, 1968), 41.

66. Hugh Scott, "University City: Brainsville on the March" *Philadelphia Inquirer Magazine*, 19 July 1964, 4.

67. Descriptive brochure on the University City Tower, 1961, FF "Community Relations—West Philadelphia Corporation—UC Tower 1960–65," Box 154, UPA 4, UPA.

68. Leo Molinaro, Letter to Joseph P. Worley, 28 September 1961, FF "University City Science Tower," Box 154, UPA 4, UPA.

69. Peter H. Binzen, "University City Tower Shifted," *Evening Bulletin*, 31 August 1961.

70. For example, in 1967 NIH awarded $1.5 million to the first year of the Regional Medical Program housed in a UCSC building, whose purpose was "to identify the region's needs and resources and to plan how these resources can best be utilized to reduce the incidence, morbidity, and fatality of heart disease, cancer and stroke" and NASA awarded an undisclosed sum to a UCSC tenant whose research "will lead to the most effective utilization of the valuable biomedical information and provide the most accurate and reliable predictions of the effects of long-term space exposure on the behavior and properties of the body" (WPC, *University City* 5: 4 [June 1967], FF "WPC V, 1965–70," Box 188, UPA 4, UPA).

71. The switch from high-rise to low-rise was accompanied by a shift in the Science Center's location, from the east to the north side of Penn's campus. President Harnwell seems to have had the idea for this move, suggesting that this location would be "better integrated into the over-all land use pattern of University City" (Harnwell, Letter to Richard Graves [Executive Vice President of the Philadelphia Industrial Development Corporation], 16 March 1961, FF "WPC," Box 154, UPA 4, UPA).

72. Group for Planning and Research, *Preliminary Draft: Trends in Research and Development: Demand for Facilities in the University City Urban Renewal Area Unit III*, July 1963, 76–80, Pamphlet Collection 322–1, TUA.

73. By 1960 the total population in the areas north of Market Street in West Philadelphia were majority-black; several of the census tracts to the north of the proposed site of the UCSC were more than 95 percent black. See U.S. Census Bureau, *U.S. Censuses of Population and Housing: 1960. Census Tracts, Philadelphia, Pa.-N.J. Standard Metropolitan Statistical Area* (Washington, D.C.: Government Printing Office, 1961).

74. Editorial, *Evening Bulletin*, 31 August 1961.

75. Memorandum, 30 August 1961, FF "UC Tower, 1960–1965," Box 154, UPA 4, UPA.

76. Harnwell, Text of Remarks at UCSC Groundbreaking Ceremony, 9 January 1961, FF "Community Relations—West Philadelphia Corporation—UC Tower 1960–65," Box 154, UPA 4, UPA.

77. Wilcox, "Research and Development and Local Universities and Colleges."

78. Elizabeth P. Deutermann, "The Innovation Industry," *Business Review of the Federal Reserve Bank of Philadelphia*, August 1965, reprinted in *Mainsprings of Growth* (Federal Reserve Bank of Philadelphia, March 1967), Pamphlet Collection 298–2, TUA, 73.

79. Klarfeld's "Private Taking, Public Good?" provides a thorough account of the extent of displacement and resultant community conflict spurred by renewal around Penn.

80. Betty M. Jacob, Letter to Robert Geddes, 21 March 1963, Box 154, UPA 4, UPA.

81. The class-conscious racial conflict in West Philadelphia occurred during critical years of struggle for African American civil rights and economic rights, and of escalating racial consciousness. For discussion of these movements nationally, see Manning Marable, *Race, Reform, and Rebellion: The Second Reconstruction in Black America, 1945–1990* (Jackson: University Press of Mississippi, 1991 [revised 2nd ed.]) and Todd Gitlin, *The Sixties: Years of Hope, Days of Rage* (New York: Bantam Books, 1987). For examinations of the politics in other cities, see Ronald Formosiano, *Boston Against Busing: Race, Class, and Ethnicity in the 1960s and 1970s* (Chapel Hill: University of North Carolina Press, 1991) and William Chafe, *Civilities and Civil Rights: Greensboro, North Carolina and the Struggle for Black Freedom* (New York: Oxford University Press, 1980).

82. Unsigned memorandum on "Relocation of Residents," September 1968, Box 188, UPA 4, UPA.

83. West Philadelphia Corporation, *Annual Report* 1962, Box 154, UPA 4, UPA.

84. Harold F. Wise, Letter to Robert J. Painter, 9 August 1961, Box 154, UPA 4, UPA.

85. Harnwell, Letter to Gustave G. Amersterdam, 2 March 1964, FF "Community Relations—West Philadelphia Corporation," Box 154, UPA 4, UPA.

86. Harnwell noted the local media's attention to the controversy and delay in his remarks to a luncheon meeting of the WPC on 19 September 1966. Also see Harnwell's remarks to Annual Meeting of West Philadelphia Corporation, 22 November 1966, Box 188, UPA 4, UPA.

87. Memorandum to the WPC Board of Directors, 20 May 1963, Box 154, UPA 4, UPA.

88. Harnwell, Remarks to luncheon meeting of the West Philadelphia Corporation, September 19, 1966, FF "Community Relations—West Philadelphia Corporation," Box 188, UPA 4, UPA.

89. Molinaro, Memorandum to the WPC Board of Directors, 20 May 1963.

90. Most undergraduates seem to have tolerated, and perhaps agreed with, the protesters but did not join their effort in great numbers. There were a few small efforts on the part of conservative students to present an alternative undergraduate view. In 1969, for example, the "Committee to Combat Campus Coercion" circulated a petition on campus disagreeing with the demonstrators and their demands of student "rights" (FF "Quadripartite Committee on University/Community Development [Community Relations], 1965–70," Box 188, UPA 4, UPA).

91. Goldstein, "Vietnam Research on Campus: The Summit/Spicerack Controversy at the University of Pennsylvania, 1965–67."

92. "Urban Renewal Land Acquisition Begins in Redevelopment Units 3 and 4," *University City* newsletter 5:3 (March 1967), Box 154, UPA 4, UPA.

93. Leo Molinaro, Letter to Francis J. Lammer, 25 August 1964, FF "Community Relations—West Philadelphia Corporation," Box 154, UPA 4, UPA.

94. For example, Chicago officials used urban renewal to create a barrier of large-scale private development between the downtown Loop and the majority-black South Side (Hirsch, *Making the Second Ghetto*, especially chap. 4).

95. Decentralization of job opportunities compounded the shortages created by overall decline in well-paying unskilled work in the wake of deindustrialization. In 1950 Philadelphia contained 67.5 percent of the region's jobs; by 1970 it had only 51.2 percent (Adams et al., *Philadelphia*, 17). The suburbanization of jobs was particularly detrimental to black workers of this period, who because of discriminatory housing policies and limited economic means were rarely able to move out of the city. In 1968 the economist John Kain theorized the geographic disjunction between low-income minority residence patterns and blue-collar jobs as "spatial mismatch" (Kain, "Housing Segregation, Negro Employment, and Metropolitan Decentralization," *Quarterly Journal of Economics* 82 [May 1968]: 175–97).

96. "Dr. Mather's summing up," Editorial, *Philadelphia Evening Bulletin*, 26 June 1969, Subject File "UCSC Editorials," *Evening Bulletin* Collection, TUA.

97. "Science Center Pathway," Editorial, *Philadelphia Evening Bulletin*, 22 November 1976, Subject File "UCSC Editorials," *Evening Bulletin* Collection, TUA.

98. For an analysis of ongoing outreach efforts, see Lee Benson and Ira Harkavy, "The Role of Community-Higher Education-School Partnerships in Educational and Societal Development and Democratization," *Universities and Community Schools Journal* (a publication of the University of Pennsylvania Center for Community Partnerships), Fall–Winter 2002.

99. In the time period covered by this chapter, high taxes were less of a factor in location choices than they would be in the 1970s and beyond; the correspondence of involved officials reveals little concern with city tax rates and more concern with city amenities and built environment. For analysis of the economic effects of local taxes, see Andrew Haughwout, Robert Inman, Steven Craig, and Thomas Luce, *Local Revenue Hills: A General Equilibrium Specification with Evidence from Four U.S. Cities*, National Bureau of Economic Research Working Paper no. W7603 (March 2000). For a history of the Philadelphia wage tax, see "The Sterling Act: A Brief History" (Philadelphia: Pennsylvania Economy League, 1999).

100. Analysis by David Birch cited in Pennsylvania Economy League, "An Assessment of Early-Stage Venture Capital in Greater Philadelphia: 1986 to 1996," January 1998.

101. Many of these efforts have been facilitated by the Center for Community Partnerships, founded in 1992. See www.upenn.edu/ccp (accessed 25 August 2003).

Chapter 5
Selling the New South: Georgia Tech and Atlanta

1. Emory and Georgia State were not ignored by local economic development campaigns of this sort, but they were not employed as an economic development partner and high-tech economic asset like Georgia Tech. Medical research powerhouse Emory played a key role in this period in building up the metropolitan area's health care and medical research structure, a development also greatly

aided and abetted by the growing presence of the U.S. Centers for Disease Control (CDC). The purpose of this chapter, however, is to trace the relationship between Georgia Tech and local leaders, and explore the process of high-tech and defense-related development—one that had different institutional dynamics than the growth of medical research in Atlanta, which was a process spurred in large part by the presence of the CDC (a presence that predated the Cold War). For more on the role of Emory University in the growth of medical sciences in Atlanta, see Thomas H. English, *Emory University, 1915–1965: A Semicentennial History* (Atlanta, Ga.: Emory University, 1966); for more on the history of the CDC, see Elizabeth W. Etheridge, *Sentinel for Health: A History of the Centers for Disease Control* (Berkeley and Los Angeles: University of California Press, 1992).

2. These efforts often centered around large, ambitious events that sought to bring national and international attention to the city, a trend that began with the Cotton States and International Exposition of 1895 and continued through the Atlanta Olympics of 1996. See Dana F. White and Timothy J. Crimmins, "How Atlanta Grew: Cool Heads, Hot Air, and Hard Work," in *Urban Atlanta: Redefining the Role of the City,* ed. Andrew Marshall Hamer (Atlanta: College of Business Administration, Georgia State University, 1980), 25–44.

3. Speech delivered at the Banquet of the New England Club, New York, 21 December 1886, in *Life of Henry W. Grady Including His Writings and Speeches,* ed. Joel Chandler Harris (New York: Cassell Company, 1890), 83–93. Sherman's presence is noted in Gary M. Pomerantz, *Where Peachtree Meets Sweet Auburn* (New York: Scribner, 1996), 59. For analysis and critique of Atlanta's mythmaking, see Charles Rutheiser, *Imagineering Atlanta: The Politics of Place in the City of Dreams* (New York: Verso, 1996).

4. Ronald H. Bayor, "Atlanta: The Historical Paradox" in *The Atlanta Paradox,* ed. David L. Sjoquist (New York: Russell Sage Foundation, 2000), 43. Class divisions were not limited to the white community; wide political and cultural gulfs existed between educated, middle-class blacks and the poor. This had an important effect on the black community's ability to mobilize politically, as discussed in Ronald H. Bayor, *Race and the Shaping of Twentieth-Century Atlanta* (Chapel Hill: University of North Carolina Press, 1996) as well as Clarence N. Stone, *Regime Politics: Governing Atlanta, 1946–1988* (Lawrence: University Press of Kansas, 1989). Racial violence also had undertones of gender as well as class divisions; see Nancy MacLean's study of another industrial conflict during this period in Atlanta, "Gender, Sexuality and the Politics of Lynching: The Leo Frank Case Revisited," in *Under Sentence of Death: Lynching the South,* ed. W. Fitzhugh Brundage (Chapel Hill: University of North Carolina Press, 1997).

5. For discussion of the "New South" political ideology and Atlanta as the presumptive epitome of this ideology, see Harold E. Davis, *Henry Grady's New South: Atlanta, a Brave and Beautiful City* (Tuscaloosa: University of Alabama Press, 1990).

6. Robert C. McMath Jr., Ronald H. Bayor, James E. Brittain, Lawrence Foster, August W. Giebelhaus, and Germaine M. Reed, *Engineering the New South: Georgia Tech, 1885–1985* (Athens: University of Georgia Press, 1985).

7. The institution's name was not changed to the "Georgia Institute of Technology" until 1948. To minimize confusion, however, this chapter will refer to it as "Georgia Tech" throughout.

8. N. E. Harris quoted in "Formal Opening," *Atlanta Constitution*, 6 October 1888, quoted in McMath et al., *Engineering the New South*, 49.

9. For examples, see Georgia Institute of Technology, Annual Report Files, Boxes 18–19, Series 86–05–01, GTA.

10. Georgia Institute of Technology Board of Regents, 1 July 1934, quoted in McMath et al., *Engineering the New South*, 186.

11. McMath et al., *Engineering the New South*, 172. Discussion of Tech football games as a mainstay of white Atlanta social life in the postwar era is found in Seymour Freegood, "Life in Buckhead," *Fortune* 64 (September 1961), 108–10 et seq.

12. Truman A. Hartshorn and Keith R. Ihlandfeldt, "Growth and Change in Metropolitan Atlanta" in Sjoquist, *The Atlanta Paradox*, ed.

13. Bayor, "Atlanta: The Historical Paradox," 48.

14. *Report of the Forward Atlanta Commission: Being a Detailed Statements of the Administration of the Forward Atlanta Fund for the Year 1926, 1927, 1928, 1929* (Atlanta: Forward Atlanta Commission, 1929); "Industry Spreads in Atlanta," *Business Week*, 10 September 1949.

15. Industrial Bureau, Atlanta Chamber of Commerce, *Key to Atlanta* (Atlanta, 1928), 1.

16. White and Crimmins, How Atlanta Grew," 30.

17. Bayor, "Atlanta: The Historical Paradox," 44.

18. Arthur C. Nelson, *Deciding Factors for Regional Decision-Making in Metro Atlanta* (Atlanta: Research Atlanta, June 1999), x.

19. Hartsfield, *Annual Message of the Mayor to the City Council*, 6 January 1947, FF 1, Box 34, Series IV, William Berry Hartsfield Papers, Emory University Special Collections (hereafter WBHP, EUSC). The one interruption to his tenure was when he was voted out of office in 1940, losing by only eighty-three votes to Roy LeCraw. LeCraw was a former president of the local Chamber of Commerce who ran on a promise to reduce the vigilance with which Atlanta police gave speeding tickets. Fortunately for Hartsfield, LeCraw took a military leave of absence in 1942, and Hartsfield was reelected to his old job in a special election (Harold H. Martin, *William Berry Hartsfield: Mayor of Atlanta* [Athens: University of Georgia Press, 1978], 32–36).

20. As early as 1949, manufacturing employment exceeded agricultural employment in Georgia (Engineering Experiment Station, Georgia Institute of Technology, "Little Known Facts about Georgia's Economy," *IDeas* 2:1 [March–April 1960], EES-Industrial Development Division, Subject Files, GTA).

21. Community Improvement Program, City of Atlanta, *Economic Report No. 1*, February 1966, 21, FF 2, Box 6, City Range T-6, AHC. Contemporary observers expressed concern that the shift was precipitating an "urban crisis"—not in large cities like Atlanta but in small cities in farming areas, which were nearly becoming ghost towns as their able-bodied residents moved to the city for work (Gene Britton, "Tech and State Experts Study Scared Counties," *Atlanta Journal-Constitution*, 12 July 1959).

22. Schulman, *From Cotton Belt to Sunbelt*, 140. It is particularly valuable to keep in mind Schulman's point that defense dollars in and of themselves were not what remade the economy of the South, but what he terms the "constellation of defense-related programs" and industries that accompanied this military spend-

ing, increasing industrial capacity, shifting demographics, and making the South more like the rest of the nation economically and socially (135–73).

23. Russell chaired the Senate Armed Forces Committee from 1951 to 1967, with the exception of the years of a Republican majority, 1953–55, when he was minority leader. Vinson chaired the House Armed Services Committee from 1947–65.

24. For discussion of Russell's political career and his leadership of the Southern opposition to civil rights legislation, see Fite, *Richard B. Russell*.

25. Richard S. Combes and William J. Todd, "From Henry Grady to the Georgia Research Alliance: A Case Study of Science-Based Development in Georgia," in *Science-Based Economic Development: Case Studies Around the World*, ed. Susan U. Raymond, *Annals of the New York Academy of Sciences* 798 (1996), 63. Another of the federal facilities locating in Georgia during this period was one that responded to the problems of the "old" South rather than the new: the U.S. Public Health Service's Centers for Disease Control. The facility opened in Atlanta as the "Communicable Disease Center" in 1946 and had "a mission to work with state and local officials in the fight against malaria . . . typhus, and other communicable diseases," as there still were periodic epidemics of these tropical maladies in the region (www.cdc.gov/od/media/timeline.htm, accessed 11 January 2001). Although an organization that now employs thousands of scientific professionals, the CDC is not discussed in this chapter, as prior to 1970 it was less a research organization than a public health entity. It also had little relationship with the research activities under way at Georgia Tech nor did it figure significantly in the regional leadership's economic development strategies.

26. "Atlanta: Aviation Center of the South," *Atlanta Magazine* 1:2 (June 1961), 16–19; "Brief Resume of Facts and Figures on the Population and Economy of Greater Atlanta," 27 August 1959, 4, FF 6, Box 1, Atlanta Bureau of Planning Files, City Range A-7, AHC.

27. Kenneth C. Wagner and M. Dale Henson, *Industrial Development in Georgia Since 1947: Progress, Problems, and Goals* (Atlanta: Industrial Development Branch, Engineering Experiment Station, Georgia Institute of Technology, 1961).

28. "C141 Herald Cargo Profits, Colonel Says," *Atlanta Journal*, 22 April 1963. For other mention of Lockheed, see Atlanta Bureau of Planning, "Brief Resume of Facts and Figures on the Population and Economy of Greater Atlanta," 27 August 1959, FF 6, Box 1, Atlanta Bureau of Planning Files, City Range A-7, AHC; "Lockheed Looks to the Future," *Atlanta Magazine* 1:2 (June 1961) 34–38; Gerald T. Horton, "Atlanta and the World Market," *Atlanta Magazine* 1:10 (February 1962), 25–28, 51–57.

29. William A. Emerson, Jr., "Where the Paper Clips Jump . . . and 'M' Stands for Men, Money, Millions," *Newsweek*, 19 October, 1959, 94–96.

30. One mention of this phrase is in Hartsfield's undated notes, FF 6, Box 19, Series III, Subseries 4, WBHP, EUSC.

31. Martin, *William Berry Hartsfield*, 80.

32. For extended discussion of the power dynamics of Atlanta during this period, see Clarence Stone, *Economic Growth and Neighborhood Discontent: System Bias in the Urban Renewal Program of Atlanta* (Chapel Hill: University of North Carolina Press, 1976).

33. William A. Emerson Jr., "Surge in the South: The Long Reach of Atlanta," *Newsweek*, 8 March 1954.

34. Rutheiser, *Imagineering Atlanta*, 147.

35. Lochner Report and related materials, Bureau of Planning Files, City Range A-8, Box 6, AHC.

36. *Funds Available for Highway Purposes, 1951, a Study Committee Report on Federal Aid to Highways*, Submitted to the Commission on Intergovernmental Relations, (Washington, D.C.: GPO, June 1955), table 1.

37. In his inaugural address as president of the American Municipal Association in 1952, Hartsfield "urged federal legislation to encourage highway construction" (Martin, *William Berry Hartsfield*, 97). By the 1990s, downtown Atlanta was at the hub of three interstate highways, and the metropolitan area as a whole had 261 miles of interstates within its boundaries (Atlanta Regional Commission, *Atlanta Regional Transportation Planning Fact Book* [December 1998], 9). The Atlanta region's prodigious road building resulted in its becoming one of the most congested and polluted metropolitan areas in the United States by the end of the twentieth century; see *Moving Beyond Sprawl: The State of Metropolitan Atlanta* (Washington, D.C.: Brookings Institution Center on Urban and Metropolitan Policy, 1999).

38. As Ron Bayor has demonstrated, these roads also performed the convenient function of blocking black residential expansion into white neighborhoods (*Race and the Shaping of Twentieth-Century Atlanta*, 74 et seq.).

39. Metropolitan Planning Commission, *Up Ahead: A Regional Land Use Plan for Metropolitan Atlanta* (February 1952), 9.

40. Douglass Carter, "Atlanta: Smart Politics and Good Race Relations," *The Reporter* 17:1 (16 July 1957).

41. Metropolitan Planning Commission, *Up Ahead*, 5.

42. Ibid., 5, 7, 73.

43. Metropolitan Planning Commission, *Metropolitan Growth Problems: A Follow-up of the Comprehensive Plan for the Metropolitan Area*, October 1957, 6–7, Box "City of Atlanta Planning Publications," City Range T-4, AHC.

44. "Industry Spreads in Atlanta," *Business Week*, 10 September 1949.

45. Metropolitan Planning Commission, *Metropolitan Growth Problems*, 52.

46. This was the result of a massive voter registration drive spearheaded by leaders of the black community (Bayor, *Race and the Shaping of Twentieth-Century Atlanta*, chap. 2).

47. Hartsfield, Letter to unspecified "Gentlemen," 7 January 1943, FF 1, Box 29, Series III, Subseries 7, WBHP, EUSC. Also see Hartsfield, Remarks before Buckhead Civitan Club, 24 March 1941, FF 1, Box 29, Series III, Subseries 7, WBHP, EUSC. Discussion of Hartsfield's pragmatic, business-driven approach to racial progressivism can be found in Freegood, "Life in Buckhead."

48. Hartsfield, undated notes, FF 2, Box 29, Series III, Subseries 7, WBHP, EUSC.

49. Hartsfield repeated this phrase often, including in William Emerson's 1959 *Newsweek* article, which is likely what brought it national attention ("Where the Paper Clips Jump . . .").

50. Emerson, "Surge in the South."

51. An unnamed "native" quoted in ibid.

52. Metropolitan Planning Commission, *Metropolitan Growth Problems*, 1.

53. Hartshorn and Ihlandfeldt, "Growth and Change in Metropolitan Atlanta."

54. McMath et al., *Engineering the New South*, 214–15. Federal R&D did not change everything. The EES's bread and butter well into the late 1940s continued to be industrial surveys and conducting research on matters relevant to Georgia and Southeastern industries like lumber and paper, agriculture, and mining. "The Experiment Station will undertake work on any industrial or business problem in the fields of economic, management, engineering or technical research which affects the people of this state," wrote the *Atlanta Journal* in 1943 (John Mebane, "Tech Winds Up Economic Survey in 26 Counties," *Atlanta Journal,* 17 September 1943). In 1947 the Atlanta Federal Reserve Bank noted that the EES was "one way that colleges and universities can directly assist Southern industry to better economic conditions" (Charles T. Taylor quoted in John Mebane, "Tech Research Cited As Aid to Industry," *Atlanta Journal,* 4 March 1947).

55. Ivan Allen Jr., *Mayor: Notes on the Sixties* (New York: Simon and Schuster, 1971), 150. The state's rural bias in spending priorities grew out of the county unit voting system for statewide offices that gave sparsely populated rural counties nearly the same political weight as densely populated places like Atlanta's Fulton County. Under the system, which *Time* called "one of the most bizarre devices in U.S. state politics," each county received between two and six "unit votes" that went to candidates who received the majority of the popular vote in that county. The tally of all the unit votes determined the winner of any statewide election. After being found unconstitutional by the Supreme Court, county unit voting was outlawed in 1961. See "Georgia: There'll Be Some Changes Made," *Time*, 11 May 1962.

56. Carter, "Atlanta: Smart Politics and Good Race Relations."

57. "1944 Approved Development Plan of Georgia School of Technology," Records in Box 6, 85–11–01, GTA.

58. *Annual Report 1945–46*, 14, FF 7, Box 18, 86–05–01, GTA.

59. *Annual Report 1947–48*, 1, FF 9, Box 18, 86–05–01, GTA. The Georgia state university system's perpetual funding shortages during this period stemmed from a state prohibition on deficit spending. As McMath et al. observe, this meant that public funding for higher education "was extremely sensitive to short-term economic fluctuations and generally incapable of keeping up with the inflationary spiral" (*Engineering the New South*, 416).

60. While the institution's financial problems were severe at times, the negative tone of these reports probably stemmed in some part from the rather gloomy attitude of Van Leer. When Edwin D. Harrison succeeded him as president, the reports became considerably more optimistic. Harrison was upbeat and diplomatic; in the 1957–58 *Annual Report*, his first, he wrote, "A number of positive steps forward have been taken. . . . It is with a deep sense of gratitude that we all extend our appreciation for the generosity of our state in making it possible to improve our salary picture" (*Annual Report 1957–58*, 1, FF 19, Box 18, 86–05–01, GTA).

61. "$1,000,000 Research, Tech Total," *Atlanta Constitution*, 19 September 1947.

62. McMath et al., *Engineering the New South*, 214–15, 263.

63. Georgia Tech Research Institute, *Annual Reports* FY 1968 and FY 1970; *Treasurer's Report* FY 1971, FF 37, Box 11, 86–05–01, GTA.

64. "Industrial Associate Program," FF 11, Box 12, 86–05–01, GTA.

65. George W. Morris Jr., *Calculators and Computers: A Manufacturing Opportunity in Atlanta*, Prepared for Forward Atlanta, the Atlanta Chamber of Commerce by the Industrial Development Division, Engineering Experiment Station, Georgia Institute of Technology, August 1962, 10.

66. McMath et al., *Engineering the New South*, 311, 319–36.

67. Stone, *Regime Politics* 39. The first steps toward expansion did not use federal dollars. Although the campus expansion plan of 1944 was slow to get under way, in the next seven years, Tech purchased nearly $13 million worth of land for campus expansion. *Report of Construction*, August 7, 1951, FF 8, Box 5, 85–11–01, GTA.

68. McMath et al., *Engineering the New South*, 337–38; Bayor, *Race and the Shaping of Twentieth-Century Atlanta*, 80.

69. Each of these visits and transactions was duly noted for administrative records. For examples of these see Georgia Tech Urban Renewal and Land Analysis Files, ca. 1941–74, 92–02–04, GTA.

70. "Hemphill Project Praised, Scored at Open Hearing," *Atlanta Constitution*, 14 November 1951.

71. McMath et al., *Engineering the New South*, 381–82. For further discussion, see Stone, *Community Power Structure* and Bayor, *Race and the Shaping of Twentieth-Century Atlanta*.

72. Metropolitan Planning Commission, *Up Ahead*, 34.

73. "Rough Draft Comments on Study Areas," Confidential Memorandum, 3 February 1959, FF 1, Box 1, Atlanta Bureau of Planning Files, AHC.

74. Harrison, Letter to Mayor Ivan Allen Jr., 4 December 1962, FF 7, Box 3, 86–05–01, GTA.

75. In a 1961 talk to area business leaders, the director of Atlanta's urban renewal program indicated that "if a school expansion project is proposed in which the school 'credits' account for the 1/3 portion of funds normally provided by the city, such a limited project could be processed without waiting for city funds" (Minutes of meeting of North West Atlanta Businessmen's Association, 20 April 961, FF 7, Box 3, 86–05–01, GTA).

76. Various documents relating to 1962 report (called Keck Report), FF 17, Box 2, 92–04–02, GTA.

77. Harrison, Report to Mayor and Board of Aldermen of Atlanta, 4 December 1964, FF 7, Box 3, 86–05–01, GTA.

78. Arthur D. Little, Inc., Georgia *Tech: Impetus to Economic Growth, Report to Georgia Tech National Alumni Association*, November 1963.

79. Harrison, Letter to Earl H. Metzger (Director of Redevelopment, Housing Authority of City of Atlanta), 10 March 1965, FF 7, Box 3, 86–05–01, GTA.

80. Dr. J. E. Boyd, "The 27th Year," presentation or speech to unspecified audience, July 1961, FF 42, Box 11, 86–05–01, GTA.

81. Between 1946 and 1956, nearly half the firms moving to Atlanta (96 of 211) located outside city limits. The total industrial square footage of these suburban firms, not surprisingly, was close to 3 million square feet more than the total in the city. See internal notes with annotation "copy of data given to Mr. Rowland

(with Dr. Benchler) 8/29/56," appended to "Comparison of manufacturing and population trends of United States with those for Atlanta, Georgia, Standard Metropolitan Area," MPC response to Scripps Foundation Questionnaire, 1954, FF 8, Box 1, Atlanta Bureau of Planning Files, City Range A-7, AHC.

82. Metropolitan Planning Commission, *We're Feeling Like a Million: 1959 Population-Housing Report, Atlanta Standard Metropolitan Area* (Atlanta: MPC, 1959), 2. By the 1990s, the jurisdictional fragmentation of the Atlanta region would become a liability, not an asset, as it compromised Atlanta's ability to create regional strategies around land use and transportation planning. See *Moving Beyond Sprawl.*

83. Atlanta Chamber of Commerce, *Atlanta: A National City* (Atlanta, ca. 1972), 3.

84. "Brief Resume of Facts and Figures on the Population and Economy of Greater Atlanta," 27 August 1959, FF 6, Box 1, Atlanta Bureau of Planning Files, City Range A-7, AHC.

85. William A. Emerson Jr., "Where the Paper Clips Jump . . ."

86. Boyd, "The 27th Year."

87. By 1965 the average weekly wages for Georgia workers in transportation industries was $131.46; the U.S. average for transportation was $137.71, but the U.S. average weekly wage for all industries was $107.53 (United States Department of Labor, Bureau of Labor Statistics, quoted in Amy Collins, *Industrial Development in Georgia, 1958–1965* [Atlanta: Industrial Development Division, Engineering Experiment Station, Georgia Institute of Technology, 1967], chart 10).

88. "Plant Location: Where the People Are," *Duns Review and Modern Industry* 83: 2 (March 1964), 106–7.

89. Amy Collins, *Industrial Development in Georgia, 1958–1965* (Atlanta: Industrial Development Division, Engineering Experiment Station, Georgia Institute of Technology, 1967), iii.

90. For analysis of the Southern labor movement prior to the civil rights period, see F. Ray Marshall, *Labor in the South* (Cambridge, Mass.: Harvard University Press, 1967); for discussion and analysis of the Southern labor movement during the postwar civil rights era, see Alan Draper, *Conflict of Interests: Organized Labor and the Civil Rights Movement in the South, 1954–1968* (Ithaca, N.Y.: ILR Press, 1994).

91. EES, "Little Known Facts about Georgia's Economy," *IDeas* 2: 1 (March–April 1960), EES-Industrial Development Division, Subject Files, GTA.

92. Wagner and Henson, *Industrial Development in Georgia Since 1947,* 32.

93. Collins, *Industrial Development in Georgia, 1958–1965,* iii.

94. Curtis Driskell, "The Force of 'Forward Atlanta," *Atlanta* 4:3 (August 1964), 37–41.

95. Gerald T. Horton, "Atlanta and the World Market," *Atlanta* 1:10 (February 1962), 25–28, 51–57.

96. Atlanta Region Metropolitan Planning Commission, *Economic Potentials: R&D, The Outlook for Research and Development in Metropolitan Atlanta,* December 1962, 49.

97. "Space Crescent Transforms Gulf Area," *Business Week,* 24 March 1962, also quoted in *Economic Potentials: R&D.*

98. Appendix I, *Procedures Manual*, Engineering Experiment Station, Georgia Institute of Technology, 1960, FF 44, Box 11, 86–05–01, GTA.

99. For a comprehensive exploration of Scientific Atlanta and its effect upon the regional economy, see Richard S. Combes, "Technology, Southern Style: Case Studies of High-Tech Firms in Atlanta, 1836–1984," Ph.D. diss., Georgia Institute of Technology, May 2002, 75–123.

100. Dr. J. E. Boyd, "The 27th Year."

101. "Opportunities on the Fringe . . ." undated (probably 1960s), EES-Industrial Development Division, Subject Files, GTA.

102. Driskell, "The Force of 'Forward Atlanta.' " Although founded as a publicity gimmick, *Atlanta* magazine quickly moved into more substantive and less slanted journalism; by the late 1960s, it was an independent publication ("City Magazines Are the Talk of the Town," *Business Week*, 18 February, 1967, 184 et seq.).

103. George W. Morris Jr., *Calculators and Computers: A Manufacturing Opportunity in Atlanta*.

104. Industrial Development Division, Engineering Experiment Station, *Atlanta's Potential in the Aerospace Age*, Prepared for Forward Atlanta, the Atlanta Chamber of Commerce, July 1963, 4. The publication was "not in the same league with the stereotyped notion of a Chamber of Commerce brochure," wrote the *Atlanta Journal*, "and it couldn't have come out at a better time" (William McClure, "Tech's Aerospace Report Makes Area a Contender," 22 July 1963).

105. The leading local newspapers, the *Atlanta Journal* and *Atlanta Constitution* (soon merged into one publication) had publishers and editors that were solidly inside the civic elite and likely more than willing to assist in the effort to promote Tech's research capabilities.

106. Robert Joiner, "Industry Sends Tough Problems to Tech," *Atlanta Journal and Constitution*, 11 March 1962.

107. Frank Wells, "Tech Lab Turns Out Missile Nose Cones," *Atlanta Journal and Constitution*, 24 January 1965, C1.

108. Other reports prepared by EES researchers for the Chamber of Commerce included W. C. Eisenhauer, *Electronic Testing and Measuring Instruments: A Manufacturing Opportunity in Atlanta*, September 1962, and George W. Morris Jr., *Antibiotics: A Manufacturing Opportunity in Atlanta*, June 1962. The MPC published *Economic Potentials: R&D, The Outlook for Research and Development in Metropolitan Atlanta* in December 1962.

109. Wagner and Henson, *Industrial Development in Georgia Since 1947*, 32.

110. George B. Leonard Jr., "The Second Battle of Atlanta," *Look*, 25 April 1961.

111. Freegood, "Life in Buckhead," 190.

112. "Glad to See You: Reporters in Atlanta," *Newsweek* 58 (11 September 1961), 93–94.

113. Bayor, *Race and the Shaping of Twentieth-Century Atlanta*, 226. Bayor points out that "the Atlanta desegregation process was very similar to segregation policies used in northern schools at the same time—for example, race-based school site selection, difficult transfer policies for blacks but not for whites, and the underutilization of white schools" (227).

114. Hartsfield, Annual and Final Message to the Board of Aldermen, 2 January 1962, FF 1, Box 34, Series IV, WBHP, EUSC.

115. Ibid. Hartsfield's connection of Atlanta's desegregation to Cold War ideological battles was not as far-reaching as it seems. See Mary Dudziak, *Cold War Civil Rights: Race and the Image of American Democracy* (Princeton, N.J.: Princeton University Press, 2000).

116. Joseph R. Daughen, "There's More Fancy than Fact in Atlanta's Racial Reputation," *Philadelphia Evening Bulletin*, 19 May 1965.

117. James L. Townsend, "The Miracle in Atlanta," *Town and Country*, February 1963; Judd Arnett, "Atlanta's Mayor Points Way to Sane Integration," *Detroit Free Press*, 31 May 1961.

118. "Boom Town," *Time* 80 (at 17 August 1962), 20.

119. Bayor, *Race and the Shaping of Twentieth-Century Atlanta*, 229.

120. U.S. Dept of Commerce, quoted in "Danger Flags of Success," *Atlanta* 4:3 (August 1964), 53.

121. Raleigh Bryans, "Sandy Springs Annexing Fails," *Atlanta Journal*, 12 May 1966.

122. Letter to Earl Patton, 19 December 1969, FF 4, Box 29, Series III, Subseries 7, WBHP, EUSC.

123. "Wooing White-Collar Workers to Suburbia: Office Parks," *Business Week*, 8 July 1967, 96–98.

124. Celestine Sibley, "Atlanta: Manageable, Many-Sided, Magnificent," *Saturday Evening Post*, November 1974, 101.

125. "Wooing White-Collar Workers to Suburbia: Office Parks."

126. Atlanta Chamber of Commerce, *Atlanta: A National City*, 2.

127. "Research Park Thrives in Academic Neighborhood," *Business Week*, 10 December 1966.

128. McMath et al., *Engineering the New South*, 364–65; Michael I. Luger and Harvey A. Goldstein, *Technology in the Garden: Research Parks and Regional Economic Development* (Chapel Hill: University of North Carolina Press, 1991), 76–99.

129. James A. Donovan, *Atlanta Data Processing, 1969*, Prepared for the Atlanta Chamber of Commerce by the Industrial Development Division, Engineering Experiment Station, Georgia Institute of Technology, June 1969.

130. Frederick C. Apple, "Industrial Spinoff from Georgia Tech: A Study of the Impact of a Technological Center on Its Surroundings," discussion paper 12, Program on Regional Industrial Development, Georgia Institute of Technology, May 1969, FF 43, Box 11, 86–05–01, GTA.

131. Schulman, *Race and the Shaping of Twentieth-Century Atlanta*, 170–71; McMath et al., *Engineering the New South*, 411. Tech made another Stanford connection in 1976, after Pettit recruited Donald Grace, the associate dean at Stanford, to become director of the EES.

132. McMath et al., *Engineering the New South*, 347, 412.

133. *GTRI Annual Report FY 1970*, 1 July 1969 to 30 June 1970, FF 37, Box 11, 86–05–01, GTA.

134. *GTRI Treasurer's Report FY 1971*, FF 37, Box 11, 86–05–01, GTA.

135. This highly unbalanced growth also meant that the "dirtier" industries like heavy manufacturing and trucking stayed on the (more heavily black) south

and west sides of the region. See Hammer and Company Associates, "Preliminary Survey of Trucking Industry, Atlanta Metropolitan Area," Prepared for Lockheed Air Terminal, Inc., Burbank, California, September 1962, FF 1, Box 19, Series III, Subseries 4, WBHP, EUSC. For discussion of unbalanced growth, see *Moving Beyond Sprawl.*

136. "Atlanta, the Hopeful City," *Fortune* 74 (August 1966), 156. For further discussion of the industrial park geography of Atlanta, see Truman A. Hartshorn, with contributions from Sanford Bederman, Sid Davis, G. E. Alan Dever, and Richard Pillsbury, *Metropolis in Georgia: Atlanta's Rise As a Major Transaction Center* (Cambridge, Mass.: Ballinger Publishing Co., 1976), 33.

137. "Wooing White-Collar Workers to Suburbia: Office Parks."

138. Paul A. Duke, Letter to Dr. Arthur G. Hansen, 1 August 1969, FF1, Box 3, 86–05–01, GTA.

139. Cover note to news clipping (no longer in file) sent by Duke to Hansen, dated 6 September 1969, FF1, Box 3, 86–05–01, GTA.

140. Memorandum on "A Model Research Park Facility," undated, FF 1, Box 3, 86–05–01, GTA.

141. Paul Duke, Memorandum to Hansen, May 22, 1970, FF 1, Box 3, 86–05–01, GTA.

142. Memorandum to Hansen, undated, FF 1, Box 3, 86–05–01, GTA.

143. McMath et al. 445.

144. Bayor, *Race and the Shaping of Twentieth-Century Atlanta*, 51.

145. See Raymond W. Smilor, George Kozmetsky, and David V. Gibson, "The Austin/San Antonio Corridor: The Dynamics of a Developing Technopolis," in *Creating the Technopolis: Linking Technology Commercialization and Economic Development* (Cambridge, Mass.: Ballinger Publishing Company, 1988), 145–84.

Conclusion:
The Next Silicon Valley

1. The extensive debate over the question of how to define city and suburb began in the early 1970s, when observers realized the extent to which industry had suburbanized and heralded this change as an entirely new urban form: "the ensuing flurry of articles and books introduced neologisms such as 'outer city,' 'satellite sprawl,' 'new city,' 'suburban "city,"' 'urban fringe' and 'neocity' to describe this phenomenon." (William Sharpe and Leonard Wallock, "Bold New City or Built-Up 'Burb?" *American Quarterly* 46:1 [March 1994], 1–30). Some of these critiques were the intellectual inheritors of the anti-suburban movement of the 1950s, and derided suburbs as lacking the cultural vitality and energy of the city. But others acknowledged that American ways of living and working had fundamentally changed, and that the new decentralized, low-rise city was a consequence of that. The attempt to first redefine the city was accompanied by a Johnson Administration effort to re-imagine the shape and demographic composition of suburbs with the "New Towns" program; see Nicholas Dagen Bloom, *Suburban Alchemy: 1960s New Towns and the Transformation of the American Dream* (Columbus: Ohio State University Press, 2001). In the 1990s, one work dominating popular debates over the redefinition of city and suburb was Joel Gar-

reau's. In *Edge City: Life on the New Frontier* (New York: Doubleday, 1991), who also argues that the suburbanization of work responded in part to the entry of women and mothers into the workplace. For a response to Garreau and more nuanced explorations of "edge cities" that highlight functional differences from place to place, see Richard D. Bingham, William M. Bowen, Yosra A. Amara, Lynn W. Bachelor, Jane Dockery, Jack Dustin, Deborah Kimble, Thomas Maraffa, David L. McKee, Kent P. Schwirian, Gail Gordon Summers, and Howard A. Stafford, *Beyond Edge Cities* (New York: Garland Publishing, 1997). Robert Fishman explicitly linked the changed urban geography with the rise of the high-tech, post-industrial economy, calling such satellite communities "technoburbs" (Fishman, *Bourgeois Utopias*, 184).

2. Mounting costs for the Vietnam War and President Johnson's new anti-poverty programs contributed to this decline. One observer wrote at the time, "money for science has that discretionary look; you don't *have* to spend it, and if you don't the worst that can be expected is a few anguished letters" (D. S. Greenberg, "Money for Science: Budget Faces Pressure from Vietnam Conflict," *Science* 150 (31 December 1965), 1790). Also see Donald F. Hornig quoted in Greenberg, "LBJ's Budget: Lean Fare Set Forth for Research and Development," *Science* 155 (27 January 1967), 435.

3. Martin Kenney and Richard Florida, "Venture Capital in Silicon Valley: Fueling New Firm Formation," in *Understanding Silicon Valley*, 98–123; Thomas F. Hellman, "Venture Capitalists: The Coaches of Silicon Valley," in *The Silicon Valley Edge*, 276–94.

4. See Katz, *Reconstructing American Education*; Hollinger, "Money and Academic Freedom a Half-Century after McCarthyism."

5. Initiative for a Competitive Inner City and CEOs for Cities, "Leveraging Colleges and Universities for Urban Economic Revitalization," *Metropolitan Philadelphia Regional Review*, Spring 2003, 5. This article is a distillation of a longer publication, *Leveraging Colleges and Universities for Urban Economic Revitalization: An Action Agenda*, A Joint Study by Initiative for a Competitive Inner City and CEOs for Cities (Boston, 2003).

6. For discussion of new immigrants in Silicon Valley, see AnnaLee Saxenian, "Networks of Immigrant Entrepreneurs," in *The Silicon Valley Edge*, 248–68. While the population of Asian professionals in Silicon Valley increases, Latino blue-collar workers are among the most marginalized. See Pitti, *The Devil in Silicon Valley*.

7. In the year 2000, for example, the tech-dominated economy of the San Francisco Bay Area had an economic output per capita that was 84 percent higher than the national average (San Francisco Bay Area Council, *After the Bubble: Sustaining Economic Prosperity* [San Francisco: Bay Area Council, January 2002]).

8. This is the subtitle—and central theme—of *The Silicon Valley Edge*, ed. Lee et al.

9. For discussion of Hewlett Packard's "HP Way" and other developments in Silicon Valley's corporate culture, see Kaplan, *The Silicon Boys and their Valley of Dreams*, and Malone, *The Big Score*.

10. Texas Transportation Institute, *Urban Mobility Study 1999*, Table 4: Annual Delay Per Driver, 1982 to 1997, http://mobility.tamu.edu, 24 January 2002.

11. Metropolitan Atlanta, whose thirst for decentralization has resulted in its being one of the most car-dependent and sprawling metropolitan areas in the nation, was found in violation of the Clean Air Act in 1999 and had federal transportation funds suspended. The San Francisco Bay area, despite its strong environmental politics, was nonetheless also found in violation of air quality laws in early 2002 (Jane Kay, "U.S. Blocks $716 Million in Transit Work; Bay Area Funds Put on Hold, Clean Air Program Called Inadequate," *San Francisco Chronicle*, 23 January 2002). The cost of housing is a good indicator of household wealth, see National Association of Home Builders, *Housing Affordability Index, First Quarter 2000* (Washington, D.C.: NAHB, 2000).

12. See for example Richard Florida and Gary Gates, *Technology and Tolerance: The Importance of Diversity to High-Technology Growth* (Washington, D.C.: Brookings Center on Urban and Metropolitan Policy, 2001) and Edward L. Glaeser, Jed Kolko, and Albert Saiz, "The Consumer City," National Bureau of Economic Research Working Paper no. W7790 (July 2000), both of which argue that educated workers seek communities that provide the cultural and environmental amenities for active, cosmopolitan lifestyles, and that have a diverse population that includes sexual as well as ethnic minorities.

13. New measures often respond to the policy proposals outlined by the "new regionalists" of the 1990s. Some key works: David Rusk, *Inside Game, Outside Game* (Washington, D.C.: Brookings Institution Press, 1999); Orfield, *Metropolitics*; Rusk, *Cities Without Suburbs* (Washington, D.C.: Woodrow Wilson Institute Press, 1993); Neil Pierce, *Citistates: How Urban America Can Prosper in a Competitive World* (Washington, D.C: Seven Locks Press, 1993).

Index

POLITICS AND SOCIETY IN TWENTIETH-CENTURY AMERICA

CPSIA information can be obtained at www.ICGtesting.com
Printed in the USA
BVOW08s1032080715

407880BV00004B/228/P